Mood and Trope

Mood and Trope

The Rhetoric and Poetics of Affect

JOHN BRENKMAN

The University of Chicago Press
Chicago and London

The University of Chicago Press, Chicago 60637
The University of Chicago Press, Ltd., London
© 2020 by The University of Chicago
Published 2020
Printed in the United States of America

29 28 27 26 25 24 23 22 21 20   1 2 3 4 5

ISBN-13: 978-0-226-67312-7 (cloth)
ISBN-13: 978-0-226-67326-4 (paper)
ISBN-13: 978-0-226-67343-1 (e-book)
DOI: https://doi.org/10.7208/chicago/9780226673431.001.0001

Library of Congress Cataloging-in-Publication Data

Names: Brenkman, John, author.
Title: Mood and trope : the rhetoric and poetics of affect / John Brenkman.
Description: Chicago : University of Chicago Press, 2019. |
    Includes bibliographical references and index.
Identifiers: LCCN 2019025716 | ISBN 9780226673127 (cloth) |
    ISBN 9780226673264 (paperback) | ISBN 9780226673431 (ebook)
Subjects: LCSH: Emotions in literature. | Affect (Psychology) in literature.
Classification: LCC PN56.E6 B74 2019 | DDC 809/.93353—dc23
LC record available at https://lccn.loc.gov/2019025716

for Donald L. Epley
uncle mentor friend

Contents

Introduction

> The ontological meaning of feelings emerges precisely from the character that [is] most striking in them, that is, their complete groundlessness.
>
> GIANNI VATTIMO, *Art's Claim to Truth*

Mood

Beware of "turns." The *linguistic turn* brought out how a philosophical tradition that for a couple of millennia spoke of thought, mind, understanding, knowledge, spirit, and soul (*psyche*) began to look at the fundamental role of language in human cognition and, consequently, questioned many cherished concepts associated with thought, mind, understanding, knowledge, spirit, and soul. The ensuing century of preoccupation with language, signs, discourse, text, metaphor, and semiosis has prompted a rejoinder against all that textuality and primacy of the signifier in the form of the *affective turn*. Linguistic turn, affective turn. The work actually achieved under these excellent slogans, sound bites evocative of intellectual revolutions, turns out to be not so much *coupures épistémologiques* as valuable discoveries of hitherto unnoticed folds in the preceding discourse. The task is not to celebrate breaks, but to explain folds.

Thought and knowledge are inseparable from language and discourse; language and discourse are inseparable from affect and mood. How, then, to conceptualize this triad whose elements are inseparable yet distinct, simultaneous yet noncoincident?

Just such an endeavor is at the heart of the early chapters of *Being and Time*, as Martin Heidegger explores the "equiprimordiality" of *mood, understanding*, and *speech*. He begins with an intriguing remark about Aristotle: "It is not an accident that the earliest systematic Interpretation of affects that has come down to us is not treated in the framework of 'psychology.' Aristotle investigates the *pathê* [affects] in the second book of his *Rhetoric*."[1] The first affect or mood (*Stimmung*) that Heidegger considers is fear. Fear is also one of the emotions analyzed in the *Rhetoric* (1382a–83b), where its opposite is confidence, and fear is of course associated with pity in Aristotle because of his analysis of tragedy in the *Poetics*; in the *Rhetoric*, pity is set over against indignation (1385b–87b). Fear, confidence, pity, indignation. Heidegger, though, starts from fear in order to prepare a reflection on anxiety (*Angst*) as the basic modern state-of-mind, or mood.[2]

The first questions to explore then revolve around the triad mood–understanding–speech; ancient fear and modern anxiety; rhetoric, poetry, and philosophy.

Heidegger makes nothing easy and may seem an inauspicious starting point. I'm sometimes inclined to think that anyone who doesn't find something to learn from him should probably not waste their time reading him—and time-consuming it is. For those who do not find it a waste of time—*temps perdu*, in Proust's phrase—I find Gianni Vattimo's attitude the most useful: namely, that Heidegger's thought and language ultimately have to be deflated if we are to grasp the extraordinary insights, discoveries, and still uncharted explorations his writings afford. Even as Heidegger strains language to the edge of distortion, his readers' challenge is to resist the distortion but enjoy and exploit the strain. Take Dasein. It "normally" means existence and frequently human existence specifically. Heidegger stresses its components, *Da-sein*, being-there. More colloquially in English, one could even say "thereness" to stress the spatiality of the term and shave off a bit of the theological and philosophical loftiness of the German *Sein* when used as a noun rather than as the ubiquitous infinitive *to be*. As though to keep it aloft, Heidegger's translators endow the English with an unnecessary capitalization: Being for *Sein*, Being-there for *Dasein*, Being-in-the-world for *In-der-Welt-sein*. Dasein, in redesignating human existence as being-there, has given rise to the notion that Heidegger's thought is antihumanist, a notion that finds superficial support in the polemical edge of the postwar essay "Letter on 'Humanism'" and more substantial and worrisome support in Heidegger's intense, deeply embedded Nazi sympathies. Nonetheless, the assumption of antihumanism does not square with the very first line of the first chapter of *Being and Time*, the chapter devoted to "a preparatory analysis of Dasein": "We are ourselves the entities to be analysed" (H 41). Or with the first use of the term in the introduction: "This entity which each of us is himself and which includes inquiring as one of the possibilities of its Being, we shall denote by the term '*Dasein*'" (H 7). Human being/being human is the unwavering focus of *Being and Time*. Three decades later, in the midst the meditations on being, the meaning of being, and the history of being that are often taken as a departure from the existential focus of the early work, one finds the following assertion: "Being, however, is a call to man and is not without man."[3] Heidegger does not in any way rebut the uniqueness and centrality of human being (as distinct from other ways of being). He challenges, rather, how to understand it.

The human being is, in Heidegger's metaphor, thrown into the world, into a specific world already made, sustained, and occupied by others. Every individual Dasein finds itself already there, unaware of how it got there, uncertain of its bearings, alert to the indistinct landmarks it is in the midst of. Dasein thus entails being-in-the-world and being-with-others. It is also "an entity for which in its Being this very Being is an issue" (H 141), that is, the question and questioning of the meaning of our being is an essential aspect of our being itself.

Heidegger's whole reflection on affect, emotion, feeling, and the like is organized as an exploration of mood (*Stimmung*), attunement (*Gestimmtsein*), or state-of-mind (*Befindlichkeit*), terms he uses almost interchangeably, as an original and inescapable aspect of being-in-the-world and being-with-others. There are, however, two other equally original and inescapable aspects of this being-in and being-with. These he calls "understanding" and "speech" (or "discourse"). Mood–understanding–speech are, in Heidegger's phrase, *equiprimordial*. None is more original than the others, none is the source or cause of the others, none determines the others, none dominates or subordinates the others. And yet none occurs without the others, and each continually affects and is affected by the others.

This equiprimordial triad poses an intriguing philosophical possibility. One must reconcile statements in apparent tension with one another. Heidegger says, for example, in introducing mood, that while in actuality "Dasein can, should, and must, through knowledge and will, become master of its moods," nevertheless "ontologically mood is a primordial kind of Being for Dasein, in which Dasein is disclosed to itself *prior to* all cognition and volition, and *beyond* their range of disclosure. And furthermore, when we master a mood, we do so by way of a counter-mood. We are never free of moods" (H 136). When he then introduces understanding, he says, "State-of-mind is *one* of the existential structures in which the Being of the 'there' maintains itself. Equiprimordial with it in constituting this Being is *understanding*. A state-of-mind always has its understanding, even if it merely keeps it suppressed. Understanding always has its mood" (H 142–43). The simple solution to the tension is that Heidegger means by cognition (*Erkenntnis*) something less fundamental than understanding (*Verstand*), something more formalized, procedural, and objectifying. Nevertheless, the idea of the equiprimordiality of mood and understanding requires a kind of dialectical thinking without the dialectic, that is, a dialectic without intrinsic orientation, an operation of

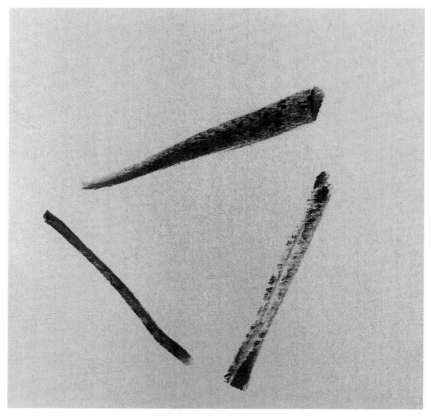

FIGURE 1. Mood–understanding–discourse

mutual affecting without mutual determination: a play and indeterminacy that the mutual effects never resolve into a necessary outcome.

My crude visual image and didactic illustration of this figure (fig. 1) of thought is a kind of triangle whose sides don't meet but are charged with activity and energy, like synapses perhaps, such that every charge or modification of one sets off a charge or modification of the others, but none is origin, cause, or master, and the effect of their continual mutual modification follows no predetermined or necessary course. What then makes the threefold mood–understanding–speech equiprimordial aspects of Dasein's being-in and being-with? Keep in mind that the conceptual challenge that Heidegger has given himself is to develop a phenomenology of human existence without anchoring it in consciousness per se and by breaking down and eluding any postulation of subject and object, an inner reality and an outer world, even a clear boundary between interiority and exteriority. Dasein is not a subject over against an object. Rather, it is always already in a world, and it finds itself there in the form of its "state-of-mind" (*Befindlichkeit*), which in everyday experience is manifest as mood. "A mood assails us. It comes neither from 'outside' nor from 'inside,' but arises out of Being-in-the-world, as a way of such Being. . . . *The mood has already disclosed, in every case, Being-in-the-world as a whole, and makes it possible first of all to direct oneself toward something*" (H 136–37). Hubert L. Dreyfus proposes translating *Befindlichkeit* as affectedness rather than state-of-mind. It is the capacity of being affected.[4] Indeed, it must be added, the inability to be unaffected. That translation has some advantages in clarity over the inappropriate evocation of "mind" in "state-of-mind," but it misses the *state-I'm-in* aspect. In any case, mood is a kind of vibration that "discloses" (Heidegger's word) all at once my own existence, my inherence in a world, and the world and the entities within it as mattering to me.

Heidegger thus approaches the "phenomenon of fear" not as a subjective state but as a phenomenon to be analyzed from "three points of view": "(1) that in the face of which we fear, (2) fearing, and (3) that about which we fear" (H 140). The phenomenon of fear is itself a kind of threefold. Consider the following formulation: "Fearing about something, as being afraid in the face of something, always discloses equiprimordially entities within-the-world and Being-in—the former as threatening and the latter as threatened" (H 141). Fear is the vibration that discloses all at once my existence (as threatened), the world (as where I dwell and "out of which something like the fearsome may come close"), and the fearsome (as the particular entity that threatens). All three are disclosed by (or in) the mood—and are disclosed as related to one another, so long as we resist the notion that they at first exist independently and subsequently come into relation. In my metaphor, they unfold together in and as mood.

Heidegger couches the analysis of fear in spatial terms: "That which is detrimental, as something that threatens us, is not yet within striking distance [*in beherrschbarer Nähe*], but it is coming close. In such drawing-close, the detrimentality radiates out, and therein lies its threatening character" (H 140). A question I leave aside for the moment is the fluctuation between metaphorical and literal senses of space in Heidegger's language, beginning of course with designating human existence as being-*there*. Is the threat that comes from hearing a bear in the woods literally close by, whereas the threat from hearing of impending layoffs is metaphorically close by? What I want to emphasize now, though, is that the second leg of the triad—understanding—has crept into the account of mood. For fear entails possibility, not immediate occurrence, and an assessment (what Heidegger calls "circumspection"), not sheer perception: "Circumspection sees the fearsome because it has fear as its state-of-mind. Fearing, as a slumbering possibility of Being-in-the-world in a state-of-mind . . . , has already disclosed the world, in that out of it something like the fearsome *may* come close" (H 141; my italics). A few pages later he says, "As understanding, Dasein projects its Being upon possibilities" (H 148).

Understanding also projects its own possibility in the sense that it can develop, expand, become articulate. That development Heidegger calls "interpretation." The sense in which understanding or interpretation is equiprimordial with mood—is enfolded with it—is clearest, I think, when Heidegger argues that interpretation is not added onto perception or sensation, as though "we have experienced something purely present-at-hand"—as a kind of mere unidentified object—"and then taken it *as* a door, *as* a house." Rather, the door or the house is already "encountered as such . . . in our understanding of the world." Understanding is equiprimordial with Dasein's bodily, sensory, mooded being-in-the-world. The point is made more vividly in the essay "The Origin of the Work of Art": "We never really first perceive a throng of sensations, e.g., tones and noises, in the appearance of things . . . ; rather we hear the storm whistling in the chimney, we hear the three-motored plane, we hear the Mercedes in immediate distinction from the Volkswagen. Much closer to us than all the sensations are the things themselves. We hear the door shut in the house and never hear acoustical sensations or even mere sounds. In order to hear a bare sound we have to listen away from things, divert the ear from them, i.e., listen abstractly."[5]

This sort of understanding is the foregrasping of entities within the world that is "articulated as such in interpretation" as "the meaning." The third leg of the triad emerges thus: mooded understanding reaches toward articulation because language is equiprimordially there with state-of-mind and understanding. Dasein's being-in-the-world, let's recall, includes its being-with-others. Speech (or discourse, as it is translated here [*Rede*]) is constitutive of being-with. "Such Being-with-one-another is discursive as assenting or refusing, as demanding or warning, as pronouncing, consulting, or interceding," and so on (H 161). In crossing a street, you hold out your arm to signal to your companion, friend, or child to *be careful*—that is discourse in Heidegger's sense. Nevertheless, the triad mood–understanding–speech displays its equiprimordial threefoldedness most emphatically in and as poetry: "Being-in and its state-of-mind are made known in discourse and indicated in language by intonation, modulation, the tempo of talk, 'the way of speaking.' In 'poetical' discourse, the communication of the existential possibilities of one's state-of-mind can become an aim in itself, and this amounts to a disclosing of existence" (H 162).

Naming by Misnaming

The notion that literary works are the form of discourse where "the *communication* of the existential possibilities of one's state-of-mind can become *an aim in itself*" defines poetry or literature's specificity with reference to its autotelic nature, but does not construe this being-its-own-aim as aesthetic autonomy or in a formalistic manner. The mooded dimension of language—in any of kind of discourse—lies in "intonation, modulation, the tempo of talk, 'the way of speaking.'" I take the phrase "the way of speaking" to suggest not only style but also figures of speech, metaphor, trope—the *in-a-manner-of-speaking* aspect of discourse—thus opening the avenue for exploring literature within this Heideggerian problematic of language and mood.[6]

Let's look at a short passage from Flaubert's "Hérodias" from *Trois contes* (*Three Tales*), the story in which he reimagines the imprisonment and beheading of John the Baptist. The Tetrarch Antipas imprisons him at the behest of his wife, Herodias, after John the Baptist humiliates her in public for the adulterous origins of their marriage. Antipas abandoned his first wife for her, and she herself was his brother's wife. John the Baptist's prophesying the coming of a new king of the Jews unnerves Antipas all the more, especially as the Roman proconsul has arrived to scrutinize his rule and inventory his citadel. When the proconsul insists that a mysterious underground vault be unsealed, Jokanaan (as he is called in the story) is seen in the cell beneath: "A human being lay stretched on the ground, his long hair running down into the hair of the animal hides which covered his back." He rises and rails, "Woe unto you . . ." against the Pharisees, the Sadducees, the people, and Herod Antipas himself and evokes the coming messiah: "O son of David, your reign shall know no end!" Then, sensing Herodias's presence in the crowd above, he unleashes at her the following curse, whose mood, affect, emotion is manifest in its rhetoric—in the twofold sense of trope and mode of address:

> "Ah! It is you, Jezebel! You who stole his heart by the squeak in your shoe! You whinnied like a mare. You set up your bed on the mountain-tops to perform your oblations! But the Lord shall tear away your earrings, your purple robes and your linen veils, the bracelets on your arms, the rings about your feet and the little golden crescents that quiver on your brow, your silver mirrors, your fans of ostrich plumes and the mother-of-pearl pattens which make you seem so tall, your proud display of diamonds, the scents in your hair, the paint on

your nails and all the adornments of your womanhood. There are not enough
rocks in all the world for the stoning of adultery like yours!"

She looked around for someone to defend her. The Pharisees lowered their
eyes hypocritically. The Sadducees looked away, afraid that they might offend
the Proconsul. Antipas looked as though he were about to die.[7]

His rage and contempt are first expressed in belittlement, mockery, and sarcasm: "Ah! It is you, Jezebel! You who stole his heart by the squeak in your
shoe! You whinnied like a mare. You set your bed on the mountain-tops to
perform your oblations!" There follows the extraordinary conceit in which
the divine punishment in store for her is figured as God's stripping her
clothes and jewelry from her body. John the Baptist—the half-naked celi-
bate purist—teeters between a lover's erotic attentiveness to every detail as
he undresses his beloved (down to "the little golden crescents that quiver on
your brow"!) and a sadist's or rapist's humiliation of his victim with every
ripping away: "The Lord shall tear away your earrings, your purple robes and
your linen veils, the bracelets on your arms, the rings about your feet and
the little golden crescents that quiver on your brow, your silver mirrors, your
fans of ostrich plumes and the mother-of-pearl pattens which make you seem
so tall, your proud display of diamonds. . . ." Until the humiliation arrives
at surreal torture: "But the Lord shall tear away . . . the scents in your hair,
the paint on your nails and all the adornments of your womanhood." The
conceit of God's punishing stripping Herodias bare reaches there its zenith.
Just for an instant, as John the Baptist culminates his curse with a hyperbole:
"There are not enough rocks in all the world," which immediately in turn
surpasses itself: "There are not enough rocks in all the world for the stoning
of adultery like yours!": the sentence refigures—re-tropes—each detail of the
divine lover-rapist's punishment into a stone cast crushing Herodias's body
and skull, as though every phrase hurls another stone: "The bracelets on your
arms, the rings about your feet and the little golden crescents that quiver on
your brow, your silver mirrors, your fans of ostrich plumes. . . ." Stripping is
refigured as stoning. It is the layering of tropes—sarcasm, conceit, hyperbole,
refiguration—that conveys John the Baptist's layered emotions: his contempt;
his sexual fascination and arousal; his revulsion at adultery, luxury, beauty,
and femininity; his delight in cruelty; his godlike pride.[8]

This brief text may be an emphatic instance of the relation of trope and
mood, but it is also exemplary of literary expression. And in keeping with
Heidegger's notion that in literary discourse "the communication of the existential possibilities of one's state-of-mind can become an aim in itself," I
am willing to claim further that it is therefore in literary discourse that we

encounter and can analyze the relation of communication and state-of-mind as such.

Three hypotheses guide inquiry into the rhetoric and poetics of affect. First, mood and trope are so intimately connected that there is not the one without the other. The equiprimordiality of discourse and mood is the equiprimordiality of trope and mood. I define trope or figure of speech broadly as the act of *naming by misnaming*. Second, affect—however apparently singular, immediate, and forceful—is complexly structured; there is a many-sidedness or layeredness to emotion. Third, the key to the discursive manifestation of affect lies in the *énonciation*, not the *énoncé*—that is, not in the content, but in the saying or articulation itself. (A therapist today would no doubt admonish John the Baptist, "Now, Jokanaan, there is no need to shout and say such violent things. I just want you to tell Hérodias what you are feeling right now.") Poetry enables affect to be studied with some precision because affect resides in the language of literature not in speaking *about* feelings but in the very speaking and way of speaking.

From Heidegger to Aristotle

With these three hypotheses in mind—mood-trope; the complex structure of emotion; *énonciation* rather than *énoncé*—let's look for initial guidance in Aristotle on rhetoric, since it is there that Heidegger locates the inaugural philosophical exploration of affect. Forensic and political oratory—the endeavor to persuade one's peers to take a particular decision—has in its arsenal of persuasiveness the arousal and dampening of emotions. Aristotle's reflection places the emotions as part of Dasein's being-with, most obviously in the orator's relation to his audience but also in their relation to one another. Being-with is also even more immediately manifest in the emotions themselves insofar as almost all the instances Aristotle discusses involve passions aroused in relation to others: pity, envy, anger, shame, jealousy.

Aristotle's discussion of fear, from which Heidegger clearly took many elements for his own, situates danger spatially as "the proximity of the frightening" and furnishes the following definition of fear: "*Let fear, then, be a kind of pain or disturbance resulting from the imagination of impending danger, either destructive or painful*" (1382a).[9] Heidegger too stresses both proximity and potentiality as features of fear. I want to suggest that the close connection between emotion and the orator's discourse lies in the fact that intrinsic to the emotion itself is an act of imagination. Fear "result[s] from the imagination of impending danger," and the orator's task if he seeks to arouse fear in his listeners is to make them "think," that is, imagine or believe, that "they are in a position to suffer by pointing out that others, greater than them, have in fact suffered" (1383a).[10]

The role of imagination and the element of persuasion show up, unexpectedly perhaps, in Descartes's treatise *The Passions of the Soul*. Rüdiger Campe discusses how the treatise "clearly inherits and continues the tradition of the pathe in the vein of Aristotle's Rhetoric" but "revises the traditional presentation through a narrative account of passion's genesis," in contrast to "the one, continuous, world in which scenes of affects unfold" in Aristotle.[11] However, even as Descartes displaces the social and rhetorical field of Aristotle's thought with the soul's inner genesis of passion, the elements of imagination, representation, and persuasion reappear:

> Our passions, too, cannot be directly aroused or suppressed by the action of our will, but only indirectly through the *representation* of things which are usually joined with the passions we wish to have and opposed to the passions we wish to reject. For example, in order to arouse boldness and suppress fear in ourselves, it is not sufficient to have the volition to do so. We must apply ourselves to consider the reasons, objects, or precedents which *persuade us* that the danger is not great; that there is always more security in defense than in flight; that we shall gain glory and joy if we conquer, whereas we can expect nothing but regret and shame if we flee.[12]

The suppression of fear is here accomplished not by possessing confidence, as in Aristotle, but by arousing boldness in oneself. Nevertheless Descartes's analysis interestingly evokes the very kind of martial and masculine values that pervade Aristotle's interpretations: after the arguments that diminish the danger and recall principles of strategy, one must persuade oneself with the imagination of glory over against the prospect of regret and shame.

The virile values of the Athenian *polis* are evident throughout *The Art of Rhetoric*, as when Aristotle explains that "insulted virtue with power" is fearsome since—and this is self-evident for Athenians—"virtuous men would obviously choose to do harm after being insulted in all cases, and are able to do so in the present one [i.e., with power]." So, too, the emotions vary with one's rise and fall according to social hierarchy as well as differences in power: among the fearsome are "those who are fearsome for one's superiors; for they would be more able to harm us, if they could harm even them" (1382b).[13] The distribution of power, talents, and wealth among superiors, inferiors, and equals inflects every emotion's shape and intensity. It is certainly possible to examine this relation of emotion to social difference and hierarchy as a kind of map of domination.[14] There is a contrasting advantage in looking at Aristotle's analysis of the emotions as an exemplary, perhaps still the most powerful, analysis of a structure of feeling in Raymond Williams's sense: a constellation of social perceptions and values and convictions by which a society, or social group, conducts itself and experiences its world.[15] Athenian society, in which the public square, debate, and rhetorical competition were supremely important, made the art of persuasion in politics and the court the privileged site for Aristotle's analysis of the prevailing structure of feeling.

The first emotion Aristotle considers is anger, and I think it illuminates more connections to Heidegger's equiprimordial triad as well as Williams's structure of feeling. Peter Sloterdijk's *Rage and Time* (*Zorn und Zeit*) begins with the observation that the first keyword in Western literature is wrath.[16] Homer calls upon the muses so that he may "sing Achilles' wrath." Not just to sing about Achilles' wrath, but to sing it. Of course, Aristotle too quotes the *Iliad* in defining wrath. What is striking in Aristotle's definition is the complexity of the emotion. Anger enfolds belittlement, opinion, value, pain, desire, and pleasure—and all on account of the working of imagination: "*Let anger, then, be desire, accompanied by pain, for revenge for an obvious belittlement of oneself or one of one's dependants, the belittlement being uncalled for.*" Aristotle defines belittlement as "a realization of an opinion about what seems to be of no value." This painful entanglement with another comes in three possible forms of belittlement: contempt, spite, and insult. How, then, are desire and even pleasure enfolded in the pain of being the object of another's underserved contempt, spite, or insult?

> With all anger there must be an attendant *pleasure*, that from the *prospect of revenge*. For it is pleasant to think that one will achieve what one seeks, and nobody seeks those things that are obviously impossible for him. Thus the following is a fair comment about wrath:
>
> > Which sweeter far is than ooze of honey
> > And grows in human hearts . . . [*Iliad*, 18:109]
>
> For a certain pleasure accompanies it for this reason and because men dwell on their revenge in their thoughts. . . . Thus the imagination arising on these occasions produces a pleasure like that of dreams. (1378a–b)[17]

As in Descartes, the passion is an auto-affection effected and sustained by means of imaginative representation. A structure of feeling is not only feelings, or even predominantly feeling, just as mood is not more primordial than understanding and speech and does not even exist without them. Anger, like fear and like pity, requires imagination. Enfolded in anger is the pleasurable imagining of revenge. Enfolded in fear is the imagination of impending harm. And enfolded in pity is the imagination of one's own like suffering.

The rhetorician arouses such imaginings in order to persuade to decision and action. The poet's imaginative deployment of language is, according to Heidegger, "the communication of the existential possibilities of one's state-of-mind" as "an aim in itself." And, according to Descartes, the imagination is what arouses the passions of the individual soul in a kind of auto-affection. Emotion, which is easily thought of as purely sensory and bodily real, prelinguistic and precognitive, has as its very condition of possibility understanding, speech, and imagination.

The one instance in Aristotle's analysis of fear in which the fearsome is not that of other human beings suggestively leads back to Heidegger and the concept of Dasein in another way. I refer to Aristotle's juxtaposition of the two contrary conditions under which men are confident and unafraid: "If they think that many things have come off and that they have not suffered, or if they have frequently got into danger and escaped it. For men become free from suffering in two ways: either by not having been put to the test or by having protections, as, with the dangers at sea, those unfamiliar with storms are confident for the future and those who have protection because of their experience" (1383a).[18] So, the two human beings who are unafraid of the storm at sea are the expert sailor and the idiot. The former's lack of fear in the face of a coming storm comes from the fact that he has weathered many intense storms, while the other is utterly innocent and ignorant of storms at sea. For everyone else in the boat, the brewing storm arouses fear. *The brewing storm arouses fear.* Heidegger questions just the sort of subject-predicate structure in that sentence. Rather, mood is the vibration within which Dasein's fear frees the storm to appear, to arise from sea and sky *as* storm. Otherwise, the churning of waves, the pull of tides, the air currents, the condensation of airborne moisture, electrical currents exploding in the air—none of this amounts to a storm. None of this *is* a storm until Dasein fears. Dasein's fear discloses the storm in-the-world. I suspect that some such imagery and imagining is what so struck Heidegger in the choral ode to *anthropos* (to Dasein) in *Antigone*, where the first image of human daring and achievement is sailing:

> Many are the wonders, none
> is more wonderful than what is man.
> This it is that crosses the sea
> with the south winds storming and the waves swelling,
> breaking around him in roaring surf.[19]

This takes us back to Heidegger's ill-disguised humanism. Were it not for Dasein's ingenuity in crafting boats, invention of the art of sailing, and courage in the face of its own mortality, the sea would not lie between two shores, the winds would not storm, the waves would not swell, and the surf would not roar.

In *Being and Time* the analysis of fear is but a prelude to the analysis of anxiety (*Angst*). Having Aristotle's analysis of the ancient Greek structure of feeling in mind, we can perhaps more readily grasp how powerfully Heideggerian *Angst* defines modernity against antiquity. Echoing the phrasing of his analysis of fear, Heidegger brings out the difference between fear and anxiety: "That in the face of which one has anxiety is not an entity within-the-world. . . . That in the face of which one has anxiety is characterized by the fact that what threatens is *nowhere*" (H 186). It is unimaginable in the Greek structure of feeling that one could vibrate to a threat that was nowhere. Without proximity, tangible form, recognizable likenesses and unlikenesses, nothing threatens in the Athenian lifeworld. For the modern structure of feeling, however, the truly threatening is nothing, is nowhere, is unidentifiable. Modernity makes existence itself something to flee: "*That in the face of which one has anxiety [das Wovor der Angst] is Being-in-the-world as such*" (H 186).

The concept of anxiety is conveyed in a rich imagery of movement in space, raising anew the question of the literal and metaphorical meaning of space in Heidegger's language regarding Da-sein, being-*there*. Dasein in its *Angst* falls, flees, turns away, and turns back, and these movements are unlike flight in fear because the threatening is nowhere, or at once nowhere and closer than close: "That which threatens cannot bring itself close from a definite direction within what is close by; it is already 'there,' and yet nowhere. It is so close that it is oppressive and stifles one's breath, and yet it is nowhere" (H 186). In Heidegger's space language, anxiety is Dasein's twistings and turnings as it tries to turn away from its own being-in-the-world: "That in the face of which it flees is *not grasped* in thus turning away [Abkehr] in falling; nor is it experienced even in turning hither [Hinkehr]. Rather, in turning away *from* it, it is disclosed 'there'" (H 185). Literally or metaphorically movement in space? No easy answer. And note the bent syntax of the sentence: "In turning away *from* it, it is disclosed 'there.'" Is the second "it" that which turns away or that which is turned away from? They are of course the "same," since in anxiety Dasein is turning away from Dasein, human existence is turning away from the thereness which it itself is. A wrenching, torque, twisting, swerve, "trope." Dasein is enfolded-upon-and-in-strife-with-itself.

Let me venture another way of considering the spatiality of Dasein Heidegger evokes here with this kind of pirouette by which Dasein in turning from itself, from its own being-*there*, points to—indexically brings out—*there* where it fleeingly turns away. (Something like that.) Dasein's space is not that of geometry or cartography. It is, rather, space as it is traversed, referenced, and experienced in dance. The dancer turns as to flee, only to point up the very space from which he or she cannot possibly escape. But the analogy to dance brings out a complication that I think takes us even closer to Heidegger's understanding. The dance is not the same for the spectator and the dancer, yet it only exists because of the dancer *and* the spectator, that is, it exists *between* them. It is their being-with-one-another. The dancer moves not only foreseeing his or her next movements but also with some sort of image of what the spectator is seeing, though that image can be but an approximation or a partial memory of what the studio's mirror showed the dancer in rehearsal. The spectator merely watches, but what is seen provokes an imaginative proprioception of the dancer's experience. The dancer reaches for an approximation of the dance as visible spectacle; the spectator reaches for an approximation of the dance as felt movement. The dance does not happen without the one and the other, without their being-with-one-another. And yet never can the twain meet. *That's* Dasein. The dance is the world, the dancer and the spectator exist as being-in and being-with, that is, in-the-world and with-one-another.

It's only a metaphor, so the problematic of Heideggerian space—from being-*there* to the spatiality of mood in the analysis of *Angst*—will have to remain sketchy. The ancients do, though, provide another suggestive hint. In the *Poetics* Aristotle proposes that "two causes seem likely to have given rise to the art of poetry, both of them natural"—by "natural" he means spontaneous and untaught, capacities that human beings exhibit from childhood. The first is imitation, in the sense of mimicry; the second is melody and rhythm: "Given, then, that imitation is natural to us, and also melody and rhythm (it being obvious that verse-forms are segments of rhythm), from the beginning those who had the strongest natural inclination towards these things generated poetry out of improvised activities by a process of gradual innovation" (48b).[20] A comparable reflection is found in book 2 of *Laws*, where Plato too sees the spontaneous origin of rhythm and melody. But he first identifies the shared animal spirits of humans and animals and then marks the difference effected by human talent, a difference indicating that art is a gift of the gods: "No young creature whatsoever, as we may fairly assert, can keep its body or its voice still; all are perpetually trying to make movements and noises. They leap and bound, they dance and frolic, as it were with glee, and again, they utter cries of all sorts. Now animals at large have no perception of the order or disorder in these motions, no sense of what we call rhythm or melody. But in our case the gods of whom we spoke as given us for companions in our revels [the Muses, Apollo, and Dionysus] have likewise given us the power to perceive and enjoy rhythm and melody. Through this sense they stir us to movements and become our choir leaders. They string us together on a thread of song and dance, and have named our choirs so after the delight (*chora*) they naturally afford" (653e–54a).[21] So just as poetry in my hypothesis is the privileged site where the equiprimordiality of mood, understanding, and speech can be grasped, Aristotle and Plato suggest that saying that the nature of our human existence in space, that is, Dasein's fundamental being-in-space, is to be found in dance is perhaps not a metaphor after all.

The juxtaposition of Heidegger and Aristotle brings out a cluster of orienting themes. The impossibility of *Angst* in the Athenian lifeworld underscores Heidegger's contribution to our understanding of modernity. Aristotle's analysis of the ancient Greek structure of feeling shows, as does the Flaubert passage in another way, that emotions are complex configurations, compounds of imagination, social perceptions, wishes, sensation. Heidegger's triad of mood–understanding–speech brings out the significance of Aristotle's linking of affect and persuasion, which in turn concretizes the Heideggerian notions of Dasein as being-*in*-the-world and being-*with*-one-another. Rhetoric—in its two-pronged sense of the art of persuasion and the art of the trope, its mode of address and its naming-by-misnaming—is indissociable from emotion, affect, mood. And, more strongly yet, emotion, affect, and mood are indissociable from rhetoric.

There is a temptation to identify and catalogue emotions as psychological facts independent of their social embeddedness and to let go of rhetoric's link to affect and affect's link to rhetoric. Heidegger scholars themselves express frustration with how to account for the passage from the base mood *Angst* to the actual variety of moods and feelings in everyday experience. Matthew Ratcliffe explores the problem by advancing a distinction between "ground moods" and "focused emotions" but quickly points out the limitation of such stipulated definitions torn from experiential contexts. He is driven to speculate: "It could be argued that . . . specifically focused experiences reshape background mood, thus enabling different kinds of experience, and so on. Perhaps this is what happens when major life events 'sink in'—what starts off as a focused emotion leads to a change in how one finds oneself in the world."[22] *Angst* itself is slippery as a term if it is supposed to name a psychological fact, since, as Ratcliffe suggests, anxiety or dread in Heidegger's description overlaps with what is often called, or experienced as, depression. I question whether the solution is to erect a psychic architecture that inevitably falls back on stipulating the meaning of particular emotions as if they were stable entities. Illusory objectification is not the answer to interpretive uncertainty; the hermeneutics of affect has to acknowledge the impossibility

of certainty in the way that literary interpretation does. Ratcliffe gets closer
to the matter in signaling the slipperiness of the essential terms themselves—
mood, *Stimmung*, feelings—in relation to the "varieties of mood": "People
talk of all-enveloping feelings of significance, insignificance, detachment, estrangement, absence, isolation, alienation, belonging, unreality, disorientation, disconnection, familiarity, unfamiliarity, anxiety, objectless dread, awe,
ecstasy, and many, many others. There are all sorts of more nuances and lengthy
descriptions too, as exemplified by good literature."[23] A qualification is called
for. Literature is an exemplary, nuanced site of varieties of mood and emotion
not by means of description, but via trope—that is, via its poetic and rhetorical
powers.

A Philosophical Quartet

Two related polarities in modern thought provide the theoretical webbing of
Mood and Trope: Nietzsche versus Kant and Deleuze versus Heidegger. My
choices are neither imperative nor arbitrary. What turns out to have been the
origins of this project was an interest in how various philosophers have discussed the emotions and passions. Other combinations would fruitfully serve
to organize a discussion of affect. This philosophical quartet is especially apt
because their differences and oppositions are a fertile terrain of controversies
in modern thought and, even more, because each of the four ultimately cen-
ters the question of affect on literary and aesthetic experience. The literary
critic and theorist is not bound to—or capable of!—philosophical systematic-
ity. The vocation of criticism is attuned, rather, to the singularity and plurality
of literary and artistic creations. *What is art?* is a less pressing question than
What does this work do? What do these works do? The emphasis in my subtitle
should fall on the *rhetoric* and *poetics* of affect, with *of* bearing all the playful
ambiguity of the genitive.

A two-tiered dialogue is to be animated. The differences among Kant,
Nietzsche, Heidegger, and Deleuze bring questions of art, language, and affect to bear on the set of charged terms associated with Kant: enlightenment,
modernity, and universalism. Interwoven is a second dialogue that confronts
the quartet with an intentionally heterogeneous set of authors and artists, including Harold Pinter and Edgar Allan Poe, Charles Baudelaire and Li-Young
Lee, Shakespeare, Tino Sehgal and Rineke Dijkstra, Percy Bysshe Shelley and
Jorie Graham.

For me it is not a question of being Heideggerian or of subscribing to applied Deleuzianism. Nor does doubting that Kant's thought has simply been
overcome by Nietzsche's require becoming a Kantian. A guide to the most

productive attitude to take toward these four philosophers is supplied by Deleuze in his explanation of his commentaries on Kant: "When you're facing
such a work of genius, there's no point you saying you disagree. First you have
to know how to admire; you have to rediscover the problem *he* poses, his particular machinery. It is through admiration that you will come to a genuine
critique. The mania of people today is not knowing how to admire anything;
either they're 'against,' or they situate everything at their level while they chit-
chat and scrutinize."[24]

The quartet's value lies in becoming attuned to the dissonance they produce. From his earliest thinking in *The Birth of Tragedy* to the notes for the
never-achieved *Will to Power*, Nietzsche pursues a relentless assault on Kant's
conception of aesthetic judgment, disinterestedness, and the categorical imperative. While Heidegger and Deleuze both place themselves in the lineage
of Nietzsche, they also creatively engage Kant's thought rather than merely
rejecting it. By the same token, Heidegger's Nietzsche is not Deleuze's. Deleuze takes from Nietzsche the vitalism that privileges urge, desire, and self-
enhancing power, while Heidegger takes from Nietzsche the idea that humans
are interpreting beings for whom every "is" arises from a more or less unacknowledged interpretation of being. Nietzsche both straddles and thwarts his
two astute commentators, as when he jots in a 1885–86 notebook entry, "moral
valuating is an *interpretation*, a way of interpreting. . . . *Who interprets?*—
Our affects."[25] Between Deleuze and Heidegger lies a seemingly unbridgeable fault line separating vitalism and hermeneutics, sensation and being,
"transcendental empiricism" and "fundamental ontology." And yet, as Deleuze grapples with sensation in Francis Bacon's painting and Heidegger with
the disclosure of being in van Gogh's, their otherwise incommensurate views
surprisingly tend to converge. What is the significance of the incommensurability? What is the significance of the convergence? Such questions inform
the encounter I orchestrate among the philosophers and between them and
the poets and artists.

The philosophical quartet's approach to affect via aesthetics combined
with my taking poetry as the terrain for testing their reflections makes the
trajectory of *Mood and Trope* somewhat oblique to major contributions to
affect theory. Groundbreaking work over the last decade and more has often focused on a particular emotion or state-of-mind and explored how its
significance branches out into the social world and public contexts. In Eve
Sedgwick's work on shame and Ann Cvetkovitch's on depression, the theoretical exploration is strongly inflected with personal testimony; Cvetkovitch
begins *Depression: A Public Feeling* with a frank autobiographical journal.[26]
The foundational projects in affect theory have come predominantly from

feminist and queer theory and other politically and ideologically inflected trends, including those expressing radical resistance or even revolutionary expectation with regard to, variously, racism, neoliberalism, liberal democracy, globalization, or capitalism per se. My project could not have taken shape without that work and those projects, and while I maintain a certain distance from the political claims of much affect theory, affect theorists' insights inspire and impinge upon much of what I address. As always in a rich field of inquiry, it is the fissures among and within the theories themselves that invite continued probing.

Two questions stand out that stimulate markedly different responses in affect theory: Can reliable distinctions be made among such terms as *affect*, *feeling, emotion, passion*, and *mood*? And how does *affect* relate to the cognitive and linguistic dimensions of experience?

In the psychotherapeutic vernacular *affect* frequently refers to how someone manifests or expresses feelings through gesture, tone, posture, and facial expression. Someone is said to lack affect when others cannot readily discern what emotions the person might actually be feeling. The explanation of such a lack of affect can run from mere inhibition or repression to so-called narcissistic disorders all the way to sociopathy and psychopathy. In this conception, emotion is internal and subjective, while affect is manifest and intersubjective.

Brian Massumi anchors a strand of affect theory that upends the therapeutic lexicon and gives affect the meaning of "being affected," independent of feeling and emotion. He stakes out the claim for the "autonomy of affect," a claim based on the notion that responses in the autonomic nervous system operate in advance of emotional and cognitive responses. Relying heavily on various experiments that isolate and measure electrodermal activity, heart rate, breathing, or brain activity, Massumi elaborates their results in a Deleuzian vocabulary of intensity and the virtual. He stipulates *affect* to be bodily responses—intensities—occurring below the threshold of consciousness and separate from any cognition, intention, or awareness. In experiments where children watching a film gave different valuations of the film on happy–sad and pleasant–unpleasant scales depending on whether it was shown with a factual voice-over narration, an emotional voice-over, or no voice-over at all, "the original nonverbal version elicited the greatest response from their skin," that is, the greatest "*autonomic* reaction." Massumi concludes that this is evidence of the "primacy of the affective in image reception" and that "the primacy of the affective is marked by a gap between *content* and *effect*: it would appear that the strength or duration of an image's effect is not logically connected to the content in any straightforward way."[27] Such strength and duration are what he calls "intensity." Affect (the body's being affected below the threshold of consciousness) is sharply distinguished from emotion (a quality of consciousness): "An emotion is a subjective content, the sociolinguistic fixing of the quality of an experience which is from that moment onward defined as personal. Emotion is a qualified intensity, the conventional, consensual point of insertion of intensity into semantically and semiotically formed progressions, into narrativizable action-reaction circuits, into function and meaning. It is intensity owned and recognized."[28] The distinction becomes dichotomy. Emotions are ascribed to a social order of convention, consensus, function, and meaning, while affect's intensities are endowed with disruptive potential (virtuality). Language is order and structure; image is intensity and event. "Structure is the place where nothing ever happens, that explanatory heaven in which all eventual permutations are prefigured in a self-consistent set of invariant generative rules." In the event, by contrast, "nothing is prefigured. . . . It is the collapse of structured distinction into intensity, of rules into paradox. . . . Intensity is the unassimilable."[29]

This pseudopolitical and avant-gardist vocabulary swells into a programmatic yet vague political vision: the Left needs to learn from the Right's success in mobilizing through images and affects. Further backing for this view is drawn from other neurophysiological experiments that demonstrate a lag between bodily stimulus and perception, even a blank in perception for stimuli lasting less than half a second. One experiment clocked brain waves, subjects' finger-flexing, and their sense of the flex's timing. There was "a half-second lapse between the beginning of a bodily event and its completion in an outwardly directed, active expression." These half-second lags—which are reminiscent of the temporality of perception in Freud's mystic writing pad in Derrida's classic commentary "Freud and the Scene of Writing"[30]—are cast by Massumi in a Deleuzian idiom: "Brain and skin form a resonating vessel. Stimulation turns inward, is folded into the body, except that there is no inside for it to be in, because the body is radically open, absorbing impulses quicker than they can be perceived, and because the entire vibratory event is unconscious, out of mind. Its anomaly is smoothed over retrospectively to fit conscious requirements of continuity and linear causality."[31] As it stands, this formulation is unobjectionable and quite eloquent. The problem comes in ascertaining how it matters.

The attempt to derive political strategy and tactics from neurophysiology, as though such a project could simply forego delineating mediations between the time-lag presumed endemic to human perception and the mobilization, organization, and sustaining of political movements and opinion, is scarcely plausible. At the level of everyday experience, there is a more basic flaw. Massumi postulates that affect in his sense of the term is more primordial, on account of its autonomy, than cognition and language, understanding and discourse. His prime example suggests otherwise. For his account of the kids watching the film overlooks the fact that a film, even without voiceover, requires of the viewer two complex cognitive processes, namely, the capacity to decipher an image *as* image and to follow and grasp a sequence of images *as* a narrative, capacities already well cultivated in nine-year-olds. Those skin reactions could not occur without the aesthetic-cognitive-imaginative apprehending of images and narrative. The experiment was not designed to take account of the capacity to decipher images and apprehend narratives, even though without that capacity the subjects' autonomic reaction would lack any relevance whatsoever. There is no reason to fault the experiment's design, but every reason to be alert to what the experiment can and cannot disclose.

All sensation and all perception rely on subsensory and imperceptible processes. Consider hearing. Unfelt and unheard sound waves imperceptibly vibrate the tympanic membrane, whose unfelt percussive movement transforms the sound waves into mechanical waves by vibrating, still subsensorily, against a bony structure filled with a fluid that then moves in waves that transform into electrical impulses registered by fifteen to twenty-five thousands cells—the marvelously named "hairy cells of the Corti"—deep within the inner ear and are—finally!—transmitted by the cochlear nerve to the brain. Only then is something heard. What matters in the realm of experience and behavior is that all the subsensory and imperceptible stimuli and movements give rise to perceptions that allow individuals to understand, move, act, respond, *soon enough*. Orientation in time has to be soon enough, orientation in space close enough. A bullet will strike you before you hear the gunshot, but when a car approaches as you cross the street or someone calls out to you or something falls on the floor, you turn and look, accurately, to the left or the right. Studies suggest that this is because the brain processes the difference in time it takes for the sound waves to reach your left ear and your right.[32] Given that sound travels 1,126 feet per second and the distance from one ear to the other is a matter of give-or-take seven inches, the difference registered in the brain and then acted upon by body and eye is in the nanoseconds. Soon enough, close enough. One hears the spoon hit the floor to the left. One hears the door slam, one hears the wind in the chimney. How the temporal delays, missed stimuli, and retrofittings matter is in the relative coherence of the practices, actions, behaviors they enable.

It is not a question of giving primacy to consciousness. Massumi gets argumentative traction from countering the centrality of consciousness and the phenomenological concept of intentionality as articulated for example in Edmund Husserl's *Cartesian Meditations*. Heidegger's project in *Being and Time* by contrast, as already pointed out, is a phenomenological analysis that does not center on consciousness and intentionality. Mood is the first instance of that decentering, as is the equiprimordial triad mood–understanding–discourse. Maurice Merleau-Ponty, whose unique contribution to the phenomenological and Heideggerian tradition I will draw on at crucial moments, makes a strong case for not postulating the bodily, biological, physiological dimension of human being as pre- or nonhuman, since such a postulate reinstates some variant of the idea that humans are rational animals, that is, animals to which the capacity of reason or speech is added. Whether the emphasis or affirmation then falls on the rational or the animal, the conception is misguided. Merleau-Ponty argues that it is necessary, instead, "to grasp humanity first as another manner of being a body."[33] There is a specifically human bodily being. Massumi risks losing this specificity in postulating that our ordering, narrativizing, and conceptualizing powers are mere fixity and social control composed in arrears of "affect." The kids' skin's autonomic responses are enfolded in an experience that includes understanding in the form of image deciphering and narrative apprehension.

Lauren Berlant distinguishes affect and emotion differently from Massumi as well as from the common therapeutic conception. For her, there is always an ample and indeterminate range of possible relations between an affect and its manifestations, between feelings and their perceptibility by others, indeed between one's own feelings and their meaning. She sees "a distinction between a structure of affect and what we call that affect when we encounter it. I may be or feel overwhelmed, I may be composed or feel composure; my panic might look like a stony silence, my composure might be a manic will to control, or not. What looks like a shamed response in one decade, may look angry in another one. One can experience the world not being there for one because of one's singularity or because one's singularity includes *the kind of thing* one appears to be to others."[34] Feeling has multiple registers.

At the same time, Berlant proposes that a particular affective configuration defines the dynamic tying individuals to the institutional, economic, and political conditions of contemporary American society. This configuration she calls "cruel optimism." Optimism is understood as attachment to an object, person, situation, or circumstance that seems to hold the promise of satisfying one's desires and needs and sustaining one's existence. The promise and hope can intensify the attachment even when the desire and need are repeatedly thwarted by the attachment itself. The question that arises is "what happens when the loss of what's not working is more unbearable than the having of it, and vice versa."[35] Hence optimism's cruelty. Berlant aligns with Massumi and others in arguing "that affective atmospheres are shared, not solitary, and that bodies are continuously busy judging their environments and responding to the atmospheres in which they find themselves."[36]

Much of the power of *Cruel Optimism* derives from the fact that its account is at once subtly testimonial—pervaded by a sense of *I know whereof I speak*—and insistently theoretical. Its theoretical intent, as I see it, is to overcome the limitations of the concepts of reification and commodification in the Lukácsian–Frankfurt School tradition as well as the Althusserian notion of ideology as interpellation, all of which were designed to explain Western workers' adaptive rather than revolutionary response to capitalism.[37] Berlant eschews these concepts as oversimplified but perhaps keeps the motive behind them. In any case, she faults them for failing to grasp "the messy dynamics of attachment, self-continuity, and the reproduction of life that are the material scenes of living on in the present." Sensitive to the injustices and struggles involving gender and sexuality, race, and income inequality and at the same time expressing a moral-aesthetic resistance, even rejection of the incentives and imperatives of capitalist society, Berlant's project "tracks the fraying relation between post–Second World War state/economic practices and certain postwar fantasies of the good life endemic to liberal, social democratic, or relatively wealthy regions."[38] The theoretical reflection offers a diagnosis of the present experience of affluent societies: "Amidst all the chaos, crisis, and injustice in front of us, the desire for alternative filters that produce the sense—if not the scene—of a more livable and intimate sociality is another name for the desire for the political. This is why an intimate attachment to the political can amount to a relation of cruel optimism."[39] So, too, the endeavor and stress of trying simply to live with and live the imperatives and incentives of society give rise to cruel optimisms. The apparent aporia is, rather, Berlant's rethinking of the relation between social integration and political opposition. In place of the polarity of reified versus revolutionary consciousness, cruel optimism is meant to describe the ineluctably "messy" imbrication of subjection, resistance, and revolt. While cruel optimism is not a specific emotion, affect, or mood, it does purport to convey the specificity of the contemporary period's atmosphere and affective dynamic. In its suggestion of a collective experience, and at times of a yearning for the experience of collectivity, the concept has a rough resemblance to ideas of zeitgeist, period feeling, or a generational sensibility.

An approach to mood as the collective experience of a generation is exemplified by Hans Ulrich Gumbrecht's *After 1945: Latency as Origin of the Present*. His testimony from personal recollection combines with historical research to describe the mood (*Stimmung*) that underlay and inflected the experiences and mentality of Gumbrecht's own generation of Germans, whose childhood and youth unfolded in the immediate aftermath of World War II. The atmosphere in which his generation found itself he calls "latency." This latency is *Stimmung* in the double sense of "an all-embracing atmosphere and a subjectively experienced mood." Gumbrecht makes a case for the investigation of collective moods or atmospheres on the ground that "calling *Stimmungen* to mind can give us retrospective certainty that something neglected or overlooked—or even lost altogether—made a decisive impact on life at a certain moment in history and formed part of each subsequent present from that moment on."[40]

In Heidegger's terms, *Stimmung* is an aspect of being-with-others. The emphasis can fall either on collective (and collectivizing) moods or on individual (and individuating) moods. In the seminar Heidegger gave in 1929–30, two years after the publication of *Being and Time*, the mood he takes up is ennui or boredom. The stress falls on its collective nature and in particular its hold on the generation that fought in the Great War, suffered Germany's surrender and reparations, was thrown into the uncertainties of Weimar politics, and by the year of the seminar found itself in the midst of a global economic crisis: "Everywhere there are disruptions, crises, catastrophes, needs: the contemporary social misery, political confusion, the powerlessness of science, the erosion of art, the groundlessness of philosophy, the impotence of religion. Certainly there are needs everywhere."[41] Reform and the actions of all manner of "groups, associations, circles, classes, parties" attempt to address the needs but according to Heidegger miss the import of the "profound boredom in our Dasein," which stems from a different kind of need:

> what oppresses us most profoundly and in a concealed manner is the very *absence of any essential oppressiveness* [*Bedrängnis*] *in our Dasein as a whole*.
>
> The absence of an essential oppressiveness in Dasein is the *emptiness as a whole*, so that no one stands with anyone else and no community stands with any other in the rooted unity of essential action. Each and every one of us are servants of slogans, adherents to a program, but none is the custodian of the inner greatness of Dasein and its necessities.[42]

Nothing weighs heavily enough to incite satisfying action, so human existence is paradoxically weighed down by boredom. "Has man today," Heidegger asks, "become boring for himself?"[43] Had Heidegger not been a reactionary, and had he had a novelistic sensibility, he might have rendered this condition with insights something like those of *Berlin Alexanderplatz*. But in the event his philosophical *cri de coeur* stirs him to a rhetoric that readies his own ear to heed—hear and obey—the rallying cry of Hitler. The 1929–30 seminar hooks together a German generation's supposed collective state-of-mind and the anticipatory hope for deliverance and entry into a new communal unity. Caught between the disdain for reform and the yearning for solidarity and "the rooted unity of essential action," he and his generation await an annunciation: "The most extreme demand [*Zumutung*] must be announced to man."[44] Philosophy itself cannot sound such a collective demand; philosophers can only affirm or reject those that arise from social and political strife. Heidegger chose to affirm Nazism. His political decisions and allegiances do not refute his philosophical project as a whole, for they do not organically follow from it, even though for Heidegger himself there was undoubtedly a sense of consistency.

While the analysis of boredom ties that affect to a generation and its experience of a decade, the analysis of *Angst* in *Being and Time* is pegged to the *longue durée* of modernity and to the other slope of thrownness and being-with-others, namely, the ordeal of individuation and its oscillations between estrangement and resoluteness, between being left to one's own devices and acting in one's own name, isolation and belonging, heteronomy and autonomy. The historical span is that of the modern era—Heidegger likes to date it from Descartes—whose economic, scientific, and philosophical developments tore at the symbolic and religious bonds that were the fabric of traditional societies. Modern individuals are at once bereft of premodern forms of "affective sociality," to borrow Berlant's term, and delivered into new and uncertain forms of freedom. The notion that Heidegger pairs with the individuating force of *Angst*, being-toward-death, also reflects the eclipse of religious consolation; being-toward-death is the horizon of experience that individuals must make their own once the afterlife ceases to be the goal, expectation, and hope of *this life*.

Throughout *Mood and Trope* I hew predominantly to the *longue durée* perspective on modernity rather than any more specific historical focus, except incidentally (Baudelaire and 1848, Li-Young Lee and the Sukarno regime's violence against Chinese immigrants, Shelley and Alpine tourism). The broader perspective facilitates fashioning dialogues among philosophers from the late eighteenth to the late twentieth century and poetry from Shakespeare to Jorie Graham. I do not consider it superior to more historicizing perspectives. Each sees things the other does not. I also hew more closely to affect's individual rather than collective slope. Aside from my reservations about identifying particular affects with specific political or ideological orientations,[45] I shy away from attributing certain states of mind to an entire period or generation. For those who boldly take that step, the underlying methodological question is distinguishing where the theorist's own sensibility finds itself reflected in the collective mood from where it has projected itself onto it.

My attention is directed primarily to aesthetic experience, which on the one hand relies on just such an ambiguity between receptivity and projection but on the other must confront the question of affect in the singularity of poets and artists and their works rather than with collective manifestations. Taking *Angst* to be the base mood of modern existence, that is, the affect from which other feelings and passions arise, helps bring to light the quality of artistically rendered emotions, including jealousy (Pinter), self-tormenting grief (Poe), spleen (Baudelaire), fury (Lee), vengefulness (Shakespeare), and others.

I have staked this project on several premises regarding poetry, philosophy, and affect. First, literature, especially poetry, goes furthest in plumbing the powers and possibilities of language, and philosophy exercises thought's furthest reach in precision and consistency. Furthest not fullest, since neither poetry nor philosophy can ever exhaust the possibilities or reach of language and thought. Second, the question of affect needs to be addressed primarily by means of aesthetic theory, a premise tacitly shared by the quartet of Kant, Nietzsche, Heidegger, and Deleuze. Third, affect can be studied with some precision in poetry because it resides there not in speaking *about* feelings but in the very speaking and way of speaking. And, finally, the interpretation of poetry straddles three distinct, never fully synthesizable theoretical fields—poetics, aesthetics, and rhetoric—which foreground, respectively, creativity, receptivity, and persuasion. Poetry is the site that stirs theoretical reflection in all three disciplines but never lets theory wholly resolve them. In that sense, there is an incommensurability between poetry and theory; between poetry and philosophy. That strife animates what follows.

Part One: The Poetics of Affect brings the Heideggerian triad mood–understanding–discourse to bear on a many-sided inquiry on the nature of affect from Kant's "transcendental aesthetic" to Deleuze's "transcendental empiricism" to Nietzsche's Dionysian/ Apollonian conflict, and on literary interpretation via engagement with Pinter, Poe, Baudelaire, and Li-Young Lee. A strength of Heidegger's primordial triad is that it articulates in a philosophical register the inseparability of the affective, cognitive, and linguistic dimensions of human experience and action. Literature and its interpretation are the emphatic site of that inseparability.

Part Two: Feeling and the Vocation of Criticism unfolds from a basic question. Can the relevance of Kant's aesthetic theory be rethought in light of Nietzsche's powerful criticisms, Deleuze's innovative commentaries, and Heidegger's attempted appropriations? The three chapters in this section are an attempt to revise and reinvigorate several Kantian themes—affect and judgment, the beautiful and the sublime, form and formlessness—in light of the hydra-headed critique of enlightenment, modernity, and universalism,

indeed even of the human, associated with Nietzsche, Heidegger, and Deleuze. And to do so without merely rejecting those critiques. To accomplish
that dual task requires two apparently contradictory lines of argument. Going
back to Nietzsche's inaugural response to Kant, it is necessary to pry aesthetic
judgment loose from its parallel with the categorical imperative. And, on the
other hand, it is necessary to reaffirm the appeal to universal agreement that
Kant lodges within aesthetic experience itself and that the others of the quartet so vehemently reject.

PART I

The Poetics of Affect

/1/ Before inaugurating modern aesthetic theory in the *Critique of Judgment*, Kant explored the aesthetic in the root sense of perceiving and sensing (*aist-hesis*). The "transcendental aesthetic" postulates that in order for external objects to be perceived in space and time, the mind must sense space and time without the presence of any such external object—a sensing of itself. Space and time are the mind's *self-affection*. This touchstone of modern philosophy shapes debates regarding affect, sensation, and space and time, as well as aesthetic theory. Merleau-Ponty contests the disembodied nature of Kant's postulate by examining the ambiguities of touching/being touched/touching oneself. Daniel Heller-Roazen and Judith Butler, in intriguingly different interpretations of Merleau-Ponty, address the otherness in self-affection, Aristotelian friendship for the one and the traumatic core of selfhood for the other, reflecting the difference of ancient and modern structures of feeling. Self-arousing passions such as jealousy are turned outward in Aristotle but inward in modern settings. Harold Pinter's *Betrayal* dramatizes jealousy's involuted rage, an affecting of oneself rather than a violence inflicted on another. A juxtaposition of Poe and Freud brings to light the question of affect and self-affection in aesthetic theory itself. Does reception retrace the artwork's creation, or are the motives and gratifications of creation radically divergent from the gratifications and affects in reception? Heidegger's approach to mood, emotion, or state-of-mind as attunement questions the Kantian inside/outside in perception and feeling. Beyond that, it sits at the heart of such central concepts as the "ontological difference," "present-at-hand" and "ready-to-hand," "equipment" and "artwork," and the temporality of *Angst*.

/2/ Lyric poetry plumbs the link between mood and trope, that is, feeling and language, affect and expression. There is a *passion of the signifier*, whether the figurative action of poetry or the animating motives of critical method. Paul de Man exemplifies the linguistic turn in literary studies, especially in readings of Rousseau and Baudelaire. Counterposed to some of his most powerful insights, which implacably lead to the binary logical impasse of interpretation he calls "aporia," is the triadic mood–understanding–discourse. In poetic discourse, trope provokes interpretation, and interpretation discloses mood. The affective labyrinth of Baudelaire's poetry and its duality of *spleen* and *ideal* occasion an attempt to give methodological consistency to the Heideggerian triad. Two problematics come to the fore. The question of subjectivity, interiority, selfhood, and identity is posed by poetry that knits or knots together mood–*I*–trope. And the question of pathos and form, the relation of the poet's suffering and creativity, is acute with Baudelaire, whose verse forms have often been interpreted as the salutary imposition of order on the emotional and existential chaos of his life and character. Against such a therapeutic view, Maurice Blanchot and Erich Auerbach support a consideration of Baudelaire's poetry as giving form to, rather than constraining or healing, the disorder of his soul. Another angle on mood and trope as well as pathos and form is found in the poetry of Li-Young Lee, for whom exile, family, and the past century's "diary of fires" create layers of memory and dream, imagination and witness. Via Lee and Baudelaire the question of the lyric *I* comes into focus anew, reviving the dialectical approaches of Hegel and Nietzsche to the "self" in poetic creation.

/3/ Heidegger's most extensive contribution to aesthetic theory is "The Origin of the Work of Art," the essay that develops his seminal notions of earth and world; the distinction of mere things, equipment, and artworks; and truth as an effect of the difference between what an artwork represents and what it discloses. Gilles Deleuze's most concrete reflection on art is his *Francis Bacon: The Logic of Sensation.* For Heidegger, the question of being is at the heart of philosophy and of art; for Deleuze, it is the question of life and sensation—ontology versus vitalism. Heidegger begins with something like the adolescent who awakens to the world inherited from others and questions what it is, that it is, how it can become one's own. Deleuze begins with being alive: "Even when one is a rat. . . ." Two such incommensurate philosophical orientations unexpectedly converge when it comes to reflecting on the nature of the artwork. In Heidegger's aesthetics, earth plays a role analogous to sensation in Deleuze's. Out of their shared concern to foreground the materiality of art and not reduce it to matter (*hylē, materia*) to which the artist gives form (*morphē, forma*), Deleuze and Heidegger converge around three theses on art: its difference from what it represents, its paradoxical standing as "the self-positing of the created," and its exceeding of any communicative relation between creator and recipient. From these emerges an enigma about aesthetic receptivity itself. In Deleuze's terms, the affect of an artwork is independent of both creator and recipient, and the work is only experienced by viewers, listeners, or readers "if they have the strength for it." But what is this independence? And what is this strength? Shakespeare's Sonnet 120 provides a test, bringing the discussion of affect and art back to the rhetoric of poetry and bridging the divide that would separate sensation and affect from hermeneutics. Interpretation is the way to the work's affect. Finally, Heidegger's way of connecting language, art, and truth is interrogated via Deleuze's bracketing of "truth" in favor of the idea that science, philosophy, and art are three distinct—indeed, coequal but incommensurate—modes of thinking. Art, he asserts, thinks in percepts and affects.

Affect, Self-Affection, Attunement

nam quotiens liquidis porreximus oscula lymphis,
hic totiens ad me resupino nititur ore.
posse putes tangi: minimum est, quod amantibus obstat.

For, often as I stretch my lips toward the lucent wave, so often with upturned face he strives to lift his lips to mine. You would think he could be touched—so small a thing separates our loving hearts.

O V I D , *Metamorphoses* III, 451–53

Touch

Long before Kant inaugurated modern aesthetic theory in the *Critique of Judgment*, he explored the aesthetic in the root sense of perceiving and sensing (*aisthesis*). Under the heading of the Transcendental Aesthetic in the *Critique of Pure Reason*, he addresses the conditions of possibility of feeling and perception. When Descartes explains in *The Passions of the Soul* that an emotional state cannot be directly willed but can only be "aroused or suppressed . . . indirectly through the representation of things" that are associated with it, he tacitly introduces auto-affection into the discussion of affect. The notion of auto-affection makes its appearance in modern thought in various guises, usually in connection with attempts to grasp the fundamental conditions of sensory and perceptual experience. The *locus classicus* is the Transcendental Aesthetic.

Kant postulates that space and time are the "two pure forms of sensible intuition, serving as principles of *a priori* knowledge," in the sense of "pure intuition and the mere forms of appearances" without which no empirical objects could appear to the mind and which are themselves prior to any such appearance and do not require the presence of any empirical object.[1] "By means of outer sense, a property of our mind, we represent to ourselves objects as outside us, and all without exception in space. . . . We can never represent to ourselves the absence of space, though we can quite well think it as empty of objects. It must therefore be regarded as the condition of possibility of appearances, and not as a determination dependent upon them."[2] As the pure (and necessary) form of sensible intuition and of appearances, space is empty. Time is comparable, but with a twist. Like space, time is necessary for appearances to be sensed and is independent of them: "Neither coexistence nor succession would ever come within our perception, if the representation of time were not presupposed as underlying them *a priori*. . . . We cannot, in respect of appearances in general, remove time itself, though we can quite well think time as void of appearances. Time is, therefore, given *a priori*. In it alone is actuality of appearances possible at all."[3] Time is not simply comparable to space, however, since as "the form of inner sense, that is, of the intuition of ourselves and of our inner state," time is "the formal *a priori* condition of all appearance whatsoever. Space, as the pure form of all *outer* intuition, is so far limited; it serves as the *a priori* condition only of outer appearances." While "all outer appearances are in space," "all appearances whatsoever, that is, all objects of the senses," inner and outer, "are in time."[4]

It is easy to see why this crux right at the outset of the First Critique became a point of reference and controversy for philosophers ever after. It led Kant himself to acknowledge that his claim that time is "an inner sense in respect of the form of that sense," that is, that time is the pure form of our inner sense of ourselves, touches on a vexing question: "The whole difficulty is as to how a subject can inwardly intuit itself; and this is a difficulty common to every theory."[5] It is beyond the scope and capacity of my project to resolve the difficulty; I want simply to mark it so that it can be recognized in the various theoretical texts to be encountered. The shape of the difficulty for Kant lies in keeping up the distinction between pure contentless self-sensing by which the subject intuits itself (time as pure a priori intuition) over against any notion of self-consciousness as a foundational knowledge of self. Inner sense is self-affection, not self-knowledge: "It can be nothing but the mode in which the mind is affected through its own activity (namely, through its positing of its representation), and so is affected by itself."[6] Self-consciousness in the epistemological sense of the endeavor "to seek out (to apprehend) that which lies in the mind" cannot be foundational because it presupposes, and is limited by, the self-affection of inner sense as time: the mind "intuits itself not as it would represent itself if immediately self-active, but as it is affected by itself, and therefore as it appears to itself, not as it is."[7] *As it appears to itself, not as it is*: one difficulty may thus be resolved by distinguishing inner sense as self-affection from self-activity in the sense of the sovereign positing of knowledge, but another difficulty lingers: auto-affection implies some sort of joining of receptivity and activity.

The problem of human—or sentient—beings' inward intuiting of themselves is a question, then, of the fold along whose crease suffering and doing, undergoing and acting, passivity and activity, feeling and making felt are joined and distinguished. If our thinking were to start not from the transcendental aesthetic but from a supposed immediacy of bodily experience, the exemplary auto-affection might be the sense of touch, since to touch is to make oneself be touched and to be touched is to feel oneself touching. And what if it is literally a question of touching oneself, from licking one's lips to showering, from masturbation to interlocking the fingers of one's hands or simply touching one hand with the other? This last is the example used by Maurice Merleau-Ponty in a reflection on touching and being touched that crops up at crucial points in the draft and fragments of his unfinished work *The Visible and the Invisible.*

According to his reflection, even as I touch my other hand while it is touching something else, the two (or three) events of sensation do not really coincide. The term *coincidence* is given a richly ambiguous temporal, logical, and symbolic significance:

> We spoke summarily of a reversibility of the seeing and the visible, of the touching and the touched. It is time to emphasize that it is a reversibility always imminent and never realized in fact. My left hand is always on the verge of touching my right hand touching the things but I never reach coincidence; the coincidence eclipses at the moment of realization, and one of two things always occurs: either my right hand really passes over to the rank of touched, but then its hold on the world is interrupted; or it retains its hold on the world, but then I do not really touch *it*—my right hand touching, I palpate with my left hand only its outer covering.[8]

The sense of noncoincidence, nonunity, interrupted reversibility leads Merleau-Ponty to postulate that "this hiatus between my right hand touched and my right hand touching" implies that within tactility itself lies the untouchable.[9] From the undeveloped "working notes": "To touch and to touch oneself . . . do not coincide in the body: the touching is never exactly touched. This does not mean that they coincide 'in the mind' or at the level of 'consciousness.' Something else is needed for the junction to be made: it takes place in the *untouchable.*"[10]

Merleau-Ponty is here in the midst of working out his idea of flesh, through which he rethinks being-in-the-world in the light of thoroughly embodied Dasein. Heidegger establishes that the world is not something wholly outside me since I am *in* the world. For Merleau-Ponty, the sense of sight and the sense of touch *bring to appearance* the visible and the tangible; the world occurs as the visible and tangible, and I am in the world as sight and touch but also as visible and tangible to others and so to the world. There is, in his marvelous metaphor, an "intertwining" or "chiasm" of touching and the tangible and seeing and the visible. Again with reference to the hand as felt from within, as touching something and as touched by the other hand: "Through this crisscrossing within it of the touching and the tangible, [my hand's] own movements incorporate themselves into the universe they interrogate, are recorded on the same map as it: the two systems are applied upon one another, as the two halves of an orange."[11] The crisscrossing or chiasm of embodied Dasein and the world is what Merleau-Ponty calls "flesh," the flesh of human existence and the flesh of the world. His fragmentary note on the untouchable hints, I think, at his realization that if touching and being touched actually coincided, if they were fully or perfectly reciprocal, then Dasein and world as well as self and other would congeal or fuse into an unfeeling and unfelt mass. It is in that sense that touching and being touched "take place in the untouchable." The reversibility of touching into being touched or of being touched into touching occurs across a gap.

Or, drawing on Merleau-Ponty's other metaphor, within the chiasm there is an invisible intangible chasm. Staying with hand experiments, if you press the tip of your thumb to the tip of the forefinger and hold them together, you soon cease to feel the contact at all, either the touching or the being touched.

The suggestiveness of these notions of chiasm and the untouchable, these images and metaphors of embodied being-in-the-world, has inspired penetrating reflections by Daniel Heller-Roazen and Judith Butler. Both of them link Merleau-Ponty's problematic to the philosophical tradition and draw out the implications for ethics as well as ontology, even as they head toward contrasting conclusions.

Heller-Roazen relates the untouchable to Aristotle's reflections on sensation and touch and Thomas Aquinas's commentaries on Aristotle. Those two philosophers are essential landmarks in Heller-Roazen's deft and learned book *The Inner Touch: Archaelogy of a Sensation* as he takes up from multiple points of view both ancient and modern the difficulty of accounting for how we inwardly intuit ourselves. From what can appear to be certain inconsistencies and contradictions in Aristotle's various discussions of the senses and sensation, the human in relation to the animal, and the nature of the soul, Heller-Roazen develops a quite unified reflection that hinges on the understanding of touch. For Aristotle, touch is a sense, like sight, hearing, smell, and taste, but at the same time it is *primus inter pares*: "'there is a common faculty that accompanies all the senses, by which one senses that one is seeing and that one is hearing.' . . . Complex sensation and the sense of sensing, too, are now said to number among the capacities of a single common dimension of sensation. Together they form the function of a 'dominant sense organ' . . . , which, we read a few lines later, 'remains for the most part simultaneous with touch.'"[12] Aquinas refines this idea to the point of considering touch to be the foundation of sensitivity itself. He also follows Aristotle's motif of treating touch as the sense more developed in humans than animals, as opposed to the sense of smell, and of associating the degree of individuals' refinement or sensitivity of touch to their temperament, moral amplitude, and intelligence. "When Aristotle in [the *Metaphysics*] defines the most fully realized of all intellectual acts, the activity proper to a god, he invokes no power other than that of the tactile being. The greatest of all intelligences, we read in a decisive passage of Book Lambda, 'becomes the intelligible by touching and by thinking, in such a way that intelligence and intelligible become the same.'"[13]

Touching and thinking: Heller-Roazen sees the possibility that these distinct components of intelligence are joined in some fundamental way, intertwined, as Merleau-Ponty might say: "What would it mean for touch to be the root of thinking and for thinking, in turn, to be in its most elevated form a kind of touch?"[14] Merleau-Ponty himself plays on thought's tactile, prehensile, and manual connotations as "grasping." Heller-Roazen turns to the fragments on the untouchable in *The Visible and the Invisible* to clarify a subtle irregularity in Aristotle's reflections on the senses; unlike the other senses as he analyzes them, touch has no clear object, organ, or medium. Heller-Roazen sees a kinship between this Aristotelean obscurity and Merleau-Ponty's untouchable. What is it that touching and thinking reach toward but do not touch, even as this untouchable is the source—or condition of possibility—of thinking and touching? Once again Heller-Roazen finds a response in Aquinas: "Although he differentiates the sense of sensing from the thought of thinking, he still believes them open to a single terrain: our life. 'When we sense that we are sensing and when we think that we are thinking,' the angelic doctor concludes, 'we sense and we think that we are.'"[15] Drawing on the pagan Aristotelean and Christian Thomist philosophical lineages, Heller-Roazen is thus able to specify (or redesignate) the untouchable as life—as *being* in the sense of *our life*: "Our being is the common element to which both perception and intellection ultimately lead."[16] And leaning more toward Aristotle than Aquinas, he gives ethical weight to this very orientation or disposition toward life on the part of touching and thinking because it grounds (or exposes) the nature of friendship: "'Life,' the Philosopher maintains, 'is a thing good and pleasant in itself.' . . . That, he explains, is why to feel affection for the intimate 'other self' (*heteros autos*) that is the friend is above all to feel affection for the good and pleasant thing that is his life: to sense an existence jointly and in common."[17] Ethics, from this perspective, stems from the affirmation of being as living, life itself being the untouchable ground of thinking and touching.

Judith Butler delves into a seminar Merleau-Ponty gave a decade before working on *The Visible and the Invisible*, in particular his commentary on the late seventeenth- and early eighteenth-century philosopher Nicolas Malebranche. As in much of her work, Butler is ultimately concerned with the originary division, destitution, insufficiency, wound, loss, or traumatic hole that at once afflicts human subjectivity but also enables it. At issue is the nature of the primordial scission and its ethical as well as psychological consequences. Her illuminating analysis of Merleau-Ponty's seminar shows that he is drawn to that aspect of Malebranche's thought which recognizes that feeling is an essential dimension of human being and knowledge but can neither be attributed to nor have originated in oneself. Malebranche, according to Butler, "sought to rectify Descartes's understanding of mind, arguing that the order of ideal intelligibility is disclosed through sentient experience," not solely through clear and distinct ideas, as is the case with mathematical truths. By the same token, then, "it is not possible to have such clarity and distinctness with respect to one's own self, considered as a *sentiment intérieure*."[18] If sentience and inner feeling underpin "the idea of our own being" but do not derive from our own mind (the *I* of the *cogito*), then our very self-sensing is not an auto-affection. "Malebranche contends, against Descartes, that 'nothing is more certain than an internal sentiment [feeling] to establish knowledge that a thing exists,' but there is no way for sentiment itself to furnish the grounds for the existence of anything; it attests to an existence that is brought into being by an elsewhere, a constitutive alterity."[19] For Malebranche, such a constitutive alterity must be God. The *I* and the being in the proposition *cogito ergo sum* are "not a direct inference, but a manifestation of the divine 'word' as it makes itself present in experience itself."[20]

Malebranche presents Merleau-Ponty with the necessity of thinking through a distinctive constellation of notions while transposing them from the theological domain. The soul and the body are not separate in the Cartesian manner; rather, sentience and feeling give rise to the sense of one's own being and the being of things in the world. Therefore, ideas do not arise solely from the mind, and it is not possible for the mind to apprehend or bring to consciousness the sentient source of ideas or the source of sentience itself. In Malebranche, following Butler's interpretation, "grace, understood as the moment of being touched by God and as the rupture that such a touch performs, reveals to us the divine life, where that life is understood, if 'understanding' is the word, as an interruption of understanding, a sudden interruption of our time and perspective by that of another."[21] Extrapolating into her own terms, this interruption "establishes the field of experience through a traumatic inauguration, that is, in the form of a break, a discordance, or a cleavage of temporalities"; it is thus that she glosses Malebranche's precept *I can feel only what touches me* by attributing the touch to a constitutive alterity and characterizing feeling as "the sentient relation to an animating alter-ity."[22] Accordingly, what Merleau-Ponty finds compelling in Malebranche is a constitutive nonknowledge inseparable from life and being. From the semi-nar: "I only know that by experience I can think the past; my memory is not known to me by being seized directly as an operation. My reference to the past is not my work. I receive certain memories that are given to me. I am therefore not a spirit who dominates and deploys time, but a spirit at the disposition of some powers, the nature of which it does not know. I never know what I deserve [vaux], whether I am just or unjust. There is a way I am simply given to myself, and not a principle of myself."[23] Therein lies the first approximation of the flesh and the untouchable explored a decade later. The noncoincidence that Merleau-Ponty attributes to touching and being touched suggests an enabling passivity in the sense of, in Butler's words, "a kind of *primary undergoing* for which we have always and only an obscure and par-tial knowledge" (my italics); the association of freedom with self-originating activity in opposition to passivity is overturned in the postulation instead of "a realm of primary impressionability" or "a certain passivity as the condition of freedom."[24] Butler leaves open the question of whether Merleau-Ponty's own work provides "a fundamental inquiry into the animating conditions of human ontology,"[25] and she concludes instead with the ethical implications, resonant with Emmanuel Lévinas, of the constitutive otherness at the heart of subjectivity itself and with the psychoanalytic awareness of our radical de-pendence as newborns on others' care: "Our inability to ground ourselves is based on the fact that we are animated by others into whose hands we are born and, hopefully, sustained."[26]

Even this quick sketch of various conceptual and metaphorical approaches to the enigma of auto-affection confirms Kant's observation that it is a "dif-ficulty for every theory." Our inward intuiting of ourselves is construed as a self-contained circuit in Kant's transcendental aesthetic, where the mind's (self-)sensing of time and space without contents is postulated as the pre-condition of its perception of external and internal objects. Merleau-Ponty eschews the transcendental perspective in order to think through embodied Dasein's being-in-the-world as a mesh of sentient, perceptual, and affective processes and exemplifies them in touching and being touched. In then tak-ing account of the impossibility for touching and being touched to "coincide," he offers the paradoxical notion that the site of touching and being touched is the untouchable. That paradox generates responses from Heller-Roazen and Butler that overlap and then diverge. Heller-Roazen draws on Aristotle and Aquinas and affiliates the untouchable with being in the sense of "our life": "Our being is the common element to which both perception and intellection lead. Element, but not object: for neither the faculty of sensation nor that of thought could grasp the fact 'that we are' (*nos esse*) as one thing among others. The fact is untouchable, although, 'not something transcendent.' "[27] Butler draws on Malebranche to formulate the subject's primary animation by an Other(ness) whose conceptualization-symbolization is unsettled, ranging from the divine grace of God's Word to primary caregiving (a.k.a. maternal love). The ethical field opens in Butler's view through the pertubations of this obscure and untouchable other that is within the self, without which the self would not *be*, and thanks to which it vacillates between abjection and love. Heller-Roazen, in keeping with the image of ancient Athens's sun-drenched, open-air solidarities, postulates that thought and perception orient themselves heliotropically toward the life-affirming ethics of friendship. Thus, an ethics arising from the subject's "traumatic inauguration" and inner discord (Butler) versus an ethics that spontaneously values flourishing and living well and manifests itself in delight in the other's flourishing and well-being (Heller-Roazen). Hence too the various determinations of the other: Friend or inscrutable source of self? Divine grace or maternal love or living's inborn search for happiness? Let's note in passing that a philosophical vitalism might well assert that the pure passivity that is the condition of activity is simply life, *bios*, as the animating force that in befalling the organism animates it and causes it to strive. Heidegger—who has an allergy to vitalism, deconstructs any theology of grace, and remains unaware of the philosophical significance of mothering and infancy—designates Dasein's feeling that its own being and its world are not of its own making as *thrownness*.

Betrayal, or, Involuted Rage

This cacophony of theories highlights two sets of problems that, to come back now to the question of the rhetoric and poetics of affect, recur irrepressibly and seem perpetually unresolved.

The first concerns the tensions or differences between ancient and modern structures of feeling, which are vivid in the juxtaposition of Heller-Roazen and Butler. The unperturbed affirmation of life's eudemonistic aim contrasts starkly with the constitutive emptiness or trauma associated with modern subjectivity. Consider rage. Self-affection as self-arousal and self-persuasion in the ways considered by Aristotle and Descartes is reflected in everyday experience by such expressions as "getting worked up," "nurturing a grievance," "poking at a wound," and "brooding." Even jealous rage in response to betrayal is seldom purely spontaneous; it has to be sustained, built up again and again from the rhythmic, repetitive revival of the enraging representation—the image of the other's witnessed or imagined act with someone else—and, as Aristotle avers, the fury finds sustenance in the fantasized pleasures of revenge. An ancient Greek marshals the thymotic passion of jealousy toward action. If his or her modern counterpart undertakes any sort of violence, it is considered not a natural act, but acting-out. In the modern structure of feeling, self-affected murderous rage is sanctioned only if its path bends back toward self-pity, moral righteousness, a sense of victimhood, or some eventual mix of forgetting and forgiving. Such involuted rage can be seen as a civilizational advance not only because it repudiates physical violence, but also because it etches the modern individual's complex, indeed contradictory, interiority.

The affective involutions of jealous rage in post-thymotic times are portrayed with pathos and biting humor in Harold Pinter's *Betrayal*. Jerry, who until two years ago had been carrying on a long affair with Emma, the wife of Robert, his best friend, finds out from her that she and Robert are splitting up and that she has told him about the affair. Jerry is led to believe that she told him the previous night. With a sense of urgency he invites Robert over to talk and expresses his dismay at Emma's act—"The fact is I can't understand . . . why she thought it necessary . . . after all these years . . . to tell you . . . so suddenly . . . last night . . ." and—apparently not hearing Robert say, "Last night?"—blames her for breaching his and Robert's friendship: "Without consulting me. Without even warning me. After all, you and me. . . ."[28] It turns out that Emma confessed the affair four years ago while it was still going on. Jerry is now even more perplexed and agitated.

JERRY: But we've seen each other . . . a great deal . . . over the last four years. We've had lunch.
ROBERT: Never played squash though.
JERRY: I was your best friend.
ROBERT: Well, yes, sure.
JERRY *stares at him and then holds his head in his hands.*
Oh, don't get upset. There's no point.
Silence
JERRY *sits up.*
JERRY: Why didn't she tell me?
ROBERT: Well, I'm not her, old boy.
JERRY: Why didn't you tell me?
Pause
ROBERT: I thought you might know.
JERRY: But you didn't know for *certain*, did you? You didn't *know*!

ROBERT: No.
JERRY: Then why didn't you tell me?
Pause
ROBERT: Tell you what?
JERRY: That you knew. You bastard.
ROBERT: Oh, don't call me a bastard, Jerry.
Pause
JERRY: What are we going to do?
ROBERT: You and I aren't going to do anything. My marriage is finished. I've
    just got to make proper arrangements, that's all. About the children.[29]

Whether Jerry has harbored the fact of his transgression over the years as a
source of guilt, aggression, pride, or fear is left unknown. What the play dramatizes is that he is crushed that his betrayal of Robert elicits no response.
And that it didn't even elicit a response four years ago in the midst of the affair
itself. Betrayal turns inside out. It's Jerry who feels betrayed. He feels betrayed
by Robert's indifference. He feels betrayed that Emma would expose him to
his best friend without consulting or warning him. He feels betrayed that the
couple left him in the dark about the revelation of his betrayal, reducing him
to the victim of dramatic irony as he remained ignorant of the others' shared
knowledge of his own secret. Jerry finds himself diminished and disregarded.
"*Let anger, then, be*," according to Aristotle's definition, "*desire, accompanied
by pain, for revenge for an obvious belittlement of oneself*." But in the emotional convolutions of *Betrayal*, Jerry is belittled by the fact that his betrayal
of Robert aroused no desire for revenge in Robert himself. His crime has not
even warranted an accusation; his resulting belittlement is pain unaccompa-
nied by desire. The thymotic capacity to become impassioned over a threat to
one's sense of self turns inward and flattens not only for Jerry but for Robert
as well.

The second problematic regards the nature of affect once affecting oneself and being affected by oneself are taken into account. Latent too within
the question of auto-affection is its relation to affecting and being affected
by another. Auto-affection can be postulated as a circuit perfectly closed on
itself only when held to be without content, without objects or their representation. As soon as there is an empirical dimension in self-sensing and
self-intuiting, some kind of interval or discrepancy comes into play between
affecting and being affected. Kant himself acknowledges as much when, in
distinguishing the mind's self-affection from self-knowledge, he asserts, in
all consistency with his inaugural position, that the mind "intuits itself . . . as
it is affected by itself, and therefore as it appears to itself, not as it is."[30] *As it*

appears to itself, not as it is: the contents of the mind, just as will be the case with the objective representations of what is outside the self, do not grasp the thing-in-itself but only its appearance. Kant's conception can be taken in the spirit of limitation, which is how he meant it: our experience of ourselves takes place within the limitations of human finitude. Or it can be construed more radically, as it is for example by Slavoj Žižek, to indicate that in the deepest recesses of the self resides an uncanny and unknowable Thing that haunts consciousness precisely because one strives to know oneself and in the very endeavor encounters the presence of the unrepresentable Thing.[31] Here again are resonances—let's say a family resemblance—with Aristotle's opacity, Merleau-Ponty's untouchable, and Butler's constitutive alterity. However it is that the discrepancy in self-affection marks the intrusion of an inscrutable other within the self, it surely raises by implication questions about the intersubjective chiasm of affecting another, being affected by another, and the other's affecting and being affected by oneself. It is as though four vectors traverse the simplest *we touched*. Touching one another, like touching oneself, hides reciprocal asymmetries behind apparent symmetry.

Poe's Raven and Freud's Jokes

Symmetries and asymmetries in affecting and being affected are especially pertinent to aesthetics and poetics. Literature and art throw a special light on the question, and nothing illumines auto-affection quite so brightly as the theory and practice of Edgar Allan Poe. The thesis of "The Philosophy of Composition" is seldom taken at face value, for Poe claims that the composition of a poem has nothing to do with the frequently purveyed idea of "a species of fine frenzy—an ecstatic intuition—" but results straightforwardly from deduction and logic. He lays out the features of "The Raven" not simply as the end product of the creative process, but as the series of inaugural decisions he made before his pen ever touched paper, deductions made purely by determining the best choice in each category of composition: The ideal length for a poem to sustain uninterrupted attention: *a hundred lines*. The source of the purest, most elevated pleasure: *Beauty*. The highest tone to accompany the contemplation of Beauty: *sadness* ("melancholy is . . . the most legitimate of all poetical tones"). A structural pivot: a *refrain*. How to heighten the monotonous and repetitive refrain's effect: *variation* of what the refrain applies to. Two further deductions: "Since its application was to be repeatedly varied, it was clear that the *refrain* itself must be brief. . . . This led me at once to a single word as the best *refrain*." And because the refrain "must be sonorous and susceptible of protracted emphasis," he is "inevitably led to the long *o* as the most sonorous vowel, in connection with *r* as the most producible consonant." Therefore, "the very first word" that came to mind to meet this necessity of sound as well as the "predetermined" melancholic tone was . . . "Nevermore."

A hundred lines; Beauty; melancholy; a sonorous one-word refrain, "Nevermore," variously applied—in the case of each decision, what is chosen, Poe emphasizes, is simply the most universal or the purest possibility in each category. Two decisions remained: First, how to justify a one-word refrain that was too monotonous for a human being to speak? A parrot would be too obvious; a raven was "infinitely more in keeping with the intended *tone.*" Secondly, " 'what, according to the *universal* understanding of mankind, is the *most* melancholy?' Death was the obvious reply." And, so, by these precise deductions Poe has the structure, theme, and situation of his poem and its ultimate dramatic interaction: "I had now to combine the two ideas, of a lover lamenting his deceased mistress and a Raven continuously repeating the word 'Nevermore.'—I had to combine these bearing in mind my design of varying, at every turn, the *application* of the word repeated; but the only intelligible mode of such combination is that of imagining the Raven employing the word in answer to the queries of the lover."[32]

It is thus that Poe demonstrates his thesis "that no one point in [the poem's] composition is referable either to accident or intuition—that the work proceeded, step by step, to its completion with the precision and rigid consequence of a mathematical problem."[33] While there can be little doubt that Poe derived this implacably logical and conscious process of the poem's creation by means of a back-formation from the finished poem, his account highlights a striking feature of "The Raven" itself, namely, that its "unity of impression" arises from the yoking of surprise and deliberateness. The aggrieved speaker is startled by the raven's "Nevermore" and at first ruminates on its presence and even allows himself to believe, to venture the hope, that its visitation is a sign he will be released from his oppressive mourning.

> Then, methought, the air grew denser, perfumed from an unseen censer
> Swung by Seraphim whose foot-falls tinkled on the tufted floor.
> "Wretch," I cried, "thy God hath lent thee—by these angels he hath sent thee
> Respite—respite and nepenthe from thy memories of Lenore;
> Quaff, oh quaff this kind nepenthe and forget this lost Lenore!"
>   Quoth the Raven "Nevermore."

And then, having taken this "Nevermore" as a reply, one that negates his hope of forgetting his dead beloved, he begins to address the raven directly. The next "Nevermore," and then another and another, are anticipated by his own ever more despairing questions and pleas, indeed are elicited by them in mounting self-torment. The poem culminates in auto-affected despair:

> "Prophet!" said I, "thing of evil!—prophet still, if bird or devil!—
> Whether Tempter sent, or whether tempest tossed thee here ashore,
> Desolate yet all undaunted, on this desert land enchanted—
> On this home by Horror haunted—tell me truly, I implore—
> Is there—*is* there balm in Gilead?—tell me—tell me, I implore!"
>   Quoth the Raven "Nevermore."
>
> "Prophet!" said I, "thing of evil!—prophet still, if bird or devil!
> By that Heaven that bends above us—by that God we both adore—
> Tell this soul with sorrow laden if, within the distant Aidenn,
> It shall clasp a sainted maiden whom the angels name Lenore—
> Clasp a rare and radiant maiden whom the angels name Lenore."
>   Quoth the Raven "Nevermore."
>
> "Be that word our sign of parting, bird or fiend!" I shrieked, upstarting—
> "Get thee back into the tempest and the Night's Plutonian shore!
> Leave no black plume as a token of the lie that thy soul hath spoken!
> Leave my loneliness unbroken!—quit the bust above my door!
> Take thy beak from out my heart, and take thy form from off my door!"
>   Quoth the Raven "Nevermore."

Poe says he "first established in mind the climax, or concluding query" and began by composing the middle stanza quoted above (the sixteenth of the poem's eighteen stanzas) so that "this word 'Nevermore' should involve the utmost conceivable amount of sorrow and despair." As regards the speaker's *Befindlichkeit*, he "propounds [his queries] half in superstition and half in that species of despair which delights in self-torture—propounds them not altogether because he believes in the prophetic or demoniac character of the bird (which, reason assures him, is merely repeating a lesson learned by rote) but because he experiences a phrenzied pleasure in so modeling his questions as to receive from the *expected* 'Nevermore' the most delicious because the most intolerable of sorrows."

The aesthetic ideal of "unity of impression" requires the poem to achieve, in Poe's phrase, a "totality, or unity, of effect." What is meant by effect and unity of effect? The poem should produce *an* effect for its reader, that is, just one, toward which all elements of the poem contribute, and the effect in question is of course emotional. The poem effects an affect in the reader that the poet designs from the outset. This design is matched in "The Raven" itself by the speaker's act of effecting an affect in himself. It is as though the bereaved lover's frenzied intensification of his own despair were the inverted double of the poetic act's unfrenzied calculations. The culminating stanzas fuse the speaker's auto-affection and the poet's allo-affection. Such a marriage of self-torment and rational design, superstition and reason, sorrow and pleasure puts the poetics of "The Raven" in line with Poe's narrative innovations in his detective stories and gothic tales. Through C. Auguste Dupin he introduces ratiocination as the structuring principle of detective fiction, and in uncanny stories such as "The Black Cat" he chops storytelling's "symbolic" and "real" planes into a logical distinction that formalizes the difference between narrator and author.[34] The poem, like the stories, melds derangement and ratiocination. In Poe's theoretical image of poetry, poetic composition is the calculated production of an affect in the reader; in the poem itself, the poet's calculation is doubled in the lyric *I*'s self-affecting frenzy. The theory and the practice are a variation on, perhaps even an inspiration for, the idea that aesthetic reception retraces the process of artistic creation in reverse, as though creation and reception fit hand in glove.

A very suggestive account of the asymmetry rather than symmetry between creation and reception is developed in *Jokes and Their Relation to the Unconscious*. The art of the joke is another form of verbal creativity that is intended to produce a precise effect, an eruption of laughter rather than the gratifications of the anticipated shudder of fascinated horror or the eagerly awaited surprise solution of the crime. In the chapter "The Motives of Jokes—Jokes as a Social Process," Freud begins with the observation that the joke's creator has a need to tell the joke: "If one comes across something comic, one can enjoy it by oneself. A joke, on the contrary, *must* be told to someone else. The psychical process of constructing a joke seems not to be completed when the joke occurs to one: something remains over which seeks, by communicating the idea, to bring the unknown process of constructing the joke to a conclusion." His hypothesis: "It is possible that my need to communicate the joke to someone else is in some way connected with the laughter produced by it, which is denied to me but is manifest in the other person."[35]

In this period of his thought, Freud uses the language of "psychical energy" and postulates the zero-sum economy of its investments in various "paths of association" and especially in energy-consuming efforts to inhibit, suppress, or repress disturbing or taboo ideas and associations in order to keep them from becoming conscious. Just as dream work expends psychical energy to construct the nocturnal hallucinations by which repressed thoughts can come to consciousness so well disguised as not to startle the dreamer awake, so joke work—that is, the creative process of inventing a joke—finds a way to put an inhibited, suppressed, or repressed idea into a conscious verbal form. The difference between the joke's creator and its hearer—whom Freud calls the "first person" and the "third person"—lies in their respective expenditures of psychical energy in relation to the joke. The hearer "has bought the pleasure of the joke with very small expenditure on his own part. . . . The words of the joke he hears necessarily bring about in him the idea or train of thought to the construction of which great internal inhibitions were opposed in him too. He would have had to make an effort of his own in order to bring it about spontaneously as the first person; he would have had to use at least as much psychical expenditure on doing so as would correspond to the strength of the inhibition, suppression, or repression of the idea."[36] Since laughter at a joke "is an indication of pleasure," Freud's hypothesis is that the laughter is prompted by "the lifting of the cathexis which has been previously present"; in the hearer's experience, "owing to the introduction of the proscribed idea by means of auditory perception, the cathectic energy used for the inhibition has now suddenly become superfluous and has been lifted, and is therefore now ready for laughter."[37]

Whereas dream work succeeds in not startling the dreamer, joke work succeeds only if, in hearing the joke, "our attention has been caught unawares."[38] It is the sudden superfluousness of inhibition that occasions laughter. There is commonality between teller and hearer in the inhibition to be overcome, but not in the expenditure required to overcome it: "A joke is . . . a double-dealing rascal who serves two masters at once. Everything in jokes that is aimed at gaining pleasure is calculated with an eye to the third person, as though there were internal and unsurmountable obstacles to it in the first person."[39] It costs the hearer very little to laugh at the joke, but it costs the teller a great deal to create it. Although Freud surmises that the teller may derive pleasure "by the roundabout path" of inducing the other's laughter, he remains tentative in explaining—beyond the notion of psychic expenditures—the difference between the pleasure that the joke affords the hearer and the motives that it gratifies in the teller, the source of the desire to make another laugh. The difference, however, is ineluctable. It can only be imagined how Freud might have confirmed, sharpened, and enriched his thinking had he been able to witness the last century and more of stand-up comedy, including the heartbreaking trail of brilliant comedians' depression, alcoholism, addiction, overdoses, and suicides.[40] The *jouissance* of creating the joke and the *jouissance* of laughing at it occur across a chasm that in the brief moment of the telling and the flash of the punch line feels like an intimate bond between kindred spirits, a solidarity that is at once real and illusory, an asymmetry of affecting and being affected and of auto- and allo-affection.

The models of creativity and reception furnished by Poe and Freud are in one sense polar opposites. The symmetry of expression and reception that joins the self-affecting *I* and the aesthetically affected reader of "The Raven" contrasts sharply with the asymmetry of Freud's joke teller and joke hearer. The polarity underscores how tentative and potentially plurivalent any theory of artistic creativity needs to be. Poe and Freud are also, however, united in viewing the creator's intent to be to adduce a particular affect in the reader or auditor. Such is not the case with artistic and literary creativity in general. The gothic tale and the detective story belong to that genre of literary works that attract readers eager to experience a distinct and particular effect that they anticipate in advance, just as we return to the "The Raven" not so that the rereading will alter or deepen our understanding but in order to feel the same thing all over again. Poe helped invent genre fiction and its reliable provocation of readers' desired and expected affects. The import of Freud's foray into the psychological sources of literary creativity in "Creative Writers and Day-Dreaming" is limited by the bias toward popular forms, in particular stories that are barely disguised versions of egoistic (masculine) heroic and erotic wish fulfillment, which are a questionable model for the modern novel. Neither Freud nor Poe provides a sufficiently complex account of artistic creativity, and yet their polarities of auto-affection and allo-affection, artistic calculation and creative frenzy, the fulfillments and despairs of artistic achievement set the parameters for any inquiry into creativity.

The notion that a literary creation is designed for a particular emotional effect construes literature as an instance of rhetoric. It subsumes the literary under the rhetorical. Such a notion was anathema to most twentieth-century critics and especially to the New Critics, who sprang from T. S. Eliot's precepts on poetic autonomy and whose innovative attention to poems' images and metaphors transformed literary analysis. Kenneth Burke was a maverick within this tradition in disputing the separation of poetics and rhetoric; he argued that poetry bridges the two aspects of rhetoric: figures of speech and the art of persuasion. His contemporaries drew the line at persuasion: the poem expresses but does not persuade; even better, it should not mean but be. Burke grants that poetry does not persuade in the Aristotelean modes of forensic and political rhetoric, that is, the persuasion to decision or action. Poetry does not solicit decisions and actions. Rather, it is a *persuasion to attitude*:

> Insofar as a choice of *action* is restricted, rhetoric seeks rather to have a formative effect upon *attitude* (as a criminal condemned to death might by priestly rhetoric be brought to an attitude of repentance and resignation). Thus, in Cicero and Augustine there is a shift between the words "move" (*movere*) and "bend" (*flectere*) to name the ultimate function of rhetoric. This shift corresponds to a distinction between act and attitude (attitude being an incipient act, a leaning or inclination). Thus the notion of persuasion to *attitude* would

permit the application of rhetorical terms to purely *poetic* structures; the study of lyrical devices might be classed under the head of rhetoric, when these devices are considered for their power to induce or communicate states of mind to readers, even though the kinds of assent evoked have no overt, practical outcome.[41]

Persuasion to attitude is akin to a "way of seeing." The poem in Burke's account alters the reader's angle of vision or valuation or recognition regarding some aspect of reality and experience. Poetry is rhetorical in the sense that it effects a shift in attitude by the way it says something. A tension that runs through modern criticism concerns what difference the way-of-saying makes. One extreme could take its motto from Alexander Pope's neoclassical definition according to which the poetic art articulates the already-thought in a pleasant and memorable new way—"True wit is Nature to advantage dressed, / What oft was thought, but ne'er so well expressed"—while for the Romantic and modern traditions the way of saying makes all the difference. Heidegger will go so far as to identify poetry with projective saying: "Projective saying is saying which, in preparing the sayable, simultaneously brings the unsayable as such into a world."[42] Deleuze will attribute to literature and art a specific power of thought, different from that of philosophy and science but on a par with them in displacing the already-thought of *doxa*: "Art thinks no less than philosophy, but it thinks through affects and percepts."[43] Burke himself comfortably vacillates between *doxa*-expressing and *doxa*-transcending or *doxa*-negating interpretations of poetry. I align with a range of modern critics who gravitate toward Heidegger's end of the spectrum—from Maurice Blanchot to Theodor W. Adorno, from Paul de Man to Julia Kristeva—and see in poetry an original opening onto realms of language, experience, and being unmatched by other forms of discourse and thought.

The Ontic Jolt

Poetry's bearing on a central Heideggerian problematic is clarified by Burke's formulation of the persuasion-to-attitude. It resembles the notion running through John Berger's art criticism that a painting lets something be seen for the first time, not only in the sense that the painting is a new and unique object in our field of vision and in the world, but more fundamentally in the sense that it alters, displaces, and reorients our relation to the visible: it shifts our way of seeing and thus makes something visible for the first time.

Just such an unexpected reorienting is at stake in Heidegger's earliest approach to what he calls the "ontological difference." In *Being and Time* he

examines the realm of preunderstandings, opinion, the "they," everyday-
ness, thrownness, and so on, in arguing that human existence (Dasein) is immersed in the world of facticity and the ontic. The ontological reflection he
wants to pursue emerges as a kind of questioning, but it has to emerge out of
ontic experience and perception, not from a preestablished or transcendent
higher plane. There is no direct route to the meaning of being. Heidegger pursues—or dramatizes—this wresting of the ontological from the ontic through
the notion that Dasein is defined by being-in-the-world. His phenomenological "descriptions" dramatize—or conceptualize—the shift from an ontic to an
ontological perspective as those moments when our everyday understanding
of *what is* is jarred into an interrogation of *what it is* and *that it is*. The jarring
is an event within the ontic, an interruption within the everyday.

   Let me illustrate by referring to Heidegger's argument that whereas an abstract logic would say that a mere thing is a more basic entity than a tool, the
phenomenological account shows that we do not have a relation to mere things
except through an event in our everyday use of tools. In his jargon the mere
thing is "present-at-hand" and the tool "ready-to-hand"—the hand again,
replete with the prehensile-cognitive admixture of grasping, apprehending,
comprehending, seizing hold. The upshot of the argument (paras. 15–16)
is that it is through interruptions of the ready-to-hand, as when a tool breaks,
that the present-to-hand (the mere thing) happens phenomenally. From a
purely logical viewpoint this is paradoxical, perhaps even nonsensical: the
present-to-hand appears only *mediately*, glimpsed in the breakdown of the
tool and never given in itself. For Heidegger, the turn "towards understanding the phenomenon of the world ontologically" arises from this glitch in
everyday experience.[44]

   The interruption occurs in the form of a missing tool, a broken tool, the
wrong tool, a tool worthless for *this*, and so on, and Heidegger proposes a
typology of such interruptions as "modes of conspicuousness, obtrusive-
ness, and obstinacy [*Auffälligkeit, Aufdringlichkeit, Aufsässigkeit*]," for "when
equipment cannot be used, this implies that the constitutive assignment of
the 'in-order-to' to a 'towards-this' has been disturbed." Normally such "assignments," that is, the intentions, uses, and purposes materialized in the tool
and the capacities and skills for using it, are themselves "not observed; they
are rather 'there' when we concernfully submit ourselves to them [*Sichstellen
unter sie*]. But *when an assignment has been disturbed*—when something is
unusable for some purpose—then the assignment becomes explicit" (H 74).
The "there" refers of course to the *there* of being-there (Da-sein); the
becoming-explicit happens thanks to the "*break* in [the] referential contexts"
of everyday practice and prompts a new possibility in experience, since what

is momentarily broken is the ready-to-hand's inconspicuous, unobtrusive, and pliant belonging to the web of Dasein's concerns and everyday activities. "Our circumspection comes up against emptiness, and now sees for the first time *what* the missing article was ready-to-hand *with*, and *what* it was ready-to-hand *for*." With this interruption, break, and emptiness, "the environment announces itself anew" (H 75).

What is the nature of this new experience? It lies on the very edge of the difference between the ontic and the ontological. Entities have been roughly divvied up into mere things and tools, the present-at-hand and the ready-to-hand. Logically, the mere thing would come first and the tool would be a thing-plus-its-uses. Phenomenologically, the tool has precedence over the mere thing, since Dasein first encounters objects in the world as things to handle and use. When the use and handling break down, Dasein glimpses the "environment" to which itself and the tool belong. Or, rather, to which the tool *did* belong, for as it is emptied of its tool-being "the presence-at-hand in what is ready-to-hand" is brought "to the fore." The tool is part of the flesh of the world so long as it is usable; it loses its worldhood in the very event that makes its belonging to a world apparent: "Whenever the world is lit up in the modes of concern which we have been Interpreting, the ready-to-hand becomes deprived of its worldhood so that Being-just-present-at-hand comes to the fore" (H 75). Since tools are inconspicuous so long as they work and so long as I am immersed in the world, my being-in-the-world clouds what it is to be in the world. "In this *familiarity* Dasein *can lose itself* in what it encounters within-the-world and be fascinated with it " (H 76; my italics). This formulation anticipates the distinction, widely and easily misunderstood, that Heidegger makes between inauthenticity and authenticity. They are not separated by a boundary, nor does authenticity stand firmly above inauthenticity. They relate as a kind of pulsation. When immersed in the world, I scarcely notice the world, the implements it offers, or my immersion in it. But when an implement breaks, I suddenly take note of its being a tool as it ceases being a tool; I awaken to my environment; I sense my own existence in its capacity to be interrupted.

The tool analysis reveals a chiasm: when I use the tool, I lose sight of my being-in-the-world; when the tool breaks, I glimpse its tool-being and my now-disrupted involvements with it. The tool is grasped in its worldly being only when, having broken, it loses its worldhood. This chiasm or pulsation defines the rhythm, indeed the predicament, of Dasein's ontic experience.

The ontological inquiry, by contrast, has to take *world* as its point of departure: "Only on the basis of the phenomenon of the world can the Being-in-itself of entities within-the-world be grasped ontologically" (H 76). However, as with the difference between inauthenticity and authenticity, ontological inquiry's difference from ontic experience does not amount to a firm separation. Another chiasm arises. The ontological inquiry, in its effort of "working out both the phenomenon and the problems of worldhood" (H 76), begins where the taken-for-granted ("familiarity") is no longer taken for granted, and yet its task of explicating the taken-for-granted cannot be accomplished without its own immersion in the taken-for-granted itself. The ontological problematic is hooked to the ontic predicament. Recall the inaugural claim of Dasein analysis: "We are ourselves the entities to be analysed" (H 41). There are in effect three kinds of entities roughly sketched out in *Being and Time*: mere things, tools, and human beings. Humans are the entity in the world whose existence entails asking the meaning of being-in-the-world; world, being, and human being are, for it, a question. The pulsation in ontic experience between self-forgetting immersion in the world and the jarring interruption of that immersion opens the possibility of ontological inquiry. But it does not dictate its direction. That is the predicament which gives *Being and Time* its élan of spiraling, inconclusive questioning. The ontic jolt opens ontological inquiry, but the sought-after meaning of being keeps slipping beyond the reach of Dasein's grasp—here, too, a hint of untouchability, alterity.

What I am calling the ontic jolt corresponds to what Burke calls "persuasion-to-attitude" when it comes to the rhetorical powers of poetic language. Ontologically, the poem works like a broken tool. In light of Heidegger's notion that in poetry "the communication of the existential possibilities of one's state-of-mind . . . become[s] an aim in itself" (H 162), how is the relation between the ontic jolt and attunement (*Gestimmtsein*), mood (*Stimmung*), or state-of-mind (*Befindlichkeit*) to be understood? After all, *attunement* carries the musical connotation of being-in-tune-with, as does the German,[45] while *jolt* suggests a dissonance, jarring, or disruption. By the same token, the fundamental mood or attunement of modern life is identified in *Being and Time* as *Angst*, precisely the feeling of being out of tune with the things of the world. Anxiety is dissonance as a mood, out-of-tune attunement. The stakes that modern poetry poses for the questions raised by Heidegger's thought will begin to come into sharper relief as this jumble of terms—ontic jolt, attunement, mood, *Angst*—is disentangled and brought to bear on the question of trope and the lyrical *I*.

A start on this task will also serve to conclude the discussion of affect and self-affection. It seems clear that Heidegger considers that the notion of *mood*, along with its near-synonyms *attunement* and *state-of-mind*, establishes that feeling or being-affected is a primordial dimension of human existence and so belongs on the ground floor, so to speak, of philosophical inquiry. Being-in-the-world and being-with-others are disclosed in mood. So is mood the basis, in Kant's phrasing, of the subject's intuiting itself? The answer for Heidegger, I think, is simply yes; or perhaps he would simply consider the question to be moot. In his seminar on Nietzsche he said: "Feeling, as feeling oneself to be, is precisely the way we are corporeally. . . . In feeling oneself to be, the body is already contained in advance in that self, in such a way that the body in its bodily states permeates the self. . . . We do not 'have' a body; rather, we 'are' bodily. Feeling, as feeling oneself to be, belongs to the essence of such Being."[46] In the terms set forth in *Being and Time*, the "inner" sensing of oneself is not purely internal, because it is inseparable from being-*in*-the-world and -*with*-others; that is, sensing oneself is at the same time a being-outside-oneself.

The conceptual and linguistic puzzle of mood's straddling of inner and outer receives fuller expression in Heidegger's exposition of Dasein's temporality as "ecstases." Dasein is ineluctably outside itself, for example, in being ever "ahead-of-itself" insofar as its immersion in matters of concern involves anticipation. That is an ontic manifestation of the question. More fundamentally, human time does not constitute a simple flow of nows with past ones susceptible of being remembered and future ones of being anticipated. For this movement of remembering and anticipating to happen at all requires that time itself be an ecstatic going out of itself within and as human existence: "The future, the character of having been, and the Present show the phenomenal characteristics of the 'towards-oneself,' the 'back-to,' and the 'letting-oneself-be-encountered-*by*.' . . . *Temporality is the primordial 'outside-of-itself' in and for itself.* We therefore call the phenomenon of the future, the character of having been, and the Present, the '*ecstases*' of temporality" (H 328–29). "Temporality temporalizes," says Heidegger. It plunges Dasein to and fro in, to borrow Yeats's phrase, "what is past, or passing, or to come" in such a way that all three ecstases pass through and affect one another. Heidegger works out the ecstases of temporality in the second half of *Being and Time*, where he in effect works back through all the elements in the first half, which was devoted to existential analysis of Dasein (being-*there*), now in terms of temporality. Thus, the equiprimordial triad mood—understanding—speech is reexamined in light of each element's specific temporality, its distinctive rhythm of authenticity and inauthenticity, and the unity of the whole (para. 68).

The temporality of state-of-mind is especially pertinent. The thesis is that whereas "understanding is grounded primarily in the future" insofar as it is the plying toward "*a potentiality-for-Being*" (H 336), "one's *state-of-mind* . . . temporalizes itself *primarily in having been*" in the sense that "the existentially basic character of moods lies in *bringing one back to* something" (H 340).

Heidegger's meaning is a bit obscure at this point; what he seems to mean is that because moods are in continual flux, being in a mood orients one "back" toward the markers of one's own continuity across the changes in mood, that is, in a different vocabulary, one's self or "identity." But that is not quite right. Things becomes clearer when he goes on to analyze the temporality of *Angst*: "The world in which I exist has sunk into insignificance. . . . Anxiety is anxious in the face of the 'nothing' of the world; but this does not mean that in anxiety we experience something like the absence of what is present-at-hand within-the-world. The present-at-hand must be encountered in just *such* a way that it does *not* have *any* involvement *whatsoever*, but can show itself in an empty mercilessness" (H 343). Anxiety's disclosure of "an insignificance of the world" opens Dasein to two contrary, indeed oscillating possibilities. On the one hand, "this insignificance reveals the nullity of that with which one can concern oneself—or, in other words, the impossibility of projecting oneself upon a potentiality-for-Being which belongs to existence and which is founded primarily upon one's objects of concern" (H 343). Colloquially, *nothing matters*. On the other hand, and contrariwise, the very "revealing of this impossibility . . . signifies that one is letting the possibility of an authentic potentiality-for-Being be lit up," since "anxiety brings one back to the pure 'that-it-is' of one's ownmost throwness . . . brings one back to one's throwness as something *possible* which *can be repeated*" (H 343).

The repetition of what? That too can seem obscure, but therein lies the distinctive temporality of anxiety. Dasein's throwness, "its naked uncanniness," is obscured by everyday involvement in the world, as shown in the tool analysis. In anxiety, however, insofar as now nothing matters to Dasein, Dasein is brought back to its throwness—nothing matters but I am still *there*—and "becomes fascinated with it": "This fascination . . . not only *takes* Dasein back from its '*worldly*' possibilities, but at the same time *gives* it the possibility of an *authentic* potentiality-for-Being" (H 344). What "can be repeated" is one's individuated-individuating potentiality, which has been disclosed before and is now disclosed again. Heidegger first outlines such repetition with respect to the temporality of understanding, where there is an oscillation between two modes of temporalizing the future, waiting-for and anticipating. Waiting-for is oriented toward one's surrounding, enveloping concerns, toward "what is feasible, urgent, or indispensable in our everyday business"; the future is faced as purely what might befall one and is in that sense "inauthentic" (H 337). The arc of anticipation, by contrast, points toward what one can do or become. Once again a chrono-choreographic image is brought to bear, for it is as though stepping forward draws one to oneself: "The authentic coming-toward-oneself of anticipatory resoluteness is at the same time a coming-back to one's ownmost Self, which has been thrown into its individuation. This ecstasis makes it possible for Dasein to be able to take over resolutely that entity which it already is. In anticipating, Dasein *brings* itself *again forth* into its ownmost potentiality-for-Being. If *Being*-as-having-been is authentic, we call it '*repetition*'" (H 339). A clarification is now possible: the repetition, in bringing one back to "one's ownmost Self," does not establish the selfsameness of that Self through time in the sense of a smooth continuity of identity but rather resituates one as the one who is yet again capable of projects. The plunge through the nothingness *of* the world all the way back to the thrownness of one's own existence *in* the world, connecting past and present, renews one's future orientation in projects and decisions. This "resoluteness" is, however, ever-susceptible to "falling" again into those merely "'*worldly*' possibilities," because the very field in which resoluteness can manifest itself is nothing other than the world. The authentic-inauthentic pulsation permeates the entire realm of experience and action.

Angst is an attunement; it is attunement to the *nothing*. It at once saps human creativity and arouses it. How that pulsation or vacillation specifically bears on the creativity whose outcome is the artwork or poem is the question that will recur in various guises throughout all that follows. As dissonant attunement, *Angst* is the precondition of the ontic jolt. As I read Heidegger's text, there is a discernible parallel between the ontological opening exemplified by the breaking of a tool and the vacillation in anxiety between *nothing matters* and *potentiality-for-being*. And yet to say that *Angst* saps *and* arouses, numbs *and* provokes creativity, leaves much unanswered. What is it that at once stimulates and tranquilizes? Avital Ronell addresses the conundrum in a few luminous and provocative pages on *Being and Time* in her *Crack Wars* by questioning how Heidegger maintains (para. 41) that addiction, along with willing, wishing, and urge, is a derivative of care (*Sorge*) and concern (*Besorgen*), which define Dasein's primordial immersion in-the-world and determine *Angst* as its fundamental mood. What makes affectedness (*Befindlichkeit*), that is, the capacity to be affected, more primordial than the capacity to be addicted? For, as Ronell asserts, addictability exemplifies the very crossing of the inner/outer dichotomy so crucial to Heidegger's own project. "Much like the paradigms installed by endorphins, Being-on-drugs indicates that a structure is already in place, prior to the production of that materiality we call drugs"; conversely, insofar as the drug is a technology, addiction is, playing on Heidegger's own understanding of technology, "Dasein's internalization of *Gesell* according to the chemical prosthesis."[47] Ronell speculates on Heidegger's reluctance to sully *Angst* with toxins:

> One might hazard that Dasein needs to face its intoxication—fascination and vertigo—soberly, that is, with the tensed fist of anxiety. That's why Dasein is split over where to go: it is drawn toward the experience of fascination and passivity even as it is drawn (or draws itself) toward the experience of death.
>
> Of course, the same could be said of the suicidal rush of the addicted Dasein. Except that the addicted Dasein doesn't detach itself from the experience of passivity in order to *decide* upon repetition in time; rather it is inhabited by a compulsion that blindly bypasses finitude's markers. Heidegger may not say it quite this way, but he does go to the trouble of protecting Dasein from making a habit of addiction, urge, wishing and tranquilized "willing," as he puts it. He will do it again in other works, as when he himself injects tranquilizers into the Nietzschean corpus in order to subdue the ravages of *Rausch* (intoxication).[48]

Heidegger also associates addiction (*Hang*) and urge (*Drang*) with life forces. "Dasein's hankering as it falls makes manifest its *addiction* to becoming 'lived' by whatever world it is in. . . . Dasein has become blind, and puts all possibilities into the service of the addiction. On the other hand, the *urge* 'to live' is something toward which one is impelled, and it brings the impulsion along with it of its own accord. It is 'toward this at any price.' The urge seeks to crowd out [*verdrängen*] other possibilities" (H 195). *Technē* and life are vexing notions in Heidegger's thought. His antagonism toward vitalism, that is, any foregrounding of *living* in the analysis of human being, and his multiple interpretations of *technē* will return in relation to Deleuzean sensation (chapter 3), Nietzschean *Rausch* (intoxication, frenzy; chapter 5), and Heidegger's own effort to distinguish the human from the animal without recourse to the notion of the *animale rationale* (chapter 6).

The ontic jolt—however anxiety, frenzy, and urge are ultimately related—occurs in poetry in its powers of persuasion-to-attitude and arises from its capacity to name-by-misnaming. Naming-by-misnaming and persuasion-to-attitude are avatars of classical rhetoric's two branches, figures of speech and the art of persuasion. Poetry, and specifically modern poetry, is marked by the predominance not only of trope and mood but also of the *I*.

It is noteworthy that when Heidegger comments on time and space in the Transcendental Aesthetic in *Kant and the Problem of Metaphysics*, his first major work after *Being and Time*, he leans hard on what can be meant by the *self* in *self-affection*. If time is the self-affection of the self's pure a priori intuition of itself, then in effect there is no self prior to or outside temporality itself. Kant stresses that the intuition of oneself is not self-knowledge but self-affection, and Heidegger interprets and radicalizes that statement as implying that it is not that the self affects itself in time, or even as time, but that the self-affection of time is the condition of possibility of the self. The question of time and being precedes the question of knowledge. But which comes first, time or human being? As the analysis of the ecstases of temporality shows, time ecstasizes as *human* being-in-time, since the ecstases of time are entwined with human experience and its oscillation between inauthentic and authentic. Temporality is ineluctably human, but humans cannot master time. So, too, *being* is a question only insofar as human existence is *there* to ask it; Dasein is the being for whom the meaning of being is a question. Heidegger thereby breaks the purely formal nature of time in Kant's Transcendental Aesthetic and at the same time breaks with the privileging of knowledge over being in the Cartesian *I think, therefore I am* by recovering, or enlisting, Kant's grounding of philosophy in the finitude of human existence. Being-in-space, being-in-time, and being-in-language are ultimately the threefold determination of Dasein's finitude—that is, in Heidegger's theme, Dasein's being-toward-death.

On the immediate horizon, then, lies the question of the difference between the (deconstructed) Cartesian *I* and the (still unformulated) poetic or lyrical *I*.

Mood and Trope in the Lyric

The metaphor is perhaps one of man's most fruitful potentialities. Its efficacy verges on magic, and it seems a tool for creation which God forgot inside one of His creatures when He made him.

JOSÉ ORTEGA Y GASSET, "The Dehumanization of Art"

Passions of the Signifier

No critic took a sharper linguistic turn than Paul de Man. Heidegger's thought permeates his own even though de Man seldom mentions him. He took from Heidegger premises that underlie his own work from at least the early 1960s until his death in 1983. Foremost is the idea that human beings inhabit language in the sense that being-in-language establishes human existence within its world, that is, in Heidegger's terms, establishes Dasein as being-in-the-world. What a world is, what the beings in it are, what human being is—all this "occurs" or "happens" in language, and it happens in time because there is no transcendent truth or ultimate reality to settle the meaning of being. Transposed to literary criticism, the reader encounters in the literary text a concealing/deconcealing of meaning, and since this encounter takes place in time, the text itself is not tethered to any moment in history where its meaning could have been or could be fixed once and for all. The text has no original, ultimate, or permanent meaning. In 1964 de Man challenged formalistic conceptions of literary form: "A text that exists in time cannot be projected in a definitive and well-rounded shape. It has to be integrated into a continuous interpretation, for it is itself a fragment in the incessant interpretation of Being that makes up our history."[1]

It is reasonable to speculate that de Man's reserve regarding Heidegger has to do with the fact that during the German occupation of his native Belgium, de Man, then in his early twenties, collaborated with the Nazis and wrote cultural criticism with a fascist and pro-German slant for *Le Soir* after the Nazis took control of the Brussels daily.[2] Of greater conceptual import is the fact that de Man shied away from any appropriation of Heidegger that hinted at epochal transformation. In another essay from 1964, he disputed views of Heidegger as prophetic or utopian: "Utopian prophecy in any form is alien to him, a dangerous misconception of time as a determined, particularized entity, the very opposite of the open and free time of man's historical project."[3] Even though the prophetic-utopian impulses of Heidegger's thought and teaching during the Third Reich have since come to light, what matters here is that various warnings against the danger of attaching any philosophical or hermeneutic exploration to some definitive image of society or humankind are scattered throughout de Man's work. He is among those readers of Heidegger who, like Dreyfus, Vattimo, Sloterdijk, and Richard Rorty, seek to tame Heidegger and turn the deconstruction of Western metaphysics and the inquiry into human existence away from millenarian overtones and revolutionary expectations.

Of the philosopher's attention to poetic language, de Man wrote, "Since man is defined as the philosophical animal, the being that interprets itself by means of language, true poets can often go further in man's essential project than philosophers, not because . . . they are closer to nature, but because they are closer to language."[4] Yet no matter how inspiring one finds Heidegger on poetry, there is no method to his criticism: he sheds precious little light on how to read poetry, he cares nothing for literary history, and he ignores form. I see de Man as seeking to give methodological consistency to the Heideggerian problematic of language's deconcealing/concealing oscillation. He carries that problematic into the heart of critical method itself, arguing in *Blindness and Insight* that every methodologically consistent interpretation brings to light a complex set of linguistic and symbolic relations within a text at the cost of obstructing others. As with the eye itself, whose blind spot at the point of attachment to the optic nerve enables sight, critical insight takes shape around what the critic fails to see. Every reading is at the same time a misreading. This is not to say that all readings are equally valid. You cannot get a text "right," but you can get it wrong.

At the very core of the radical skepticism for which de Man has often been scorned lies a passion for literature. The most pervasive feature of language for de Man is its bottomless capacity to deceive, dissemble, lie, mislead, occlude. Ever-capable of saying one thing while meaning another, language is the very motor of deception and self-deception, error and fabulation. In everyday life, in our dealings with one another, in every context where human purposes are at work, where suasion—whether intimate, pragmatic, or political—holds sway, there is no surefire escape from deceptions and self-deceptions. This anguish of untrustworthiness is something that de Man usually expresses obliquely by way of glossing or ventriloquizing some other author, but the poignancy comes from himself. Two examples: Elaborating on a passage in Rousseau, de Man distinguishes the fear of falling from fear of another person: "No one can trust a precipice, but it remains an open question, for whoever is neither paranoiac nor a fool, whether one can trust one's fellow man";[5] and from a late essay—the posthumous reconstruction of a lecture—commenting on Schlegel's concept of irony: "Words have a way of saying things which are not at all what you want them to say. You are writing a splendid and coherent philosophical argument but, lo and behold, you are describing sexual intercourse. Or you are writing a fine compliment for somebody and without your knowledge, just because words have a way of doing things, it's sheer insult and obscenity that you are really saying. There is a machine there, a text machine, an implacable determination and a total arbitrariness . . . which inhabits words on the level of the play of the signifier which undoes any narrative consistency of lines."[6] The more recent biographical evidence of de Man's own history of swindles, bigamy, perjury, and falsified credentials reveals how deeply embedded in his early life the rhetorico-linguistic powers of dissembling actually were.[7]

Literature for de Man becomes the refuge from the endless maelstrom of bad faith. But *refuge* is not really the right term, for literature does not quell the duplicity of language. On the contrary, it exposes and plumbs its resources and proliferates the possibilities of saying one thing to mean another more fully than any other kind of discourse. Literature—that is, "literary language," in de Man's phrase—is the one place where language's inexhaustible capacity to say something other than what it means and mean something other than what it says is in full bloom yet without any intention to deceive. Literature holds the possibility of freedom within the endless swerve of meaning—the freedom from the other's dissembling and from one's own motives to deceive. In *The Gay Science* (sect. 344) Nietzsche asks what the will to truth is: is it the will not to allow oneself to be deceived or the will not to deceive? And in *The Genealogy of Morals* (Third Essay, sect. 25) he postulates that "art, in which precisely the *lie* is sanctified and the *will to deception* has a good conscience, is much more fundamentally opposed to the ascetic ideal than is science."[8] The passion that animates de Man's criticism is to pursue every giddying turn of the signifier in this literary space free from deceit.

An inaugurating moment of deconstruction and the linguistic turn lies in de Man's engagement with Rousseau on metaphor and the origin of language. His affinity for Rousseau undoubtedly has many facets: his complex, virtually unclassifiable relation to the Enlightenment and to romanticism; his practice of writing across fictional and nonfictional genres; and the historical misreadings of his texts, including by the Jacobins of 1789. Moreover, Rousseau himself loathed the capacity for deception, which he first encountered in Parisian "society" when he arrived in Paris after abandoning his native republican Protestant Geneva for *ancien régime* France. The artifice of language and gesture in salon culture unnerved him; he retreated to writing in order better to present himself in the absence rather than presence of others, only to discover that the vocation of writing itself was a torment of creation and of publicness. As an endeavor to please and persuade, writing plunges the writer into the very temptation to deceive that he had fled to begin with. Forever agitated at having to pursue a career of talent as a writer, Rousseau denounces "that fatal inequality introduced among men by the distinction of talents and the disparagement of virtue."[9] Rousseau in a nutshell, then: impossible to affix a place in intellectual and literary history, unconstrained by genre, susceptible to horrific misreading, and tormented by duplicity. He is de Man's ideal author.

In his *Essay on the Origin of Languages,* Rousseau asserts that "just as the first motives that made man speak were passions, his first expressions were Tropes. Figurative language [*le langage figuré*] arose first, proper [or literal] meaning [*le sens propre*] was found last. . . . At first men spoke only poetry; only much later did it occur to anyone to reason."[10] He illustrates this Romantic dictum with a fable, the interpretations of which by de Man and Jacques Derrida are in effect the origins of deconstruction.[11] When natural man initially encounters others, he is frightened and sees them "as larger and stronger than himself" and in his fright spontaneously utters an arbitrary sound: GIANT. Only later does he realize that the other is actually another like himself, whereupon he produces a second sound to designate the stranger *and* himself in their likeness: MAN. Henceforth "he will restrict the name *Giant* to the false object that had struck him during his illusion. This is how the figurative word arises before the proper [or literal] word does, when passion holds our eyes spellbound and the first idea which it presents to us is not that of the truth. What I have said regarding words and names applies equally to turns of phrase. Since the illusory image presented by passion showed itself first, the language answering to it was invented first; subsequently it became metaphorical when the enlightened mind recognized its original error and came to use expressions of that first language only when moved by the same passions as had produced it."[12]

A quite different, apparently contradictory account of the origin and evolution of language is found in the Second Discourse. Here the hypothetical first speakers emitted a distinct sound for each distinct object of perception—in de Man's terms, each signifier actually had a kind of one-to-one relation to a real object of perception—so that before, say, the word *oak* came to refer to an indefinite number of trees resembling one another, the speaker produced a unique sound for every tree he saw: A, B, C, D, and so on. The

Essay on the Origin of Languages and the Second Discourse present contrary fables. The one says that the first language was figurative and prompted by passion, while the other says that the first words were so literal and so tied to perception as to be proper nouns, one word per object. De Man deftly points beyond the apparent contradiction. The implication of the second fable is that every common noun in language is in effect itself a metaphor: it subsumes perceptually distinct objects under a single sign on the basis of their resemblance (metaphor is the trope that works off the resemblance of nonidentical things). The conclusion de Man draws is that this simplest common noun, *oak*, is therefore a conceptualization-metaphorization that alludes to an impossible one-word-per-object literalness: "The sheer metonymic enumeration of things that Rousseau describes in the *Discourse* ('if one oak was called *A*, and another was called *B* . . .') is an entirely negative moment that does not describe language as it is or used to be at its inception, but that dialectically infers literal denomination as the negation of language. Denomination could never exist by itself although it is a constitutive part of all linguistic events. All language is language about denomination, that is, a conceptual, figural, metaphorical metalanguage."[13] The first fable postulates the origin of language in impassioning illusion that creates metaphors (*giant*) in the wake of which literal language (*man*) is minted; the second fable postulates that every instance of literal language (*oak*) is a metaphor alluding to a tacit but impossible literalness (A, B, C, D . . .). De Man resolves the apparent contradiction by transforming it into an aporia: language operates between metaphors induced by illusions and illusions of literalness. At this moment, the very idea of sharply, reliably distinguishing the fictive and the historical, the figurative and the literal, the literary and the theoretical in Rousseau's text goes up in smoke.

Baudelaire's Spleen

The deconstructive linguistic turn applied to poetry attains one of its farthest reaches in de Man's late essay "Anthropomorphism and Trope in the Lyric," a posthumously published work that seems complete in its structure and argument but remains incomplete insofar as de Man had not yet pulled its aporetic string absolutely tight. It concerns two poems by Baudelaire, "Correspondances" and "Obsession." The first has been a benchmark for poets and critics alike attempting to identify the essence of Baudelaire's poetics, the precedent and inspiration he set for French *symbolisme*, and the link between romanticism and modernism. "Obsession," which is easily overlooked, as it comes right after the four great "Spleen" poems in the 1861 edition of *Les fleurs du mal*, is shown by de Man to have such an intimate and intricate relation to "Correspondances" in its words and images as to amount to a kind of operation on the earlier poem. He calls "Correspondances" the "infratext" of "Obsession," not just an intertext but the text that "Obsession" in de Man's terms "reads" and without which "Obsession" itself could not be written. Elsewhere de Man discusses Michael Riffaterre's related idea of the "hypogram," the notion that any poem has lying implicitly beneath it another poem—existent or not—which it answers.[14] I prefer a more Bakhtinian or Barthesian way of thinking about this. For Mikhail Bakhtin, all discourse intricately answers other discourses; extend the idea and it becomes plausible to say that any text is a tissue of responses to pieces of other discourses, so that, hypothetically at least, the discursive amalgam it answers is implicit within or beneath it. For Roland Barthes, writing is a process of differentiation; every text comes into being as its active difference from others, whether actual or imagined, anonymous *doxa* or authored works. Bakhtinian dialogism and Barthesian difference make clear that the hypogram is not tacit so much as virtual and can only be suggested or approximated in any effort to identify what a particular text is responding to. Hence the intriguing possibility posed by "Correspondances" and "Obsession" if de Man's premise is accepted: we have in "Correspondances" the text that "Obsession" differentiates itself from and responds to, its hypogram, verbatim.

My chapter title is a gesture of homage to de Man, even as my aim is to test out the hypothesis that affect is inseparable from rhetoric and that this very inseparability is exploited to extreme precision in poetry. The uncompromising purity of de Man's version of the linguistic turn relegates the poetic linkage of rhetoric and affect to the margins; that said, it is hard to imagine that without that purity contemporary criticism would have developed comparable attentiveness to the figurative complexity of poetic texts. In the critical tradition against which de Man does battle—Coleridge's valorization of organic symbol over artificial allegory, W. K. Wimsatt's Coleridgean theory of the structure of Romantic nature imagery, and the "correspondent breeze" by which M. H. Abrams's classic essay defines the poetic ideal of romanticism— the relation of the human mind and nature achieves a two-way harmony in which the perception of Nature gives rise to poetic images that at once describe the natural world and express the poetic self's thoughts and feelings. The duality of mind and Nature, subjective experience and outer reality, description and expression resolves itself into a symbolic mirroring or echoing or co(r)-responding unity via poetry.

"Correspondances" is a long-standing exemplar of just that sort of symbolism, organicism, and unity:

> La Nature est un temple où de vivants piliers
> Laissent parfois sortir de confuses paroles;
> L'homme y passe à travers des forêts de symboles
> Qui l'observent avec des regards familiers.
>
> Comme de longs échos qui de loin se confondent
> Dans une ténébreuse et profonde unité,
> Vaste comme la nuit et comme la clarté,
> Les parfums, les couleurs et les sons se répondent.
>
> Il est des parfums frais comme des chairs d'enfants,
> Doux comme les hautbois, verts comme les prairies,
> —Et d'autres, corrompus, riches et triomphants,
>
> Ayant l'expansion des choses infinies,
> Comme l'ambre, le musc, le benjoin et l'encens,
> Qui chantent les transports de l'esprit et des sens.[15]

Nature is a temple where living pillars sometimes let out confused words; there man passes through forests of symbols, which observe him with familiar looks.

As lengthy echoes that from afar mix with one another in a dark and deep unity, vast as the night and as daylight, scents, colors, and sounds respond to one another.

There are scents fresh as baby flesh, mild as oboes, green as meadows,— and others, corrupt, rich, and triumphant,

having the expanse of infinite things, like amber, musk, benzoin, and incense, which sing the transports of the mind and senses.

Nothing delights de Man more than shaking symbolico-organic unities, and his commentary addresses two salient uncertainties in the poem. First, while the inaugural trope "Nature is a temple" seemingly establishes the man-nature relation as one of reverence and harmony and may well allude to a passage in Chateaubriand where the trees in the forest are said to have been the first churches, isn't it possible, de Man asks, that the space evoked here is not outdoors at all, but rather the city itself? " 'Vivants pilliers' . . . certainly suggests the erect shape of human bodies naturally enough endowed with speech, a scene from the paintings of Paul Delvaux rather than from the poems of Victor Hugo."[16] The indistinct words and familiar looks might then be the city crowd so often evoked by Baudelaire. De Man teasingly says that the very fact that such a reading "seems far-fetched and, in my experience, never fails to elicit resistance" should itself be a prod to deeper interrogation.[17]

He might have offered rather more direct support for his claim by referring to the episode in which Baudelaire was asked to contribute to a volume of nature poems honoring the man who designed the forest at Fontainebleau. Baudelaire replies ironically that he presumes he is supposed to write about "woods, tall oaks, greenery, insects—and the sun no doubt." He mocks the notion that "the soul of God dwells in plants" and declares, "I have always thought that there is something impudent and deplorable about rejuvenated and flourishing *Nature*. . . . In the depths of the woods, confined beneath arches similar to those of sacristies and cathedrals, I think of our astonishing cities," adding—as though birdsong pulled him through the mythological metamorphosis of Philomela and Procne in reverse—"and the prodigious music that rolls from the heights seems to me the translation of human lamentations" (*OC* I, 1024–25). The two poems he then contributes to the volume, "Le crépuscule du soir" and "Le crépuscule du matin," summarize, he says, "the reveries with which I am assaulted in the twilight hours." The poems evoke dusk and dawn in the city not via the setting and rising sun but through the fatigue, agitation, desires, and defeats of workers, prostitutes, beggars, scholars, thieves, women in labor, and the sick and dying. For Baudelaire, nature is not Nature.

The second uncertainty identified by de Man concerns the idea of correspondence itself. The synesthesia that is said to unify the human sensorium and celebrate the analogies of the human and the natural finds expression in language whose tropes and grammar more than once suggest something other than analogical unity. For example, the verb *se répondent* in the phrase "scents, colors, and sounds respond to one another" seems at first blush to be a ringing affirmation of the thematic centrality of synesthesia, but de Man finds in this figure a catachresis—the nearly imperceptible metaphor that designates something for which no proper or literal term exists—so that the harmonizing meaning of *se répondent* is rather more arbitrary than organic. The decisive jarring, though, is in the line "like amber, musk, benzoin, and incense," listing scents that have "the expansion of infinite things"; de Man notes that all the previous instances of the word *comme* (like, as)—and there are six of them in the fourteen-line poem—establish analogies among the different senses and between sense and the objects of sense, creating likenesses among unlike things. This seventh *comme* has a completely different logic, for it announces examples, not analogies, and initiates an enumeration of one thing after another. There is thus a clash between the line's semantic purpose of illustrating the sense of infinite expansion and its syntactical effect of perforating analogical wholeness

with potentially endless examples: "For what could be more perverse or cor-
ruptive for a metaphor aspiring to transcendental totality than remaining stuck
in an enumeration that never goes anywhere?"[18] It should also be stressed that
synesthesia itself as a neural-sensory phenomenon, drug-induced or spontaneous, is associated with metaphor and simile because to taste something
when seeing something else—or to hear oboes in a particular smell—is a kind
of living metaphoricity.[19] *Metapherein*: to carry, transfer, transport. From his
reading of Swedenborg to his experiences of hashish and alcohol, Baudelaire
sought to bind a poetics and an all-encompassing sensory-spiritual universe; it
informs his conception of the Ideal.[20]

As a question of form, de Man is implying that the entire thematic and symbolic unity of "Correspondances" as a totality of correspondences depends on
the way all its elements relate to one another by analogy, that is, as likenesses-
from-unlikeness, whereas the syntax and logic of line 13 break that unity. Language's figurative possibilities and its syntactic effects upset the reading that
affirms the poem's symbolico-organic unity. The unity of perception and expression, nature and man, objectivity and subjectivity, is knocked out of kilter
first by the built-in ambiguity of metaphor: is *nature* as it encloses, addresses,
watches, and transports man the tenor of the metaphorical vehicle *temple*, or is
nature is a temple the metaphorical vehicle whose tenor is human existence in
its urban dwelling-place? And this unity is undone secondly by the syntactical
rat-a-tat-tat of "Comme l'ambre, le musc, le benjoin et l'encens," which, right at
the sonnet's climactic moment, cuts against all the synesthetic harmonies.

I see yet a further consequence of these (to use a de Manian word) disruptions. The meaning of "the transports of the mind and senses" is so indeterminate and unspecifiable as to amount to a third unbalancing of the symbolico-
organic unity. The last line of "Correspondances" has a tone of culminating
affirmation, the celebration of those "other" scents that have "the expanse of
infinite things" and "sing the transports of the mind and senses" (*chantent les
transports de l'esprit et des sens*). The meaning, though, is utterly elusive. What
are these "transports of the mind and senses"? And by what synesthesia do "corrupt, rich, and triumphant" scents *sing* the transports of the mind and senses?
And to where, and into what, are the mind and senses transported? What is the
nature of the ecstasy that takes mind and senses beyond themselves? How is it
that the *unité* of sense and mind gets carried beyond itself? The tacit paradox
in this last question—unity becoming other than itself—is, I infer, what de
Man discerns in the two senses of the infinite: is infinity the unity of all beings
echoing and answering one another in the mind and senses, or is infinity the
endless series stretching beyond all mental or sensory comprehension?

The brilliance of de Man's insight into the little preposition *comme*, which can, like *like* in English, set up a simile or a string of examples, brings out how similitude affirms correspondence and endless examples negate it. In de Man's terms, enumeration punctures totality. The power of these disruptive moments against the organicism of Anglo-American and French criticism of Romantic and post-Romantic poetry is very persuasive. By the same token, though, de Man's deconstruction of the man/nature, self/nature, subject/object construct accepts the dualities themselves. There are never but two terms, and the controversy is whether poetic language synthesizes them or not. Since de Man rejects the synthesis but affirms the dualities, his point of arrival is ultimately the aporia, the impasse of undecidability between vehicle and tenor, between literal and figurative, and between reference and allegory. I fully subscribe to the notion that poetic language volatilizes the vehicle-tenor relation in metaphor, the literal-figurative relation in semantics, and the semantics-syntax relation in discourse. This problematic can be opened up in directions other than aporia if re-conceived via the Heideggerian triad of mood–understanding–discourse instead of dualities of inner/outer, or self/nature.[21]

Susan Stewart offers an incisive criticism of de Man's tendency to fix upon duality and render it as impasse or aporia, as in another essay in *The Rhetoric of Romanticism*, "Autobiography as Defacement," where he "sees *prosopopoeia*, or the giving of a face or voice, as both a central function of Romantic texts and a key to symbolization in general. But de Man's project was also to point to the ways in which the linguistic basis of this form of anthropomorphization is always a kind of *defacement*, inadequate to its object. . . . I would argue that this approach constantly reinscribes the very allegory it seeks to discover. The mutability of facial expression, the incommensurability between the Romantic poet's apostrophe to nature and nature's response, are not 'problems' or 'indeterminancies' limiting Romantic texts but are rather the very basis of their emergence to expression. There is an insistence in this school of deconstructive criticism on a static representation of the person. Anything less than reification seems like disfigurement, but disfigurement can also be considered as alteration, difficulty, complexity." She calls for an emphasis on "the human image as a consequence of representational practices rather than a prior referent. Only in this way can human subjectivity be viewed in historical terms."[22]

So, too, the task in reading Baudelaire is to grasp the strife within his poetic practice in light of what it creates. The apparent harmony of "Correspondances" and the dissonance evoked by "Obsession" are two manifestations of attunement (*Gestimmtsein*) in Heidegger's sense. How, then, to explore the Heideggerian triad without losing de Man's insight that "Correspondances" is the hypogram or infratext of "Obsession"? For starters, the question of the relation between the two attunements arises from the very fact that "Obses-sion" redeploys the words and images of "Correspondances." "Obsession" takes up its hypogram's words and tropes of attunement and radically, even violently transforms them. The relation between the two attunements is there-fore a relation between tropes; in effect, in each poem we encounter trope as mood and mood as trope.

That Baudelaire titled the section of *Les fleurs du mal* in which the two poems appear "Spleen et Idéal," *spleen* indicating a melancholic *Befindlich-keit* of remorse, depression, disappointment, and *idéal* indicating elevation, reverence, tranquility, calls upon the reading of these two poems to grapple with the interaction, not just the contrast, of spleen and ideal. "Obsession," in its octave, recasts the correspondences of inner and outer worlds as an at-tunement filled with fright, grief, bitterness, animosity, and self-mockery; the sestet discloses a wish and its nightmarish fulfillment:

> Grands bois, vous m'effrayez comme des cathédrales;
> Vous hurlez comme l'orgue; et dans nos coeurs maudits,
> Chambres d'éternel deuil où vibrent de vieux râles,
> Répondent les échos de vos *De profundis.*
>
> Je te hais, Océan! tes bonds et tes tumultes,
> Mon esprit les retrouve en lui; ce rire amer
> De l'homme vaincu, plein de sanglots et d'insultes,
> Je l'entends dans le rire énorme de la mer.
>
> Comme tu me plairais, ô nuit! sans ces étoiles
> Dont la lumière parle un langage connu!
> Car je cherche le vide, et le noir, et le nu!
>
> Mais les ténèbres sont elles-mêmes des toiles
> Où vivent, jaillissant de mon oeil par milliers,
> Des êtres disparus aux regards familiers.
>
> (*OC* I, 75–76)

Great woods, you frighten me like cathedrals; you scream like the organ; and in our condemned hearts, chambers of eternal grief where old death rattles vibrate, the echoes of your *De profundis* respond.

I hate you, Ocean! your leaps and your tumults: my spirit meets them within itself; the bitter laughter of the defeated man, full of sighs and insults: I hear it in the sea's enormous laughter.

How you would please me, O night! without these stars whose light speaks a well-known language! I seek the empty, and the dark, and the bare!

But darkness is itself a canvas where live, gushing from my eye by the thousands, beings that have vanished from ordinary sight.

The elements of "Correspondances" that recur in "Obsession" are so extensive as to confirm that "Obsession" relates to "Correspondances" by reading
it (de Man), answering it (Bakhtin), differentiating itself from it (Barthes)
(see fig. 2).

The sonnet's sestet, like each quatrain, starts out with an address—"O
Night"—but with the difference that its complaint contains a kind of wish,
a desire expressed negatively and in the conditional: "How you would please
me, O Night, without these stars." He seeks "le vide, et le noir, et le nu," "without these stars that speak a well-known language." The sestet itself then makes
a turn at the beginning of the second tercet: *Mais*. . . . Utter darkness does not
yield the bare void and blackness he seeks; even as it obliterates all natural
correspondences, the darkness devoid of forest, sea, and stars becomes "a
canvas where live . . . beings that have vanished from ordinary sight [*regards
familiers*]." The last stanza of "Obsession" thus echoes and reverses the first
stanza of "Correspondances," where the forests of symbols observe man "with
familiar looks [*regards familiers*]."

These lines lead de Man to characterize the poem's theme as "the enigma
of consciousness as eternal mourning" and as culminating in "the hallucinatory obsession of recollection." It is worth questioning, though, whether
the tercet is a visual image at all. The octave is distinguished by its auditory
imagery: howls, church organ, death rattles, the vespers hymn *De profundis*,
crashing waves, bitter laughter, sighs, insults, the enormous laughter of the
sea. The first tercet contrasts with the octave via its visual reference to the
starry night but also complements it with an auditory metaphor: "Those stars
whose light speaks a familiar language." The second tercet seemingly invites
a visual imagining insofar as the darkness becomes a canvas and beings gush
from the eye. Vanished beings gush *from* the eye, but does that really imply
that they are beheld by it? Is vision involved? The very fact that they gush "by
the thousands" suggests that none of these vanished souls, things, experiences, or moments is held in view. The image evokes, rather, endless vanishing. Loss never ceases. The image is more kinesthetic or proprioceptive
than visual: the bodily feeling in the unseeing eye of a tearless outpouring of
memory and grief, a grief beyond consolation or catharsis and memories too
numerous to hold. The absolute darkness furnishes "le vide, et le noir, et le
nu" that Baudelaire seeks, but this void occasions, bodily and mentally, the
sheer sensation of memory's perpetually vanishing beings. All the synesthetic
richness of sights, sounds, and scents—whether harmonious, as in "Correspondances," or discordant, as in the previous three stanzas of "Obsession"—
collapses in aggrieved sensation, and the mind's entire focus, direction, and
exercise of active thought is eclipsed by an unimpeded rush of memory. The

"Correspondances"	"Obsession"
temple	**cathéderale**
Laissent…sortir de confuses paroles	**Vous hurlez**
Let out confused (indistinct) words	you howl
	parle un langage connu
	speaks a well-known language
des forêts de symboles	**Grands bois**
forests of symbols (symbol forests)	Great woods
l'homme	**l'homme vaincu**
Man	the defeated man
des regards familiers	**aux regards familiers**
with familiar looks	to ordinary sight
de longs échos	**les échos**
long echoes	the echoes
	où vibrent de vieux râles
	where old death-rattles vibrate
une ténébreuse…unité	**les ténébres**
a dark…unity	darkness
une…profonde unité	**vos *De Profundis***
a…deep unity	your *De Profundis*
Vaste	**énorme**
vast	huge
se répondent	**Répondent**
respond to/reply to/answer one another	respond/reply/answer
Vaste comme la nuit	**ô nuit!**
vast as the night	O night!
	le noir
	the dark
de l'esprit	**mon esprit**
of the spirit (mind)	my spirit (mind)
les hautbois	**l'orgue**

FIGURE 2. Text and infratext

imageless sensation in which the senses collapse and thought is eclipsed *is* "the transports of the mind and senses" in "Obsession."

Baudelaire did not invent the trope of darkness-as-canvas for this poem. "Obsession" reworks several antecedents and alternatives so as to create an altogether new meaning. In *Un mangeur d'opium* one finds: "Les enfants sont, en générale, doués de la singulière faculté d'apercevoir, ou plutôt de créer, sur la toile féconde des ténèbres tout un monde de visions bizarres" (*OC* I, 480)—Baudelaire's amplifying translation of Thomas De Quincey: "Many children, perhaps most, have a power of painting, as it were upon the darkness, all sorts of phantoms."[23] Poe's "Shadow—A Parable," which Baudelaire translated in 1855, furnishes more than one future image. The story is narrated by a Greek, one of a group of seven men spending an evening in drunken revelry in a room where lies the corpse of another man, dead from the plague. "Black draperies, likewise, in the gloomy room, shut out from our view the moon, the lurid stars, and the peopleless streets." From the "sable draperies" emerges a "shadow neither of man nor of God, nor of any familiar thing," who sets the guests trembling when it identifies itself as SHADOW from the regions of the dead; the narrator's final words as rendered by Baudelaire: "Le timbre de la voix n'était pas le timbre d'un seul individu, mais d'une multitude des êtres; et cette voix, variant ses inflexions de syllabe en syllabe, tombait confusément dans nos oreilles en imitant les accents connus et familiers de mille et mille amis disparus!" (*OC* I, 981). The text he translates: "The tones in the voice of the shadow were not the tone of any one being, but of a multitude of beings, and varying in their cadences from syllable to syllable, fell duskily upon our ears in the well-remembered and familiar accents of many thousand departed friends."[24]

The dark as a canvas on which nightmares and hallucinations appear occurs in "Les ténèbres," written perhaps a few months before or after "Obsession":

> Je suis comme un peintre qu'un Dieu moqueur
> Condamne à peindre, hélas! sur les ténèbres;
> Où, cuisinier aux appétits funèbres,
> Je fais bouillir et je mange mon coeur.
>
> (*OC* I, 38)

I am like a painter that a mocking God condemns to paint, alas, upon the darkness, where I, a cook with funereal appetites, bring my heart to a boil and eat it.

Richard Howard eschews literalness in translating this stanza and, while losing the significant auto-affection of "Je fais bouillir . . . mon coeur," evokes the purport and tone:

as if a scoffing God had forced
my hand to fresco . . . silhouettes!
Here with grisly appetite
I grill and devour my heart.[25]

An unintended interpretive gloss is found in Stephen Crane's poem "In the Desert":

In the desert
I saw a creature, naked, bestial,
Who, squatting upon the ground,
Held his heart in his hands,
And ate of it.
I said, "Is it good, friend?"
"It is bitter—bitter," he answered;

"But I like it
"Because it is bitter,
"And because it is my heart."

"Les ténèbres" is the first of the four poems under the heading "Un fantôme," poems in which there is no tormenting Other, diabolical or divine. The Baudelairean ghost dwells in the gap that separates the reality of Jeanne Duval's half-paralysis and his own memories of their first love. The second of the Fantôme poems, "Le parfum," elaborates an audacious analogy between the memory-evocative scent of "The grain of incense filling a church / Or a sachet's ingrained musk" and the remembered smell of the lover in her youth:

De ses cheveux élastique et lourds,
Vivant sachet, encensoir de l'alcôve
Une senteur montait, sauvage et fauve,

Et des habits, mousseline ou velours,
Tout imprégnés de sa jeunesse pure,
Se dégageait un parfum de fourrure.
(*OC* I, 39)

From her thick and supple hair—a living sachet, a bedroom censer—arose a feral animal smell.
      And velvet and chiffon clothes, steeped in her pure youthfulness, gave off a whiff of fur.

"Un fantôme" does without a ghost, for while Baudelaire takes much inspiration and many images and considerable vocabulary from Poe, he changes the registers of metaphoricity. Likewise, in "Obsession" he alters the tenor of the

darkness-as-canvas metaphor by eliminating vision and visuality from it altogether. There is an utter absence of the senses of sight, smell, and hearing as
they partake in attunement and responsiveness to the world and can be troped
as synesthesia—whether the harmonious attunement of "Correspondances"
or the dissonant attunements of "Obsession." I have suggested that the darkness as "a canvas where live, gushing from my eye by the thousands, beings
that have vanished from ordinary sight" evokes by contrast a bodily sensation
of memory *as* uninterrupted loss, rather than the recollection, memorializa-
tion, or preservation of the lost beings. A palpitating, palpable, unseeing eye.
That is not an absence of attunement. Yet, what sort of attunement is it?

Angst in Heidegger's sense of the term is attunement to the nothing. The
1929 essay "What Is Metaphysics?" describes the bouts of a loss of interest in
things, the falling away of beings as a whole, and hence the mood in which
the nothing makes itself felt:

> With the fundamental attunement of anxiety we have arrived at that occur-
> rence in Dasein in which the nothing is manifest and from which it must be
> interrogated.
>
> How is it with the nothing? . . .
>
> In anxiety beings as a whole become superfluous. In what sense does this
> happen? Beings are not annihilated by anxiety, so that nothing is left. How
> could they be, when anxiety finds itself precisely in utter impotence with re-
> gard to beings as a whole? Rather, the nothing makes itself known with beings
> and in beings expressly as a slipping away of the whole. . . .
>
> Da-sein means: being held out into the nothing.
>
> Holding itself out into the nothing, Dasein is in each case already beyond
> beings as a whole. Such being beyond beings we call *transcendence*. If in the
> ground of its essence Dasein were not transcending, which now means, if it
> were not in advance holding itself out into the nothing, then it could never
> adopt a stance toward beings nor even toward itself.
>
> Without the original manifestness of the nothing, no selfhood and no
> freedom.[26]

"No selfhood, no freedom"—this last claim can seem a non sequitur if the self
is understood as a firm, pregiven, or guaranteed identity and if freedom is
construed as the power of one's will or the absence of constraints. Heidegger
contests all those definitions. As in *Being and Time*, *Angst* "individualizes
Dasein" in the sense that the attunement to the nothing, this transitory moment where nothing of what one concerns oneself with matters, paradoxically
makes manifest one's "ownmost potentiality-for-Being"; Dasein thus confronts "its *Being-free for* the freedom of choosing and taking hold of itself."[27]
This same dynamic movement, in effect the perpetual vacillation between

"authenticity" and "inauthenticity," is at work in that other facet of *Angst*, the feeling for one's own finitude, which Heidegger called being-toward-death.

During Jeanne Duval's convalescence, and shortly before the poems grouped as "Un fantôme" were written, Baudelaire himself suffered what is believed to have been a mild stroke. There is no need to shift to biographical interpretation to acknowledge that Baudelaire's debility, however slight or transitory, and his response to Duval's paralysis surely impinge on these poems, in which memory, loss, grief, and fright are all figured as embodiments and attunements. The poems' figural complexities and rhetorical structures can be resolved into purely linguistic operations and logical impasses only at the cost of a large swath of responsiveness and understanding. Trope evokes mood, and it names moods by misnaming things.

Let's consider once more the last words of "Correspondances," which seem to name and affirm the affective, even spiritual and perhaps transcendent nature of attunement: "Qui chantent les transports de l'esprit et des sens." There are so many reduplicated words and echoes of "Correspondances" in "Obsession" that the correspondence and corresponding between the poems is worded in "Obsession," and yet neither key word of that last line—neither "sing" nor "transports"—returns in the language of the second poem. In the synesthesia of "Correspondances," on the one hand, the triumphant rich corrupt scents "sing," a metaphor as far-fetched as any, and what they sing—the transports of the mind and the senses—remains opaque. The whole of "Obsession," on the other hand, conveys transports of the mind and the senses, though now through the correspondence of the howling wind and the inner shrieking of the heart, the hearkening of the world's frightful plaintive remorseful noise, and ultimately pure blind soundless aggrieved sensation. In "Obsession" it is the poem itself that "sings" the "transports" of the mind and the senses, that is, the carrying of thought, perception, and feeling beyond themselves. *Sing[ing]* and *transports* drop from the *énoncé* of "Correspondances" into the *énonciation* of "Obsession," that is, drop from being lexical items in the one poem to becoming the verbal action of the other. "Les transports de l'esprit et des sens" belong to Spleen, not Ideal. By the same token, then, taking "Correspondances" as the infratext of "Obsession," the Spleen poem gives actuality and meaning to "les transports de l'esprit et des sens" in "Correspondances."

An altogether new question arises then regarding the relation of the two poems, and of Spleen and Ideal, namely, not merely their difference but also their hinge or, better, the crease in the fold that differentiates and connects them. Since "Obsession" follows and rewrites "Correspondances," it can be tempting to conclude that spleen despoils the ideal and that dissonance disturbs harmony, even that the rewrite deconstructs the infratext. The opposite temptation exists as well, namely, the conclusion that the Baudelairean Ideal somehow transcends Spleen and transforms the melancholic and violent disorder of the poet's sensibility and experience into luminous order and beauty. At the risk of overstating the paradigmatic relevance of these two poems, the relation of Spleen and Ideal here hinges on how the semantically blank closing line of "Correspondances" is given meaning by "Obsession." I say *by* rather than *in* "Obsession" because it is the poetic utterance itself, not a theme proferred in the poem, that "sings" the transports of the mind and the senses.

Beyond the alternative between the deconstruction of the Ideal by Spleen and the transcendence of Spleen by the Ideal lies a third possibility, namely, that spleen fuels and sustains the ideal and that the ideal rebounds on spleen and intensifies it. Spleen is the ground and source of Ideal, that is, the Ideal not as aspiration but as image actively created by the poet and, because created by him, carrying, encysted within it, all the tonalites and echoes of his dread, his dissipation, and his decline. The seriality of "like amber, musk, benjamin, and incense," in which de Man sees a grammatical puncturing of "the expanse of infinite things" in "Correspondances," has its affective counterpart in "Obsession" in the trope of the visionless streaming of vanished beings.

Maurice Blanchot grasps the inseparable intertwining of Spleen and Ideal through the image developed in "Le masque" of a statue that from the front shows a woman epitomizing every nuance of the Baudelairean ideal, in particular the ideal of femininity. The opening stanzas in Richard Howard's translation read:

> It is a legacy of Tuscan skill;
> in ripples of her surging musculature
> see the holy sisters, Power and Grace,
> sustain this woman's beauty in a form
> so faultless as to seem miraculous—
> taking pride of place above rich beds
> to charm a prince's leisure, or a pope's . . .
>
> Notice the faint voluptuous smile that shows,
> that *shares*, the consummation of Desire;
> observe that teasing glance which penetrates
> the subtle coquetry of gauzy veils
> around a face whose every feature speaks,
> not just the parted lips too shy to boast:
> "When Lust commands me, even Love obeys!"

Look how the languor in her posture adds
a sweet submission to such majesty;
come close—walk around her loveliness . . .

The poem is dedicated to the sculptor Ernest Christophe, in whose studio
Baudelaire saw the plaster statuette that inspired the poem. The face just described is a mask, behind which lie the real face and head:

What blasphemy of art is this! Upon
a body made to offer every bliss
appear . . . two heads! Some kind of monster? No—

one is merely a mask—a grinning cheat
this smile articulated so cunningly!
Look there: contorted in her misery,
the actual head, the woman's countenance
lost in the shadow of the lying mask . . .
Pathos of true beauty! the bright tears
trickle into my astonished heart;
your lie intoxicates me, and my soul
slakes its passion in your brimming eyes!

The double-barreled erotic charge of her intoxicating façade and tormented
interior finds echoes throughout *Les fleurs du mal*, but the ending of "Le
masque" introduces another meaning of the anguish hidden behind the mask,
a doubling that refers not only to the statue:

—Why is she weeping? Surely such a face
would put all mankind, vanquished, at her feet!
What secret evil feeds on her firm flesh?

—She weeps, you fool, for having lived! and for
living—yet what she laments the most,
what makes her body tremble head to toe,
is that tomorrow she will have to live,
and all tomorrows after—like ourselves![28]

The idealizing notion of sculpture's permanence is reversed into the splenetic
recognition that for the immortal statue, as for the mortals who contemplate
it, there is no release from time and experience. In Blanchot's words, "art and
the artwork (which Christophe's statue represents in these verses) affirm, behind the hope of surviving, the despair of ceaselessly existing."[29] And it is in
this context that Blanchot comments on the sestet of "Obsession": "The nothing (*le néant*) cannot be counted on to put an end to anything. . . . Heidegger's
Being-toward-death, far from characterizing authentic possibility, would rep-

resent for Baudelaire just one more imposture. We do not have death ahead of us, but existence. Which, however far forward I move, is always still ahead, and however low I sink is yet lower still, and however unreally I affirm myself (for example, in art) infests that unreality with an absence of reality that is still existence."[30] Let's take Blanchot's insight one step further. Rather than separating being-toward-death and inexhaustible existence, Baudelaire fuses them. The true Baudelairean lament is voiced by another, later lyricist—Hank Williams: "I'll never get out of this world alive."

Pathos and Form

I take Spleen to be the precondition and impetus of Baudelaire's poetic creativity. It gives rise to the Ideal, which in turn rebounds on the splenetic mood, renders it abject, and yet agitates it into renewed creativity. *The Ideal, then, is the precondition and impetus of Baudelaire's poetic creativity.*

How to understand the apparent incompatibility of the first and last of these statements? Is it a simple contradiction on my part? Or an aporia concocted by theory? Or an ambiguity in Baudelairean poetics? If Spleen and Ideal mutually affect and mutually effect one another, with neither having precedence over the other, a further difficulty arises regarding Baudelaire, a question that bears on literary and artistic creativity in general. What is the relation of the self-standing poem or artwork to the dynamics, sufferings, and predicaments of its creator's existence? There is a certain extremity to this question when it comes to Baudelaire. The disorder of his life was intensified by drugs, alcohol, and syphilis and stretched from before his first published poetry and prose in 1845, when he was twenty-four, until 1867, when he died at forty-six, wracked by venereal disease, brain damage, partial paralysis, and aphasia.

The finest modern critics grapple with the puzzle of form and pathos in Baudelaire's poetry. An early essay of the great critic Jean Starobinski got the relation exactly wrong, in my view: "The traditional constraints of versification allow him to overcome destructive and destructuring drives [*pulsions*], to defer the threat they pose by the simple fact of giving it form. In the rigorous form of the sonnet, speaking destruction builds an indestructible object; speaking the void develops into a discourse without gaps."[31] Adorno, questioning in general the tendency to attribute compensatory and curative powers to art or, conversely, to evoke neurosis to explain artists "who in fact merely objectified in their work the negativity of life," marvels that "psychic normality is raised to a criterion of judgment even in the case of someone like Baudelaire, whose greatness was so unequivocally tied up with the absence of a *mens sana*."[32]

The association of Baudelaire with failure has presided over interpretations of the poetry for the last seven decades thanks to the psychosocial biographical study that Jean-Paul Sartre devoted to the poet in 1946. Sartre's
Baudelaire still rewards an attentive reading, both for the richness of its insights and for its blindnesses. Developing key themes of his own philosophical reflections, Sartre charges Baudelaire with failing to establish a project in
his life, instead letting himself be ruled by the helter-skelter of his passions
and pathologies, and so in effect choosing failure (in Heidegger's terms, an
existence of addictions and urges rather than resoluteness):

> Few existences have been more stagnant than his. For him the die was already
> cast at the age of twenty-one. Everything had stopped. He had had his chance
> and lost forever. By 1846 he had spent half his capital, written most of his po-
> ems, given his relations with his parents their definitive form, contracted the
> venereal disease which slowly rotted him, met the woman who would weigh
> like lead on every hour of his life and made the voyage which provided the
> whole of his work with exotic images. . . . Long before he was thirty his opin-
> ions were formed and for the rest of his life he did no more than ruminate
> over them.[33]

Sartre does not entertain the possibility that the poetry—however supposedly
slim and repetitive the total production—*is* Baudelaire's project. There would
be no reason to write a psychosocial biography of Baudelaire were it not for
the poems and prose poems, and yet they barely figure in Sartre's study, and
then only toward the end. Tellingly, perhaps, the one sheer inaccuracy in the
above overview is the assertion that Baudelaire had written most of his poetry
by the time he was twenty-five. As compelling and often persuasive as the
bulk of Sartre's account of the poet's psyche and life is, it does not address the
one question which must have prompted the inquiry in the first place. How
do *these* poems arise from *that* life?

Blanchot addresses just this question in "L'échec de Baudelaire," the essay
I cited above, not so much to contest Sartre's interpretation of Baudelaire's
propensity to failure in all the sexual, financial, and pragmatic aspects of his
life and even in his artistic aspirations, but to displace the question to the site
where it matters, namely, to the scene of writing itself. Few critics have been
as attentive as Blanchot to the act and experience of writing as they are disclosed by what is actually written (poem, novel, essay, or philosophical work),
and while Blanchot's essays have their own distinctive consistent and dense
style, he has an uncanny grasp of the singularity of each writer's act and experience of writing. Nor is it a matter of texts' "self-referentiality." Literature,

Blanchot asserts, "in truth has meaning and value only as a passion lived by the writer." Passion is undoubtedly meant here in the entire spectrum of its meanings, from intensities of motive and feeling to scarcely tolerable suffering. There is, however, a kink in this apparent idealization of the text and heroization of the writer: "Poetry is a means of putting oneself in danger without running any risk, a mode of suicide, of self-destruction, that comfortably makes way for the surest self-affirmation." Using a card-playing metaphor, Blanchot says that "every poet has *mauvaise foi* in his hand; there is nothing to be done against it, but with it he can do anything and even save his *bonne foi*, he can get lost and yet succeed." How the hand is played determines the role of unavoidable bad faith, and that is what Sartre misses in his encounter with Baudelaire: "Poetic creation is not pure except within uncertainty [*l'équivoque*]." The passion of the signifier cannot avoid, it turns out, the risk of a fake risk. "It is right to recall this," Blanchot insists, "because this criticism is exacted by literature itself and because literature in truth has meaning and value only as a passion lived by the writer, in the imposture to which he feels himself an accomplice."[34]

Blanchot teases out a kind of *débat*, a dispute or struggle, that goes on within Baudelaire's life and thought. All the affirmations of pure reveries, the contemplated ideal, synesthetic intoxications, the "truly spiritual," and idleness are contested by the very poetics he is committed to: "The poetic requirement always remains for him the requirement of a *parole* that is ordered, organized, carefully wrought, thought-out, and as lucid as possible."[35] It is thanks to that very quality that his poems allow his inner violence, not to be contained as Starobinski proposes, but to break into appearance and be held there lucidly before the poet and his *semblables* and *frères*. Emblematic for Blanchot is the prose poem "La Chambre double." The room in its first appearing:

> A room that is like a dream, a truly *spiritual* room, where the stagnant atmosphere is nebulously tinted pink and blue.
>
> Here the soul takes a bath of indolence, scented with all the aromatic perfumes of desire and regret. There is about it something crepuscular, bluish shot with rose; a voluptuous dream in an eclipse. . . .
>
> To what good demon am I indebted for this encompassing atmosphere of mystery, silence, perfume and peace? O bliss!

There is a knock at the door, and "a Spectre enters" in the guise of a bailiff, a complaining mistress, or an editor's messenger demanding "the last installment of a manuscript." Debts, lovers, deadlines. The poet is recalled to consciousness of the shabby room where he finds himself: "This filthy hole, this abode of eternal boredom is truly mine" where lie his "manuscripts covered with erasures or unfinished." The "Eternity that reigns" in the first room is now displaced:

> Yes, Time reigns; he has resumed his brutal tyranny. And he pokes me with his double goad as if I were an ox. "Then hoi, donkey! Sweat, slave! Man, be damned and live!" (*Vis donc, damné!*)[36]

What Blanchot draws from this brief allegory is that while the Spectre and the clock pendulum's crying "I am Life, unbearable and implacable Life!" break the spell of the poetic reverie, they are in fact the demand of poetry itself, that is, the poetry that must be written not dreamed: "The pure dream is thus nothing other than impurity. Its double is the still present banality that only the illusion hid. What does it matter, the complacent poet will say, if I delude myself with this false eternity that is but the forgetting of time? Yes, but the poetic condition wants him: the satisfaction has scarcely gotten under way when the knocking strikes, awake!, and it is poetry itself that strikes this *loud, terrible* knock, which shows what the dream is: hypocrisy, nothingness [*néant*]."[37]

There are really three moments here, not just reverie and stark reality, dreamt Ideal and awakened Spleen, for what reveals each of them and connects them inextricably together is the act of writing that produces the poem, in this case "La chambre double" itself, an act that finds its resources in Spleen *and* Ideal but belongs to neither. Blanchot signals this, I think, when he points out another persistent *débat* in Baudelaire's practice: poetry demands discipline, work, and exactitude, which Baudelaire clearly supplies (in a struggle against the lassitude and intoxications to which he is inclined), but at the same time, as Baudelaire remarked, "in art there is something not adequately noted: the share left to man's will is much less great than is believed."[38] In Blanchot's terms, the text is carefully wrought and as lucid as possible, but the work, like the lucidity, stands apart from both the elevation and the debasement that it discloses, even as it itself has not been wholly willed since it arises from the elevation and the debasement themselves. Nor can work and lucidity transcend elevation and debasement or govern the poet's everyday life. That is the passion lived by *this* writer.

Insights interestingly parallel to Blanchot's are to be found in Erich Auerbach's remarkable essay from 1950, again with Sartre in the background, "The Aesthetic Dignity of the 'Fleurs du mal.'" The very juxtaposition of Baudelaire and dignity startles. The "dignity" of the profligate, the addict, the perennial debtor and dependent, the sexual degenerate, the debilitated syphilitic? Auerbach regards the triad Spleen–Ideal–poem from the standpoint of style. He credits Baudelaire with the innovative "breach" in modern poetry and art of

the (neo)classical separation of high, middle, and low styles: "In classical aesthetics, subject matter and the manner of its treatment came to be divided into
three classes: there was the great, tragic, and sublime; then the middle, pleasing, and inoffensive; finally the ridiculous, base, and grotesque."[39] Baudelaire
overthrows the unity of manner and matter. He embraces the *grand style*—
forms, diction, tone—and the basest contents, feelings, and urges. Auerbach
starts, much as he does for each chapter of *Mimesis*, from an exemplary passage or text, in this case the fourth "Spleen" poem (the one just before "Obsession"): "Quand le ciel bas et lourd pèse comme un couvercle" (When the sky
weighs low and heavy like a lid). The last stanza:

> —Et de longs corbillards, sans tambour ni musique,
> Défilent lentement dans mon âme; l'Espoir,
> Vaincu, pleure, et l'Angoisse atroce, despotique,
> Sur mon crâne incliné plante son drapeau noir.
> (And a long line of hearses without drums or music,
> Files slowly through my soul; Hope vanquished weeps
> And vile despotic Dread
> Plants her black flag over my bowed skull.)[40]

In Richard Howard's translation:

> —And giant hearses, without dirge or drums,
> parade at half-step in my soul, where Hope,
> defeated, weeps, and the oppressor Dread
> plants his black flag on my assenting skull.

Auerbach's stylistico-affective commentary focuses on this stanza:

> Hope has given up looking for a way out; she is weeping; hideous Dread
> [*l'Angoisse*] hoists her black flag over the bowed skull, and so this magnificent
> poem ends. As a picture in the grand style of total abjection and collapse, the
> last stanza, especially the last line, outdoes all the rest. For the rhythm and the
> images—the procession of hearses, the victor hoisting a flag over the enemy's
> captured citadel—all these are in the grand style; but the victor is Dread, of
> the poet nothing remains, no soul, no brow, not even a head; what has bowed
> down beneath the black flag is only a skull, *mon crâne incliné*. He has lost all
> dignity, not before God, for there is no God, but before Dread.[41]

What was taken to be an "inconsistency of style" by Baudelaire's detractors
because of "the contradiction between the lofty tone and the indignity both
of [the poem's] subject as a whole and many of its details" marked an artistic revolution and new structure of feeling: "It became possible to take subjects seriously that hitherto belonged to the low or middle category, and to

treat them tragically. The subject matter of Flaubert or Cézanne, Zola or Van Gogh, is not 'neutral'; one cannot say that their originality consisted solely in the novelty or perfection of their techniques; *there can be no significant technique without new content.* The truth is rather that the subject matter became serious and great *through the intention of those who gave it form*" (my italics).[42]

The new content of *Les fleurs du mal* was the very disorder of the poet's own life, the pathos that is given form by the poetry or, as I prefer to see it, that *finds form in* the poetry. For while Starobinski treats the pathos as pathology and poetic form as a salvific container of unruly drives, desires, and passions, Auerbach stresses the psychic and existential "content" as what is worked up in the poetry's form and style. He cites a letter of Baudelaire from 1866: "Into this abominable book I have put all my thought, all my heart, all my (travestied) religion, all my hatred" (Dans ce livre atroce, j'ai mis toute ma pensée, tout mon coeur, toute ma religion [travestie], toute ma haine).

The fundamental flaw in the pathos/form, pathology/container conception lies in the binaries themselves, as though the disturbed poet's disorder were simply the opposite of the poem's order. As Françoise Meltzer makes abundantly clear in her recent study of Baudelaire, his disturbances are not mere psychic disorder. They are a sheaf of intensely irreconcilable responses to the events, conditions, and ideas of his era. His early enthusiasm for Pierre-Joseph Proudhon, resonant with the hopes awakened by the February Revolution in 1848, survived his bitter disappointment with the June Insurrection and its repression and his disdain for the subsequent dictatorship of Louis Bonaparte and the culture of the Second Empire, and it persisted alongside his eventual embrace of the reactionary thought of Joseph de Maistre: "Baudelaire cannot give up Proudhon because the poverty of the Paris underclass is crushing, demanding alms at every turn in the city's ever wider streets, continually attesting to extreme social injustice and inequity. But he also cannot give up Maistre, because the evil that can be attributed to capitalist greed (in both rich and poor), the inequality between the classes, the guilt and subsequent rage or pity such inequality produces, overwhelms the poet who seeks (and finds) in Maistre a theological justification for such suffering and a dark system of retribution that accounts for human misery."[43] Proudhon and Maistre. Anarchistic loathing of the bourgeoisie and pseudo-aristocratic nostalgia for Church and royalty. Contempt for the poor and horror at poverty. Fear of religion's decline and sexualized mockery of its rituals. Disgust at commerce and craven money-grubbing.

The affective vicissitudes and inconsistencies that rage across Baudelaire's sensibility and poetics cannot be accounted for by recourse to some psychological or ideological-political norm. From his experience at twenty-seven of the 1848 revolution, insurrection, and repression until his death in 1867, fifteen years into the rule of Napoleon III and with no way of foreseeing the Empire's end, the Franco-Prussian War, or the Paris Commune, there is no tangible vision of the future that he can produce or lay hold of. Auerbach describes the era and the literary task it presented in *Mimesis*, there with novelists in mind, as one in which the writer must be "continually conscious that the social base upon which he lives is not constant for a moment but is perpetually changing through convulsions of the most varied kinds."[44] Meltzer's metaphor for Baudelaire's psychohistorical turmoil is "seeing double." His experience of time in his historical moment values the past insofar as it is irretrievably lost and anticipates the future as an unpredictable, inscrutable horror: "The exhausted man . . . is caught between melancholia and chaos, between past and future, neither of which is desirable. The world is vile because it cannot provide succor."[45]

"A mind so fine that no idea could violate it"—so wrote T. S. Eliot in a remark about Henry James that no one is able to take, as it was apparently intended, unironically.[46] Baudelaire's mind and sensibility are the inverse. Violation is the precondition of his creativity. Powerful ideas, from anarchistic critiques of private property to reactionary appeals to the sword and the robe, from colonialist exoticism to Pascalian pessimism, are the acid bath that washes across his sensibility and lets its *desseins* emerge in words. Baudelaire is passive in the extreme. He undergoes, he suffers, he succumbs, he is enamored, he is intoxicated, he is afflicted, he is addicted. So, too, then, he is aesthetically receptive to an unprecedented extreme. Perhaps what is so inexplicable and uncanny for Sartre is that Baudelaire struggles with all his exhausted might to make what he so passively undergoes into poetry.

Li-Young Lee's Fury

Let's turn to another poet, a contemporary of ours, and pursue in counterpoint to Baudelaire the questions of mood and trope and pathos and form in the lyric. Li-Young Lee's 1990 collection *The City in Which I Love You* is woven with allusions to his early childhood in Indonesia, born to Chinese parents, his father imprisoned by the Sukarno regime, the family threatened in the anti-Chinese pogroms of the late 1950s, fleeing to various Asian noncommunist havens and ultimately landing, when the future poet is barely eight years old, in rural Pennsylvania, where his father sets up shop in yet another strange land and, now a Protestant minister, builds a congregation in a small town northeast of Pittsburgh.

The poems convey the oscillations between what the poet himself recalls and what his father has told him, between the real and the imagined fragments that haunt his insomnia, between nighttime dreams and poetic reveries, between his image-burdened past and his image-seeking present, between here and elsewhere. His sense of self is at once inseparable from images and memories of his father and yet unachievable unless separated from the father. "These days I waken in the used light / of someone's spent life"—so begins the first poem in the volume's opening sequence, "Furious Versions," signaling but not yet divulging that the father is dead. In the nether moments of passing out of sleep into day or into insomnia, the oscillations of time and place turn him away from himself into his father, through his father back to himself, toward his father—an existence enfolded-upon-and-in-strife-with-itself:[47]

> I lie
> dismantled. I feel the hours. Do they veer
> to dusk? Or dawn?
> Will I rise and go
> out into an American city?
> Or walk down to the wilderness sea?
> I might run with wife and children to the docks
> to bribe an officer for our lives
> and perilous passage.
> Then I'd answer
> in an oceanic tongue
> to *Professor, Capitalist, Husband, Father.*
> Or I might have one more
> hour of sleep before my father
> comes to take me
> to his snowbound church
> where I dust the pews and he sets candles
> out the color of teeth.
> That means I was born in Bandung, 1958;
> on my father's back, in borrowed clothes,
> I came to America.

The images from different moments in time, and from fantasy as readily as memory, from dream as easily as reverie, juxtapose and combine. Aren't such protean confusions the very wellspring of poetic images? The confusion and play of images bring history down upon Lee's musings:

> And I wonder
> if I imagined those wintry mornings
> in a dim nave, since

> I'm the only one
> who's lived to tell it,
> and I confuse
> the details; was it my father's skin
> which shone like teeth?
> Was it his heart that lay snowbound?
> But if I waken to a jailer
> rousting me to meet my wife and son,
> come to see me in my cell
> where I eat the chocolate
> and smoke the cigarettes they smuggle,
> what name do I answer to?

The poem concludes by articulating how the entire flow of involuntary and voluntary memory, however modified by dream, nightmare, or reverie, shapes him: "Memory revises me."

The poet is someone in whom the ordinary cascade of memory, perception, and fantasy searches the shapeliness that might yield a poem:

> Memory revises me.
> Even now a letter comes from a place
> I don't know, from someone
> with my name
> and postmarked years ago,
> while I await
> injunctions from the light
> or the dark;
> I wait for shapeliness
> limned, or dissolution.
> Is paradise due or narrowly missed
> until another thousand years?
> I wait
> in a blue hour
> and faraway noise of hammering,
> and on a page a poem begun, something
> about to be dispersed,
> something about to come into being.

The final image, according to which the poem emerges from (or as) "something / about to be dispersed," suggests a notion of form not as container of unruly drives or objectification of the subjective but as fragments which, if they do not dissolve, will spread or reach out toward shape: "I wait for shapeliness / limned, or dissolution."

For Baudelaire the affect that stirs creativity—the arousal of the artistic state Nietzsche will call *Rausch* (frenzy, intoxication, rapture)—is spleen. For Li-Young Lee the affect that arouses, and is aroused in, writing is fury:

> here, amidst
> drafts—yet
> these are not drafts
> toward a future form, but
> furious versions
> of the here and now . . .

Furious: frenetic, rapid, mad, enraged. *Versions*: drafts, revisions ("Memory revises me"), variants. The sequence's title sets out the trope that names both the poems themselves and the rage *within* that shapes the poet, the fury out of which he must wrench his reality and identity. Poems and self are "furious versions / of the here and now." The here and now is all there is, and yet its very impermanence stems from the ever-recurring layers and fragments of memory and history.

In the final poem of the sequence Lee places himself, cast in the third person, in history at century's end even as his creativity wakens in a lonely night of insomnia, where he is to be known not by his name but by the noise his pencil and soul make:

> Tonight, someone, unable
> to see in one darkness,
> has shut his eyes
> to see into another.
> Among the sleepers, he is one
> who doesn't sleep.
> Know him by his noise.
> Hear the nervous
> scratching of his pencil,
> sound of a rasping
> file, a small
> restless percussion, a soul's
> minute chewing,
> the old poem
> birthing itself
> into the new
> and murderous century.

The twentieth century's murderousness touched his own childhood and family in Indonesia, "one year of fire / out of the world's diary of fires." He witnesses the violence his father withstood: "A pistol butt turns my father's spit to blood." Is it truly what he saw and remembers? Or is it something he was told? Ambiguity presides over his memories and witnessing because remembering was from the beginning a paternal command:

> The booted ones herd us
> to the sea.
> Waves furl, boats
> and bodies drift out, farther out.
> My father holds my hand, he says,
> *Don't forget any of this.*

Paternal commands do not assure obedience: "Because he / made me recite a book a month, I forget / everything as soon as I read it" ("My Father, in Heaven, Is Reading Out Loud"). By the same token, he may owe his artistic gaze and vocation to his father's injunctions: "My father said, *Never take your both eyes / off of the world*, before he rocked me" ("Arise, Go Down"). Lee's historical awareness is looped through his father's commands, stories, and heroism, a possible image for which is his mending the boy's pants:

> His love for me is like his sewing:
> various colors and too much thread,
> the stitching uneven. But the needle pierces
> clean through with each stroke of his hand.

The father's story (physician to Mao, scholar, Indonesian prisoner, escapee and rescuer, rich Hong Kong evangelist, willful exile, small-town American minister) looms over the entire family as legend and inhabits the son's life as a myth. The predicament after the father's death—waking "in the used light / of someone's spent life"—might have been how to sift fact from legend and demythify the father's life and the family's history. But more essentially the son has been formed by the myth and legend themselves, and the poetry mobilizes their images and narratives to give expression to his experience within the swirl of fact, fiction, legend, and memory.

Reflecting on his father in a frequently cited interview with Bill Moyers in 1988, Lee explained, "He was for me a huge character. He made it obvious early on that he was the template by which all his sons and his daughter were to measure our lives. He always set himself up as a goal for us, and he wasn't modest about it." Moyers asked, "Did you ever feel devastated by him, as some sons do by a strong father?" Lee answered, "No! You know, that's one thing I have no doubt about. My mother once pointed to me and said, 'You are the stone on which your father's patience broke.' . . . Of course, she didn't tell me that until he was dead, but I realized that I had a lot of strength to be able to stand up against him. I never wanted to leave home. I always knew I would only grow stronger by struggling against him, and I was never afraid of him. I was in awe, but I never feared him."[48] Lee's poetry is remarkably free of resentment, not only in this oedipal struggle but also in relation to the injuries of racism that he registers and the trials of the displacements, exile, and prejudice that mark his passage from barely known Asian homelands to rural America. *Ressentiment* seems alien to this writer, whose own alienness leaves him estranged from China ("in a way I feel there is nothing to return to") and never truly at home in America: "In my most pessimistic moods I feel that I'm disconnected and that I'm going to be disconnected forever, that I'll never have any place that I can call home."[49]

The rage in Lee's "furious versions" is not an impulse to destroy, whether turned inward or outward. In the ancient Greek structure of feeling *thymos* encompasses such passions as anger, jealousy, vengefulness, envy, and pride, which are aroused when one's sense of oneself is threatened or negated. *Thymos* is the capacity to become impassioned, indeed enraged, by such a threat or negation. As with the transformation of ancient fear into modern *Angst*, the pathos of endangered self-esteem is today more often associated with the "narcissistic wound" than with Homeric rage. The fury limned in Lee's poetry is neither that of borderline disorders nor that of Achilles' rage. It is best set, perhaps, in the context of the decentered plurality of contemporary societies and the multiple global migrations seeking security, freedom, or wealth and fleeing poverty, violence, oppression, or natural or ecological catastrophe. Just as Western culture can no longer claim that it is in itself and as itself the realization of universal values and truth, virtually every society on the globe must by the same token come to terms with how to establish a body politic whose participants are not racially, ethnically, religiously, or linguistically homogeneous. Vattimo astutely asserts that the fact of plurality, multiculturalism, and ethnic, sexual, and religious diversity in the contemporary world "means to experience freedom as a continual oscillation between belonging and disorientation."[50] How this global predicament seeps into the marrow of a poet's experience and takes hold of his creativity is palpable throughout Li-Young Lee's work. His is a *thymos* roused by the negations and affirmations of identity in the endlessly rocking cradle of belonging and disorientation. The drafts, revisions, and versions are drafts, revisions, and versions of poem and of self, since the poem does not so much issue from the *I* as the *I* issues from the poem.

Lee's poetry has been something of a lightning rod in debates among scholars in Asian American studies, especially as those debates concern the very foundations and directions of that scholarly field itself and its possible roles as a site of identity formation and political consciousness.[51] His writing seems to stand athwart various strongly held valuations of such concepts and phenomena as assimilation, ethnicity, the literary canon, essentialism, authentic tradition, imperialism, and the ascription of Asian American identity itself. Does he privilege his integration into the Western poetic canon over his own ethnicity? Does the wide recognition of his work—prizes, fellowships, venues such as the *New Yorker* and the *Norton Anthology of Poetry*—indicate that he feeds established poetic and cultural views that obscure difference? Are his allusions to Chinese language and culture authentic? Do they orientalize a tradition from which he is separated? There is one charge against Lee that especially needs to be rebutted: the claim that his writing affirms a vacuous universalism and humanism blotting out ethnic specificity, racial oppression, and other political realities. According to Wenying Xu, "Lee's interpersonal ethics originate from his transcendentalist impulse to render cultural differentiation meaningless. Yet it is precisely his cultural difference that make him a fascinating poet."[52] A harsher assessment yet comes from Dorothy Wang: "While critics and Lee himself have mythologized his history as the son of a Chinese Indonesian political prisoner under President Sukarno's regime in Indonesia, this type of political residue—distant, foreign, a question of other Asian countries' 'human rights' violations—is neutralized in Lee's poetry by the Romantic sensibility and lyricality of his language and by readers' own reading proclivities, into a 'universal' 'human' experience of dislocation."[53]

I suspect that a moment in the Moyers interview has fueled this criticism. Moyers remarked that the family's "journey—China, Indonesia, Hong Kong, Macao, Japan, Seattle, Pittsburgh—is a story of the twentieth century, the century of refugees." Lee replied, "In a way, I feel as if our experience may be no more than an outward manifestation of a homelessness that people in general feel. It seems to me that anybody who thinks about our position in the universe cannot help but feel a little disconnected and homeless, so I don't think we're special. We refugees might simply express outwardly what all people feel inwardly."[54] If some such statement were made by someone like me, who has never been forced from one home to another by flood or gun, never fled a land never to be able to return, never abandoned possessions simply to survive, never been torn loose from my mother tongue to pursue the vocation of writing, it would be objectionable and rather obscene. Well, we are all homeless in a way. Said by an exile who is also a poet, it has very specific connotations. Dwelling in his adopted language, Li-Young Lee's poetic project takes up his own experience, memory, reverie, and family legends and continually turns the "outward" and "inward" round one another in order to rasp, scratch, percuss the furious versions of self that reach out toward, that is, invite in, the imaginative capacities of his readers. Such a project is not an abstract, naïve, lazy, or ideological universalism. It is an instance, from the standpoint of writing, of what I call the ordeal of universalism, as the poet's singular experience exceeds, reaches beyond, its own locale, boundaries, identity, in being articulated.

I, Not I

Since the advent of romanticism, poetry has provided philosophy with its most compelling and most troublesome instance of subjectivity.[55] Lyric is the art form most closely associated with the *I*. The *I* is as essential to lyric as mood and trope. Lyric takes shape *as* the triad mood–*I*–trope, and yet this extremity of subjectivity is not solipsism: poetry is pure subjectivity but not subjective. That puzzle unsettles the categories of subjectivity and objectivity themselves. Even when the word *I* does not appear in the poem, the lyric remains the most condensed and ample articulation of an *I*, the fullest self-expression a writer is capable of. I'll cite yet again Heidegger's comment in *Being and Time*: "In 'poetical' discourse, the communication of the existential possibilities of one's state-of-mind can become an aim in itself, and this amounts to a disclosing of existence" (H 162). Such is the vocation of poetry at least since Wordsworth and Keats, Baudelaire and Dickinson. Where but in the poem do modern human beings speak fully? Whitman affirms the poetic *parole pleine* with exuberance: "I . . . sing myself." Mallarmé testifies, as did the Romantics more covertly, to the death of the *I* in this full speaking, for as the emotional and linguistic labor of creating the poem reaches its desired conclusion the completion itself causes the poet to disappear from the poem or to die *into* the poem or, stated the other way round, to be left stranded outside the poem, surviving and flung back into inarticulate, incomplete stammering, only to begin drafting all over again.

Hegel wryly remarks that lyric "is especially opportune in modern times when every individual claims the right of having his own personal point of view and mode of feeling."[56] This individual right, and, more important, the desire to exercise it, is the historic achievement of modern liberal society; it has also therefore been thoroughly, sometimes exclusively, associated with the bourgeoisie and has stuck uncomfortably in the craw of rebels against the bourgeois lifeworld, be their rebellion political, moral, or aesthetic. Octavio Paz captures the irony with only slight exaggeration: "All modern poets, aside from a half-dozen aristocrats, have belonged to the middle class. They have all had a university education. . . . They were all products of that great historical creation of modernity, the bourgeoisie. And for that very reason they were all, without, exception, violent enemies of modernity. Enemies and victims. Hence—yet another paradox—they were fully modern."[57] Paz is fully aware that the torments of the antibourgeois bourgeois, of whom Baudelaire is an exemplar, do not, however, exhaust or adequately explain the paradoxes of modern lyric's *I*.

The threads of the conceptual knot posed by modern poetry include Whitman's "I sing myself," the Mallarméan poem as the poet's tomb, and Lee's "furious versions" of poem and self. Nietzsche sets up the question of lyric subjectivity in *The Birth of Tragedy* (sect. 5)[58] with regard to the prevailing aesthetic values of "objectivity" and "pure contemplation devoid of interest," values he does not outright challenge:

> Hence our aesthetics must first solve the problem of how the "lyrist" is possible as an artist—he who, according to the experience of all ages, is continually saying "I" and running through the entire chromatic scale of his passions and desires. Compared with Homer, Archilochus appalls us by his cries of hatred and scorn, by his drunken outbursts of desire. Therefore is not he, who has been called the first subjective artist, essentially the non-artist?

Reversing field, Nietzsche answers this fake rhetorical question by dissociating lyric and the subjective: "The 'I' of the lyrist . . . sounds from the depth of his being: its 'subjectivity,' in the sense of modern aestheticians, is a fiction." Lyric partakes of both the Dionysian and the Apollonian through a distinctive meshing of music and image, that is, the "primal unity" of music, which dissolves all individuality, and the "dream inspiration" that creates images and effects the *principium individuationis*. Picking up on a remark by Schiller that his creative process begins in an imageless "*musical mood*" and " 'the poetical idea only follows later,' " Nietzsche deploys the Dionysian/Apollonian theme to entertain how the lyric's *I* emerges from the dissolution of the poet's subjectivity:

> In the first place, as a Dionysian artist he has identified himself with the primal unity, its pain and contradiction. Assuming that music has been correctly termed a repetition and a recast of the world, we may say that he produces the copy of this primal unity as music. Now, however, under the Apollinian dream inspiration, this music reveals itself to him again as a *symbolic dream image*. . . . The artist has already surrendered his subjectivity in the Dionysian process. The image that now shows him his identity with the heart of the world is a dream scene that embodies the primordial contradiction and primordial pain, together with the primordial pleasure, of mere appearance.

Nietzsche's ecstatic contradictions have a corollary in the sober Hegelian dialectic, as it too confronts the question of poetry's nonsubjective subjectivity:

> The central point of unity in a lyric must therefore be regarded as the inner life
> of the poet. But this inner life itself is partly the individual's pure unity with
> himself and partly it is fragmented and dispersed into the most diversified
> particularization and most variegated multiplicity of ideas, feelings, impres-
> sions, insights, etc.; and their linkage consists solely in the fact that one and
> the same self carries them, so to say, as their mere vessel.[59]

Qui parle? In Hegel's perspective, the poetic voice is achieved as the poet takes
up some fragment of the ideas, feelings, impressions, or insights which are
transitory occurrences in the flow of his or her experience and affixes that
fragment as the full and complete expression of the lyric's *I*. From Nietzsche's
perspective, such transfiguration is the infusion of the Dionysian in the Apollonian and its reworking by it: "The inchoate, intangible reflection of the primordial pain in music, with its redemption in mere appearance, now produces a second mirroring as a specific symbol or example." Or, as he puts it in
one of his most striking metaphors: "The Dionysian-musical enchantment of
the sleeper seems to emit image sparks, lyrical poems, which in their highest
development are called tragedies and dramatic dithyrambs."

For both Nietzsche and Hegel, poetry is uniquely the site where the *I*
achieves itself in its full expressiveness. For Hegel, this self-achieving *I* surpasses the elusiveness of everyday experience and the fluctuations of ordinary
selfhood:

> In order to be the centre which holds the whole lyric work of art together the
> poet must have achieved a *specific* mood or entered a specific situation, while
> at the same time he must identify *himself* with this particularization of himself
> as with himself, so that in it he feels and envisages *himself*. In this way alone
> does he then become a self-bounded subjective entirety and express only what
> issues from this determinate situation and stands in connection with it.[60]

For Nietzsche, the lyric *I* that thus overcomes the ordinary conditions of existence and identity becomes—or disappears into—an Other: "Insofar as the subject is the artist . . . , he has already been released from his individual will,
and has become, as it were, the medium through which the one truly existent
subject celebrates his release in appearance."

In the letter where John Keats famously distinguished his own poetic
from his immediate predecessors' by coining the phrase *the wordworthian or
egotistical sublime,* what he goes on to say about his own poetic vocation can
astonish: "A Poet is the most unpoetical of any thing in existence; because he
has no Identity—he is continually in for [possibly intending *informing*]—and
filling some other Body—The Sun, the Moon, the Sea." This resonates, per-

haps discordantly, with Hegel's attempt to unravel poetry's conceptual knot by identifying who speaks in the poem as the poet insofar as the poem latches onto something in the "fragmented and dispersed" flow of "the variegated multiplicity of ideas, feelings, impressions insight, etc.," of the poet's "inner life" and endows that fragment with the poet's fullest expressiveness: "The poet must have achieved a *specific* mood or entered a specific situation, while at the same time he must identify *himself* with this particularization of himself as with himself, so that in it he feels and envisages *himself*." Complete identification with a mere fragment of inner life is the paradox by which the poem delivers the appearance of concrete identity. Keats, for his part, vacillates between an apologetic pathos: "Not one word I ever utter can be taken for granted as an opinion growing out of my identical nature—how can it, when I have no nature?" and a poetic aspiration to Shakespearean genius: "It is not itself—it has no self—it enjoys light and shade; it lives in gusto, be it foul or fair, high or low, rich or poor, mean or elevated—It has as much delight in creating an Iago as an Imogen. What shocks the virtuous philosop[h]er, delights the camelion Poet."[61] So, between Keats and Hegel the question *Who is speaking?* teeters into an alternative: *does* I *become* Not I *or does* Not I *become* I?

The twists and turns of both Hegel and Nietzsche attest to the philosophical difficulty poetry poses. It confounds the distinction of subjectivity and objectivity, selfhood and otherness, particular and universal, agent and medium. Modern criticism has responded to the paradoxes of the lyric *I* with approximate, largely inadequate distinctions such as empirical self and poetic self, biographical self and persona, poet and speaker, and so on. Such distinctions beg the question of the relation of the poet to the speaker, the person to the persona, and so on. Overlooked is the very act of writing that creates the supposed poetic self, persona, or speaker. T. S. Eliot's "objective correlative" and Wordsworth's seemingly contradictory "emotion recollected in tranquillity" and "spontaneous overflow of feeling" have proved fruitfully ambiguous formulas for the enigma of poetic voice.

Paz works a wide range of reflections off the idea of poetry as "the other voice," from his notion that modern poetry refuses assimilation to either politics or religion to the idea that it is the voice of antimodern modernity. At bottom the poet's speech is the attuned listening to something else: "All poets in the moments, long or short, of poetry, if they are really poets, hear the *other* voice. It is their own, someone else's, no one else's, and everyone's."[62] Li-Young Lee testifies to the attentiveness and intoxication of listening for the voice: "I think when a person is in deep prayer, all of that being's attention is focused on God. When a person is in love, all of that being's attention is focused on the beloved. I think in writing poetry, all of the being's attention is focused on some inner voice. I don't mean to sound mystical, but it really is a voice and all of the attention is turned toward that voice. That's such an exhilarating state to be in that it's addictive."[63]

De Man's essay on Baudelaire recently thrust itself into a debate over the meaning of lyric, voice, and the *I* thanks to its inclusion by Virginia Jackson and Yopie Prins in their invaluable critical anthology *The Lyric Theory Reader*. "Anthropomorphism and Trope in the Lyric" anchors the section titled "Post-Structuralist Reading" and occasions the editors' spirited polemical edge against, altogether and at once, poststructuralism, deconstruction, close reading, New Criticism, and Romantic and post-Romantic conceptions of lyric. De Man is taken as the exemplary specimen of the whole kit and caboodle, despite the dozens of essays in which he disputes genre, periodization, and canonical readings. Jonathan Culler sharply rebuts Jackson and Prins in *Theory of Lyric*, his own invaluable study of lyric as a genre and the array of theoretical problems it poses to modern criticism.

The debate turns around the aporetic maneuver in de Man's analysis of the relation of "Obsession" to "Correspondances." De Man in brief: critics have treated "Correspondances" as the exemplary modern (Romantic, post-Romantic) lyric because of its theme of infinite harmonies of self/nature and mind/senses (*esprit/sens*), even as the unity-puncturing effect of the line "Comme l'ambre, le musc, le bejoin et l'encens" escapes those readers' notice: "In the paraphernalia of literary terminology, there is no term available to tell us what 'Correspondances' might be. All we know is that it is, emphatically, *not* a lyric."[64] "Obsession" is a "reading" of "Correspondances" that, according to de Man, transposes all its elements into lyric via anthropomorphizing apostrophes to nature ("Grands bois, vous . . ."; "Je te hais, Océan!"; "ô nuit") and the introduction of *I* ("vous m'effrayez"; "Je te hais . . ."; "Mon esprit . . ."; "Je l'entends . . ."; "Comme tu me plairais . . ."; "Car je cherche . . ."): "The canon of Romantic and post-Romantic lyric poetry offers innumerable versions and variations of this inside/outside pattern of exchange that founds the metaphor of the lyrical voice as subject."[65] A lyrical reading in effect lyricizes the text by bringing all its linguistic and intellectual processes into alignment with one another under the aegis of an illusory self: "What we call the lyric, the instance of represented voice, conveniently spells out the rhetorical and thematic characteristics that make it the paradigm of a complementary relationship between grammar, trope, and theme."[66] "Obsession" is the original misreading of "Correspondances" as lyric. Looked at the other way round, the two poems yield de Man's concluding aporia:

Whenever we encounter a text such as "Obsession"—that is, whenever we read—there always is an infra-text, a hypogram like "Correspondances" underneath. Stating this relationship, as we just did, in phenomenal, spatial terms or in phenomenal, temporal terms—"Obsession," a text of recollection and elegiac mourning, *adds* remembrance to the flat surface of time in "Correspondances"—produces at once a hermeneutic, fallacious lyrical reading of the unintelligible. The power that takes one from one text to the other is not just a power of displacement, be it understood as recollection or interiorization or any other "transport," but the sheer blind violence that Nietzsche, concerned with the same enigma, domesticated by calling it, metaphorically, an *army* of tropes.[67]

To summarize (despite the unsettled syntax of the second sentence above),[68] "Correspondances" is not a lyric, while "Obsession" reads "Correspondances" as a lyric by rewriting it through anthropomorphisms, figurations of interiority, and the metaphor of voice as subject secured by the *I*; ultimately, beneath every text that is read lyrically lies its unintelligible hypogram; the reader is buffeted between fallacious interpretation and unintelligibility.

I have already argued that Heideggerian attunement and the triad mood–understanding–discourse break through the dualities of mind/nature and interiority/exteriority that implacably lead de Man to generate aporias. His conclusions here lie askew the issues I have raised via Baudelaire and Lee and Hegel and Nietzsche. De Man's notion of the "inside/outside pattern of exchange that founds the metaphor of the lyrical voice as subject," combined with his interpretations of apostrophe and prosopopoeia alluded to earlier, can be taken all the way to the claim that any representation of the speaking subject is anthropomorphic. Designations of *anthropos* are anthropomorphic. To construe that paradox as aporia is to miss what is perhaps the most powerful aspect of Rousseau's fable of the giant, namely, the insight that human beings are the entity that designates itself—*l'homme*—and does so within a drama of passion, metaphor, and recognition. Rather than impasse, the predicament and creativity of Dasein's self-designations is a site of its freedom—so long as freedom is not construed as sovereign dominion.

I find in Hegel's commentary on lyric, which is undoubtedly one of de Man's implicit targets, an illuminating account of the lyric subject. The poem arises from a mere fragment of the poet's experience with its "variegated multiplicity of ideas, feelings, impressions, insights, etc.," but in creating the poem the poet "must identify *himself* with this particularization of himself as with himself." That identification, however it manifests itself in the poem, is indeed a fiction, a metaphor, a rhetorico-poetic construct. Yet this difference of the poetic subject from the poet's self is not a falsehood or fallacy. The "linkage" of ideas, feelings, impressions, and insights in the poet's experience "consists solely in the fact that one and the same self carries them, so to say, as their mere vessel." The so-called empirical self is neither fixed nor "real," and the poetic subject is neither identical to that self nor "fictive." Rather than aporia, lyric volatilizes what is meant by empirical, real, false, identity, self, and subject.

The definition of lyric that de Man deploys in saying that "Correspondances" is not a lyric, whereas "Obsession" is, is a straw man. The appearance of "I" in a poem's *énoncé* is an unreliable landmark of subjectivity. One would be hard-pressed to find a poem more likely to be identified as lyric, indeed as Romantic lyric, than Keats's "To Autumn," a poem in which the pronoun "I" does not occur, nor does any shifter by which to specify the identity, circumstance, locale, or character of the "speaker." So too, of course, with "Correspondances." The fact that "Obsession," to cite de Man's somewhat tendentious phrasing, "asserts its right to say 'I' with full authority" has little bearing in itself on the nature of the poem's expressivity.[69] De Man becomes in turn the straw man for Jackson and Prins. They first seize on the meaning he assigns to *lyric*, since it resonates with their own effort to cast the modern understanding of lyric inaugurated by romanticism as now simply outdated ("the self-enclosed and self-expressive lyric" defines "the old normative lyric"),[70] whether in the name of experimental and postmodern poetry, premodern and neoclassical poetics, or the array of poetic practices that were supposedly marginalized as "various historical verse genres gradually became 'lyric' as reading practices shifted over the nineteenth century and were consolidated in the twentieth century."[71] The affinity Jackson and Prins find with de Man in "saying that the poem is not a lyric unless reading makes it so" is short-lived, for they consign him and poststructuralism *tout court* to their dustbin of outdatedness: "Post-structuralism did not unravel the lyric; instead, post-structuralist critics tended to make the lyric even more of a modern icon than did their predecessors in the twentieth century, since by doing so they could demonstrate the difficulties and hazards, perhaps even the impossibility, of thinking about lyric in any other way."[72]

Culler grants that "we need a more capacious notion of lyric to counter the modern notions of lyric intelligibility linked to the voice of the subject,"[73] thus distancing his own project from de Man's apparent disdain for the concept of genre, but he also criticizes Jackson and Prins for collapsing developments in the history of poetry (the modern lyric) and various critical stances and procedures for understanding those developments. In his discussion of theories of lyric Culler cites a definition of the term offered by the classicist Alessandro Barchiesi that is coherent enough to capture how readers recognize a lyric and yet supple enough to account for a lyric's capacity to surprise and move, that is, recognition of genre and astonishment at a particular work, an astonishment that can never be reduced to the work's success in conforming to the genre. The definition also emphasizes an aspect of the reading experience and the rhetorical action of lyric that is ingrained in criticism but seldom explicitly reflected on, namely, that in lyric the reader is at once addressed, directly or obliquely, *and* drawn to rehearse or voice the utterance as his or her own. "Shall I compare thee to a summer's day?" vibrates for the reader as *I* and *thee* and as both and as neither. Says Barchiesi, "Lyric can be tentatively (transhistorically) defined as a first person utterance whose performative conditions are reconstructed by a re-performing reader, who typically positions himself somewhere in a continuum whose extremes are a generic voice and some individual idea of the author."[74] *Generic voice* ostensibly refers to those stylized modes of address associated with the impersonal, disembodied, Orphic, or prophetic, and so on. "Correspondances" and "To Autumn" lie at that end of the spectrum, while "Obsession"—or a Shakespearean sonnet—seems to lie at the other end.

The idea that reading lyric constitutes a reperformance of the poetic first-person utterance could be thought through and formulated along many paths, including Kenneth Burke's notion that reading reenacts the poet's symbolic act, though the polarity I have discussed between Poe's raven and Freud's jokes cautions against any single relation of reader to work. Culler advances his own quite perspicacious gloss on Barchiesi's comment by stressing that reading always affords some range of possibilities for receiving and imagining the lyric voice: "The 'authoredness' of lyrics is important—they are not found language but composed for us by an author—but readers have considerable scope in choosing whether to treat them as the thought of a particular author or as general wisdom."[75] Let's add that "choosing" along that vast continuum is part and parcel of the reperforming reader's interpretation of the poem and responsiveness to its rhetorical operations, principally trope and mode of address.[76]

That poetry, standing in for art in general, upends the philosophical categories of subjective and objective is acknowledged, though indirectly, in the *Critique of Judgment*, the Third Critique of the philosopher for whom subjectivity and objectivity are benchmark concepts. In placing the question of aesthetic judgment and the claim *this is beautiful* as a relation between the judging subject and the judged object, Kant postulates subject-object and then proceeds to let that relation and those categories unravel. In §32, he asserts: "The judgment of taste determines its object with regard to satisfaction (as beauty) with a claim to the assent of *everyone*, as if it were objective."[77] *As*

if it were objective, since only what is objectively so of an object lays claim
to the assent of everyone, whereas in aesthetic judgment, as Kant says in §8,
"there can . . . be no rule in accordance with which someone could be compelled to acknowledge something as beautiful."[78] From there it follows that
the as-if-objective is counterpoised by an as-if-subjective: "The judgment of
taste is not determinable by grounds of proof at all, just as if it were merely
subjective" (§33).[79] Aesthetic judgment is as-if-subjective because it is without
ground and proof, and it is as-if-objective because it excites a claim to universal agreement regarding the object. As-if-objective *and* as-if-subjective =
neither objective *nor* subjective.

Just as aesthetic judgment eludes the categories of subjective and objective, the object's beauty itself hovers between subjective and objective; the
beautiful is subjective in that it is a particular kind of satisfaction, a pure
pleasing and favoring, in Kant's language, "disinterested and *free* satisfaction"
in the sense that "no interest, neither that of the senses nor that of reason, ex-
torts approval" (§5).[80] The beautiful is nothing other than this particular kind
of satisfaction, but this very satisfaction is felt *as if* it were objective: "The
person making the judgment . . . will speak of the beautiful as if beauty were
a property of the object" (§6).[81] In drawing attention to the breakdown of the
subject-object categories even as they are deployed to account for aesthetic
judgment, I am not disputing the direction of Kant's reflection. Rather, and
on the contrary, I see his struggle with these fundamental categories as shedding light on the fact that art and aesthetic judgment embroil us in experiences and procedures that intensify and exceed how we conceive ourselves as
subjects. The various *as-if* formulations in the *Critique of Judgment* point to
a kind of recursive paradox: the beautiful can be attributed purely to the play
of the recipient's faculties only insofar as the recipient attributes it to the thing
that occasions the feeling and judgment of the beautiful.

When art is looked at from the standpoint of its creation, as it is by Nietzsche, rather than its reception, the recursivity reappears. Artistic creativity
rebounds on the creators as something created elsewhere or by another or by
a more-than-human or other-than-human agent. That is what Paz suggests
with the idea of the other voice and what Nietzsche expresses in his reflection on the lyric *I* cited above when he writes that the artist "has already been
released from his individual will, and has become, as it were, the medium
through which the one truly existent subject celebrates his release in appearance." The recursivity endemic to human creativity arises in and as poetry:
"The images of the *lyrist* are nothing but *his very* self and, as it were, only different projections of himself, so he, as the moving center of this world, may
say 'I': of course, this self is not the same as that of the waking, empirically real

man, but the only truly existent and eternal self resting at the basis of things, through whose images the lyric genius sees this very basis." Nietzsche offers an elaboration of this notion of the "truly existent and eternal self" through two striking metaphors. According to the first, since human "existence and the world" have no objective or moral justification for being, no ordained purpose, "it is only as an *aesthetic phenomenon* that existence and the world are eternally *justified*," justified in the eyes of some kind of divine artificer: "We may assume that we are merely images and artistic projections for the true author, and that we have our highest dignity in our significance as works of art." In *The Birth of Tragedy* this "one truly existent subject" and divine artificer is in effect the tragic dramatist insofar as he himself simply *is* the creative force of the Dionysian and the Apollonian yoked together. The human creativity that creates the subjectivity beyond the subject leads Nietzsche to a second metaphorical image of impossible recursivity: "The genius in the act of artistic creation coalesces with this primordial artist of the world" and "in this state" is "like the weird image of the fairy tale which can turn its eyes at will and behold itself; he is at once subject and object, at once poet, actor, and spectator."[82]

Sensation and Being

as if emotion had ever been able to create anything artistic
NIETZSCHE, *The Birth of Tragedy*

Deleuze's Rat

Deleuze elaborates an approach to sensation and affect that ostensibly makes a decisive break with Heidegger's hermeneutic orientation. Heidegger's starting point is the adult—or, perhaps more palpably, the adolescent—who is caught up in everyday life with others and shares with them a more or less unexamined sense of the world they inhabit together. The being-in-the world of this indistinctly individuated Dasein is from the outset immersed in the triad mood–understanding–speech. Deleuze's innovative contribution to empiricism and vitalism has a very different conceptual starting point, namely, the living organism's sensory, perceptual, proprioceptive, and kinesthetic agitations and movements.

The last essay Deleuze wrote is titled "Immanence: A Life"—*a life* not in a biographical or autobiographical sense but rather in the sense of being a living being. The essay is magisterial for its philosophical scope, astounding for its brevity, and sharply poignant for being the final effort of a great mind exerting itself against debilitating illness, which was soon to be ended by suicide. The pure immanence of being alive grounds Deleuze's vitalism. He exemplifies this notion of *a life* with the observation—not altogether accurate, especially if the observer happens to be a mother—that "very small children all resemble one another and have hardly any individuality, but they have singularities: a smile, a gesture, a funny face—not subjective qualities. Small children, through all their sufferings and weaknesses, are infused with an immanent life that is pure power and even bliss."[1] The crucial difference, then, is between the pure immanence of a life and the life led and lived by an individual. The latter presupposes the former. That the difference between the lived life and *a life* is at once enormous and infinitesimally small is evinced by Deleuze's remarks on what he finds to be an unparalleled description of "what *a* life is" in Charles Dickens's *Our Mutual Friend*, where Roger Riderhood, known as Rogue, is brought unconscious and near death to Miss Abbey's tavern. Riderhood is despised by all for the life he has led, but "as he lies dying" he is valued as a life: "Suddenly, those taking care of him manifest an eagerness, respect, even love for his slightest sign of life. Everybody bustles about to save him, to the point where, in his deepest coma, this wicked man himself senses something soft and sweet penetrating him." As he recovers, though, "his saviors turn colder, and he becomes once again mean and crude."[2]

In an alternative philosophical framework, this phenomenon might appear as the pull of human dignity and a reverence for living things. It's what stirs a citizen's revulsion at an execution, a passer-by's rush to aid an injured stranger, a farmer's pang for the slaughter of a calf, hog, or chicken, a medic's attention to a wounded enemy combatant. It is what sustains a mother whose life has been shattered by her son's violent accidental death, urging her to carry on in her daily existence, to keep going to work, and to fight off the impulses to end it all, since to abandon her own survival, her now even more painful struggle to survive, would negate life itself, the very loss of which is the source of her harrowing grief. From one philosophical angle of vision, she honors her dead son by upholding the sanctity of life; from another, she is buoyed by life's pure immanence, its "pure power and even bliss." Either perspective can give rise to a sense of life, even a burdened life, as a *gift*, whether in the religious register of a divine endowment; the psychoanalytic register of the Oedipal debt of existence; the Arendtian theme of "natality," according to which the condition of possibility for inauguration and inception in human affairs lies in the "infinite improbability" of every individual's own existence; or perhaps even Roger Riderhood's brief after-awareness of the "something soft and sweet penetrating him."[3] This is not the occasion to debate these alternative conceptions or track the interpretive labyrinth of their varied inflections in experience—except as a sketch of the encounter between *vitalism* and *hermeneutics*.

Deleuze calls his empiricism a "transcendental empiricism." The transcendental field he defines "as a pure stream of a-subjective consciousness, a pre-reflexive impersonal consciousness, a qualitative duration of consciousness without a self." In simple empiricism, "sensation is only a break within the flow of absolute consciousness"; in transcendental empiricism, by contrast, "however close two sensations may be," what is brought into focus is "the passage from one to the other as becoming, as increase or decrease in power (virtual quantity)."[4] Nietzschean becoming, Spinozan immanence as the pulsation of power as enhancing or diminishing capacity, and the Bergsonian temporality of duration (*durée*) are the "blast of original concepts" that find "the power of their becoming when they pass into one another" in Deleuze's thought.[5]

In the conclusion of *What Is Philosophy?* Deleuze and Félix Guattari explicate the interpretation of vitalism to which they adhere through a series of provocative statements. Among them is one of the most marvelous sentences in modern philosophy: "Even when one is a rat, it is through contemplation that one 'contracts' a habit."[6] At issue is how to account for the fact that sensation is not pure chaos playing across the embodied nervous system: "Sensation is excitation itself, not insofar as it is gradually prolonged and passes into the reaction but insofar as it is preserved or preserves its vibrations. Sensation contracts the vibrations of the stimulant on a nervous surface or in a cerebral volume: what comes before has not yet disappeared when what follows appears. This is its way of responding to chaos."[7] The succession of overlapping sensations is, in the language of "Immanence: A Life," a becoming, a perpetual "increase or decrease in power (virtual quantity)." Thus, the phenomenon that behaviorism designates as the conditioned reflex—as in the learning process by which a rat acquires a habit—"presuppose[s] a brain-force as faculty of feeling coexistent with tissues," but in order for the habit to form, to be "contracted," there must be "a pure internal Awareness," that is, "a pure contemplation without knowledge": "This can be seen even in the cerebral domain par excellence of apprenticeship or the formation of habits: although everything seems to take place by active connections and progressive integrations, from one test to another, the tests or cases, the occurrences, must, as Hume showed, be contracted in a contemplating 'imagination' while remaining distinct in relation to actions and to knowledge. *Even when one is a rat, it is through contemplation that one 'contracts' a habit.*"[8]

The pure immanence and transcendental field we share with rats are a far cry from what Heidegger means by primordiality. He assigns primordiality to Dasein's being always already in a world and with others through immersion in mood–understanding–discourse. Heidegger's antipathy to vitalism is pronounced, whether in his dismissive references to Bergson in *Being and Time* or in the distance he takes from the biological and physiological jargon in *The Will to Power* by which Nietzsche seems to reduce artistic creativity to "a life-process conditioned by rapture. The creative state is accordingly 'an *explosive* state.' That," Heidegger harrumphs, "is a chemical description, not a philosophical interpretation. If in the same place Nietzsche refers to vascular changes, alterations in skin tone, temperature, and secretion, his findings involve nothing more than changes in the body grasped in an extrinsic manner, even if he draws into consideration 'the automatism of the entire muscular system.'"[9]

Deleuze's break with hermeneutics seems to be matched by a no less radical break with any treatment of the sort I have developed thus far of the literary text as rhetoric, with rough references to Aristotle, Kenneth Burke,

Bakhtin, and de Man: "Aesthetic figures, and the style that creates them, have nothing to do with rhetoric."[10] Rhetoric in Aristotle's analysis is inseparable from *doxa* as the domain of opinion, deliberation, assumptions, debate, common sense, and structures of feeling, whereas *thinking*, according to *What Is Philosophy?*, arises in its absolute separation from *doxa*. Thinking in this strong sense of the term occurs in the incommensurate but coequal fields of philosophy, science, and art: "Art thinks no less than philosophy, but it thinks through affects and percepts."[11] Thinking is the form of creativity in general, while its specific forms are science, philosophy, and art: "The great aesthetic figures of thought and the novel but also of painting, sculpture, and music produce affects that surpass ordinary affections and perceptions, just as concepts go beyond everyday opinions."[12] To specify what *surpassing* and *going beyond* the ordinary and everyday means—beyond the ontic-doxic, let's say—would amount then to an investigation of creativity.

The Artwork between Heidegger and Deleuze

The burden of my argument throughout this chapter will be to show, first, that there is in fact a wide area of convergence between Deleuze and Heidegger, especially at the core of their most compelling aesthetic concepts; and, second, that rhetoric in the double sense of naming-by-misnaming (trope) and persuading-to-attitude (ontic jolt) clarifies something essential regarding poetry as art that both Deleuze and Heidegger leave obscure.

Starting, then, with the area of convergence. For Deleuze as for Heidegger, the artwork is torn from the web of objects and practices that constitute what is called "equipment" in "The Origin of the Work of Art" (that is, utensils and tools broadly conceived and their uses) and from that realm of perceptions and beliefs which in *Being and Time* is called "the they" and "idle chatter" into which the individual Dasein is "thrown." What Deleuze calls *doxa* Heidegger calls "the they." Deleuze and Heidegger also share the view that the artwork is a thing whose thingly character differentiates it from other kinds of things, specifically in Heidegger's vocabulary from mere things as well as from equipment, and yet this thingness is not extraneous to what makes the artwork art. Rejecting aesthetic theories that view the painter's canvas and pigment and the sculptor's stone or iron as materials incidental to the artwork's ideality or as mere matter formed by the artist into representation or expression, Deleuze and Heidegger look to conceptualize the artwork's materiality and thingness as integral to its aesthetic nature. Heidegger does so through his conception of earth in relation to world, Deleuze through his notion of sensation.

Earth and world in "The Origin of the Work of Art" correspond to nature and culture, except that Heidegger shuns these terms in order to explore how to conceptualize *physis* without evoking either Romantic or scientific conceptions of Nature. Heidegger construes the early Greeks' use of *physis* to mean the "emerging and arising in itself and in all things" that occurs as things "first enter into their distinct shapes and thus come to appear as what they are." *Physis* "clears and illuminates, also, that on which and in which man bases his dwelling. We call this ground the *earth*."[13] As for *world*, the term snakes through Heidegger's work without a settled definition, from being-in-the world (*in-der-Welt-sein*) in *Being and Time* (1927) through earth/world in this essay (1936) to world picture (*Weltbild*) in "The Age of the World Picture" (1938).

World has two semantic edges in the earth/world conception. The first suggests lifeworld in a phenomenological and ethnographic sense, the horizon within which everyday labor, habits, interactions, and concerns take place and give the inhabitants' lifetime a semblance of coherence. Such a world is explicated from a van Gogh painting of a pair of shoes which Heidegger, famously and probably erroneously, takes to be a peasant woman's. The much-cited passage where Heidegger gives his account of what the painting shows smacks of elegiac projection and yet at the same time evocatively demonstrates that what one truly sees in a painting—that is, what the painting brings to appearance—is never simply the object represented:

> From the dark opening of the worn insides of the shoes the toilsome tread of the worker stares forth. In the stiffly rugged heaviness of the shoes there is the accumulated tenacity of her slow trudge through the far-spreading and ever-uniform furrows of the field swept by a raw wind. On the leather lie the dampness and richness of the soil. Under the soles slides the loneliness of the field-path as evening falls. In the shoes vibrates the silent call of the earth, its quiet gift of the ripening grain and its unexplained self-refusal in the fallow desolation of the wintry field. This equipment is pervaded by uncomplaining anxiety as to the certainty of bread, the wordless joy of having once more withstood want, and trembling before the impending childbed and shivering at the surrounding menace of death. The equipment belongs to the *earth*, and it is protected in the *world* of the peasant woman. From out of this protected belonging the equipment itself rises to its resting-within-itself.[14]

The second semantic edge of *world*, by contrast, exudes grandeur, universal compass, and decisions of historic consequence. It emerges in Heidegger's imagining of a Greek temple.[15] Erected from stone and resting upon the stony ground, the temple encloses and thereby manifests the god dwelling within it and thus establishes the world of the Greeks, for whom the temple is what places them with one another and in proximity to their gods, attaches their community to its locale, and "makes visible the invisible space of air" and the sky above: "It is the temple-work that first fits together and at the same time gathers around itself the unity of those paths and relations in which birth and death, disaster and blessing, victory and disgrace, endurance and decline acquire the shape of destiny for human being. The all-governing expanse of this open relational context is the world of this historical people."[16]

This poetics of space brings out at once the utter independence of earth from world and their complete interdependence, the temple being the joint and rift between them—the "rift-design,"[17] as Heidegger says in a coinage decidedly more modern than his example: "World and earth are essentially different from one another and yet are never separated. The world grounds itself on the earth, and earth juts through world."[18] The temple stone is earth jutting through world. The temple as artwork thus "moves the earth itself into the Open of a world and keeps it there. *The work lets the earth be an earth.*"[19] The artwork as the design of the earth/world rift seemingly works differently in architecture and painting. The painting, unlike the temple, has a representational aspect that leads Heidegger to elaborate earth/world in terms of the agrarian lifeworld which the shoes ostensibly serve: "This equip-ment belongs to the *earth*, and it is protected in the *world* of the peasant woman. From out of this protected belonging the equipment itself rises to its resting-within-itself."[20]

Heideggerian earth and Deleuzean sensation amount to different ap-proaches to the same problem: how to conceptualize the artwork's aesthetic dimension as indissociable from its material dimension, ultimately perhaps how to overcome the very distinction of material and aesthetic dimensions. The two approaches tend toward a convergence, but there remains a gap. The gap between Deleuze and Heidegger in this instance is also a gap within Heidegger's own aesthetic thought, for on the face of it his interpretation of *physis* does not include Dasein's own bodily existence, despite the strong if tacit sense of embodiment in the notion of Dasein's attunement and mood in *Being and Time*. There is in short an unthought-out relation of *physis* and *Stimmung*.

Without for the moment attempting to resolve the gap internal to Hei-degger, I want to explore more fully the convergence between Heidegger and Deleuze. The following passage from *What Is Philosophy?* (1991) brings the rich derivations of rule from example in Deleuze's study of Bacon (1981) to bear on a more general aesthetic theory and will serve as the reference-point:

Art preserves, and it is the only thing in the world that is preserved. . . . If art preserves it does not do so like industry, by adding a substance to make

a thing last. The thing became independent of its "model" from the start. . . .
And it is no less independent of the viewer or hearer, who only experience it
after, if they have the strength for it. What about the creator? It is independent
of the creator through the self-positing of the created, which is preserved in
itself. What is preserved—the thing or the work of art—is *a bloc of sensations,
that is to say, a compound of percepts and affects.*

Percepts are no longer perceptions: they are independent of a state of
those who experience them. Affects are no longer feelings or affections; they
go beyond the strength of those who undergo them. Sensations, percepts, and
affects are *beings* whose validity lies in themselves and exceeds any lived [ex-
perience]. They could be said to exist in the absence of man because man, as
he is caught in stone, on the canvas, or by words, is himself a compound of
percepts and affects. The work of art is a being of sensation and nothing else:
it exists in itself.[21]

Three themes stand out: (1) the artwork's specificity as a thing to endure and
be preserved cannot be explained by the durability of its materials *per se* but
rather by its difference from what it represents ("its model"); (2) in separating
itself from its creator, the artwork becomes "the self-positing of the created";
and (3) the artwork is thus a being in itself not reducible to an expression *of*
the artist or *for* the viewer or listener. There are corollaries to all three themes
in Heidegger's thought. Deleuze and Heidegger enjoy their greatest proximity around their respective understandings of the artwork's lastingness, self-
positing, and independence from creator or receiver.

Three Theses on Art

(1) *The artwork's specificity as a thing that is preserved and endures does not
lie essentially in its material durability but rather in its difference from what it
represents.* This notion emerges from Deleuze's reflection on the difference
that Bacon's paintings establish between the Figure and the figurative. Figurative here has the meaning of representational; for Bacon, to paint figuratively
would immerse the persons and things on the canvas in some implied relationship or story or as their sheer likeness to something else. His techniques
for banishing such implications include isolating the person on the canvas
and avoiding tableaux of several figures. Many great paintings are composed
in that way, but in Bacon's words " 'the story that is already being told between
one figure and another begins to cancel out the possibilities of what can be
done with the paint on its own.' "[22] He gives himself the task of using the primary medium of his art—paint—without letting it mediate or be mediated by
something not on the canvas. At the same time, Bacon turns away from the

available alternative to figurative painting, namely, abstraction. Neither abstract nor figurative, the Figure in a Bacon painting is isolated on the canvas, and the rounded area where he stands, the chair he sits in, or the bed he lies on leaves the surrounding area of the canvas implying or signifying nothing. In his triptych paintings he eschews thematic or narrative links among the panels. Observes Deleuze: "Painting has neither a model to represent nor a story to narrate. It thus has two possible ways of escaping the figurative: toward pure form, through abstraction; or toward the purely figural, through extraction or isolation. If the painter keeps to the Figure, if he or she opts for the second path, it will be to oppose the 'figural' to the figurative."[23]

The vocabulary of neither/nor, escape, banish, and eschew gives the misleading impression that Bacon's procedure is essentially a mode of negation, a practice of creation by privation. To correct this impression, it is necessary to lean hard on the last phrase in the passage just quoted: "If the painter keeps to the Figure . . . , it will be *to oppose the 'figural' to the figurative.*" Opposition here connotes active tension, not logical or semantic division. The figurative does not simply disappear in the presence of the figural, as it does in abstract painting. Deleuze confronts this problem, seemingly obliquely, by questioning the idea that the creative act entails putting something on an empty canvas; on the contrary, he argues, there is always a surfeit of "clichés and probabilities" already "on the canvas and in the painter's head" before brush is put to canvas. A more ample understanding of the relation of the Figure and the figurative emerges:

> the Figure is still figurative; it still represents someone (a screaming man, a smiling man, a seated man), it still narrates something, even if it is a surrealistic tale (head-umbrella-meat, howling meat . . .). We can now say that the opposition of the Figure to the figurative exists in a very complex inner relationship [*se fait dans un rapport intérieur très complexe*], and yet is not practically compromised or even attenuated by this relationship. There is a first, prepictorial figuration: it is on the canvas and in the painter's head, in what the painter wants to do, before the painter begins, in the form of clichés and probabilities. This first figuration cannot be completely eliminated; something of it is always conserved. But there is a second figuration: the one that the painter obtains, this time as the result of the Figure, as an effect of the pictorial act. For the pure presence of the Figure is indeed the reconstitution of a representation, the re-creation of a figuration ("this is a seated man, a Pope that screams or smiles . . .").[24]

Deleuze continues to speak of this reconstitution or recreation effected by the pictorial act as a deformation. However, it is "a deformation in place, the emergence-in-place of the Figure,"[25] that is, not a violence done *to* the Figure's body or face. For me, that is the difference between Bacon and Willem de Kooning. In Bacon, violence traverses the body and face, arising from the Figure rather than being inflicted upon it. Deleuze refers to the fact that Bacon believed he had failed whenever a painting conveyed a violence done from without: a painting must not be "sensational." Here arises the crucial distinction Deleuze makes between sensation and the sensational: "The violence of sensation is opposed to the violence of the represented (the sensational, the cliché). . . . [Bacon's] painting makes movement very intense and violent. But in the end, it is a movement 'in-place,' a spasm, which reveals a completely different problem characteristic of Bacon: *the action of invisible forces on the body*."[26] Here then is how I construe the statement in *What Is Philosophy?* regarding the artwork's lastingness that "the thing became independent of its 'model' from the start": neither abstract nor representational, Bacon's paintings search for "'what the paint can do on its own'" in order to let the Figure emerge in the "deformation," which is not the deformation *of* the prepictorial images or model so much as the event of sensation which the thus-emerged Figure *is*.

Heidegger takes a different path in addressing the inner complexity of representation. For him, a strict distinction of representational and nonrepresentational art is not at first glance decisive, since he insists that the truth of a representational work does not lie in *what* it represents. Just as much as the Greek temple in which the god is disclosed without being represented, Vincent van Gogh's painting is an event of disclosure, since "the equipmentality of equipment first genuinely arrives at its appearance through the work and only through the work" and not because the painting "draws a likeness from something actual and transposes it into a product of artistic production."[27] The stakes of the tripartite distinction of mere thing, equipment, and artwork now become clearer. The craftsman's "jug, ax, or pair of shoes" differs from the mere thing insofar as "it does not have the character of having taken shape by itself like the granite boulder"; moreover, as equipment, it is meant to be used up in its usefulness, whereas mere things, as *physis*, endure. Both artworks and handicraft are *technē*, since, unlike mere things, they are both "produced by the human hand," but the artwork is not meant to be used up but to endure, and "its self-sufficient presence" makes it "similar . . . to the mere thing which has taken shape by itself and is self-contained."[28] In sum, the artwork is like equipment in that it is humanly produced and like the mere thing because of its self-shaping and self-sufficiency; unlike the mere thing, the artwork's self-shaping is not *physis* but *technē*, and unlike equipment the artwork does not harness *physis* to useful ends that use it up but brings it forth to let it be *physis*. For Heidegger, then, it is not because of its physical properties per se that the artwork endures and is preserved, but because of its letting *physis* be: "In the creation of a work . . . , the earth itself must be set forth and used as the self-closing factor. This use, however, does not use up or misuse the earth as matter, but sets it free to be nothing but itself."[29]

Physis is thus indissociable from the essence of the artwork in two ways. The artwork's "work-material"—"stone, wood, metal, color . . . , tone"[30]—rises up as artwork and yet holds back as itself (earth). Second, the artwork gives form—rift-design—to the relation of world and earth: the temple by establishing the earthly site of the god's appearance, the painting by bringing to appearance the earthbound lifeworld of the peasant. As with Figure and figuration in Bacon, however, van Gogh's painting does represent a pair of shoes. In what terms, then, does Heidegger address the relation of the represented and the disclosed? At first blush he seems simply to overcome or bypass it altogether—or at least that is his aim—with the formulation that truth puts itself to work in the artwork: "The picture that shows the peasant shoes . . . do[es] not just make manifest what this isolated being as such is . . . ; rather, [it makes] unconcealedness as such happen in regard to what is as a whole." It is on this basis that disclosure simply overrides representation: "Truth happens in Van Gogh's painting. This does not mean that something is correctly portrayed, but rather that in the revelation of the equipmental being of the shoes, that which is as a whole—world and earth in their counterplay—attains to unconcealedness."[31] The reduction of the represented to "what this isolated being as such is" might be paired with a comment at the beginning of the essay that while the artwork "is, to be sure, a thing that is made," it "says something other than the mere thing itself is, *allo agoureuei*. The work makes public something other than itself; it manifests something other; it is an allegory."[32]

So, neither the artwork as mere thing—that is, the painted canvas framed and leaning against a wall—nor the "isolated being" it depicts count as the *work* in which *truth* happens or, in the alternative formulation, as truth putting itself to work. They are surely not to be confused with the artwork. Nor, however, are they extraneous to it. That has already been demonstrated with regard to the "work material," but not with regard to the thing portrayed. Van Gogh's painting presents a third aspect of *physis* in art not conceptualized by Heidegger. I am referring to the materiality of what is represented in the painting, namely, the shoes, their leather, the laces, the hobnails. Without this representation of the shoes in *their* materiality as worked by a craftsman, the shoemaker, neither "equipment-being" nor earth/world would be disclosed. Painters are not only occupied by the craftsmanship and toolmaking required for their own artistic activity—a fact that Heidegger acknowledges—but are also intensely attentive to the things in the world that issue from craftsmen, builders, engineers, and manufacturers. From Dutch painters' lace or

Édouard Manet's dresses and hats to Edward Hopper's filling station or David Hockney's swimming pools and patio furniture, not to mention all the bridges of stone, steel, or wood that the artist's eye schools itself on.

The question this raises bears on the relation between the representation achieved in the painting and the disclosure effected by the painting (rift-design, truth, scintillating letting-be). This question holds no matter how "wrong" Heidegger is about the shoes' agrarian provenance, since in every artwork there will be a difference between the thing represented and the being disclosed. The painting does not transcend this difference; rather, the difference is immanent to the painting—or, more simply, the painting *is* the difference. In Deleuze's terms, it is the difference between figuration and Figure. In Heidegger's terms, it would be the difference between representation and disclosure, portrayal and deconcealing. Deleuze makes it clear that Figure does not abolish figuration, and I have imposed the same clarification on Heidegger. There is in both Deleuze and Heidegger a kind of devaluing of figuration and representation; such a gesture has been widespread in modern art and aesthetics ever since Russian formalism or Brechtian *Verfremdungseffekt*, that is, the claim for art to be more or other than mere imitation, verisimilitude, mirroring, reflecting, reproduction, mimesis. The claim often relies on a caricature of realism, as though it replicates—or indeed *could* replicate—a *supposedly* stable reality. The emphasis shifts decisively, however, when put on the figuration/Figure, or representation/disclosure, relation as *difference*, a difference immanent to the artwork.

What is the nature of this difference? An unexpected clue comes from Aristotle at the very moment in the *Poetics* where he advances a definition of mimesis itself. For it is not simply the resemblance of the representation and the thing represented that constitutes the poetic structure or phenomenon of imitation:

> We take delight in viewing the most accurate possible images of objects which in themselves cause distress when we see them (e.g. the shapes of the lowest species of animals, and corpses). The reason for this is that understanding is extremely pleasant, not just for philosophers but for others too in the same way, despite their limited capacity for it. This is the reason why people take delight in seeing images; what happens is that as they view them they come to understand and work out what each thing is (e.g. "This is so-and-so"). If one happens not to have seen the thing before, it will not give pleasure as an imitation, but because of its execution or colour, or for some other reason. (48 b)[33]

In reading Aristotle, the emphasis typically falls on the idea of *the most accurate possible images of objects*, that is, the determination of mimesis as likeness. But his account emphasizes what the likeness occasions, namely, a complex structure of feeling and cognition. Mimesis adduces an awareness of the emotion the thing imitated would arouse if actually encountered— snakes, cockroaches, and corpses, for example. The mimetic image itself does not arouse a feeling of distress; enfolded with the recognition of what I would feel is my delight in recognizing the likeness: I "come to understand and work out what each thing is (e.g., "This is so-and-so"), and the experience of understanding in itself "is extremely pleasant." How, then, should the total structure of mimesis be formulated? The marvel of artistic imitation is that it triggers at once my delight in recognizing what the mimetic image represents and my awareness of the emotion it would in reality evoke. In Aristotle's example, the poetic effect or aesthetic experience lies in the difference of delight and distress. It is not likeness per se but the affective difference that defines mimesis in art.

I am not claiming that Aristotle's imitation/imitated, Heidegger's disclosed/represented, and Deleuze's Figure/figuration are the same. There are incommensurabilities to respect among the three philosophers' projects, just as van Gogh's art and Bacon's are not identical either to each other or to the hypothetical image of a corpse that Aristotle evokes. What unites the three is that in each case the non-abstract artwork, whether called "representational" or not, effects an affective difference, the recognition of which is integral to the experience of the work. Purely what is on the canvas—which both Deleuze and Heidegger call the artwork's composition—achieves this. If one sticks to an inside/outside distinction, it is necessary to recognize that the internal composition of the artwork does reference an outside. Not necessarily, however, as the visual resemblance of something outside itself. And certainly not as a fixed outer reality, for that very notion itself is suspect. We get closer with Aristotle by way of Peirce. The recognition of what I would feel in face of the actual thing is referred to by the artwork indexically: the image points to something in reality that I may have in some way experienced, which in turn informs my recognitions and delights in viewing the artwork itself ("If one happens not to have seen the thing before, it will not give pleasure as an imitation, but because of its execution or colour, or for some other reason"). The affective difference at once arises solely from the "internal" relations or composition of the artwork *and* points indexically to something that might have been encountered in the world of everyday experience. Such a formulation in turn sheds light on the Deleuzian notion that the artwork is "*a bloc of sensations, that is to say, a compound of percepts and affects,*" but that "percepts are no longer perceptions: they are independent of a state of those who experience them. Affects are no longer feelings or affections." The perceptual-affective being of the artwork is separated from perceptions and feelings of "lived experience," and yet—and this is the key to the persisting element of figuration in the Figure—the artwork points indexically to the realm of lived experiences. Without that indexicality the affective difference would not occur.

(2) *The artwork does not merely stand on its own, it is "the self-positing of the created."* The overt paradox that the artwork is at once created and self-positing is a crux of modern aesthetics, which has already been noted in Kant and Nietzsche and runs down through Heidegger, Adorno, and Deleuze. Deleuze's approach is apparent in two themes already touched on. First is his account of the artist approaching not an empty canvas but one too full of images, probabilities, models, memories, and the (posed or photographed) model, so that painting is the act of wrenching an *unpreconceived* Figure from the overabundance of figurations. Second is the idea of sensation that he develops from Cézanne and discovers anew in Bacon: "Sensation is what is painted. What is painted on the canvas is the body, not insofar as it is represented as an object but insofar as it is experienced as sustaining *this* sensation."[34] Let us combine the two themes. The Figure that emerges on the canvas is *necessarily* unpreconceived, therefore strictly *unpreconceivable*; its realization is the embodiment—in and as paint—of an utterly specific sensation ("*this* sensation"). Thus, the artwork as unpreconceivable Figure and unprecedented and inimitable sensation is, at the moment of its emergence, *self-positing* even as it has been *created*.

Heidegger approaches the paradox of self-positing and createdness by first postulating that the origin (*Ursprung*) of the artwork might be located in either the creativity of the artist or the receptivity of the viewer, listener, or reader. Both are undoubtedly necessary, the one to making and the other to preserving the artwork, and they correspond to the focus of the two traditional theoretical attitudes toward art, namely, poetics and aesthetics respectively. Nevertheless, Heidegger rejects both as the *Ursprung*. What then is the origin of the artwork? "Art is the origin of the art work and of the artist."[35] What is striking about this statement is that Heidegger also rejects any idea of an established, presupposed, or standard conception of what art is. Only the artwork manifests what is art, yet only art is the origin of the artwork. Another seeming tautology, this time one that a strict formalism could easily sustain: since formalism defines art by formal completion, the artwork is achieved when formally complete; hence the apparent tautology is actually the autotelic process of the artwork becoming art in fulfilling the goal of formal completeness. But Heidegger is not a formalist. Instead, he ranks art with the various ways that truth occurs. Truth occurs in the van Gogh painting as the coming to appearance of the earth/world rift-design of the peasant's diurnal-seasonal-gestational existence, and truth occurs in the temple as the coming to appearance of the earth/world rift-design of the ancient Greeks' city as the site of their communal project and mortal existence in the presence of their gods. "Truth establishes itself as a strife within a being that is to be brought forth only in such a way that the conflict [of earth and world] opens up in this being, that is, this being is itself brought into the rift-design."[36]

Heidegger supplies an explanation of the artwork's createdness by amplifying his distinction between craft and art, equipment and artwork: "The readiness of equipment and the createdness of the work agree in this, that in each case something is produced. But in contrast to all other modes of production, the work is distinguished by being created so that its createdness is part of the created work."[37] Another near-tautology to untangle! What comes to the fore in the artwork—what is "held forth into the Open"—is that the "unconcealedness of what is has happened here, and that as this happening it happens here for the first time; or, that such a work *is* at all rather than is not."[38] Has *happened*; has happened *here*; has *first* happened here: an event at once unprecedented and inimitable. To capture the notion that the artwork instantiates in itself the fact and the wonder that it "*is* at all" brings to mind Philippe Sollers's statement that every artwork is something that "should not have existed,"[39] that is, that arrives outside or athwart any necessity or chain of causality. For Heidegger createdness in this sense is, as it is for Deleuze, at the same time the artwork's self-positing: "Precisely where the artist and the process and the circumstances of the genesis of the work remain unknown, this thrust, this '*that* it is' of createdness, emerges into view most purely from the work."[40]

(3) *The artwork exceeds its source as the expression of its creator and its destination as an expression for its recipient.* This thesis follows from the previous two. Heidegger and Deleuze construe the artwork's separation from the artist in similar ways: insofar as the work is self-positing and self-sufficient or self-subsisting, its creator recedes, as in Mallarmé's motif of the poet dying into the poem. Heidegger's assertion that the origin of the artwork is art needs to be given one more turn: the origin of the artwork is the artwork. The claim is neither formalistic nor tautological. Creativity is a process in which the artist begins by acting from intentions and designs and increasingly turns to responding to what he or she is creating. The painter steps to the canvas and applies paint, steps back and looks at what is there, steps forward and applies more paint or removes some or smudges it, steps back and looks at what is now there, steps forward, and so on. Each step to the canvas is more and more determined by what is on the canvas. Initiative slowly

rotates from the artist to the artwork, until the artwork emerges as what has dictated itself. Such is the nonformalist conception of the autotelic nature of the artwork. It finds a concise expression in the diary of the protagonist of John Berger's novel *A Painter of Our Time*: "There comes a time in every work where suddenly the form of it takes over. Then I can do no wrong. I am Adam in paradise. And the whole of life seems to have conspired to help me. It can last five minutes. Just occasionally, like today, for a whole afternoon."[41] The fictional Janos Lavin's fleeting euphoria and the self-fictionalizing Mallarmé's entombment in the poem are different existential facets of the artist's self-transcending, self-effacing practice.

In approaching the artwork's independence of its recipient, Heidegger and Deleuze take markedly different—though not necessarily incompatible— paths. Heidegger maintains that art as the origin of the artwork "means that art lets those who naturally belong together at work, the creator and the preserver, originate, each in his own nature."[42] While the preserver's role is essential ("what is created cannot itself come into being without those who preserve it"),[43] and while even forgotten or neglected works have not wholly disappeared but subsist in a kind of latent preservation, nonetheless artworks do lose "their former self-subsistence," according to Heidegger, when the "world of the work that stands there has perished." We may "visit the temple in Paestum at its own site or the Bamberg cathedral on its own square," but "world-withdrawal and world-decay can never be undone. The works are no longer the same as they once were. . . . As bygone works they stand over against us in the realm of tradition and conservation."[44] It is clear that for Heidegger this realm is that of mere tradition and conservation, in contrast to the world-creating and world-sustaining nature of an epoch's own art. Even though the artwork can be preserved beyond its epoch because it helped create and sustain a world, Heidegger considers its survival across epochs to mark the epochal loss of world.

For Deleuze, the artwork exceeds its reception in another sense. In the passage from *What Is Philosophy?* the artwork is said to be "independent of the viewer or hearer, who only experience it after, if they have the strength for it." It is not the belatedness that really counts here, since after all an artwork cannot be seen or heard by a viewer or hearer before it is made. What matters lies in the enigmatic comment that viewers and listeners only experience the artwork "if they have the strength for it." How are we to understand *strength*? Kant considers the capacity for aesthetic receptivity to be a question of the cultivation of taste—that education of the senses and enlargement of sensibility which train one's disposition to respond to artworks. Strength might seem like a kind of Nietzschean intrusion on what is typically assumed to be Kantian refinement. But that assumption is wrong. Cultivated taste has juxtaposed to it in Kant another aspect at play in aesthetic judgment. The judgment *this is beautiful* does not apply a preexisting standard to the example at hand; rather, the rule is derived from the example. One's aesthetic education is a disposition enabling responsiveness to art, but the experience and judgment of the beautiful in the face of any actual artwork is, as Deleuze understands, unprecedented and inimitable and, as Heidegger understands, an event where something first and genuinely arrives at its appearance: "The establishing of truth in the work is the bringing forth of a being such as never was before and will never come to be again."[45] Neither the Deleuzian nor the Heideggerian terms contradict Kant; in fact, they clarify what he means by the rule deriving from the example. Whatever incommensurabilities do ultimately separate the aesthetic thought of Kant, Heidegger, and Deleuze, they intersect in asking the same question: What happens when aesthetically educated sensibility encounters an unprecedented art-event?

Shakespearean Aside

Deleuze's response raises a second question: What is the measure of the strength required for such an encounter? *Having the strength for an artwork* is an idea that seems as vague and ineffable as most statements about beauty are. How, then, to approach it? Whoever is devoted to the "literary experience," as Blanchot calls it, shares something of the Nietzschean artist's attitude in valuing only what *becomes* form. One suffers the predicament of being ultimately unable to grasp any idea or embrace any concept or affirm any value—indeed, understand anything—except in and through literary texts. To suffer this predicament is also to enjoy a rare kind of freedom. Various phrases and tropes from a poem spontaneously recur in the midst of trying to think through some question. The need to understand whatever historical or political, aesthetic or existential issue is at stake at the moment is at the same time a need to understand *that* scene, *that* passage, *that* poem. Attempting to grasp the Deleuzian issue of having the strength for an artwork's bloc of sensations or compound of percepts and affects brought me back to a Shakespeare sonnet that has often puzzled me and summoned my attention.

The uncertainties that a reader confronts in the sonnets stem from the way Shakespeare's psychological and sexual realism darkens the lover-beloved relation in the Petrarchan tradition. Freewheeling metaphors, analogies, and wit likewise transmute what expresses worshipful exaltation of the beloved and perpetually thwarted and renewed erotico-spiritual aspiration on the part of the poet-lover in the art of Petrarch or Sydney into a tangle of emotions that might best be summarized by Melanie Klein's fivefold of envy and gratitude, and love, guilt, and reparation. Sonnet 120 marks a crisis between the poet and his young male lover, whom I will call "the youth," in keeping with a quaint tradition. The poet has wronged the youth in a manner that recalls some earlier time when the youth wronged him; related poems in the sequence imply that in both cases the wrongdoing involves neglect and infidelity. The tone of address from poem to poem is varied, inconsistent, even contradictory. And it is in the tone of address that lies what Deleuze calls "the compound of percepts and affects." For example, a playful brazenness leavens Sonnet 117 ("Accuse me thus: that I have scanted all"), in which the beloved is invited to reel off an indictment of the poet-lover's misdemeanors, including his distraction and inattention, his fraternizing with strangers and taking long absences, but the poet-lover then beseeches the youth to understand the motive behind these misdeeds:

> But shoot not at me in your wakened hate;
> Since my appeal says I did strive to prove
> The constancy and virtue of your love.

I acted badly because I so desperately needed to know whether you really love me and are faithful!

From its opening line, Sonnet 120 launches another self-exoneration with similar wit but different metaphorics: *Now that I have wronged you, I have a friend in the wrong you once did me.* The poem proceeds through apparent symmetries and balances to make the harm done to the beloved in the present and the harm done by him in the past teeter as equivalents poised to foster a reconciliation:

> That you were once unkind befriends me now,
> And for that sorrow which I then did feel
> Needs must I under my transgression bow,
> Unless my nerves were brass or hammerèd steel.
> For, if you were by my unkindness shaken
> As I by yours, y'have passed a hell of time,
> And I, tyrant, have no leisure taken
> To weigh how once I suffered in your crime.
> O that our night of woe might have rememb'red
> My deepest sense, how hard true sorrow hits,
> And soon to you, as you to me then, tend'red
> The humble salve, which wounded bosoms fits!
> But that your trespass now becomes a fee;
> Mine ransoms yours, and yours must ransom me.[46]

Read along the lines suggested above, the first quatrain might be paraphrased thus: *The pain I felt then is bound to make me recognize the pain I've just inflicted on you.* Second quatrain: *For if you are suffering now as I did then, you must be going through hell and I'd be thoughtless not to know what you are feeling in light of what I felt back then.* Third quatrain: *If only our recent misery had recalled the earlier one, I could have offered you solace as you did me then.* This last quatrain, then, brings the poet-lover's confession and guilt to an expression of regret which promises in the couplet to set things right: "But that your trespass now becomes a fee; / Mine ransoms yours, and yours must ransom me." Such an interpretation brings out a semantic and affective movement of the three quatrains that goes from the acknowledgment of wrong through the recognition of the other's suffering to the expression of regret. The opening line—"That you were once unkind befriends me now"—takes on the connotation of the poet-lover's hope for forgiveness and reconciliation and is completed in the final line's symmetry: "Mine ransoms yours, and yours must ransom me."

A different angle of attention to syntax, though, alters the semantics and brings out altogether different affects. The last line contains a hint of asymmetry: *My trespass repays yours; yours must pay for me.* What difference do those differences make? The *must* might be taken as a plea, whether playful like the opening "befriends me now" or troubled like the third stanza's regret. But the *me* suggests that the two ransoms—and consequently the two transgressions—are not symmetrical: "Mine ransoms yours, and yours must ransom *me*." What upsets the symmetry and makes reconciliation uncertain and, if achieved, asymmetrical? First, it is the beloved who broke the original delight of their love: *you, not I, undid what was.* Second, the poet-lover's transgression is therefore not only a transgression comparable to the beloved's but also vengeance for it, a purposeful act of harm: it is at once worse than the beloved's act and more just. Third, the lover-poet's transgression has now righted the ledger in his own eyes ("Mine ransoms yours"), but revenge is not reconciliation, and it now falls to the beloved to somehow win him back ("and yours must ransom me"). Forgiveness alone might not be enough. A silent reversal takes place via the third quatrain. The stanza makes it seem that the poet-lover regrettably failed to reciprocate the beloved's earlier "humble salve, which wounded bosoms fits." However, the quatrain's optative mood—"O that our night of woe might have remember'd . . . / And . . . tend'red . . ."—combined with the fact that the poet-lover's *I* is not the subject of the sentence can also imply that he does not at all regret withholding a humble salve. "O that our night of woe might have remember'd" now implies that the crux is that it is the beloved who did not remember the earlier night of woe and its bearing on the new crisis. The beloved's contrition back then did not in effect salve the wound or relieve the harm done; only the poet-lover's vengeance has achieved that, so now, if the beloved truly wants the lover back, he must do something more, something else, something beyond. The balance of transgressions does not in itself produce a reconciliation; the lovers' original delight and pact has been broken, so it is for the one who broke it to invent the way to reconciliation. The couplet, contrary to convention, leaves the lovers unreconciled, even as it follows convention by clinching the meaning of the sonnet as a whole.

Indeed, the first two quatrains also reveal darker shades if their syntactical force is given precedence over their semantic balance. Now the force of the subjunctive mood: "Unless my nerves were brass or hammerèd steel." Indeed, they are brass and steel insofar as he refuses to flinch in face of the harm he has caused. So, too, in the second quatrain:

> For, if you were by my unkindness shaken
> As I by yours, y'have passed a hell of time,
> And I, tyrant, have no leisure taken
> To weigh how once I suffered in your crime.

The symmetry of the two lovers' sufferings (*mine then, yours now*) in the first two lines is slyly displaced in the second two lines, since the beloved has never been in the poet-lover's current situation. The poet-lover may well be a tyrant: *If I have inflicted comparable pain on you, you have suffered mightily and I meanwhile have eschewed all empathy, for I—willfully—have been as unmindful of you as you were of me.* The stanza conveys the cruelty of the ledger-balancing vengeance, a vengeance which still does not afford reconciliation but merely becomes its precondition: "Mine ransoms yours, and yours must ransom me." If one reads back through the entire poem with these variabilities of trope and syntax in mind, the bloc of sensations becomes palpable. It is manifest in the mode of address to the youth, as the poem overlays its offer of confession, acknowledgment, and regret with a countermovement of reminder, withholding, and demand, and overlays playfulness with bitter recollection, apology with revived accusation, a gesture of reconciliation with an expression of coldly retained rage—all wittily poised and hedged so as to avoid an open rupture with the beloved.

It is my assertion, then, that in poetry the bloc of sensations lies in the syntactico-metaphorical movements of the text and is sensed insofar as these movements are deciphered. Hermeneutics is not opposed to the aesthetics of sensation; rather, sensation is registered, takes hold, manifests itself, *in* interpretation. *Having the strength for it* lies in the capability, as Keats expressed it, "of being in uncertainties, Mysteries, doubts, without any irritable reaching after fact & reason." Having the strength for the bloc of sensations does not mean having those sensations, that is, the sensations embodied in the poet-lover's address. There is an affective difference, as in Aristotelean mimesis. Nor were those poetically embodied sensations Shakespeare's as such; that is what Deleuze and Heidegger mean by the artwork's separation from the artist.

The equiprimordial triad postulated by Heidegger as mood–understanding–discourse undergoes a transmutation thanks to the syntactico-metaphorical operations that give rise to the poetic triad trope–interpretation–affect. And here I use the term *affect* in the sense Deleuze gives it. Indeed, to take my assertion one step further, Deleuze's claim that in the artwork "affects are no longer feelings or affections" remains utterly obscure—at least with respect to poetry—unless the difference between "affects" and "feelings and affections" is linked to the trope-deciphering possibilities opened by the language of the poem. The poem's affect is not identical to whatever feelings ebb and flow through the reader, but rather is apprehended in, and as, the furthest reach and complexity of the reader's deciphering as it draws together and attempts to bind the text's entire syntactico-metaphorical variability. The New Critics may have stylized this variability into an ideal of "ambiguity," and the later de Man and deconstructionists may have logicized it into "aporia," but at the heart of poiesis is the syntactico-metaphorical variability that stimulated and underlay the sort of aesthetic attentiveness those critical movements pioneered.

Trope effects affect. In doing so it adduces readers' delight and understanding (Aristotle) and elicits their strength for affects differing from their own feelings and affections (Deleuze). In recasting the fundamentals of Deleuze's aesthetic thought in terms of poetry, I by no means intend a criticism of his view. The question of formulating an aesthetics that applies coherently to both literature and painting remains unsettled. And Deleuze is elsewhere acutely attuned to the centrality of syntax in literary experience, including its sway over "the creation of words or neologisms," that is, over what I address more broadly as *trope* in the sense of naming-by-misnaming: "Syntactic creation or style—this is the becoming of language. The creation of words or neologisms is worth nothing apart from the effects of syntax in which they are developed. So, literature already presents two aspects: through the creation of syntax, it brings about not only a decomposition or destruction of the maternal language, but also the invention of a new language within language."[47] My intent has been to give an account of the otherwise enigmatic thesis in *What Is Philosophy?* regarding the artwork: "Affects are no longer feelings or affections; they go beyond the strength of those who undergo them. Sensations, percepts, and affects are *beings* whose validity lies in themselves and exceeds any lived [experience]. They could be said to exist in the absence of man because man, as he is caught in stone, on the canvas, or by words, is himself a compound of percepts and affects. The work of art is a being of sensation and nothing else: it exists in itself." I have argued that the artwork as a being of sensation opens itself to understanding, deciphering, interpretation, by which alone it can be grasped *as* sensation; insofar as understanding, deciphering, interpretation falls short—and indeed every understanding, deciphering, interpretation necessarily does—the artwork as a being of sensation "exists in itself" in the sense that it not only opens itself to our understanding, deciphering, interpretation, but also withholds itself from them.

Language, Art, Truth

At this point the area of convergence between Deleuze and Heidegger widens again, for the artwork's ineluctable and elusive rhythm of opening and withholding touches on what Heidegger calls "deconcealing" and "concealing." Deconcealing is at once a happening in language and an event of being: "Language, by naming beings for the first time, first brings beings to word and to appearance."[48] The statement is a forerunner of the designation of language as the house of being in which Dasein dwells. Deconcealing is how Heidegger construes what he takes to be "the nature of truth that flashes out in the word *aletheia*" in ancient Greece and was immediately and variously abandoned by philosophy from Plato on through to Descartes and beyond.[49] Vattimo argues that continuing the Heideggerian project often necessitates deflating Heidegger. So it is with truth as *aletheia*. Its inflated version reserves truth to Heidegger's own meditative thought and selected passages from a handful of poems; slices of thought and poetry are arrayed against the whole of modern science, modern literature, modern art.

As regards science, the vastly more limited but still decisive claim is that the understanding of truth as "the agreement or conformity of knowledge with fact,"[50] whether in its empirical, positivist, and scientific avatars or in Descartes's concept of certitude, ignores that in order for facts to appear as something knowledge can conform to, the beings we strive to represent correctly must become available in the first place: "The entire *realm* in which this 'conforming to something' goes on must already occur as a whole in the unconcealed."[51] Just as beings arise in a realm of unconcealedness (the Open or clearing, in Heidegger's sylvan imagery), this clearing is shaded by the undeconcealed. Reality is never on full display. Undeconcealedness is a condition of deconcealedness. The uninflated description of this condition of being and human being is an important guidepost for what is vital in Heidegger's project. One mode of concealment occurs as "beings refuse themselves to us," which can be understood along the lines of *physis* withholding itself, but there are other modes of concealment as well:

> One being places itself in front of another being, the one helps to hide the other, the former obscures the latter, a few obstruct many, one denies all. Here concealment is not simple refusal. Rather, a being appears, but it presents itself as other than it is.
>
> This concealment is dissembling. If one thing did not simulate another, we could not make mistakes or act mistakenly in regard to beings; we could not go astray and transgress, and especially could never overreach ourselves. That a being should be able to deceive as semblance is the condition of our being able to be deceived, not conversely.
>
> Concealment can be a refusal or merely a dissembling. We are never fully certain whether it is the one or the other. Concealment conceals and dissembles itself.[52]

The concealed can be what refuses and withdraws or what is dissembled or simulated or what is perspectively blocked or what disguises itself. Insofar as the two senses of semblance, coming-to-appearance and mere appearance, can be so entwined as to adduce moments of uncertainty or error about a particular appearance, the very phenomenon of appearing is ambiguously disclosure and concealment.

I prefer to call the "concealed" the *undeconcealed* because it is crucial not to construe what is concealed as some determinate being simply awaiting to be uncovered. What is deconcealed is not necessarily some already constituted being, since its deconcealing is its coming into being. Deconcealing befuddles the binary alternative of *revealing* and *inventing*; it is neither a revealing of something already there nor the invention of something never before there. The category-killing event of deconcealing is exemplified and clarified by reading poetry. Recall de Man's blindness-and-insight metaphor. What is deconcealed in the course of understanding and interpreting a poem at the same time, and as the very condition of the interpretation's coherence, leaves undeconcealed other possible (or virtual) significations, percepts and affects, and metaphorico-syntactical effects. It's not simply a matter of partial or short-circuited understandings; more fundamentally, insight is enabled by the blind spot. "Truth, in its nature, is un-truth,"[53] in Heidegger's phrase, is thus a radical but not extravagant claim.

Heidegger reinflates the claim by granting only the poet and the thinker the capacity to truly have truck with this nature of truth—as though the modern scientist were not continually engaged with the deconcealing/undeconcealing and refusal/dissembling of those beings that scientific inquiry constructs and encounters as facts. A more promising account by far is Deleuze and Guattari's notion that science, philosophy, and art are coequal but incommensurate modes of thought. Even leaving aside the question of the adequacy of Heidegger's understanding of science itself, his separation of poetry and thought from science ignores how the knowledges acquired by science rebound back and become woven into the fabric of the ordinary and extraordinary experiences and understandings that are the domain from which poetry and philosophical thought arise.

This is not to reject or overtly contest Heidegger's approach to poetry, language, and truth so much as to acknowledge the need to resituate it. What gives poetry and language their distinctive role in the truth-event? In making the linguistic turn to poetry in "The Origin of the Work of Art," Heidegger must make poetry the paradigm of the arts, and his effort testifies to the difficulty of squaring the aesthetics of verbal and visual art. In citing the list of the "work-materials" of art earlier—"stone, wood, metal, color . . . , tone"—I left out one item, namely, language: "stone, wood, metal, color, language, tone" is the complete list. Language does not fit easily with the others as instances of earth jutting into world. It might if Heidegger were paralleling speech's sonority to music's tone, or if he were alluding to the mood-embodying dimension of language he identifies in *Being and Time*—"intonation, modulation, the tempo of talk"—all of which could be said to manifest *physis* in the physiological-acoustic aspect of language.[54] Heidegger draws a very different parallel: "The massiveness and heaviness of stone . . . , the hardness and luster of metal . . . , the clang of tone," and "the naming power of language."[55] Something is amiss in putting heaviness, luster, and clang on a par with the power to name. There is an obscurity, even an obfuscation in Heidegger's assimilation of naming to *physis*, especially since he eschews the irreducible bodily dimension of speech.

The obscurity of the proposed parallel between language and other artistic "work-materials" is a bit of sleight of hand to prepare for the passage in which he places the naming power of language—"poetry" broadly conceived—as the foundation of all artistic activity:

> *All art*, as the letting happen of the advent of the truth of what is, is, as such, *essentially poetry*. . . . Poesy is only one mode of the lighting projection of truth, i.e., of poetic composition in this wider sense. Nevertheless, the linguistic work, the poem in the narrower sense, has a privileged position in the domain

of the arts. . . . Language itself is poetry in the essential sense. But since language is the happening in which for man beings first disclose themselves to him each time as beings, poesy—or poetry in the narrower sense—is the most original form of poetry in the essential sense.[56]

The affirmation of a power of origination in poetry has of course rich corollaries throughout the Romantic tradition, notably in Herder, Rousseau, and Blake. The differences between those three writers' core concepts amount to a typology of the problematic of language and poetry in post-Romantic thought: Herder's hypervaluation of a language's power to forge collective identity and bind a people (*Volk*) to its native place; Rousseau's fable of the priority of the figurative over the literal at the origin of language; and Blake's assertions against ontotheology that religion in its origin is the work of poetic imagination, from the Greeks' divinities to Hebrew prophecy.

It is worth juxtaposing to Heidegger's way of claiming poetry's priority among the arts to Kant's. In the *Critique of Judgment* (§51) Kant too postulates, "at least as an experiment . . . , the analogy of art with the kind of expression that people use in speaking in order to communicate to each other, i.e., not merely their concepts, but also their sensations." Speech doubles in Kant's account. First, all the arts find an analogy in speech insofar as its threefold expressiveness through "articulation, gesticulation, and modulation" corresponds to the different arts themselves, in effect the verbal, visual, and musical arts respectively. Second, speech is the medium of verbal art itself. Kant proceeds to distinguish poetry and rhetoric as the two kinds of verbal art, giving priority and privilege to poetry. The orator "basically provides less than he promises, [the poet] more" in the sense that poetry "promises little and announces a mere play with ideas," but the result gives "nourishment to the understanding in play" and "life to its concepts through the imagination."[57] Kant goes yet further in §53: "The *art of poetry* (which owes its origin almost entirely to genius, and will be guided least by precept or example) claims the highest rank of all. It expands the mind by setting the imagination free and presenting, within the limits of a given concept and among the unbounded manifold of forms possibly agreeing with it, the one that connects its presentation with a fullness of thought to which no linguistic expression is fully adequate, and thus elevates itself aesthetically to the level of ideas."[58] It is a small step from there to saying, along with Heidegger, that since speech deploys the expressive means of all the arts through "*word, deportment*, and *tone*" (Kant), and since poetry manifests the powers of language in the fullest and most concentrated manner, poetry is the matrix of art in general.

A strong caveat has to be added to such an affirmation of poetry's ability to stimulate thinking ("nourishment to the understanding"). There is an intrinsic affinity between poetry and thought because philosophy and theory share with literature the same medium of expression, namely, language. The other arts do not provide the philosopher or theorist with an overlapping mode of expression, which does not make those arts lesser forms of thought or less thought stimulating but does demand far more of the critic, theorist, or philosopher in attempting to articulate the thought and its stimulus. A measure of the difficulty is evinced by the greatness of Deleuze's book on Bacon—and by the fact that as astute as his eye is in looking at the paintings, he still draws heavily on what Bacon has *said* about his art.

Kant touches on the fruitful yet uneasy relation between art and thought from another angle in §49 ("On the faculties of the mind that constitute genius"). Art stimulates *thought*, that is, thinking, beyond *concepts* in the sense of thoughts adequately captured in words. As regards poetry, this would suggest that *logos* splits or, better perhaps, overreaches itself. Its words exceed worded concepts. Having remarked that there are artistic creations that cannot be faulted "as far as taste is concerned" but nonetheless lack *spirit* (*Geist*), Kant clarifies his terms and introduces the idea of "aesthetic ideas" as follows: "*Spirit*, in an aesthetic significance, means the animating principle in the mind. . . . Now I maintain that this principle is nothing other than the faculty of the presentation of *aesthetic ideas*; by an aesthetic idea, however, I mean that representation of the imagination that occasions much thinking through without it being possible for any determinate thought, i.e., *concept*, to be adequate to it, which, consequently, no language fully attains or can make intelligible."[59] Creativity lies in such a representation insofar as it "by itself stimulates so much thinking that it can never be grasped in a determinate concept, hence . . . aesthetically enlarges the concept in an unbounded way."[60] This is the Kantian way of distinguishing how art and philosophy *think*. Michel Chaouli develops an extensive and penetrating commentary on the notion of "aesthetic ideas" and its complex, seemingly contradictory relation to Kant's reflections on beauty and pinpoints the implications of a thinking that "enlarges" (or eludes) concepts: "This enlargement amounts to a transformation, for it proceeds not by adding more meanings to the dictionary entry for the concept, but by enlarging it in an unbounded way. Art does not, then, supplement concepts we know already with further meanings. . . . Rather art alters the very idea of a concept having a meaning. It presents us with concepts whose boundary of meaning has been blurred thanks to the 'multitude of related representations' that the presentation suggests."[61]

The significant difference separating Kant from Heidegger and Deleuze can be glimpsed in the nuances of these various formulations. While Kant

                                    context
                    sender ——— **message** ——— **receiver**
                                    contact
                                    code

FIGURE 3. Jakobson's linguistic functions

looks to speech, language, and poetry to explain the arts because of their
power to enable us "to communicate with one another," Heidegger and Deleuze consider art in some essential sense as transforming, transcending, or
even negating communication and communicability. When Heidegger repudiates taking communication as the essence of language, it is on the grounds
that such a conception presupposes that a subject already in possession of a
meaning (referenced to an object) takes up language as a medium or mere instrument to convey that same meaning and reference to another subject: "In
the current view, language is held to be a kind of communication. It serves for
verbal exchange and agreement, and in general for communicating."[62]

The structuralist model of communication along these lines can be found
in Roman Jakobson's classic mapping of linguistic functions (fig. 3) along a
central axis of the transmission of a message from one subject to another. The
message is formed according to the rules and items in the *code* (code/mes-
sage being a variation on Saussure's *langue/parole*); it is transmissible thanks
to some physical medium or channel (speech, writing, radio, telegraph, phone,
digital media) called the *contact*; and it makes reference to ideas or states of
affairs (*context*).[63] Let's note two controversies that, though they need not de-
tain us in light of our focus here on poetry and aesthetics, would be relevant
to sorting out the relation between communication theory and Heidegger's
conception of language. A model such as Jakobson's does not in fact presuppose any particular concept of the subject, let alone the idealist version Heidegger imputes to models of communication in general; sender and receiver
in Jakobson's conception are defined not by the quality of their consciousness
or agency in any strong sense of those terms but rather by their function in
the communicative process, the "emotive" and the "conative," respectively, in
his terminology. Second, Heidegger himself never brings the dimensions of
language he is eager to foreground back to bear on the nature of communication itself. He merely indulges in the sort of bifurcations that mockingly
put newspapers on one side of a divide and genuine poetry on the other; the
enabling sleight of hand in this case lies in the way he blurs the distinction between the claim that language is not only communication but also something
else and the claim that language is something other than communication altogether: "But language is not only and not primarily an audible and written

expression of what is to be communicated. It not only puts forth in words and statements what is overtly or covertly intended to be communicated; language alone brings what is, as something that is, into the Open for the first time."[64]

Let's look more closely at how Heidegger formulates the matter: "It is due to art's poetic nature that, in the midst of what is, art breaks open an open place, in whose openness everything is other than usual. . . . everything ordinary and hitherto existing becomes an unbeing."[65] This Heideggerian *Verfremdungseffekt* seems hyperbolic, as though everything that is is undone at a stroke and rendered unbeing by a genuine poetic act, but Heidegger immediately qualifies the statement—equivocates, in fact—by stressing what should otherwise be quite obvious: "The work in no way affects hitherto existing entities by causal connections." How then? "The working of the work . . . lies in a change, happening from out of the work, of the unconcealedness of what is, and this means, of Being."[66] That sounds less like the becoming unbeing of everything hitherto existing and more like the ontic jolt that provokes the ontological attitude, that is, the capacity of the artwork to shift our relation to what is by making something be seen or heard for the first time and so awaken our questioning regarding *what* is and *that* it is. Heidegger does give a less inflated account of the out-of-the-ordinary power of art: "For a work is in actual effect as a work only when we remove ourselves from our commonplace routine and move into what is disclosed by the work, so as to bring our own nature itself to take a stand in the truth of what is."[67] Neither the sun nor death, according to an aphorism of La Rochefoucauld, can be stared at steadily. So, too, the transports of art are intermittent, irregular, unpredictable, and largely unplanned. Even the most devoted visitor to galleries and museums looks at work after work without that jolt which, when it does come, lets something be seen for the first time. Whether in art or nature, manifestations of the Spirit of Beauty are, in Shelley's words, transitory:

> visiting
> This various world with inconstant wing
> As summer winds that creep from flower to flower;
> Like moonbeams that behind some piny mountain shower.

The episodic "remov[ing] ourselves from our commonplace routine," the transitory, the intermittent glimpse of the beautiful, the ontic jolt—these are not denied by Heidegger, but they do stand athwart the epoch-making, epoch-changing role he assigns to poetry.

The reflection on language via the consideration of poetry's enjoyment of "a privileged position in the domain of the arts" and then its status as the nature of language itself make up the final pages of "The Origin of the Work of Art" and anticipate much of Heidegger's thoughts on language in the following decades. Having bracketed or neutralized the category of communication, Heidegger puts forward his bolder claims: "Language, by naming things for the first time, first brings beings to word and to appearance." This is language as poetry in the broad sense: "Poetry is the saying of the unconcealedness of what is."[68] Such deconcealedness defines what Heidegger means by truth. Artworks and poetry in the narrow sense are, so to speak, essential instances of poetry in the broad sense: "In the work, the happening of truth is at work"; art is "the setting-into-work of truth." Looked at from the standpoint of the creators, "art is the fixing in place of a self-establishing truth in the figure. This happens in creation as bringing forth of the unconcealedness of what is." Looked at in terms of the role of the recipients, that is, the preservers, "setting-into-work . . . also means: the bringing of work-being into movement and happening. This happens as preservation. Thus, art is: the creative preserving of truth in the work."[69]

Seemingly contradictory statements about language, beings, and truth abound. Subject and predicate rotate around so loosely as to yield statements that appear utterly incompatible even as they are advanced as synonymous:

—"In the work of art, the truth of an entity has set itself to work."
—Artistic creation is a "bringing forth of the unconcealedness of what is."
—"Art is truth setting itself to work."
—"Art is the fixing in place of a self-establishing truth in the figure."
—Art is "the letting happen of the advent of the truth of what is."
—"Language, by naming things for the first time, first brings beings to word and appearance."
—"Language is the happening in which for man beings first disclose themselves to him each time as beings."
—"Art lets truth originate."
—"Truth wills to be established in the work as this conflict of world and earth."
—The viewer, listener, or reader brings "work-being into movement and happening."[70]

Does art bring truth forth or does it let it happen, or does it make it happen? Does truth will its own establishment, is it brought forth by the work, or does it set itself to work in the work? However dizzying—or irritating or maddening—this swirl of predicates may be, this is not simply yet another instance of obscurity, obfuscation, and sleight of hand on Heidegger's part. The various formulations wrestle with a genuine problem that arises from the central argument. Language is not a medium for the transmission of what the speaker already and independently possesses, be it as idea, meaning, perception, or sentiment. Rather, language is the site where human beings dwell, the atmosphere without which they could not live as Dasein, their element, as the sea is for fish. Language is the web of signs and grammar by which human beings designate themselves and through which their encompassing world appears to them. In attempting to do away with the subject-object and communication-as-medium paradigms, philosophy encounters the problem of identifying the agency of the truth-event. Is it language as it first brings beings to appearance? Or the beings disclosing themselves? Or the creators and preservers of the artwork? The strain in Heidegger's language stems from the attempt to embrace each and all of these possibilities at once in order to locate not so much the true agent or cause as the vectors that constitute and traverse Dasein as that unique being in the world susceptible to and capable of participating in a truth-event. Or, more accurately, I think, Dasein is the being who experiences certain events *as* truth.

The problem when reading Heidegger, Richard Rorty once remarked, is knowing how far to play along with him. Here it is worth going at least one more lap in order to find the edge where a crisp differentiation has to occur. I share Vattimo's view that it is necessary somehow to embrace the notion that there is "a happening of truth at work" in the artwork while disentangling this from Heidegger's "too inflated a view of the work of art as an inauguration and foundation of historico-cultural worlds."[71] I think that it is by forcing the Heideggerian problematic regarding language back to poetry in the narrow sense that the richness of that problematic can be most fully brought out. That is one of the stakes of my effort here, along with introducing the sense of plurality in literary experience which Heidegger squanders in his apocalyptico-epochal vision of modernity. How to proceed?

To begin with, it is necessary to come to terms with the three distinct actions Heidegger ascribes to language. Language inaugurates in the sense that it "alone brings what is, as something that is, into the Open for the first time";[72] language envelops Dasein, in that it "is the house of being. In its home human beings dwell";[73] and language in its poetic power as art renders "everything ordinary and hitherto existing . . . an unbeing."[74]

Now, "everything ordinary and hitherto existing" is that which is already brought to word and appearance by language in its inaugurating action and is sustained by language as dwelling. Language's third mode of action, that is, the bringing to word and appearance which renders what is already named and hitherto apparent an unbeing, is the act I am calling *naming-by-misnaming*. Why naming-by-misnaming? All that already has been brought to word and appearance by language's naming power establishes the relative stability of the ordinary and usual, that is, everyday life in the house of being. Bringing to appearance a hitherto unappearing—that is, undeconcealed—being requires a twist, a swerve, a torque on the current language. The more general terms I have used for this are *trope* or the *metaphorico-syntactic operations of language*. The action of trope does not undo "everything ordinary and hitherto existing" in a causal sense but rather, as I have argued, in the sense of jarring our relation to the ordinary and existing by making something be seen or heard for the first time. Naming-by-misnaming effects the ontic jolt. Or, to bring it back into the even less exalted vocabulary of Kenneth Burke, the poetic manifestation of rhetoric is a persuasion-to-attitude.

With the notion of naming-by-misnaming, I opt for the Rousseau-Blake axis of Romantic and post-Romantic conceptions of language and poetry. Heidegger at moments seems inclined to the Blakean view, as when he says that the Greek temple, or even a "sculpture of the god," "is not a portrait whose purpose is to make it easier to realize how the god looks; rather, it is a work that lets the god himself be present and thus *is* the god himself."[75] For Blake, divine presencing holds so long as human imagination, which creates it, sustains it. For Heidegger, "the temple, in its standing there, first gives to things their look and to men their outlook on themselves. This view remains open as long as the work is a work, as long as the god has not fled from it."[76] Is the god's flight a metaphor for the lapse of human imagination, or is human imagination a misnomer for the pathways of the gods? That ambiguity persists in Heidegger's thought. What is clear, however, is that he leans toward Herder far more than toward Blake and Rousseau when it comes to considering the originating and poetic powers of language.

As "The Origin of the Work of Art" approaches its conclusion, the question regarding the artwork that has unfolded as a question about human beings' immersion in and creativity with language gradually sloughs off the focus on human being, man, Dasein, and in their place inflects the phrase "an historical humanity" with an increasingly national and nationalist determination of the entity whose being is put to the test by the poetic:[77] "an historical people," "a people's world," "an historical people's nature," "that folk," "an historical group of men." The role of poetry in inaugurating and founding is said to be "history in the essential sense": "Poetry is founding in the triple sense of bestowing, grounding, and beginning. Art is essentially historical." And what is the sense of history here and what manifestation of Dasein is bestowed, grounded, and begun? The nationalistic tinge of Heidegger's language in 1936 is unmistakable: "History is the transporting of a people into its appointed task as entrance into that people's endowment."[78]

The essay then poses its final question: "Are we in our existence historically at the origin? Do we know, which means do we give heed to, the nature of the origin? Or in our relation to art, do we still merely make appeal to a cultivated acquaintance with the past?"[79] He leaves no doubt that the *we* refers to Germans, and as his final word he conscripts lines from "The Journey," a beautiful poem in which Hölderlin evokes and celebrates the landscape of his native Swabia; Heidegger waxes enigmatic, suggesting that the native soil is a truer guide to origin than historical reflection:

> For this either-or and its decision there is an infallible sign. Hölderlin, the poet—whose work still confronts the Germans as a test to be stood—named it in saying:

> > Schwer verlässt
> > was nahe dem Ursprung wohnet, den Ort.
> > Reluctantly
> > that which dwells near its origin departs.

An essay that sets out to identify the *Ursprung* of the artwork as art and investigate the artwork's unique powers of disclosure in the history of Dasein thus ends up associating poetry with origin as birthplace and in turn linking birthplace to national destiny. Hölderlin's celebration of the indelible tie of memory and aesthetic sensitivity to one's earliest experiences of landscape, weather, and horizon is commandeered by Heidegger to evoke Germany's ethnonationalist resurgence. He undoubtedly relished the thought that he and Hölderlin shared their native ground (*heimatlicher Grund*) with Schiller, Schelling, and Hegel.[80] He would have found it more difficult to embrace his contemporary Swabians Albert Einstein and Bertolt Brecht, both of whom had fled the homeland by the time he had written his lecture on the origin of the work of art, indeed already by the time he became the Nazi rector of the university.

Deleuze attempts to rescue Heidegger from himself on this score in an imaginative essay titled "An Unrecognized Precursor to Heidegger." The precursor is—Alfred Jarry. Jarry, whose work inspired surrealists and other avant-garde writers and artists after his death in 1907, playfully infuses French with "Greek . . . , Latin, or old French, or an old dialectic, or perhaps Breton . . . in order to bring to light a French of the future." It is thus that Deleuze prefers to see Heidegger's linguistic inventiveness: "He put an ancient Greek or an Old German to work within contemporary German, but precisely to obtain a new German."[81] Along the lines of his reflections on poetry and syntax cited earlier, Deleuze sees here "the invention of a new language within language." It is as though there are three languages, an outside language acting on the mother tongue to effect a third: "The first injects, the second stammers, the third starts with a fit."[82] Infusing such a linguistic spirit into the reading of Heidegger would

undoubtedly have the positive effect of sweeping aside all the etymological mys-
tifications that attend upon his own myriad root words and Greek antecedents.
Deleuze dismisses the whole question of roots with a cavalier flourish: "We
have heard the news that not one of Heidegger's etymologies is correct, not
even Lethé or Aletheia. But is this a well-posed problem? . . . It is sometimes
said these are nothing more than word plays. But is it not contradictory to
expect some sort of linguistic correctness from a project that explicitly sets
out to go beyond scientific and technical being toward poetic being?"[83] The
problem is, of course, that Heidegger did not treat them as wordplay. Deleuze
forces playfulness upon the Heideggerian text. That, too, is a procedure for
deflating it.

The theme of the artwork's "bestowing," "grounding," or "beginning" a
world not only brings "The Origin of the Work of Art" toward its conclusion but also sketches the epochal scheme of historicocultural worlds that
will thereafter anchor Heidegger's reflections on the history of being. Each
epoch lives a historically distinct relation to being; it unfolds and encounters a historically distinct meaning of being. The historical outline Heidegger
deploys is a quite conventional view of the West's defining epochs. There are
three: Greek and Roman antiquity, medieval Christianity, and modernity. He
situates his own thought and the crisis of the West in the 1930s and thereafter,
during the war and in the postwar period, as on the cusp of a new, still wholly
unknown era. That artworks inaugurate and found epochal worlds is virtually self-evident for Heidegger in the case of ancient Greece, in the form of
Homeric epic, Athenian tragedy, or Greek architecture. In this he has the support of the entire prodigious tradition of German classicism and historiogra-
phy. The Greek temple is thus Heidegger's primary—and clearest—example
of art as world-inaugurating and world-founding.

The preliminary reflection on the epochal nature of art, *aletheia*, and the
historicity of being gives mere hints as to the ancient meaning of being. The
most remarkable, yet unacknowledged aspect of the brief passage on the three
epochs is that only the medieval Christian meaning of being is able to be
sharply defined:

> Always when that which is as a whole demands, as what it is, itself, a ground-
> ing in openness, art attains to its historical nature as foundation. This founda-
> tion happened in the West for the first time in Greece. What in the future was
> to be called Being was set into work, setting the standard. The realm of beings
> this opened was then transformed into a being in the sense of God's creation.
> This happened in the Middle Ages. This kind of being was again transformed
> at the beginning and in the course of the modern age. Beings became objects
> that could be controlled and seen through by calculation. At each time a new

and essential world arose. And each time the openness of what is had to be established in beings themselves, by the fixing in place of truth in figure.[84]

In medieval Christian thought and experience, every being is an *ens creatum*, a creature in the sense of a being created by God, and God is determined as the Supreme Being. This determination of God as the being that is "Being" will be the key reference point for failures to grasp the ontological difference, that is, the difference between being and beings. Thomist theology violates the ontological difference by postulating being as a being, namely, God the Creator, the Father. To attribute the question of being to the ancients is something of a back-projection: "What in the future was to be called Being," that is, in the medieval Christian epoch and in violation of the ontological difference. The ancient meaning of *being*, Heidegger concedes, is yet to be understood. He further concedes, in the guise of heightened critical attentiveness, that Greek philosophy itself "does not remain in conformity with the nature of truth that flashes out in the word *aletheia*."[85] Plato in effect extinguished the pre-Socratic spark by attributing truth and eternality to the Idea, separating truth from temporality and relegating earthly phenomena to mere imitation and shadow. Therein lies Heidegger's other epochal narrative, according to which the era of Western metaphysics stretches from Plato through Descartes to Nietzsche, who outlines and partially achieves the completion or destruction of metaphysics: "The nature of truth as *aletheia* was not thought out in the thinking of the Greeks nor since then, and least of all in the philosophy that followed after."[86] Heidegger aligns his own project with the enigmatic, still-not understood flashes of the pre-Socratic encounter with being and truth.-

The elements of anachronism and fabrication in Heidegger's interpretation of pre-Socratic thought are remarked on with deflating irony by Sloterdijk as regards Fragment 119 of Heraclitus, *ēthos anthrópo daímon*, conventionally translated, or construed, as *man's character is his fate*. Dissatisfied with any such rendering, Heidegger reworks *ēthos anthrópo daímon* and infuses his translation with the separate anecdote of Heraclitus warming himself by his oven and inviting some visitors to join him there, since "here too the gods are present." Notes Sloterdijk: "Hence the saying, if one translates *ēthos* with 'stay' or 'abode' (which is problematic) and *daímon* with 'God' (which is probably a little too lofty), would mean: 'Man dwells, insofar as he is man, in the nearness of God.' . . . But that is not the end of it: Heidegger then makes a second translation suggestion, in which he turns the problematic into the grotesque by augmenting the motif of neighbourhood with that of uncanniness. Now the three little words *ēthos anthrópo daímon* supposedly mean: 'The (familiar) abode is for man the open region for the presencing of god (the unfamiliar one).' If that were truly the meaning of the statement, it would make Heraclitus the most profound commentator on Heidegger's work ever to come from ancient Greece."[87]

As for the artistic foundation of the modern world, it remains quite opaque even as Heidegger launches an early articulation of the idea that the modern age reduces being to objects of calculation and control. Van Gogh's painting is the one instance of modern art in "The Origin of the Work of Art." It is said to be, in the swirl of Heideggerian predicates, what brings forth the truth of a being and where a being first discloses itself and what lets the advent of the truth of what is happen, but the rift-design of earth and world that this artwork deconceals does not involve the modern world at all. As Heidegger interprets the painting, it does not found a world but discloses a vanishing world. It can be said, anticipating problems yet to be broached, that van Gogh's painting touches on the pressing but unsettled question of *technē* in Heidegger's thought: the painting is *technē* in the specific mode of the artwork, which he distinguishes from *technē* as craft, that is, the activity of the shoemaker who makes the shoes the truth of whose equipment-being the painting deconceals, even as the painting is made in the modern era where *technē* receives its third determination as neither art nor craft, but technology. *Technē* as craft, as art, and as technology is a conceptual knot that Heidegger obliquely acknowledges but does not resolve in his Addendum, written in 1956 and published in the 1960 edition of "The Origin of the Work of Art," where he alerts his readers that "*Ge-Stell*, frame, framing, framework," a term central to his conception of the artwork in the 1936 essay, is "used in later writing as the explicit key expression for the nature of modern technology"; it is necessary, however, "to put out of mind the modern meaning of placing or framing" "when we hear the words 'fix in place' and 'framing' or 'framework' in 'The Origin of the Work of Art.'"[88] Henceforth the words adduced to understand *technē* and applied to artworks and modern technology alike must at the same time carry utterly different meanings in relation to each, even as both belong to *technē*.

Such a puzzle signals at the very least how tentative—perhaps tenuous— the first undertakings to delineate epochs of the meaning of being actually are. It also brings out the problem of situating Heidegger's thought, especially from the moment of the 1936 essay onward, in relation to its historical moment. Vattimo's call to deflate Heidegger's epoch-inaugurating claims for art, like Deleuze's experiment in turning linguistic rootedness into poetic playfulness, comes from the desire to tear what remains inspiring and promising for contemporary thought in Heidegger's work from its deeply compromised connection to Nazism, nationalist extremism, racism, and anti-Semitism.

PART II

Feeling and the Vocation of Criticism

/4/ What is required to rethink the relevance of Kant's aesthetic theory in light of Nietzsche's powerful criticisms? The philosophical quartet divides most severely in the rejection by Nietzsche, Heidegger, and Deleuze of Kant's notion that the experience of the beautiful entails a claim for everyone else's agreement. Such universalism is anathema to Nietzsche. Aesthetic judgment in Kant is but a variant of the oppressive categorical imperative in his moral philosophy. For Deleuze and Heidegger, Kant's conception of a *sensus communis* is a delusion that dilutes the power of art and thought. They set art as well as philosophy in utter opposition to *doxa*. While there is much that is right in these criticisms, their profound illiberalism inspires a search for alternative ways of taking Kant's fundamental notions, against the grain when necessary. Moreover, there are dimensions of Kant's thought that the later thinkers, for all their critical acumen, miss or underestimate. Aesthetic judgment's supposed universal agreement is neither grounded in a standard nor required in principle nor even expected in fact. The particular pleasure in feeling *this is beautiful* is at the same time a feeling for others' experience and an urge to persuade. The enigma of that link is the wellspring of the vocation of criticism. The material and institutional preconditions of this experience and this vocation—the so-called liberal public sphere—were scarcely emergent in Kant's time and are residual and fragile in ours. Jacques Rancière renders a systematic critique of the "aesthetic regime" inaugurated by Kant, and Nathalie Heinich describes a new "artistic paradigm" that negates the very objecthood of art without which criticism's appeal for agreement becomes impossible. The contemporary artists Tino Sehgal and Rineke Dijkstra, by contrast, probe limit-experiences where the configuration of artwork, aesthetic response, and criticism is captured at the moment of its emergence or its fading. From an appreciation of Kant despite Nietzsche, it is necessary to return to Nietzsche and his typology of the affective sources of artistic creativity. Just as aesthetic judgment has to be dissociated from the categorical imperative, Nietzsche's four-cornered grid of classical, Dionysian, *ressentiment*, and Romantic pessimism has to be recast and seen as an account of the pluralistic, contradictory sources from which modern art arises. Is it possible to democratize Nietzsche not by leveling art but by grasping its inherent plurality and criticism's commitment to the ordeal—not the ideal—of universalism?

/5/ The antagonism between vitalism and hermeneutics, sensation and being, returns in Heidegger's rejection of Nietzsche's Dionysian and Apollonian sources of art, intoxication and dream. Heidegger misses the path out of this recurrent impasse by not seeing the unity of three concepts scattered across his own work: *Angst* (the base mood of modern existence), *Rausch* (the rejected Nietzschean term for the creative state), and *Riss* (the rift whose power to disclose is lodged in the very form of the completed artwork). How indeed to understand that an artwork's form is at the same time a rift? Terms such as *the beautiful* and *form* are best understood not via definitions or conceptual abstractions, but rather as they emerge, elusively, in poetic discourse itself. Shelley's "Hymn to Intellectual Beauty" is a still inexhaustible source. Contrary to the apparent Platonism of his thought, this poem ties the beautiful to the transitory, the flickering, the momentary flash of appearance against a void. Jorie Graham, the contemporary poet who most astutely engages with Heidegger's thought, provides a sustained meditation on creativity and form throughout her poetry. "The thing called form" is for her, as for Anselm Kiefer, the moment of breaking off an ongoing process, "a faltering where it ceases / to falter." Seeing past the divergence between Nietzsche and Heidegger requires just such a fusion of process and form. Graham's playful uses of the word *thing* subtly unsettle Heidegger's essay "The Thing" with its oft-cited meditation on a simple jug for serving water or wine. That essay elaborates on the fourfold of earth, sky, mortals, and divinities. Setting the stage for the final chapter, mortals—humans, Dasein, "Man"—turn out to differ from the other figures in the fourfold since mortals—we ourselves—are at once the fourfold's unrecognized source, its addressee, and a figure within it.

/6/ The beautiful is linked to modernity and enlightenment because of its dependence on the emergent public sphere, the sublime because of the disenchantment of nature. Storms cease to manifest divine wrath and instead arouse a purely aesthetic awe. The Kantian sublime branches out into four consequences that all bear on the question of modernity. This concluding chapter devotes a section to each of those consequences, respectively: the sublime's role in shaping the very idea of Nature, its renewed and altered relevance in the Anthropocene, its role in occasioning Kant's most detailed account of the emotions, and its introduction of formlessness as an aesthetic category. For Kant as for Shelley, Mont Blanc's glaciers, waterfalls, and raging Arve were the consecrated site of the sublime. A Shelleyan reading of Kant has the task, though, of wrenching aesthetic judgment from the hold of the categorical imperative, which presides over Kant's identification of the sublime with those affects aroused by the overcoming of desire, impulse, instinct. Unforeseeable by either Shelley or Kant was the industrial age's ushering in of the Anthropocene, a highly charged symbol and evidence of which today is the rapid melting of Mont Blanc's Mer de Glace, the inspiration of their very idea of the sublime. The lively philosophical debate that has emerged regarding the Anthropocene points up the need to rethink the relation of *anthropos, physis,* and *technē,* the triad that vexes Heidegger's aesthetic theory. Two theses: the Anthropocenic imagination must be anthropocentric and, second, the human itself is an anthropomorphism, since *anthropos,* ever incomplete and continually self-interpreting, has no definitive form. Motifs and themes encountered throughout previous chapters return, fuguelike, amid these new questions: Merleau-Ponty on human embodiment, controversy over Heidegger's humanism, the hinge between the beautiful in art (*technē*) and in nature (*physis*) in Kant, Deleuze's "transcendental empiricism," Heidegger's fourfold and earth/world.

4

This is beautiful, or, The Urge to Persuade

At this point the conflict between art and politics arises, and this conflict cannot and must not be resolved.

HANNAH ARENDT, "The Crisis in Culture"

Kant despite Nietzsche

The very unprecedentedness that modern art demands of itself underscores that the genuine artwork *exceeds* communicability. Aesthetic theory has to embrace, and account for, that demand. It is around the question of communicability that Nietzsche, Heidegger, and Deleuze separate themselves from Kant. Nietzsche considers the idea that aesthetic experience turns on a *sensus communis* to be absurd. For Heidegger and Deleuze, the artwork asserts itself against the realm of the "they" and *doxa* and exceeds it altogether. Neither art nor philosophy belongs to a realm of consensus.

Kant, for his part, treats the unprecedentedness of every appearance of the beautiful and the communicability of the judgment *this is beautiful* as complementary, not contradictory. Indeed, more than complementary, since the imputation of the judgment *this is beautiful* to everyone inheres in my very experience of the beautiful: "This claim to universal validity so essentially belongs to a judgment by which we declare something to be *beautiful* that without thinking this it would never occur to use this expression" (§8).[1] By the same token, however, there is no established standard or objective principle that makes something beautiful: "There can be no rule according to which anyone is to be forced to recognize anything as beautiful. We cannot press [upon others] by the aid of any reasons or fundamental propositions our judgment that a coat, a house, or a flower is beautiful. People wish to submit the object to their own eyes, as if the satisfaction in it depended on sensation; and yet, if we then call the object beautiful, we believe that we speak in a universal voice, and we claim the assent of everyone, although on the contrary all private sensation can only decide for the observer himself and his satisfaction."[2]

As if . . . and yet, if . . . although on the contrary. Kant is aware that everything about his reflection on aesthetic judgment presses against the very terms and categories in which that reflection is conducted. The experience of the beautiful is at once a singular sensation as though purely private *and* a judgment, that is, the conviction that the sensation is universally valid for others. Kant puts forward the strongest form of the conundrum—it is his central thesis—by arguing in §9 that in the judgment of taste the pleasure in question does not come before the judgment that claims the assent of everyone but follows upon it: "Thus it is the universal capacity for the communication of the state-of-mind in the given representation which, as the subjective condition of taste, must serve as its ground *and have the pleasure in the object as a consequence*" (my italics).[3] One way to resolve, or restate, the puzzle of aesthetic judgment is to recast it in pragmatic and performative terms. Insofar as art is encountered as an aspect of the public realm, my experience of an artwork is implicitly mindful of the others who participate with me in that public realm. Kant importantly calls this implicit mindfulness an "enlarged mentality"; if what he calls the *sensus communis* is construed performatively, rather than substantively, the tacit claim to the assent of everyone else that is intrinsic to my experience of the beautiful does not affirm an actually shared sensibility so much as appeal to others to attain the sensibility required to respond to *this* artwork. It is likely that just this dimension of publicness, of judgment as an appeal to the agreement of those who participate together in the public realm, explains the distance that Nietzsche, Heidegger, and Deleuze take from this moment in Kant's aesthetic theory.

The relations among the quartet do not, however, reduce to the thumbnail histories of philosophy in which Heidegger along with Nietzsche exemplifies anti-Enlightenment, and Kant and Nietzsche are conveniently cast as antipodes in modern thought, especially regarding aesthetics and ethics. Just as it turned out that the sheer polarity between Deleuzian vitalism and Heideggerian ontology frays in looking at their respective forays into aesthetic theory, so too neither the plaintiff's brief nor the defendant's holds up in *Nietzsche v. Kant* or *Kant v. Nietzsche* when it comes to the encounter with art. The more obvious oppositions and differences in these pairings can obscure salient affinities and shared, still unsettled questions.

The concept conventionally paired with the appeal to everyone's agreement in aesthetic judgment is *disinterestedness*. This gives rise to the idea that there is a universality to aesthetic judgment based on the neutralization and transcendence of all particular interests. *This is beautiful* is in turn seemingly derived from the logic of the categorical imperative in Kant's moral philosophy. Is this what Kant meant? Nietzsche thinks so, but Heidegger opens a different perspective, on both Kant and Nietzsche, in the 1936 seminar now known as *Nietzsche*, volume 1, *The Will to Power as Art*, published in 1961 and translated into English in 1979. Heidegger disputes Nietzsche's rejection of Kant's notion of disinterestedness on the grounds that it is based on a misinterpretation. It is not that Kant is right and Nietzsche wrong, but rather that Nietzsche misinterprets Kant and so misses a significant link between their respective aesthetic theories. At issue is how to construe what Kant in the *Critique of Judgment* calls "the pure disinterested satisfaction in the judgment of taste" (§2).[4]

Nietzsche bristles at the talk of disinterestedness, seeing it as a denial of will, impulse, and body—all the more so because of the moralistic overtones in Kant's way of distinguishing "pure disinterested satisfaction" from "enjoyment" or "intense gratification." But the moralism is not essential. It is even superfluous, and Heidegger looks past it: "Whatever exacts of us the judgment 'This is beautiful' can never be an interest. That is to say, in order to find something beautiful, we must let what encounters us, purely as it is in itself, come before us in its own stature and worth."[5] The tacit ethical thread in *we must let* could be brought out in hands other than Heidegger's insofar as that which has intrinsic worth can be deemed to be persons as well as landscapes or artworks. The aesthetic attitude takes nature and art as ends in themselves; the moral attitude takes other persons to be ends in themselves. "The only being which has the purpose of its existence in itself is *man*" (§17).[6] Where Kant himself most powerfully knits together the aesthetic and the moral attitude of taking persons as ends in themselves lies not in the categorical imperative of the *Critique of Practical Reason* but in the inseparability of the affective experience of the beautiful and the implicit universalizing claim for everyone's agreement— the very dimension of the *Critique of Judgment* that Heidegger, along with Deleuze, eschews: "Now I say the beautiful is the symbol of the morally good, and that it is only in this respect (a reference which is natural to every man and which every man postulates in others as a duty) that it gives pleasure with a claim for the agreement of everyone else. By this the mind is made conscious of a certain ennoblement and elevation above the mere sensibility to pleasure received through sense, and the worth of others is estimated in accordance with a like maxim of their judgment" (§59).[7] While the terms *duty* and *maxim* are borrowed from the lexical bank of the categorical imperative, the dynamic in aesthetic judgment is quite distinct for the twofold reason that there is no rule from which to derive that some particular thing is beautiful and no one can be compelled by argument or logic to affirm that something is beautiful. The universal claim is an impulse to persuade that is akin, as Hannah Arendt notes, to wooing or courting.[8]

Aesthetic judgment has a circularity about it. The power of judgment as such, even before there is a question of beauty, differs in this respect from the other faculties. Unlike the faculty of cognition, which "in accordance with concepts has its *a priori* principles in the pure understanding (in its concept of nature)," and unlike the faculty of desire, whose principle lies in "pure reason" and "its concept of freedom," the "faculty or receptivity" involved in judgment bears only on "the feeling of pleasure and displeasure" and "does not produce any concepts of objects for itself alone."[9] As Paul Guyer explains, "The doctrine that the feeling of pleasure or displeasure reflects the relation of an object to the subject rather than the properties of the object by itself is one of Kant's most entrenched views."[10] In Kant's formulation of this circularity: "The feeling of pleasure and displeasure is only the receptivity of a determination of the subject, so that if the power of judgment is to determine anything for itself alone, it could not be anything other than the feeling of pleasure, and, conversely, if the latter is to have an *a priori* principle at all, it will be found only in the power of judgment."[11] When the judgment of pleasure takes the form of *this is beautiful*, the circularity is neither tautological nor solipsistic. The two aspects of aesthetic judgment are, rather, mutually enhancing. Internal to the feeling of pleasure in the beautiful is the appeal to the assent of others, and internal to that appeal lies an affirmation of *their* stature and worth. It is the subject's inner sense of this inseparability that constitutes the experience of the beautiful: *I find this beautiful in feeling that you too must find it beautiful.* In Kant's own terms, the feeling of the beautiful is *as if* purely subjective and the claim for everyone's assent is *as if* purely objective. The mutually enhancing coincidence of the two constitutes the aesthetic judgment *this is beautiful.*

Which is to say anew that the judgment is neither subjective nor objective. The element of wooing in the claim for assent might suggest that aesthetic judgment must instead then be intersubjective. But this does not hold if intersubjectivity is meant in either a normative or an empirical sense. Aesthetic judgment is not empirically intersubjective, since actual agreement is not required. Kant is acutely aware that universal agreement, especially in the face of the unprecedentedness of artworks, is empirically uncertain, even unlikely. What matters in his account is that my tacit appeal to the assent of everyone else is inseparable from the particular satisfaction aroused within me by the beautiful as distinct from other pleasurable feelings. As to the normative, there is no aesthetic norm in nature or in art and no external or a priori rule for determining what is beautiful. My claim for everyone's assent is a judgment that others cannot agree with except through their own experience of *this* example and *their own* claim for everyone's agreement. Even as the actual experience of the beautiful contains within it a tacit appeal for everyone's agreement, there is no commitment in principle to agreement. Or to agreement as a principle. No formal or procedural ideal of consensus explains aesthetic judgment, since the very occurrence of aesthetic judgment has to be occasioned by a concrete phenomenon or object, whether in nature or art, which no rule determines to be beautiful and the pleasure in which is in Kant's words "a disinterested and *free* satisfaction."[12]

The full meaning of this phrase is the stake in Heidegger's objection to Nietzsche's understanding of Kant. However, Kant's notion that the claim to everyone's agreement is internal to the very experience of the beautiful as a disinterested and free satisfaction, a notion I have just reconstructed as ungrounded, virtual intersubjectivity, finds no place in Heidegger. I consider his account of Kantian disinterestedness compatible with that notion but questionable when uncoupled from it. Heidegger proceeds by discussing what is entailed in finding something beautiful:

> We may not take it into account in advance with a view to something else, our goals and intentions, our possible enjoyment and advantage. Comportment toward the beautiful as such, says Kant, is *unconstrained favoring*. We must freely grant to what encounters us as such its way to be; we must allow and bestow upon it what belongs to it and what it brings to us.
>
> But now we ask, is this free bestowal, this letting the beautiful be what it is, a kind of indifference; does it put the will out of commission? Or is not such unconstrained favoring rather the supreme effort of our essential nature, the liberation of ourselves for the release of what has proper worth in itself, only in order that we may have it purely? Is the Kantian "devoid of interest" a "smudging" and even a "besmirching" of aesthetic behavior? Or is it not the magnificent discovery and approbation of it?[13]

All these rhetorical questions are meant to reclaim Kant's conception of the beautiful from what Heidegger finds to be its Schopenhauerian misinterpretation in Nietzsche: "The misinterpretation fails to see that now for the first time the object comes to the fore as pure object and that such coming forward into appearance is the beautiful. The word 'beautiful' means appearing in the radiance of such coming to the fore."[14] These formulations resonate with those in "The Origin of the Work of Art" and indicate the specific affinity Heidegger wants to establish between his own aesthetic thinking and Kant's.

His next move is bolder. He aligns with Nietzsche's understanding of the nature of the pleasure at issue: "Nietzsche too defines the beautiful as what pleases. But everything depends on the operative concept of pleasure and of what pleases as such."[15] Heidegger cites *The Will to Power* 819: "The firm, powerful, solid, the life that reposes broad and majestic and conceals its strength—that is what '*pleases*'; i.e., that corresponds to what one thinks of oneself"[16]—as well as a phrase from the late notebooks concerning "the thrill that comes of being in our world now." The surprising yoking of Nietzsche and Kant follows:

> Hence we call "beautiful" whatever corresponds to what we demand of our-selves. Furthermore, such demanding is measured by what we take ourselves to be, what we trust we are capable of, and what we dare as perhaps the extreme challenge, one we can just barely withstand. . . .
>
> The beautiful is what we find honorable and worthy, as the image of our essential nature. It is that upon which we bestow "unconstrained favor," as Kant says, and we do so from the very foundations of our essential nature and for its sake. . . . [W]hat Nietzsche describes as the thrill that comes of being in our world is what Kant means by the "pleasure of reflection."[17]

Equating Kant's "unconstrained favor[ing]" and "pleasure of reflection" with Nietzsche's "thrill that comes of being in our world" is not as far-fetched as it first seems. Kant says of the satisfaction associated with the beautiful that it "directly brings with it a feeling of the furtherance of life" (§23).[18] Nietzsche frequently figures the will to power as an enhancement of life, an intensification of being alive.

While the phrase *unconstrained favor* (*die freie Gunst*) does not occur in Kant, Heidegger's italics easily leading commentators to suppose that it does, the purport is there. Kant distinguishes three kinds of satisfaction in §5, where satisfaction is defined as the relation of a representation to pleasure or pain: "The pleasant, the beautiful, and the good designate then three different relations of representations to the feeling of pleasure and displeasure. . . . That which *gratifies* a man is called *pleasant*; that which merely *pleases* him is *beautiful*; that which is *esteemed* [or *approved*] by him, i.e. that to which he accords an objective worth, is *good*."[19] When the representation of something in the mind arouses the feeling of being merely pleased, that is, purely and simply pleased, that something is beautiful: "We may say that, of all these three kinds of satisfaction, that of taste in the beautiful is alone a disinterested and *free* satisfaction; for no interest, either of sense or reason, here forces our assent. Hence we may say of satisfaction that it is related in the three aforesaid cases to *inclination*, to *favor*, or to *respect*. Now *favor* is the only free satisfaction."[20] By *free* Kant means that the satisfaction has not been compelled by need or instinct (as is the case for inclination) or by a moral law (as with respect).

In effect, the Kantian "pleasure of reflection" and "unconstrained favor" and the Nietzschean "thrill that comes of being in our world now" differ more in the rhetorical intensity of the philosophers' respective formulations than with respect to the quality or affective intensity of the aesthetic experiences they refer to, an intensity that in any case varies according to the specific occasion. The more telling difference lies in the significance of the ennoblement associated with art and aesthetic experience. Kant sharply distinguishes the free satisfaction of the beautiful from moral satisfaction—that is, the feeling, freedom, and feeling of freedom that comes from acting according to a moral law that one embraces—but at the same time, as we have seen, he postulates that the beautiful is a *symbol* of morality insofar as the free and disinterested pleasure it gives esteems "the worth of others" through the intrinsic "claim for the agreement of everyone else." It is a symbol insofar as this esteem does not, as in the use of that term in §5, affirm the objective worth of others. The worth of others' judgment is virtual, potential, anticipated, and hoped for, but not necessarily manifest.

Feeling for Others

There can be little doubt that Heidegger's uncoupling of unconstrained favoring from the esteem accorded others in the claim for universal agreement—indeed, his casting aside of reference to universalism in Kant in general—fits his aversion to democracy and liberalism. Here, though, it is important to keep in mind that the linkage between a thinker's ontology and his or her politics may be consistent and yet contingent, an articulation rather than a logical necessity. Questioning universalism need not abandon liberalism or democracy. I reject the illiberalism in Heidegger's disregard for the other-esteeming appeal for agreement, but at the same time my interpretation of that appeal to universal agreement does not presuppose the universal values and universally valid forms of rationality that are often extracted from Kant in order to taint Heidegger's thought as intrinsically illiberal, irrational, nativist, and authoritarian. Heidegger's politics were indeed illiberal, irrational, nativist, and authoritarian, but his aesthetic thinking is open to other possibilities, other articulations.

The central thesis of the *Critique of Judgment* has to be grasped in my view via discourse pragmatics. The claim or appeal to universal agreement is a discursive act even when left unstated and purely tacit, since within the experience of the beautiful is an urge to woo others' assent. This claim posits not an actual but a virtual or potential universality; it is an invitation to agreement. Universality could become actual only if everyone else in fact agreed with my judgment (but they don't) or if there were a fixed standard of beauty to which the artwork or natural phenomenon in question by right conformed (but there isn't). Aesthetic judgment occurs in the ungrounded space where my appeal to everyone else's agreement presupposes their capacity to respond to the same object with their own appeal for everyone else to agree that *this is*—or *is not*—*beautiful*. Hence the prospect of disagreement is intrinsic to my intrinsic claim for universal agreement. A logical contradiction? No. Rather, a discursive performance which is ungrounded at its inception and without guarantees in its outcome.

Kant's reference to the *sensus communis* (§40) leads many of his readers, whether they affirm or reject this conception, to construe it as positing that aesthetic judgments have a shared foundation or a necessary outcome. Such a reading is dead wrong. Having first bemoaned that *common sense* has come to refer to "the merely healthy (not yet cultivated) understanding" and is hence synonymous with "vulgar" and "indicates absolutely no merit or superiority" (in the Bernard translation; does not possess "an advantage or an honor" in Guyer and Matthews), Kant stipulates a more pertinent understanding of the *communis* in *sensus communis*, namely, "the idea of a *communal* sense [a sense *common to all* (Bernard)], i.e., of a faculty of judging that in its reflection, takes account (*a priori*) of everyone else's way of representing in thought, in order *as it were* to hold its judgment up to human reason as a whole [the collective reason of humanity (Bernard)] and thereby avoid that which, from subjective private conditions that could easily be held to be objective, would have a detrimental influence on the judgment."[21] *As it were*: like the various instances of *as if* in the *Critique of Judgment*, this nuance marks an interruption of otherwise settled terms and distinctions. Here it is not only that subjective and objective are interpenetrating rather than distinct, but also that "the collective reason of humanity" at which one's going beyond oneself aims is not a reachable destination, for, as Kant continues, "now this happens by one holding his judgment up not so much to the *actual* as to the *merely possible* judgments of others, and putting him into the position of everyone else, merely by abstracting from the limitations that contingently attach to our own judging" (my italics).[22] A tension unsettles this statement. Such abstraction from one's own contingent limitations cannot occur simply by negating the contingent in the name of the universal, since it has to unfold as the enlarging of one's sense of others' possible judgments—*judgments* in the plural. The very plurality of possible judgments implies that contingency cannot be expunged from judgment, including one's own, by the "universal." Moreover, there is little reason to assume that one is capable of envisioning *all* possible judgments. An enlarged mentality—"a broad-minded way of thinking" ("enlarged thought" in Bernard's felicitous translation)—is an intrinsically limited effort even as it overcomes its own contingent limitations. It strives for but cannot take possession of the universal.

What becomes of the universal if it cannot be possessed? That question is addressed by François Jullien in the context of anthropology and cross-cultural philosophy as he examines the consequence of recognizing that Western or European culture cannot lay claim to a privileged possession of universally valid values and ideas and therefore cannot lay claim to understanding other cultures in their specificity and particularity as though its own specificity and particularity did not figure in that act of understanding itself: "On the other hand, the *idea* of universal understanding between cultures, present or past, a horizon never reached or even attainable since it is always hiding behind all the proposed universalisms, plays a no lesser *regulatory* role in guiding the search for it."[23] He turns to the *Critique of Judgment* and, as I am doing, does a certain "violence to Kant" in order to rethink the conundrum of the universal and the singular. For Jullien, the task is "to transpose what [Kant] tells us about the judgement of the beautiful to the cultural judgement of values." Nietzsche's exposure of "the idea of a *perspective* on values" and Kant's confinement "within the fold of the European tradition alone" necessitate and justify a displacement of the "objectively universal" model of value ensconced in the latter's moral theory.[24] Finding a way beyond either, in Jullien's phrasing, "*facile universalism* (naively projecting its vision of the world onto the rest of the world)" or "*lazy relativism* (condemning cultures to imprisonment in an identity with specific values)" can look to the analytic of the beautiful because, as Kant puts it, the universal rule implied in the claim for everyone's assent cannot be formulated.[25] Kant thus clarifies for Jullien that "the universal represents an ideal."[26] My view differs in that I find that Kant helps us see not the ideal but the ordeal of universalism.

The ordeal of universalism becomes palpable not so much in the "faculty" of aesthetic judgment as in the *practice* of criticism. A touch more violence to Kant brings this out. He briefly falls back on a notion of the universal that negates embodied attunement and would render *unconstrained favoring* meaningless: "In itself, nothing is more natural than to abstract from charm and emotion if one is seeking a judgment that is to serve as a universal rule"—as though a straight line connected the abstraction from charm and emotion to a universal rule.[27] But in a digression identifying the "maxims of the common human understanding," he acknowledges that the universal has to be an orientation and aspiration, not an achievement. The maxims are "(1) to think for oneself; (2) to put ourselves in thought in the place of everyone else; (3) always to think consistently. The first is the maxim of *unprejudiced* thought; the second of *enlarged* thought; the third of *consecutive* thought."[28] These maxims echo the definition of enlightenment that Kant famously advanced six years earlier: "*Sapere aude!* Have courage to use your *own* understanding!"[29] In the *Critique of Judgment* he adds a footnote to warn against any assumption of achievement rather than striving: "We soon see that, although enlightenment

is easy *in thesi*, yet *in hypothesi* it is difficult and slow of accomplishment."[30]
Like aesthetic judgment itself, the *sensus communis* is ungrounded and uncertain. What is presumed or treated as *in common* is everyone else's *capacity*
to judge in the same discourse-mediated manner as oneself. In the case of
aesthetic judgment the felt presence of that presumption of commonality is a
constitutive element of the experience of the beautiful.

When the appeal for agreement emerges from tacitness and becomes articulate, it takes the form of criticism. That is not to say that critical discourse
literally asserts, "this is beautiful." Thankfully, it seldom does. Criticism at
its best lets the judgment arise by implication. A distinctive attentiveness to
the work is adduced through whatever facets, meanings, devices, techniques,
and contexts the critic's particular method succeeds in illuminating, and even
where the intent and purport show no concern with explicitly making "value
judgments"—say, Burke on Keats or Deleuze on Bacon, de Man on Wordsworth or Adorno on Beckett—the critic nonetheless hones an attention and
attentiveness to "Ode on a Grecian Urn," *Triptych, Three Studies from the Human Body*, "A slumber did my spirit seal," or *Endgame* that palpably conveys
the claim *this is beautiful*. But *what* is claimed to be beautiful? To anticipate
on a question still to be addressed more fully, Heidegger's view that the artwork produces the beautiful—in contrast to Kant's that the artwork itself is
beautiful—remains a crux for aesthetic theory, especially as it grapples with,
and is inspired by, modern art and literature. So, too, what can be meant by
form in Bacon and Beckett—or Baudelaire and Shakespeare—is emphatically
not a matter of well-formedness, symmetry, balance, or proportion, as it undoubtedly was for Kant, in keeping with his times' neoclassical sensibility.

As soon as the practice of criticism is brought to bear on the understanding
of aesthetic judgment, the question of the public realm arises, a question that
hovers untheorized in Kant and is shunned altogether by Heidegger once he
expunges the claim to agreement and urge to persuade from his appropriation
of the concept of unconstrained favoring. When Kant refers to what he rightly
calls "the *art* of criticism," he stresses again that while critics are capable of "cor-
recting and broadening our judgments of taste," it is "absolutely impossible" for
criticism—or theory—to provide "a principle of taste" or "the exposition of the
determining ground of this sort of aesthetic judgments in a universally usable
formula" (§35).[31] (The example does not derive from a rule, but the rule from
the example.) By the same token, the art of criticism itself does not arise spontaneously in the mind but relies on a web of political and social institutions,
habits of conversation and genres of writing, and the economy and technology
of print culture. What, then, is the relation between judgment as a "faculty"
(Kant) in the sense of a capacity of the human mind and the "public sphere"

(Habermas) in the sense of a "politically guaranteed space" (Arendt) that fosters and protects the circulation of information, opinion, and expression?

The idealist response postulates an intrinsic capacity of the mind that then incidentally manifests or externalizes itself in the institution of the public sphere, while the materialist and historical response asserts that the emergence of the public sphere and its requisite economic, technological, and legal systems enable the mind to judge. I subscribe to a materialist-historical standpoint, but without abandoning the inner dynamic of Kantian judgment when reconceived in pragmatic-performative terms.

Kant's idealism itself is laced with materialist and historical recognitions, for he witnessed the actual activity of aesthetic judgment in the conversations enlivening the bourgeois and aristocratic sites of eighteenth-century sociality and in the deeper tradition of humane letters that gave polite culture intellectual substance since the early Renaissance. He clearly recognized that what he considered a faculty of the mind could not be exercised without the semblance of a public sphere. In his 1793 essay "On the Common Saying: 'This May be True in Theory, but it does not Apply in Practice,'" he affirms—even in the midst of the extraordinarily conservative argument opposing *any* form of rebellion against established rule, tyranny included—that judgment is indissociable from publicness. The value and necessity of public discussion stem, he argues, from the fact that the sovereign's own judgments are human, not divine, and are therefore fallible: "Everyone has his inalienable rights, which he cannot give up even if he wishes to, and about which he is entitled to make his own judgements. . . . Thus the citizen must, with the approval of the ruler, be entitled to make public his opinion on whatever of the ruler's measures seem to him to constitute an injustice against the commonwealth. For to assume that the head of state can neither make mistakes nor be ignorant of anything would be to imply that he receives divine inspiration and is more than a human being. Thus *freedom of the pen* is the only safeguard of the rights of the people."[32] Rotated into its materialist restatement, this passage brings out that there is no such thing as a capacity to make one's own judgments except where there exists at least an incipient form of the politically guaranteed space and the discursive practices by which one can manifest one's own judgment *to others*, that is, others who are granted the same rights and to whom one imputes the same capacity for judgment as oneself. It is my intuition that this is in fact Kant's own meaning, for otherwise he could have taken account of the sovereign's fallibility simply by positing the right (or entitlement) to convey one's opinion of an injustice against the commonweal to the sovereign—but not publicly. By casting *"the freedom of the pen* [as] the only safeguard of the rights of the people,"* Kant affirms that judgments are one's own in an emphatic and meaningful sense only where judgment is formed in relation to the possible views of others who, unlike the fallible sovereign himself, are regarded as one's peers. Actual publicness is thus the pre- or co-condition of judgment.

Habermas's early work *The Structural Transformation of the Public Sphere* is often used as a straw man in order to criticize the liberal public sphere on the grounds that it supposedly presupposes that the participants in the politically guaranteed space for the circulation of information, opinion, and ideas are fully formed, autonomous individuals unshaped by culture, class, associations, or ascriptions. But this so-called liberal subject is a fabrication generated by critics of liberalism more than by liberalism itself. Kant does not posit individual autonomy as a given. To the contrary, autonomy is an ongoing process of emerging from dependence. The "motto of enlightenment"—"Have courage to use your *own* understanding!"—takes the form of an imperative not on the model of the categorical imperative but as a plea, indeed an aspiration, to take stock of one's own beliefs and convictions and gauge their nature and sources. The task is at once collective and radically individual: *"Enlightenment is man's emergence from his self-incurred immaturity. Immaturity is the inability to use one's own understanding without the guidance of another. This immaturity is self-incurred if its cause is not lack of understanding, but lack of resolution and courage to use it without the guidance of another."*[33] Individual autonomy is here valued but not presupposed, and certainly is not reducible to the so-called abstract liberal subject. As Arendt so profoundly understood, to value individuality in the public realm is to value plurality, actual concrete plurality. She did not look to concepts of the normative modeled on the *Critique of Practical Reason*'s categorical imperative but undertook her lectures on the *Critique of Judgment* as Kant's most important contribution not just to aesthetics but also to political theory.

In short, the faculty of judgment, when it comes to aesthetic judgment, could not exist as Kant conceives it without institutions and practices of the (incipient) liberal public sphere. The conceptual incompatibility of an inherent faculty of the mind and a historical institution of civil society, expressed in the antagonism between idealist and materialist standpoints, dissolves once the tacit appeal to the agreement of everyone else that Kant places within the experience of the beautiful is construed in discourse-pragmatic terms. The feeling-and-judgment *this is beautiful* reaches toward peers for agreement. It is a historically specific mutation of the equiprimordial triad mood–understanding–speech. Without sensing peers whose unconstrained favoring should accord with my own judgment, my own unconstrained favoring would not occur. Since this *should* does not have the backing of empirical fact, consensus principle, or objective standard, it is a discursive-performative gesture, even when unexpressed. As aesthetic judgment becomes articulate, the urge to persuade encounters the possible differences that impede the actual agreement of everyone else. Arendt, ever mindful of plurality, stresses that the constitutive being-with-one-another of judgment requires the enlarged mentality in Kant's sense, that is, the effort to stand in others' shoes and see from their perspectives as amply as possible. For her, the enlarged mentality is a capability that the public realm brings into being and that in turn sustains that realm. Its vigorous, capacious exercise is the sine qua non of democracy.

The art of criticism thrives on the enlarged mentality. Critics at their best elaborate their own response and understanding while sensing an array of other, even contrary responses that the artwork or literary text might arouse. Aesthetic attentiveness—attunement to the work—intensifies attunement to other possible responses. The urge to persuade lies just there. The conditions of criticism give it an inherent fragility. It is ungrounded, performative, its outcome uncertain, its persuasiveness never guaranteed, and its ends lie purely in its means. This fragility mirrors the fragility that Arendt saw in democracy, freedom, and the public realm in general.

Two circumstances are required for aesthetic judgment in the Kantian sense. Neither of them is assured of permanence. Aesthetic judgment depends on the institutional contexts and discursive practices that enable and stimulate the art of criticism, and on the artwork itself as an object available to oneself and others, the subjective response to which confounds distinctions of objective and subjective. Each element of this constellation of artwork, institution, and critical practice emerged in the first two centuries or so of European modernity: the relative separation of art from religion and myth (what Max Weber and T. W. Adorno called *aesthetic rationality*), the incipient forms of the liberal public sphere, and a persuasion-oriented discourse for debating the value and meaning of publicly displayed or performed or published works. Without that constellation, there can be no aesthetic judgment. While the historical origins of this constellation often prompt more or less strong repudiations in the form of denigrations of "autonomy," "bourgeois," "taste," and indeed "judgment," I want to emphasize the reverse, namely, the value of preserving the fragile constellation of artwork, public sphere, and criticism in the face of various forces that erode it. The historicity of the constellation does not in itself disqualify it. Rather, it marks the historical opening of an epoch in which we still live and act, a still-open epoch better to embrace as an adventure than to reject as error or injustice.[34]

There is considerable turbulence today in the conditions and practices of criticism, whether journalistic, belletristic, or scholarly: from journalism's frequent anti-intellectualism and scholars' recent tendency to eclipse the "literary" in favor of the "cultural" or "political" to the uncertainties produced by digital and social media. Nevertheless, for a century, since, say, Georg Lukács's *The Theory of the Novel*, criticism has developed as a major literary genre, a distinct genre of writing. And as a distinct genre of thought in its own right. The critical essay addresses philosophical, political, social, or historical problems through literary texts or artworks. I find the vitality of modern criticism most pronounced if considered in compelling but conflicting pairings: Lukàcs and Mikhail Bakhtin, Walter Benjamin and Erich Auerbach, William Empson and Raymond Williams, Roland Barthes and Fredric Jameson, Stephen Greenblatt and Marjorie Perloff, Northrop Frye and Tzvetan Todorov, Julia Kristeva and Eve Sedgwick, Maurice Blanchot and Kenneth Burke. And these are but a fraction of the tradition's major critics. Philosophers have ventured into this genre of thought as well, turning to literature and art not simply to illustrate an already-formed philosophical idea but to discover ideas in the encounter: Derrida on Mallarmé, Merleau-Ponty on Cézanne, Cavell on Shakespeare, Deleuze on Proust. Add to these the lineage of prolific non-scholarly critics from Edmund Wilson and Clement Greenberg to Addison Gayle, Jr., Susan Sontag, John Leonard, John Berger, Pierre Assouline, and James Wood, all of whom fuse interpretation and advocacy and provoke and educate their readers to apprehend art and literature in unanticipated ways. No less enlightening are the poets and novelists as critics, from T. S. Eliot and Virginia Woolf to Octavio Paz, Milan Kundera, William Gass, and Susan Howe. Much contemporary scholarly and journalistic criticism might seem not so much inspired as merely backgrounded by this multifaceted tradition, but the tradition's richness remains an unmatched, hardly exhausted, still renewable resource for future efforts to grapple with literature and art. In the work of these critics lies the fullest manifestation of aesthetic judgment as Kant first formulated it.

Aesthetic "Regimes" and Artistic "Paradigms"

The vocation of criticism as its possibility and lineaments are opened by Kant's analytic of the beautiful eventuates in a plurality of practices, methods, political inclinations and affiliations, literary and aesthetic values, discursive styles, venues, and audiences. Such a plurality, which I have just evoked in referring to an array of twentieth- and twenty-first-century critics, easily appears at odds with the universalism of Kantian judgment—unless, as I have argued, the appeal to universal agreement is recognized in its performative and discourse-pragmatic essence. As Arendt puts it, "Judgment is endowed with a certain specific validity but is never universally valid. Its claims to validity can never extend further than the others in whose place the judging person has put himself for his considerations."[35] So, too, the radical implications have to be drawn out of Kant's notion that aesthetic judgment in its encounter with the artwork does not apply a rule to an example but must derive the rule from the example, which is to say that aesthetic receptivity—whatever the shape and extent of one's cultivated and educated taste—encounters in the artwork an unprecedented event. Kant thus intuited, quite beyond the taste community of eighteenth-century polite culture that conditioned his thinking about art, what would soon emerge as the driving imperative of modern artistic and literary creation. That imperative is too limitedly understood as *Make it new!* or associated exclusively with early twentieth-century avant-gardes, for it is already explicit in Wordsworth's recognition that the poems he and Coleridge published in *Lyrical Ballads* had to create the taste by which to be appreciated. As regards the novel, the necessity of innovation typically associated with modernism already animates nineteenth-century realism as it responds to unforeseen and unforeseeable social change.[36]

In light of the unprecedentedness of artworks and the performativity of the appeal to the agreement of everyone, the *sensus communis* is—as Kant also intuited—not merely an already shared background of taste, educated sensibility, literacy, and competence, but also and more emphatically the urge and striving to enrich and extend commonality. Hence its vitality and its fragility. Whether viewed from the standpoint of the judging individual or the structure of the public realm, universalism is not a given. Rather, the ordeal of universalism takes shape as the striving to put oneself in the place of others in face of the social unevenness of learning and literacy as well as the contours and niches of the public sphere.

Kant's relevance to nearly two and a half centuries of aesthetic thinking and experiences of art is framed by Jacques Rancière as demarcating the era of the "aesthetic regime of the arts," distinguished from two earlier "regimes." The "ethical regime of images" is articulated in Plato's division of *technē* as "ways of doing and making" into the "true arts, that is to say forms of knowledge based on the imitation of a model with precise ends, and artistic simulacra that imitate simple appearances." The "poetic—or representative—regime" is first articulated by Aristotle and, according to Rancière, "identifies the substance of . . . the arts in the couple *poēsis/mimēsis*"; in "the Aristotelian elaboration of *mimēsis* . . . It is the *substance* of the poem, the fabrication of a plot arranging actions that represent the activities of men, which is the foremost issue." Tragedy's imitation of an action is not mere simulacrum because what is imitated is real human action. The tie to praxis is internal to *mimēsis*; therein lies the difference between Plato and Aristotle. What they share, though, is an understanding of art as "doing and making" and a valorization of the fabric of actual human activity, which leads Plato to devalue art because the artist (unlike the artisan) fails to fabricate a useful object and Aristotle to value tragedy because it imitates real human action.[37]

The "aesthetic regime" breaks with what these other two regimes share: "The identification of art no longer occurs via a division within ways of doing and making, but is based on distinguishing a sensible mode of being specific to artistic products." Three ideas are compressed in this formulation. First, art is no longer viewed as a practice comparable to other practices. Second, the artwork is now understood as a "specific mode of being" unlike other entities in the world. Third, in order to establish this unique ontological standing, the artwork is disconnected from all our "ordinary connections" to sensible things.[38] Rancière ties this third idea directly to Kant's separation of the beautiful in aesthetic judgment from the other faculties' grasp of sensible things as useful, desirable, knowable, consumable, good, and so on.

Rancière's picture of the "aesthetic regime of the arts" cannot be completed without Schiller's amplification of Kantian aesthetics in the *Letters on the Aesthetic Education of Man*. The threefold formulation of the aesthetic regime entangles art in various aporias: it is a product as if unproduced; it is an outcome separate from an intention; where *technē* was a knowledge and know-how, the aesthetic regime separates fine art from *technē*: "Knowledge is transformed into non-knowledge." In these ways, Rancière says, "the aesthetic regime asserts the absolute singularity of art and, at the same time, destroys any pragmatic criterion for isolating this singularity." Schiller's response to this apparent impasse is to up the ante. For him, the aesthetic regime "simultaneously established the autonomy of art and the identity of its forms with the forms that life uses to shape itself."[39] How does art, defined in its very separation from and incommensurability with all practical forms of living, doing, and acting, become life-forming? That was Schiller's puzzle. It has long been understood that Schiller formulated the aesthetic education as a life-forming, indeed life-transformative process in response to what he saw as the failure of political revolution in France after 1789 and the utter absence of revolutionary ferment in Germany itself. What hadn't happened in politics could, he hoped, happen through aesthetic experience. Art and the aesthetic education held for him the promise, perhaps the only promise, of cultivating the sense of freedom and stoking, that is, educating the love of freedom required to emancipate humankind throughout society.

Rancière's takes this general understanding of Schiller and boldly extends it to the claim that the separation of art from all practical activity, including politics, combined with the claim that the aesthetic education is the path to emancipation, becomes the dominant and defining "regime" of the arts in the modern age. At its most insightful, this thesis illuminates the impasse that afflicts aesthetic theory when it postulates art as the unique and exclusive counterpole to domination, power, commodification, or capitalism. "The tension animating both Adorno's aesthetics and the Lyotardian anti-aesthetics of the sublime becomes fully intelligible only when referred to a primitive scene, one that serves to ground both art's autonomy and the promise of an emancipated humanity in the experience of a sensorium of exception." The primal scene is Schiller, for whom "aesthetic 'free play' ceases to be a mere intermediary between high culture and simple nature, or a stage of the moral subject's self-discovery" and "becomes the principle of a new freedom, capable of surpassing the antinomies of political liberty. In a nutshell, it becomes the principle of a politics or, more exactly, of a metapolitics, which, against the upheavals of state forms, proposes a revolution of the forms of the lived sensory world."[40]

In Rancière's reckoning, Adorno takes the Schillerian fusion of aesthetic autonomy and human emancipation to an ultimate dead end. Accordingly, Adorno's *Aesthetic Theory*, the essay on Ulysses in *Dialectic of Enlightenment*, and the writings on modern music, especially Schoenberg, unwind a permanent irreconcilability in place of the promised fusion:

> Adorno shares the same central preoccupation as Schiller: to revoke the division of labour implying the separation of labour and enjoyment, of the men of necessity and the men of culture. The [art]work, for him, continues to promise what in the supreme state of agitation and repose was promised by the free appearance of the Greek statue: a world in which the separation of labour and enjoyment, symbolized by the primitive scene of Western reason, is abolished—namely, [the scene] in which the sailors sit on their benches with their ears blocked to the song of sirens, while Ulysses, tied to the mast and enjoying this song in itself, is unable to ask his subordinates to untie him so he can go and meet his enchantresses. But if the [art]work promises this reconciliation, it is only through an effort of indefinite deferral, achieved by rejecting all the forms of conciliation in which domination is allegedly still preserved in concealment. . . . The path toward emancipation is the one that exacerbates the separation, that offers the beautiful appearance only at the price of dissonance and reaffirms the good of dissensus by rejecting all forms of reconciliation between the beautiful and pleasure. The aesthetic scene, properly speaking, thus turns out to be the scene of the irreconcilable.[41]

Adorno is thus nicely distilled into a kind of allegory of his thought, and this picture does capture something of the movement of "negative dialectic" as it churns through his aesthetic reflections and criticism. However, it conveys none of the power of the criticism itself, from *The Odyssey* to Schoenberg and Beckett. It also passes over a historical trench. For while Schiller in the 1790s locates emancipation in the achievement of liberal society and some form of a constitutional-democratic polity, Adorno found it essentially impossible after 1945 to still envision emancipation as he understood and embraced it in the revolutionary and Marxist tradition.

Adorno's work is not the simple distillation of an "aesthetic regime" into a fixed theoretical stance. Rather, his sensibility and intellect, formed in the utopian and antifascist imagination of a classless society and the educated attunement to Europe's entire literary, artistic, and musical heritage, now faced the evidence and aftermath of the Holocaust, Stalinism, and Hiroshima. Repelled since the Weimar Republic by the promises of liberal democracy, what the postwar Adorno sees emerge from the defeat of fascism is the intractable victory of capitalism, consumerism, and the intellectual and artistic depredations of mass culture. There is much that can be argued with in this constellation of perspectives, diagnoses, and values, but it is not the simple, let alone inevitable, outcome of the Schillerian aspiration. Adorno does not, as in Rancière's rendition, unfold the inner logic of a "regime" into its inevitable impasse; rather, he writes passionately from inside the impasse and unfolds it out into the witnessing of his time in a scintillating rhetoric of aversion and condemnation. Zachary Samalin places the contemptuousness of Adorno's cultural criticism in a tradition reaching back to the medieval *contemptus mundi*. He draws out the ways in which disgust is implicated in contempt. Contempt's posture of superiority over the contemptible arises from the affect of disgust, which suggests that the contemptible is within not merely outside the contemptuous subject. Adorno and Horkheimer's *Dialectic of Enlightenment* operates "with a model of critical affectivity which can at least pretend—that is, rhetorically—to sit outside the dialectic of Enlightened self-interest. It is this posture of superiority which, like the conceit of a poem, allows them simultaneously to describe the products of the culture industry as structured exclusively for consumption, while affecting to maintain such a degree of control and circumscription for their own appetites so as not to feel the effects of the desire to consume. Perhaps, as we are told, 'the heroizing of the average forms part of the cult of cheapness,' but what does it matter so long as you are immune to the draw of the low? Such contemptuous condemnation, harkens back to that negative ascetic ideal of an integral self—that impermeable layer of superiority kept in place by caustic repudiation—as though to produce the rush of affect found at certain points in the chapter on 'The Culture Industry' its authors did not need to have an above average appetite for the movies."[42]

As regards theory, the grain of truth in Rancière's mini-allegory is better elaborated in light of Adorno's appropriation of Weber's notion of aesthetic rationality. Weber defines modernity in terms of the processes by which distinct "cultural spheres" emerge as various social practices and activities are increasingly separated from religion. He considers principally the economic, political, aesthetic, erotic, and intellectual spheres. His famous 1918 essays "Politics as Vocation" and "Science as Vocation" elaborate on the political and intellectual spheres respectively.[43] Weber never postulates that these spheres are wholly separated from religion, though that is a common misreading of his account of secularization. The "ethic of brotherhood," which he places at the core of religiosity, also had a secular manifestation at the core of the socialist and communist movements. The modern cultural spheres differentiate themselves from religion and come into strife with it. I see Weber demarcating an ongoing process of difference, strife, and return insofar as religious ideas, symbolizations, and values can reinhabit the precincts of any "separated" sphere, reigniting differentiation and strife.[44] Moreover, the various cultural spheres are not only differentiated and in strife vis-à-vis religion but also vis-à-vis one another; that is the point of Weber's juxtaposed essays on vocation, since the ethic and tensions within the scholarly vocation are at moments fundamentally incompatible with those of the political vocation. Weber calls a differentiated sphere's elaboration of distinctive procedures, practices, and rules a process of "rationalization." Thus, aesthetic rationality is the long, layered process by which artists increasingly relate to the techniques and forms of their art not primarily as skills acquired for realizing the aims of representation dictated by subject matter furnished by religion and myth, but rather as a body and history of artistic techniques and forms that are now free to be deployed and developed for singular, unpredetermined ends.

When Adorno takes up this notion of aesthetic rationality, he quickly narrows the field of difference and strife to art's opposition and antagonism to commodification and capitalism. He pits the aesthetic sphere exclusively over against the economic sphere, whereas the fabric of modern society involves the difference and potential strife among the several cultural spheres, including the political sphere, whose specificity is eclipsed in Adorno's thought in keeping with a doctrine going back to Marx, for whom the state and politics were but instruments of class struggle. Even as Adorno registers the demise of class struggle in reification and commodification, Marx trumps Weber in his thought.

The limit Adorno imposes on his theoretical endeavor is matched by the self-limitations imposed by Rancière. Where Adorno reduces the Weberian problematic to the aesthetic over against the economic, Rancière attributes excessive explanatory power to his model of three "regimes" of the arts. In both cases, the plurality of artistic production and its varying relation to modern political and economic process are diminished. Rancière's three-regimes model is so rigid that it needlessly impoverishes his own most original and productive concept: the "distribution of the sensible." That notion sets out to interrogate how access to what is common, in the strong sense of the basis and site of the political realm and political decision, and participation in that realm are unevenly "distributed" and "shared." Such distributed access and differentiated participation have an aesthetic dimension in the sense of giving form to perceptions and feelings, that is, to the sensible. The distribution of the sensible is a kind of "system of *a priori* forms determining what presents itself to sense experience. It is a delimitation of spaces and times, of the visible and the invisible, of speech and noise, that simultaneously determines the place and the stakes of politics as a form of experience. Politics revolves around what is seen and what can be said about it, around who has the ability to see and the talent to speak, around the properties of spaces and the possibilities of time."[45] Rancière in turns seeks to relate the distributions of the sensible that structure the political realm directly to artistic practices and forms; there is a fluid intermingling of the political and the aesthetic in his conception. But that is where the problem of the three-regimes model arises. How can three (in fact, only two) models of the arts account for the distribution of the sensible across five centuries of Western societies, their political formations, and their literature and art? On the one hand, the principal articulation of the three regimes is philosophical (Plato, Aristotle, Kant), and on the other, the poetic (Aristotelian) and aesthetic (Kantian) regimes are historical, indeed epochal, and follow a quite traditional French periodization of the classical age (roughly the sixteenth through the eighteenth century) and the modern age (since the Revolution of 1789). By asking so much of aesthetic theory Rancière actually depletes it; the more it is supposed to explain, the more simplified it becomes.

Ironically, Rancière's polemical commentary on Deleuze's aesthetic thought pinpoints its reductive connection of art and politics. Deleuze for him exemplifies yet another outcome of the Schillerian aspirations of the "aesthetic regime of the arts." He homes in on an extravagant, self-poeticizing claim made by Deleuze and Guattari in *What Is Philosophy?* that reinserts art—which "undoes the triple organization of perceptions, affections, and opinions in order to substitute a monument composed of percepts, affects, and blocs of sensation"—back into the world from which it stands apart. It is, to use their terms, a reterritorializing of the deterritorialized artwork. The reterritorialization lies in the future:

A monument does not commemorate or celebrate something that happened but confides to the ear of the future the persistent sensations that embody the event: the constantly renewed suffering of men and women, their re-created protestations, their constantly resumed struggle. Will this all be in vain because suffering is eternal and revolutions do not survive their victory? But the success of a revolution resides only in itself, precisely in the vibrations, clinches, and openings it gave to men and women at the moment of its making and that composes in itself a monument that is always in the process of becoming, like those tumuli to which each new traveler adds a stone. The victory of a revolution is immanent and consists in the new bonds it installs between people, even if these bonds last no longer than the revolution's fused material and quickly give way to division and betrayal.[46]

This might be more than a nostalgia for May '68 revoiced as the ecstatic imagination of pure becoming if it is taken to describe not revolution, as is claimed, but rather the discontinuous heritage of revolt in which aesthetic experiences and political experiences resonate with one another in varied and wholly unexpected ways. By the same token, to place the sole viable reterritorialization of the artwork in moments of revolt, even in a less hyperbolic sense than a new earth and a new people, robs aesthetic experience of its engagement with the actual worldliness of politics. Such a radical refusal is certainly intended by Deleuze and Guattari, because for them this type of engagement falls under the broad heading of *doxa*. However, aesthetic judgment and criticism belong precisely to *doxa*, which is why I have confronted Deleuzian and Heideggerian aesthetics with the Arendtian understanding of Kantian judgment as wooing, enlarged mentality, and esteem for others.

Rancière is right to point up that *futurity* means deferral in the formulation from *What Is Philosophy?*: "The 'resistance of art' thus appears as a double-edged paradox. To maintain the promise of a new people, it must either suppress itself, or defer indefinitely the coming of this people." But because of his three-regimes model, Rancière attributes this impasse not just to this particular claim of Deleuze and Guattari, but to modern art itself: "The dynamic of art for the last two centuries is perhaps the dynamic generated by this tension between the two poles of art's self-suppression and the indefinite deferral of the people it calls forth. This paradox of the politics of art refers back to the very paradox of its definition in the aesthetic regime of art, in which the 'things' called art are no longer defined, as before, by the rules of a practice. They are defined by their belonging to a specific sensory experience, that of a sensible weave subtracted from the ordinary forms of sensory experience."[47]

Several elements of modern aesthetic experience and artistic practice fail to truly fit Rancière's "aesthetic regime" or can be described in a decidedly different way. Features of the "aesthetic regime" could easily be mistaken for the three theses I have delineated as shared by Deleuze and Heidegger—the artwork's lastingness, self-positing, and independence of creator and recipient—theses that need not lead to impasses of the sort Rancière treats as inevitable. He consistently distinguishes the "aesthetic" from the "representative" regime with reference to the idea that Kant, Adorno, and Deleuze give the artwork an ontological and sensory status unlike other things and sensings. This idea is an oversimplification. First, Kant and Adorno associate the beautiful not exclusively with artworks, but also with nature, and, in Adorno's case, with eroticism. Second, the artwork's difference from other things in the world is not a pure separation. That is what Deleuze explores so extensively in regard to the difference-inseparability of figuration and Figure in Bacon's paintings. From another angle and in another idiom altogether, Niklas Luhmann's systems-theoretical reworking of Weber's cultural spheres states the paradoxical character of the artwork (its ontological distinctiveness) in the thesis that art at once asserts its difference from reality and yet becomes a part of reality: "Art establishes in the world a reality of its own while making this reality a part of the world. . . . Art splits the world into a real world and an imaginary world in a manner that resembles, and yet differs from, the use of symbols in language or . . . the religious treatment of sacred objects and events." What is the difference? "The function of art concerns *the meaning of this split*" (my italics).[48] Luhmann's formulation would apply as thoroughly to the mimetic art of the "representative regime" as to Bacon or Beckett in the "aesthetic regime."

Rancière repeatedly gives a critical edge to his account of the "aesthetic regime" by evoking the notion that the "representative regime" of Aristotelian mimesis establishes "an agreement between a productive nature—*poiesis*—and a receptive nature—an *aisthesis*," in effect defining "human nature" as the "three-way agreement" of imitation, making, and sensory-affective reception.[49] In Kant's terms, though, the receptive nature (*aisthesis*) involves judgment. And Arendt finds the distinction and separation, the radical difference, of making and judging already in the ancients, in particular Plato and Cicero. It is not a problematic unique to the modern "aesthetic regime" but cuts across Rancière's philosophical and historical categorizations. *Homo faber*, the maker as craftsman or artist, Arendt argues, does not have "the same relationship to the public realm and its publicity as the things he makes, with their appearance, configuration, and form. In order to be in a position to add new things to the already existing world, he himself must be isolated from the public, must be sheltered and concealed from it." By contrast, politics takes place in "the public . . . a space constituted by the many." Nevertheless, the judging of what is beautiful and enhances the common space of publicness is, as we have seen in Arendt's understanding of Kant, a model of political judgment. Artistic creation stems from the fabricator isolated and sheltered from the public, while political and indeed aesthetic judgments are an inherently public activity. Hence difference and strife obtain between making and receiving, *poiesis* and *aisthesis*, creation and judgment. "At this point," Arendt concludes, "the conflict between art and politics arises, and this conflict cannot and must not be solved."[50] That conclusion runs contrary to Rancière by acknowledging an unbridgeable gap between *poiesis* and *aisthesis*; it runs contrary to Deleuze and Guattari by affirming that the articulated engagement with the artwork participates in *doxa*. Criticism, as the practice of evoking aesthetic responsiveness to the artwork and articulating an interpretation of it, belongs to *doxa*. But the artwork does not. That disjunction is already formulated in Kant in terms of the artwork's unprecedentedness. Criticism is charged with letting the educated sensibility undergo the jolt of that unprecedented encounter and striving to raise its own receptiveness and urge to persuade to the new example. "The chief difficulty in judgment," Arendt writes, citing Kant, "is that it is 'the faculty of thinking the particular'; but to *think* means to generalize, hence it is the faculty of mysteriously combining the particular and the general."[51] Such is the vocation of criticism.

The other condition of criticism, namely, that the artwork exist as a shared object, has been unsettled by artistic practice itself. The last century of art has accentuated the artwork's singular, even autonomous nature; considered a unique kind of object wrested from all circuits of utility, the artwork has thus been understood as countermovement to commodification (Adorno), countermovement to nihilism (Heidegger's Nietzsche), or a bloc of "percepts and affects" surpassing "ordinary affections and perceptions" (Deleuze). That same century of art has also, though, rejected, mocked, and displaced the very idea of such autonomy, singularity, and uniqueness, beginning with Marcel Duchamp's ready-mades.

What counts as an artwork, and how institutions, markets, dealers, and the so-called art world shape what is deemed art and which works and trends are deemed valuable—these sorts of questions are the basis of Nathalie Heinich's sociology of modern and contemporary art. She in fact stipulates the meaning of "modern" and "contemporary" in a strict distinction between two "paradigms" of art. Her conceptualization, like the title of her *Le paradigme de l'art contemporain: Structures d'une révolution artistique*, draws inspiration from Thomas Kuhn's theory of the paradigm shifts that constitute scientific revolutions. Let me briefly state, and then bracket, my reservations about her conceptual frame, that is, her paradigm, in order then to draw on her deeply researched descriptions of the "contemporary" and bring into focus the volatilization of the artwork as object.

My reservations: First, the analogy of artistic and scientific revolutions is compromised by the fact that paradigm shifts in the natural sciences are invariably an advance in knowledge, a progress that does not apply to art: Cézanne is not truer than Rubens, Joyce does not supplant Dante, Ashbery does not negate Wordsworth. The validity of all six of these artists is measured by how they took the manifest and latent possibilities in their art's tradition and refashioned it or innovated on it in response to the particular conditions and needs of their own time and experience. Second, Heinich consequently presents the contemporary paradigm as succeeding and supplanting the modern paradigm, whereas the clash of these supposed paradigms exists from the beginning: no sooner do the Cubists establish "modern" art than Duchamp upends it, and indeed Duchamp himself is steeped in both the "modern" and the "contemporary" at once, painting *Nude Descending a Staircase (No. 2)* in 1912 and displaying *Bicycle Wheel* in 1913. Third, Heinich stumbles on an obstacle that every sociology of art must inevitably confront, namely, how to pass from the analysis of the conditions and contexts of artistic production, reception, valuation, and institutionalization to an account of artworks "themselves"; her thick description of the art world and detailed tracking of movements, trends, and polemics provide countless insights into "modern" and "contemporary" Art but less into modern and contemporary art. In but one example: taking up a typical widely used label, Heinich characterizes *neo-expressionism* as a kind of backlash against minimalism and other trends that by the 1980s were prevalent in galleries and museum exhibitions of "contemporary" art at the expense of "pictorial" painting. She cites the Tate's refusal at that time to mount an exhibition of Lucian Freud and designates Julian Schnabel neo-expressionism's "principal figure." To account for these artists' eventual out-of-sequence foothold in the new "contemporary" paradigm, she attributes their success to their paintings' being "no longer modern but 'postmodern,' inasmuch as they refer to the history of art rather than the artist's interiority." Succumbing to the art world's manic nominalism, she mentions Anselm Kiefer as another postmodern neo-expressionist who edges into the "contemporary" paradigm because the fragile materials he attaches to his canvases threaten the works' permanence. From the standpoint of criticism, it is difficult to see what is gained by lumping Schnabel, Freud, and Kiefer together as postmodern throwbacks to "pictorial" painting. Obscuring their distinctive artistic purposes and effects, Heinich falls prey to the very institutional-discursive dynamics she is claiming to analyze.[52] Close bracket.

Heinich places "the four major genres of contemporary art" under the rubric *the work beyond the object*: ready-mades, performance art, conceptual art, and installations. Common to these instances of the "contemporary paradigm" is the fact that "the artwork no longer resides in the object put forth by the artist." A caption, an account (*récit*), commentary, interpretation, or anecdote becomes essential to—or, she even suggests, the essence of—the artwork. The artwork cannot be what it is without its accompanying discourse. (Hence, too, the omnipresence of appending labels to trends.) Heinich interprets the inner dynamic of these sorts of projects as enacting "a rich series of operations" on art's objecthood: "The dematerialization of the work into the formless, its conceptualization in the idea, its multiplication in installations, its 'ephemeralization' in performances."[53]

Dematerialization is on the face of it the most extreme of these operations, since, after all, performance art is no more ephemeral than the performance of a play, however sharp the distinctions between them otherwise are, and installations may be a "hybridization" of the object but nevertheless do have a material presence and can be dismantled and reassembled. As for conceptual art, Heinich asks, "What could be more immaterial than an idea?" and concludes that the "object as materialization of the idea is only a pretext—and even sometimes . . . literally a pre-text." Pure dematerialization is exemplified by Yves Klein's *Exhibition du vide*, consisting of several absolutely empty rooms that visitors roam, and still more by the eight "sales of immaterial pictorial sensibility," paid in gold, which was thrown in the Seine, in exchange for a certificate, which was then burned. Among current artists, Heinich identifies Tino Sehgal, along with Ian Wilson, as "the most radical" of the "experimenters in a dematerialization."[54] That claim accords with Sehgal's own stated purpose, tinged with ecological and anticonsumerist associations, of achieving an artistic practice and aesthetic experience that add absolutely no new object to the world: an artwork as pure activity, altering nothing in humanity's life-sustaining metabolic interchange with nature and yet creating an unprecedented experience, creation without production, the transcendence both of reification and of its critique, a dereifying of the artwork itself.

Tino Sehgal, or, Criticism's Outer Edge

Sehgal's 2010 work at the Guggenheim Museum in New York seemed to attain just such dematerialization and ephemerality. Publicity for the exhibition neither named nor described the work to be found there. Simply: *Tino Sehgal*, January 29–March 10. Entering the museum, visitors first encountered a young man and woman, fully clothed, lying together on the floor in the center of the rotunda and taking up various postures of embrace in extremely slow yet flowing movements. The piece, called *The Kiss*, had been created by Sehgal several years before; the couple's postures allude to several sculptures and paintings throughout the history of Western art. The sensual but enigmatic movement of these horizontal dancers presented the visitor with the only hint of an artwork in the vast space of the Guggenheim. The walls along the famous spiraling ramp were empty. People were ascending the spiral with nothing to look at and with no discernible destination.

Where was the work?

Once the visitor starts up the ramp, a Child of eight or nine unexpectedly approaches, gives his or her name, and then announces, "This is a work by Tino Sehgal." The Child asks the visitor, "What is progress?" and turns so as to lead or accompany the visitor up the ramp and hear the answer to the question. After a turn or two a Teen approaches, and the Child paraphrases the visitor's definition of progress. The Child leaves the visitor and the Teen to continue on; unbeknownst to the visitor, a Younger Adult now follows them for a while, just close enough to pick up a thread or some key words of their conversation about progress. At some point the Younger Adult walks on ahead and, taking advantage of one of the columns and blind spots on the ramp, heads back down to meet the visitor and the Teen. The Teen leaves as the Younger Adult proceeds with the visitor on the walk upward, by now somewhere on the third of the rotunda's seven levels. Unbeknownst to the visitor, the Teen runs up two flights of a back stairway to tell an Older Adult waiting on the fifth level the broad themes of the conversation with visitor. The visitor and the Younger Adult are pointed out as they come into view across the atrium on the level below. The Teen returns back down the stairs. The Older Adult remains stationed out of view behind a large column that is very close to the railing. Reaching the narrow passageway, the Younger Adult gestures for the visitor to go through. As the visitor steps ahead, the Younger Adult spins away unnoticed. The visitor emerges to be immediately intercepted by the Older Adult, who announces, "The title of this work is *This Progress.*" As they proceed, the Older Adult unfolds an anecdote or reflection on some event for a few minutes before bringing the visitor into the conversation as they walk on to the top of the rotunda. Once there, the Older Adult continues the conversation for a few moments and then extends a hand to shake, saying, "It was a pleasure talking with you." The Older Adult then abruptly turns around, walks straight to a door, and exits down the back stairway, leaving the visitor stranded.

So, the visitor has four conversations directly or obliquely about progress while traversing the quarter-mile ascent of Frank Lloyd Wright's iconic museum in the company, successively, of a Child, a Teen, a Younger Adult, and an Older Adult. The unrehearsed conversations likely produce surprising resonances or uncanny coincidences thanks to the Younger Adult's eavesdropping and the Teen's report to the Older Adult.

There is no documentation, film, or recording of *This Progress*, no script or written instructions archived, and visitors who were taken through the piece were unaware of being overheard and reported on. How, then, could I provide my account of Sehgal's work? I was one of the Interpreters, as we were called, and did a four-hour shift as an Older Adult three times a week during the work's six-week run at the Guggenheim. For each shift, there were a dozen, sometimes up to twenty, Interpreters in each of the four groups. When the volume of visitors was high, you shook hands at the top of the ramp, did your pirouette, headed down the stairs to the staging area, and almost immediately got another report from a Teen and prepared for the next visitor (or visitors, as sometimes two or even three people would go through the piece together).

When the crowd was thinner, I often stood at the railing and was captivated, indeed almost mesmerized as I watched the visitors move along unhurried and in conversation with a Teen or Younger Adult, another such pair just twenty or thirty paces behind. It was a unique sight, at once soothing and wondrous, so undramatic as to be mundane and yet unlike anything one would see in a museum or on the street. The leisurely pace and undistracted attention to conversation suggested Renaissance gentlemen strolling the streets and courtyards of Florence or Machiavellian cardinals conspiring as they cross St. Peter's Square. From the height of the fifth level I could also look down and watch *The Kiss*, whose performers similarly conveyed utter leisure and intense attention to one another.

The Older Adults all developed their own opening monologues in consultation with Sehgal's producer and longtime collaborator Asad Raza. (All four groups of Interpreters had a coach and handler.) I developed a half dozen or so topics that could foster a conversation touching on the notion of progress: a friend's anxiety about lost intimacy in the face of his wife's in vitro fertilization; the discovery of warfarin, the rat poison and medical anticoagulant, thanks to a Wisconsin dairy farmer's desire to know why his heifer dropped dead on a bed of hay; my horror at age eleven in moving to Iowa, where the death penalty was carried out by hanging; Native Americans in the northwest who valued tribal income from their fish hatcheries over ecologists' concerns to protect native salmon; a surprising passage from *Leaves of Grass* that seems to negate any idea of progress (and expresses, by the way, a more compelling interpretation of eternal recurrence than Nietzsche's cosmological hypothesis)—

> There was never any more inception than there is now,
> Nor any more youth or age than there is now;
> And will never be any more perfection than there is now,
> Nor any more heaven or hell than there is now.

—a Paris butcher's despair because no young person would take over his thriving neighborhood business; Danica Patrick's move to NASCAR; the discontinuation of Concorde flights. For the first few days I struggled to insert a phrase or detail into the monologue that would resonate with what the Teen told me about the visitor, but I soon figured out that it was better to let such a link emerge spontaneously, as it would seem to the visitor, at some later point in the conversation. I was especially keen to create a kind of Brechtian estrangement at the top of the ramp; I looked for a moment to conclude that left something in the conversation unresolved, using the handshake with the visitor and the turn toward the door as a sudden, unexplained punctuation of our encounter.

This Progress is unscripted but highly choreographed. I realized over the six weeks how thoroughly Sehgal's early training as a dancer, including his association with the brilliant experimental dancer and choreographer Xavier Le Roy, shapes his approach to the creation of what he calls "situations." He rejects the label of performance art. *This Progress* is an original collation of happening, conceptual art, and theatrical estrangement effects, all resting upon a web of carefully choreographed movements—strolling, ascending, encountering, gesturing ("after you"), vanishing, intercepting, shaking hands, exiting—that create the shelter within which spontaneous conversations with strangers can occur. One day during a lull in the procession of visitors, Sehgal chatted with me about my prosthetic right arm; ever the choreographer, he had been observing how I shook the visitor's hand at the end of the piece: I extended my left hand, rolling it 180 degrees thumb down, in order to meet the other's outstretched right hand as seamlessly and inconspicuously as possible—an artifice to effect naturalness. He had studied this gesture and had been using it himself.

One colleague among the Older Adults always entered on the ground floor before his shift and went through the piece, experiencing it as a visitor, albeit an initiated and well-informed one. He thus had conversations with dozens of the Interpreters. I never went through the piece at all; every morning I took the staff elevator, reviewed my monologues in my head, and got ready to be an Older Adult. I didn't really understand my reluctance to experience the show at first, but eventually I realized that I was inexplicably hewing to my decidedly limited perspective on the work. I began to reflect on the fact that such limitation was an integral dimension of the work itself. Visitors were never privy to the orchestration of the Interpreters' appearances, disappearances, and surveillance. The visitor might well have an engaging, even personable series of conversations without ever knowing quite what was happening. The gaps in awareness were part of the effect. When a friend told me she had gone through the piece, I explained the Older Adults' role in intercepting visitors, prepped with information about them and their talk. She astutely observed, "So, you are the special effects!" The Interpreters themselves had only partial views. We never heard one another's conversations: Younger Adults trailing the Teens overheard fragments, the breathless Teens hurried through their reports to the Older Adults. The view from each of the staging areas was unique, and none of them offered a complete view of a visitor's entire journey up the gyre. No two conversations were ever the same. Even the view of strollers and dancers that I so relished from my perch did not necessarily attract or come into focus for others. There was no way for even the artist to take it all in at once, even though Tino Sehgal was there every day watching things unfold, making suggestions and adjustments, stealthily following an Interpreter to listen to the conversation, keeping an eye out for special visitors, monitoring the pace to avoid delays and logjams.

It undoubtedly would have been possible to record, even in real time, all the moments of *This Progress*—say, one visitor's trip through the piece as well as all the behind-the-scenes activities and special effects—with several cameras, well-placed microphones, and some nifty editing. But Sehgal disdains any such effort. His reasons are grounded in his aspiration to make art that manifests artistic creativity and aesthetic responsiveness without introducing yet another material object into the world. Moreover, the recording would only transmute the piece; it would not preserve it. A record of all the moments would still not grasp the work as a whole because the work never appears as a whole. By *a whole* I do not imply any particular conception of wholeness as unity, organicity, or totality. At issue, rather, is that no two individuals ever experience the same work. There lies the stake for aesthetic theory of *This Progress*. Being an Interpreter was an immensely engaging and gratifying experience, memories of which remain more vivid than anything else I did during those weeks. But I also came away with a kind of unease, difficult to pinpoint at first, except that something about the work lay athwart my own attempt to understand it even though I participated in it. My own critical habits and vocation encountered—or were themselves—a stumbling block. For what *This Progress* does not afford is any shared relation to it. It interrupts the urge to persuade because no two people are responding to the same thing. An exchange among Interpreters or among visitors or between Interpreter and visitor would amount to nothing other than comparing notes. It is easy to imagine an Adornoesque fulmination against such a fragmentation of aesthetic response into isolated subjective monads. But such a critique would completely miss the mark.

For me, *This Progress* makes one feel the fading away of the conditions of aesthetic judgment in the midst of an aesthetic experience. That is why the account I have just given of *This Progress* is not criticism. My attunement to the work and my analysis of it do not give rise to an appeal for everyone else's agreement. Perceptive critics who went through the work in previews or at the opening produced narratives without any claim that invited agreement or disagreement. One could differ from them, but not with them. Holland Cotter in the *New York Times* describes his encounters with the Interpreters, whose topics included scientific speculations on the color of dinosaurs and the strong strain of nostalgia for communism among Bulgarians, and concludes: "'This Progress' was awkward, rambling, indeterminate, peppered with doubt and ambiguity. (Why, I began to wonder as I walked and talked and listened, had I answered Giuliana's question as I did? What would I say if I were asked again?) Still, at the end, after Bob had disappeared, I felt stirred up, but light and refreshed, the way I sometimes—but not that often—do when I feel that I've met art in some very bare-bones way. It really is about life. It really is about communication. It really does have no answers. And it really is addictive. I was primed to go back for more." Gillian Sneed, writing for *Art in America*, mapped the generational sequence of Interpreters from Child to Older Adult in relation to her image of herself: "A child invites you to participate, and the themes it touches on are universal and accessible to everyone. It is a thoroughly thought-provoking experience to meditate on the meaning of life and to reflect on your own past and future. As a woman of 30, I was aware of my shifting roles as I progressed along the ramp. I transitioned from a protective caretaker to a mentor to a protégée in the matter of 10 minutes. I also really enjoyed the discussions I shared with these people, and the metaphorical mirror the experience provided on my own life span." And Peter Schjeldahl's review in the *New Yorker* captured with characteristic acumen and wit the essence of one kind of experience of the piece: "I arrived at the top of the building with no clear sense of how I got there. So I did it again, with different interlocutors but the same result. Now I'm remembering the encounters as a collection of short stories, of which I am the bumbling protagonist. They continue to unfold, endlessly."[55] Each testimony is valid in itself and makes no appeal to others' agreement.

The death of criticism? Killed by art itself? I don't think so. Nor do I think that the dematerialization and ephemerality enacted by *This Progress* are best understood as a paradigm shift, as though they negated or rendered obsolete a preceding paradigm. Tino Sehgal's work is, rather, the exploration of a limit experience; it marks and crosses the boundary that distinguishes and joins art and aesthetic judgment. It plunges responsiveness into a boundary experience where the conditions of aesthetic judgment drop from under aesthetic receptivity itself. It makes palpable the fading of the urge to persuade. The work is not formless; on the contrary, it limns the edge between art and judgment.

Rineke Dijkstra, or, Criticism's Inner Edge

To Sehgal's artistic rendering of the limit at which the conditions of criticism dissolve I want now to juxtapose a work by Rineke Dijkstra that artistically renders the preconditions of criticism, the precritical or protocritical fount of criticism. Dijkstra's photography and video art often deals with the experiences of adolescents and children, and *I See a Woman Crying* (*Weeping Woman*; 2009), fixes its cameras on a group of schoolchildren who are looking at Picasso's 1937 painting *The Weeping Woman* at the Tate Liverpool. I first saw the video at the Marian Goodman Gallery in New York in the summer of 2010, the experience of *This Progress* still at the forefront of my experience of new art. The work is described as a "3-channel HD video installation, duration: 12 minutes."[56] The viewer does not see the painting, as one camera is effectively in the position of the painting, though just above the children's line of sight, and the other two are just slightly to the left and right. The three video screens are in synch with one another, and their images often overlap at the edges; the cameras pan in and out, side to side, in different rhythms. It plays as though it unfolds entirely in real time, though that could be an illusion of the editing. The result is a three-screen panorama of the nine pre-teens, six boys and three girls; two girls stand at either end of the group and the third stands in the middle behind the boys, four of whom are sitting very close together and often lean an arm on the shoulder to their right. Freshly scrubbed, alert, and serious, the boys and girls, all of whom are white, are dressed in a school uniform of white shirt, gray sweater, and red tie. The background is an empty white wall. The boys have crewcuts or neatly trimmed, slightly tousled hair; a few stray hairs escape the girls' tightly pulled ponytails and pigtails.

The children look at the painting and are oblivious to the cameras, which are presumably inconspicuous, perhaps unseen; conversely, the video's viewer watches the kids looking at the unseen painting. Our eyes are on their eyes on the painting. The commanding presence of the painting as the center of their attention is intensified by its onscreen absence. The video itself is filled by the children's voices, eyes, facial expressions ranging from curiosity and wonderment to worry and empathy, and constant minuscule shifts of posture, shrugs, shivers, and signs of affection. In the nearly twelve minutes of dialogue the kids talk only among themselves; occasionally an off-camera voice is heard, the tonality and timbre that of a woman, that may be giving brief prompts to keep the kids talking as they occasionally respond by glancing to their right; yet they never address anyone but themselves, their eyes fixed on the painting. Their multivocal chorus begins with what they see:

—I can see a woman crying and loads of different shapes.
—I see a woman with part of a mouth, a chin, and around the mouth there's fingers.
—I can see the hair in different colors.
—I can see a woman expressing different things with all different colors.
—There's loads of different colors in different parts of the picture.
—I can see different colors, shapes, and feelings in the picture.
—I can see lots of bright colors.
—I can see all shapes to make parts of a face.
—It looks like she's in the house and that—
—I can see all triangles, like, but it's making the face look sad.
—I can see, like, parts of the bottom half of the face, it's a bit like a mirror, all blue and white.
—I can see patterns on . . . that looks like a T-shirt.
—It looks like she's coming out of the house of [or?] under it.
—Looks like a man's face a bit.
—Looks like women's accessories.
—It does a bit.

When talk turns to the figure's state-of-mind and the reasons for it, the kids speculate across an array of emotional states: *worried, lonely, scared, frightened, horrified, petrified, sad.* "Looks like she's seen something she'd never wanna see again," or perhaps she is mourning the loss of "her best friend" or "husband" or has done something wrong and "regrets" it or "was abandoned when she was a child or something" or is ostracized "because she is the only person she knows who looks like that" or because "she has money and no one wants to be her friend." Maybe "she's seen a ghost." Or "is a ghost" or "the living dead." "She's done something wrong." "No one likes her"; "she could just be sad about life." "She might have got thrown out of her house." "Or her partner left her or something." "Her mum could have passed away." They speculate that she is waiting for someone—"her husband's just come home, like from war"—or has just been to a funeral or a wedding. One particular affecting exchange between two of the boys brings out giggles in the group:

—It's like she went to a wedding and then she got lonely.
—Or she went to the wedding and, like, she's done something wrong, like stole the cake or something.

The speculations freely associate with one another as the kids vary or amplify or reverse one another's ideas. They consistently come back to details of the painting. The group at one point erupts into naming the colors of her hat, *pink, purple, orange, blue*. In the midst of the discussion of her sadness, one boy—who seems to be the youngest and whose face constricts in worry the more intently he looks at the picture—points out, "There are tears coming out of her eyes just where the triangle starts."

References to money, war, wrongdoing, stepmothers, housing, rejection and regret, weddings and funerals, hint at the experiences, fantasies, and anxieties that the children themselves draw on or project in trying to comprehend the painting. One girl who is generally quiet but always attentive breaks into the speculations with a complete scenario: "Maybe someone died of her family and she has seen them dying and just ran to them and she was crying because she loves her family."

Art consciousness flares among them the one time the artist is mentioned. One of the boys has a thought that would render all their speculations moot: "Maybe Picasso just wanted to do a colorful picture what is different from most pictures." This thought is immediately dropped when someone counters, "Unless it was based on a real person, and he drew, like, that was how they would feel inside." The thought that there might be a real person known to the artist behind the figure of the Weeping Woman turns the group, including the boy who suggested pure coloration as possibly the painter's motive, back to talking about feeling and the idea that Picasso "paints how people feel"—how "they might feel inside"—"That could have been his friend and his friend had a bad moment." When nearly ten minutes of concentrated effort have not yielded a consensus or decision, a blast of preteen cacophony breaks out; the Weeping Woman might be "mental" or "scared of the devil," or "she saw a horror film" or is actually crying "tears of happiness," perhaps "because someone bought her a sports car." After several references to the "tissue" she seems to hold up to her face, they speculate it might be something else—a "love letter," says a girl; "a bill she can't pay," says a boy.

The painting holds the group's attention for ten intense minutes. The untutored substratum at the core of all aesthetic experience is manifest in their free associations, projections, oscillations between form and representation and emotion, imaginings of a backstory—all of it engaging their own inchoate unarticulated experiences and anxieties, fantasies and desires. They are a chorus of what might go through anyone's head looking steadily at *The Weeping Woman*. There is a naïve viewer or naïve reader at the bottom of every critic or theorist, identifying with the hero or heroine, taking every narrated moment as real, worrying about the fate of the characters and dreading the possible outcomes, enamored of happy endings and awed at tragic ones. Without such surrender and without the sort of unbridled curiosity exhibited by Dijkstra's kids, there cannot be aesthetic judgment and criticism. And yet naïveté and curiosity do not amount to judgment and criticism. Rather, they are its precondition.

Dijkstra's achievement in this installation is twofold. The video discloses in the fluid yet fragmented talk among schoolchildren the experiential fount of aesthetic experience, and it dramatizes how the source of that experience is rapt attention to a unique artwork. Subjective fount, objective source. And yet the source is absent from the video, and the fount does not arrive at judgment and criticism. Dijkstra discloses without representing the conditions of aesthetic judgment and criticism. The theoretical allegory that I have developed in juxtaposing *This Progress* and *I See a Woman Crying* can be taken as the polarity between the disappearance of the conditions of criticism and the emergence of the conditions of criticism. True but insufficient, for *This Progress* also discloses without representing. It does not abolish aesthetic judgment; rather, it discloses—renders sensible—the vanishing point of aesthetic judgment. Like Sehgal's work, Dijkstra's is a limit experience. His manifests the dissolution of what is shown arising in hers. In keeping with Heidegger, these are artworks in that they disclose something other than what they represent; the truth they disclose is, in keeping with Kant, the truth of aesthetic judgment: shared object and urge to persuade.

Nietzschean Creativity

The constellation of artwork–publicness–criticism is vulnerable to conceptual undermining in modern thought itself, which brings us back to Heidegger's Nietzsche commentary. Since Heidegger eschews that aspect of the judgment *this is beautiful* by which the appeal for agreement esteems "the

worth of others," he must relocate what Kant calls "ennoblement and elevation" and what he himself calls the "honorable and worthy." Seeking a locale
other than the public realm in its liberal manifestation, he displaces the Kantian site of judgment in favor of what Nietzsche, in scattered remarks, calls
the "grand style." The grand style becomes the site of ennoblement, elevation,
the honorable, and the worthy. Heidegger's appropriation of the term distorts,
I will argue, its actual place in Nietzsche's aesthetic theory and obscures other
avenues that his reflections open for thinking about art and aesthetic judgment. While Nietzsche himself is of course contemptuous of the liberal public
sphere, the configuration in which the grand style plays a part exceeds the use
Heidegger makes of it.

The concept of grand style marks for Nietzsche an aspiration, a value that
artists approach rather than reach and the apprehension of which requires
an attitude he expresses with typical faux-virile bluster in *Will to Power* 842:

> The greatness of an artist cannot be measured by the "beautiful feelings" he
> arouses: leave that idea to the females. But according to the degree to which
> he approaches the grand style, to which he is capable of the grand style. This
> style has this in common with great passion, that it disdains to please; that it
> forgets to persuade; that it commands; that it *wills*—To become master of the
> chaos one is: to compel one's chaos to become form: to become logical, simple,
> unambiguous, mathematics, *law*—that is the grand ambition here.[57]

Heidegger picks up the language of command and law and carries it from
artworks to humankind's historical destiny in a manner familiar from "The
Origin of the Work of Art": "The word 'art' does not designate the concept
of a mere eventuality; it is a concept of rank." Demoting the public sphere to
entertainment and pastime, he in turn inflates art's destiny-deciding power:
"Art is not just one among a number of items, activities one engages in and
enjoys now and then; art places the whole of Dasein in decision and keeps it
there."[58]

The grand style presupposes "a classical taste," according to Nietzsche,
who proposes "to think through, without prejudice or indulgence, in what
soil a classical taste can grow. Hardening, simplification, strengthening, making
man more evil: these belong together."[59] Heidegger extrapolates that "the grand
style and wickedness belong together, emblematic of the flagrant contradictions in Dasein."[60] Mastering the chaos that one is cannot be mere orderli-
ness but must fuse contradictions into an artistic whole; strife must become
form. Heidegger turns the sense of this in a direction that does not necessarily exhaust or even grasp Nietzsche's meaning, for he wants the physiological
language of sensation, muscular automatism, *Rausch*, and the like to dissolve

into the other Nietzschean theme of art as a countermovement to nihilism. Rather than illuminating strife-becoming-form, Heidegger infuses art with the politically charged attributes of rank, distinction, standard, decision, measure, and law:

> Physiology of art apparently takes its object to be a process of nature that bubbles to the surface in the manner of an eruptive state of rapture. Such a state would evanesce without deciding anything, since nature knows no realm of decision.
>
> But art as countermovement to nihilism is to lay the groundwork for establishment of new standards and values; it is therefore to be rank, distinction, and decision. If art has its proper essence in the grand style, this now means that measure and law are confirmed only in the subjugation and containment of chaos and the rapturous.[61]

I question whether Nietzsche's mastering the chaos one is and strife-becoming-form are to be understood as "the subjugation and containment of chaos and the rapturous." That question will continue to crop up. It has already emerged in the incongruity in Heidegger's earth/world conception, which sees *physis* rise up and hold itself back within the artwork but does not count the body, sentience, or sensation as *physis*. In the passage just cited, the bodily aspect of *physis*, that is, the "process of nature," gets acknowledged, but only as what is to be constrained and subjugated by art. Followed to its logical conclusion, such a conception would efface Heidegger's own productive idea of the artwork as a rift of earth and world.

The discussion of the grand style is part of Nietzsche's revaluation—that is, devaluation—of Wagner, whose work he now labels Romantic in opposition to what he calls "classical." The classical points toward the grand style but does not fully constitute it. To sort out his scheme, which is at once classificatory and evaluative, Nietzsche distinguishes the classical from the Romantic in terms of the "antithesis active and reactive" that underlies them, but that opposition is further complicated by another: "I ask in each individual case 'has hunger or superabundance become creative here?' At first sight, another distinction might seem more plausible—it is far more obvious—namely the distinction whether the desire for rigidity, eternity, '*being*' has been the cause of creation, or rather the desire for destruction, for change, for *becoming*."[62]

There are consequently four distinct sources or logics of creativity. The desire for becoming can be active or reactive: "The desire for destruction, change, becoming *can* be the expression of an overall power pregnant with the future (my term for this, as is known, is the word 'Dionysian')," whereas the reactive desire for destruction is what he elsewhere calls *ressentiment* and here "hatred" on the part of "the ill-constituted, disinherited, underprivileged, which destroys, *has* to destroy, because what exists, indeed existence itself, all being itself, enrages and provokes it." At one pole, then, the Dionysian, and at the other, the nihilist, in the common nineteenth-century sense of the one who destroys for no purpose but destruction, a figure that Nietzsche, in his conservative reaction to the rise of the masses in politics and society, frequently identifies as an anarchist or a socialist. The desire for being or "'eternalization' . . . *can* proceed from gratitude and love—an art of this origin will always be an art of apotheosis, dithyrambic perhaps with Rubens, blissful with Hafiz, bright and gracious with Goethe, and shedding a Homeric aureole over all things." He also includes Raphael in this grouping of the classical. At the other, reactive pole of the desire for being is "Romantic pessimism," exemplified by Wagnerian music: "The tyrannic will of a great sufferer who would like to forge what is most personal, individual, and narrow—most idiosyncratic—in his suffering, into a binding *law* and compulsion, taking revenge on all things, as it were, by impressing, forcing, and branding into them his image, the image of his torture."[63] A positive value is placed on the desire for being and the desire for becoming in each's active form—the classical and the Dionysian—while their reactive forms as *ressentiment* and Romantic pessimism evoke Nietzsche's scorn and epitomize the life-denying impulses by which he defines "European nihilism."

The various polarities—Romantic and classical, being and becoming, active and reactive—sort out into a kind of grid (see fig. 4). There is significant asymmetry and incompleteness in the grid. The active desire for being is attributed not only to Goethe but also to a fourteenth-century Persian poet, an Italian Renaissance architect and painter favored by the Vatican, and a seventeenth-century Flemish baroque painter (all of whom are said to partake of a Homeric aureole), whereas all the exemplars of Romantic pessimism and its reactive desire for being are among Nietzsche's contemporaries: Wagner, Hugo, Zola, Taine. The classification in effect expresses Nietzsche's revolt against his own century, against which he pits writers and artists from the previous five centuries. Meanwhile, the slots on the grid for the Dionysian and *ressentiment* are left without examples, the former reserved perhaps for the ancient Greek namesake and the latter left indistinct, as though *ressentiment* were scarcely capable of creativity.

Is this systematic grid or "schema," as Nietzsche calls it, actually systematic? The fact that the classical hints at the grand style but does not constitute it suggests that the vaunted grand style would truly require a synthesis of

	active (+)	**reactive (-)**
becoming:	Dionysian	*ressentiment*
being:	classical	romantic pessimism
	(Raphael, Rubens, Hafiz, Goethe)	(Wagner)

FIGURE 4. Nietzsche's creativity grid

becoming and being, each in its active rather than reactive mode. Nietzsche does not identify any contemporary example except, as we will see, himself and his Zarathustra. Such a synthesis does, however, recall the early Nietzsche's account of Greek tragedy as the fusing of the antagonistic artistic impulses, the Dionysian and Apollonian. In *The Birth of Tragedy* (1872) Wagner's music and theater reclaim and revive this Dionysian-Apollonian synthesis, but in Nietzsche's notebooks and completed works of 1886–88 Wagner has come to embody the very opposite of Greek tragedy and the spirit of music.

In the 1886 preface to the reissue of *The Birth of Tragedy*, titled "Attempt at Self-Criticism," Nietzsche slyly defends his entire conceptualization of Greek tragedy but condemns himself for having taken "the latest German music" as the basis on which "to rave about 'the German spirit' as if that were in the process even then of discovering and finding itself again"; he now realizes he had "appended hopes where there was no ground for hope, where everything pointed all too plainly to an end!"[64] He mocks a passage in which he had asked of a "coming generation," "*would it not be necessary* for the tragic man of such a culture . . . to desire a new art, the *art of metaphysical comfort*?" He now repudiates the idea of metaphysical comfort, associating it with Romantics, Wagner, and Christians, and instead extols "the art of *this-worldly* comfort" and urges his "young friends" to hear the call to laughter and dancing "in the language of that Dionysian monster who bears the name of Zarathustra."[65] So now *Thus Spoke Zarathustra* stands as the reclamation of the Greek tragic experience and harbinger of a future rid of romanticism and Christianity. Where Wagner was, there shall Zarathustra be.

The substitution of his Zarathustra for Wagner recurs in *Ecce Homo*, the 1888 work in which Nietzsche reviews the entire career of his thought and writing and whose title appropriates as a reference to himself the phrase used by Pontius Pilate to present Jesus, scourged and mockingly crowned in thorns and robed in purple (John 19:5), to the crowd. Nietzsche takes a retrospective look at his 1876 essay "Richard Wagner in Bayreuth," the fourth of the

Untimely Meditations, where he still associated Wagner with the Dionysian and tragic art of the future, and now revamps its referent:

> A psychologist might still add that what I heard as a young man listening to Wagnerian music really had nothing to with Wagner; that when I described Dionysian music I described what *I* had heard—that instinctively I had to transpose and transfigure everything into the new spirit that I carried in me. The proof of that, *as strong as any proof can be*, is my essay *Wagner in Bayreuth*: in all the psychologically decisive places I alone am discussed—and one need not hesitate to put down my name or the word "Zarathustra" where the text has the word "Wagner."[66]

Nietzsche so completely occupies the territory over which he once thought Wagner ruled that everything meaningful in the early essay, he now says, was but a veiled reference to himself. And to the work he would not compose until more than six years later: "This is the strangest 'objectivity' possible: the absolute certainty about what I am was projected upon some accidental reality"—that is, Richard Wagner and his music—"the truth about me spoke from some gruesome depth." The *"style of Zarathustra,"* he now asserts, "is described with incisive certainty and anticipated" in one section of the essay, and "the *event of Zarathustra*, the act of a tremendous purification and consecration of humanity" finds "magnificent expression" in another.[67]

The paroxysms of self-aggrandizement dramatized by the titles *Ecce Homo* and *The Antichrist*, the last works that Nietzsche wrote within months and weeks of his irreversible, brain-ravaged mental collapse on January 3, 1889, touch on what he had long taken to be his mission of countering Christianity's hostility to life. In *Ecce Homo* he writes of *The Birth of Tragedy*: "A tremendous hope speaks out of this essay. In the end I lack all reason to renounce the hope for a Dionysian future of music. Let us look ahead a century; let us suppose that my attempt to assassinate two millennia of antinature and desecration of man were to succeed. . . . The attempt to raise humanity higher, including the relentless destruction of everything that was degenerating and parasitical, would again make possible that excess of life on earth from which the Dionysian state, too, would have to awaken again."[68] Even the most partisan Nietzschean has to acknowledge that well over a century has passed without the prophecy being fulfilled or its projected horizon coming any closer; Nietzsche's epochal thinking invites a Nietzschean refutation: "If the motion of the world aimed at a final state, that state would have been reached" (*Will to Power* 708).[69]

Peter Sloterdijk offers an intriguing interpretation of Nietzsche's rhetorical dilations of the self as a decisive transformation of eulogy in Western culture:

"The author of *Zarathustra* wanted to lay bare the eulogistic force of language from the ground up, and to free it from the inhibitions with which sentiment, itself coded by metaphysics, had stamped it."[70] A praise song that overcomes group narcissism (the herd), God's narcissism (medieval Christianity), and the narcissism of nineteenth-century *ressentiment* is, then, a eulogy of this life and of this world only insofar as it eulogizes oneself. Sloterdijk quotes a cascade of self-affirming, self-aggrandizing passages from *Ecce Homo*, passages that readers typically try to buffer as they read them. For example: "It is all over with all 'darkling aspiration'; precisely the *good* man was least aware of the right way.—And in all seriousness: nobody before me knew the right way, the way *up*; it is only beginning with me that there are hopes again, tasks, ways that can be prescribed for culture—*I am he that brings these glad tidings.*—And thus also I am a destiny."[71] Is this language pure naked narcissism, even psychosis? Is this gesture of radical individuality simple megalomania? Sloterdijk answers, No. I extrapolate two implications from Sloterdijk's reading. First, the practice of eulogy beyond herd–God–*ressentiment* must be a song of myself, and, second, the Nietzschean poetic is one in which, in keeping with the modernist aesthetic, the poet disappears in the poem. To use Anglo-American criticism's familiar term, Nietzschean megalomania is *impersonal*. The extreme of self-assertion lies in the poetics of impersonality. Nietzsche himself describes the experience of self-eulogizing creation as self-abandonment and loss of self, as in the following passage, which Sloterdijk does not cite but which supports his reading: "Everything great—a work, a deed—is no sooner accomplished than it turns *against* the man who did it. By doing it, he has become *weak*; he no longer endures his deed, he can no longer face it. Something one was never permitted to will lies *behind* one, something in which the knot in the destiny of humanity is tied—and now one labors *under* it!—It almost crushes one."[72]

In the essays and books Nietzsche completed during the period of the notes on the grand style in *The Will to Power*, the art he hopes for, prophesies, and claims to exemplify in the figure of Zarathustra is cast as more Dionysian than classical. That reinforces the sense not only that the grand style is a pure aspiration prefigured in a discontinuous heritage to which Nietzsche's own sensibility is attuned (Hafiz, Raphael, Rubens, Goethe), but also that the grand style itself would be not the extension of the classical, as Heidegger supposes, but rather the (impossible) synthesis of the classical and the Dionysian, that is, of the Apollonian and the Dionysian, as he originally postulated in *The Birth of Tragedy*: a creativity that is at once an active desire for being and an active desire for becoming. *Twilight of the Idols*, also from 1888, revives these terms and despite nuanced changes continues to conceive them "as kinds of frenzy" that are associated with distinct artistic processes: "The Apollonian frenzy excites the eye above all, so that it gains the power of vision. The painter, the sculptor, the epic poet are visionaries par excellence. In the Dionysian state, on the other hand, the whole affective system is excited and enhanced: so that it discharges all its means of expression at once and drives forth simultaneously the power of representation, imitation, transfiguration, transformation, and every kind of mimicking and acting. . . . The Dionysian type . . . does not overlook any sign of an affect. . . . He enters into any skin, into any affect: he constantly transforms himself."[73] Nietzsche also retains the ideal of the *Gesamtkunstwerk* he got from Wagner and associated with Greek tragedy, and therefore he laments the modern separation of the arts, such that music retains "a mere residue of the Dionysian histrionicism" and loses altogether "the muscle sense" of dance, "so that man no longer bodily imitates and represents everything he feels."[74]

Taking stock of these late writings as well as the notes in *The Will to Power*, what conclusions can be drawn regarding the grand style and the Dionysian/Apollonian sources of art?

The four corners of the being-becoming/active-reactive grid turn out not to be fixed or even stable categories. As Nietzsche reaffirms the Dionysian and Apollonian as the two sources of creativity, he does not—indeed, could not—privilege the one over the other. In that sense, and contrary to Heidegger's reading, the classical is not in itself the basis of the grand style. Nietzsche's earliest intuition that the Dionysian-Apollonian fusion was responsible for the greatness of Greek tragedy remains his aspiration for modern art and the guide for his own thought. The aspiration and guide are, however, tormented and tormenting. If, for example, Nietzsche's indictment of Wagner as Romantic pessimist—"the tyrannic will of a great sufferer who would like to forge what is most personal, individual, and narrow—most idiosyncratic—in his suffering, into a binding *law* and compulsion, taking revenge on all things, as it were, by impressing, forcing, and branding into them his image, the image of his torture"[75]—is reread in light of Nietzsche's hatred of Christianity and repulsion at his own era and culture, not to mention the still unfulfilled prophecy of his own song of myself, the indictment could apply to Nietzsche himself: Romantic pessimist and vengeful imaginary tyrant.

Nietzsche's thought is inseparable from the pathos of his thinking, that is, from the sufferings of his life of the mind and the sufferings of the life of *his* mind. That's true for everyone, no doubt, but Nietzsche's expression and display of it are unmatched in the history of philosophy, with the possible exception of Pascal. It is what makes him so adept at entering into the skin of other thinkers and writers. And what makes his criticisms so venomous:

when he spits venom, he is spitting out himself. Human venom, unlike the spider's or snake's, poisons the producer, and so the need to expel it is not the animal-rational need to defend oneself but the human-irrational need to defend against oneself. Nietzsche's migraines, intestinal disorders, and convulsive vomiting were indeed a kind of gruesome source of truth.

And one truth that comes through is that the Apollonian and Dionysian or even the apparently sheer opposition of active and reactive marks not an absolute separation but an edge, or fold, that can slant one way or the other, tilt from one into the other, as in the marvelous passage on polytheism in *The Gay Science* (§143):

> *The greatest advantage of polytheism*—For an individual to posit his own ideal and to derive from it his own law, joys, and rights—that may well have been considered hitherto as the most outrageous human aberration and as idolatry itself. The few who dared as much always felt the need to apologize to themselves, usually by saying: "It wasn't I! Not I! But *a god* through me." The wonderful art and gift of creating gods—polytheism—was the medium through which this impulse could discharge, purify, perfect, and ennoble itself; for originally it was a very undistinguished impulse, related to stubbornness, disobedience, and envy.[76]

The Apollonian power to posit an ideal and "derive from it [one's] own law, joys, and rights" is the very capacity that Nietzsche craves, yet it is itself but a transmutation of the "reactive" impulses of "stubbornness, disobedience, and envy," all of which are affects belonging to *ressentiment*. In the same vein, Nietzsche does not consistently condemn those artworks that arise from the reactive as opposed to active desire for being or becoming. In the fragments he compiled into *Nietzsche contra Wagner* (1888), largely from previous writings, he contrasts Goethe and Flaubert on the active-reactive polarity: "Is it the *hatred* against life or the *excess* of life which has become creative?" Even as he categorizes Flaubert as one for whom hatred became creative, it is by no means clear that he simply condemns or rejects his work and its aesthetic:

> Flaubert—a new edition of Pascal, but as an artist, with the instinctive judgment deep down: "*Flaubert est toujours haïssable, l'homme n'est rien, l'oeuvre est tout*."* He tortured himself when he wrote, just as Pascal tortured himself when he thought; they were both unegoistic. "Selflessness"—the principle of decadence, the will to the end, in art as well as in morals.
>
> *"Flaubert is always hateful; the man is nothing, the work is all."[77]

Nietzsche had read Flaubert's correspondence as well as the novels, whose psychological acuity he elsewhere affirms. Rather than condemnation the emphasis above falls on the pathos of the decision for art at the expense of life. That permutation of life denial surely haunted Nietzsche himself—after all, he shares many of Flaubert's hatreds. His own writings projected in Zarathustra a figure quite unlike himself and a life unlike his own. *Zarathustra, c'est pas moi.* As for Pascal, the one who asserted "le moi est haïssable," he arouses in Nietzsche a subtle brew of empathy, irony, reverence, and horror: "I do not read but *love* Pascal, as the most instructive victim of Christianity . . . the whole logic of this most gruesome form of inhuman cruelty."[78]

The four corners of the grid of creativity—classical, Dionysian, Romantic pessimism, *ressentiment*—are forces not positions, and they contend with one another, can combine with one another, can transmute one into the other. Each is a bundle of motives and affects, all of which counts further against Heidegger's tendency to see the extension of the classical into the grand style as a kind of hyper-Apollonian sovereignty (the "unconstrained disposition over" the "yoke" of "chaos and law") and as the essence of art as such ("wherever the grand style prevails, there art in the purity of its essential plenitude is actual").[79] Nietzsche in effect advances a more pluralistic view, even as he posits the grand style as his own ideal and guide. For, on the one hand, the Dionysian-Apollonian fusion will ever be aspiration and strife. And, on the other hand, all four sources of creativity do produce art; the valuing of the grand style does not make it the essence or purity of art, and even as Nietzsche asserts and affirms that value he wavers between its Apollonian and its Dionysian aspect. What the four-cornered grid ultimately suggests, then, is that any artist's work is to be viewed in light of the affects and motives that *become* creative in its making; the becoming-creative is what counts as decision, neither in the mundane sense of a choice between equally available alternatives nor in the grandiose sense of collective destiny, but as the welling up into artistic form of the active *or* the reactive desire for becoming *or* for being. Such creative welling up is the *Rausch* (frenzy, rapture, intoxication) that Nietzsche calls "the state that creates art" (*Will to Power* 821)[80] and that so troubles Heidegger that it must be deeroticized, *aufhebt* by form in the grand style, and thus dissolved into rank and law.

Recognizing that all four corners of the grid are modes of creativity and that therefore the classical, the Apollonian, and the grand style are not the essence or origin of art, a new question arises. What is the basis of the four-cornered grid? What is the foundation on which the active and reactive desires for being and becoming arise? Strictly speaking, Nothing. In the language of Vattimo's and Rorty's antifoundationalism, reality or being has no transcendent cause, purpose, or direction. This is nihilism in the sense of the condition of modernity. No supreme value holds society together;

individuals and collectives are not provided unquestionably binding rules
and goals. Nietzsche seeks to interpret this condition affirmatively: it enables
genuine freedom and the positing of ideals. Over against this affirmation are
the devaluing of existence and laments of the loss of meaning, the response
that defines the actual state of "European nihilism" in the sense of the denial
of life, whether in blind destructiveness (the nihilism of the anarchist) or in
hope of otherworldly salvation (the nihilism of Christianity). These Nietzschean archetypes of the anarchist and the Christian revolt against the very
freedom and responsibility to create meaning that the inherent lack of meaning affords.

As Nietzsche condemns Christianity's "hostility to life," his counterasser-
tion on behalf of art—which Christianity "with its absolute standards, beginning with the truthfulness of God, negates, judges, and damns"—unwittingly
describes nothing quite so well as the modern novel: "For all of life is based
on semblance, art, perception, points of view, and the necessity of perspective
and error."[81] That is just the sort of formulation that sends up denunciatory
shouts of "relativism," as though that were an intractable evil, on the part
of—how else to call them?—normativists. The lack of a novelistic ear is something that Habermasians peculiarly share with Nietzsche and Heidegger. For
the former, the novel is a stumbling block because it is, as Milan Kundera
says of Salman Rushdie's *The Satanic Verses*, "an immense *carnival of rela-
tivity*" in which "no one is right and no one is entirely wrong," and because
more generally "novelistic characters develop" only on "the imaginary terrain
where moral judgment is suspended."[82] The novel confronts Nietzsche and
Heidegger with the problem of publicness that dogs their respective denunci-
ations and appropriations of Kant. The novel shares with the art of criticism a
tacit but formative affirmation of the reading public: the novel seeks to bring
the writer's deepest aesthetic and intellectual probings to the widest possible
readership; criticism ventures the critic's most sensitive attunements and
strongest interpretations to woo everyone else.[83] That's the Kantian moment.
The Nietzschean moment lies in the fact that the novelist and the critic feel in
their bones that no norms, substantive or formal or procedural, are given in
the domain of art. That's why Arendt could take aesthetic judgment as a surer
guide to the political than the normativity of the categorical imperative. The
correlative of this understanding of judgment, political or aesthetic, is the
recognition of its fragility, that is, the fragility of the institutions, practices,
and will needed to sustain it.

Nietzsche and Heidegger stand together in their repudiation of the public
realm in its liberal and protodemocratic determination and so eschew the
urge to persuade in aesthetic judgment. Heidegger stands against Nietzsche

in recuperating Kantian disinterestedness as unconstrained favoring on a par with "the thrill that comes of being in our world now," but he overlooks the plurality that the Nietzschean grid of creativity suggests and wipes the favoring and the thrill clean of any erotic—indeed, sensuous—reverberation.

A new potential cross-fertilization of Nietzschean and Heideggerian perspectives opens up, however, with regard to the ungroundedness of the grid of creativity and the notion that the bundle of affects and motives that become creative arises from nothing. How Dasein encounters the nothing is the focus of Heidegger's renewed reflection on *Angst* after *Being and Time*. "Anxiety makes manifest the nothing. . . . The nothing unveils itself in anxiety—but not as a being."[84] This is to suggest that *Angst*, which experientially drains motive and stifles creativity, is at the same time the groundless ground from which creativity arises. The cross-fertilization leaves neither philosopher's view completely intact. Heidegger questions Nietzsche's exclusive focus on the artist's creative impulses and processes for failing to address the nature and role of the artwork itself. Nietzsche's *Rausch* is, in Heidegger's felicitous paraphrase, the "form-engendering force" of the aesthetic state, but the form that this force engenders is then neglected. By the same token, Heidegger's own conception of form is elusive and remains largely indiscernible in his commentaries on actual artworks and poems. Heidegger also questions the conception of truth by which Nietzsche posits, in another apt paraphrase, the "raging discordance between art and truth," for missing the way in which art is, in Heidegger's own view, "the becoming and happening *of* truth."[85] Yet Heidegger's notion that the artwork discloses the truth of a being as the rift (*Riss*) of earth and world somehow echoes the Nietzschean discordance. It is my view that, compelling though Heidegger's questioning of Nietzsche is, he himself fails in the Nietzsche seminar and "The Origin of the Work of Art" to return to the question of creativity after shifting the focus to the artwork. *Angst*, *Rausch*, and *Riss* are never seen in their potential conceptual unity.

Angst/Rausch/Riss

For nothing can be sole or whole
That has not been rent.
w. b. yeats, "Crazy Jane Talks with the Bishop"

Nietzsche after Heidegger

The crux between Nietzsche and Heidegger in aesthetic theory lies in the fact that as Heidegger seeks to supersede Nietzsche's conception of the will to power as art, he in effect abandons the notion of creativity itself. At issue for Heidegger is what distinguishes artworks from other kinds of human creation: "Only in and through creation is the work realized. But because that is so, the essence of creation for its part remains dependent on the essence of the work; therefore it can be grasped only from the Being of the work. Creation creates the work. But the essence of the work is the origin of the essence of creation."[1] Important though this formulation is—and I have already drawn on it to consider how at crucial moments in the creative process the artwork begins to dictate the artist's action—the artist's creative process is relegated to the background without being rethought.

In order to rethink creativity I propose to bring together the three concepts that Heidegger elaborates separately without acknowledging or exploring their unity: *Angst* (as elaborated in *Being and Time* and "What Is Metaphysics?"); *Rausch* (the Nietzschean word analyzed in *Nietzsche*, volume 1); and *Riss* (introduced in "The Origin of the Work of Art"). Each word has a rich range of meanings and connotations, and their possible translations— *Angst*: anxiety, dread, worry; *Rausch*: intoxication, frenzy, rush, rapture; *Riss*: rift, tear, rip, rent—can be combined in various ways: anxiety–rapture–rift; dread–rush–tear. I will let various English resonances emerge according to context. Recovering a concept of creativity from the constellation *Angst/ Rausch/Riss* will also address the tripartite problematic of beauty, form, and truth that separates and yet links Heidegger and Nietzsche.

Angst occupies various points in the architecture of Heidegger's thought. At the core of the analysis of Dasein as being-in-the-world, *Angst* is the "fundamental" mood of modern existence from which other moods and states of mind derive (*Being and Time*, paras. 39–40). In contrast to fear's attunement to what concretely threatens, "that which anxiety is profoundly anxious about [*sich abängstet*] is not a *definite* kind of Being for Dasein or a *definite* possibility for it. . . . That which anxiety is anxious about is Being-in-the-world itself. In anxiety what is environmentally ready-to-hand sinks away, and so, in general do entities-within-the-world."[2] Anxiety is the pivot on which teeters the widely misunderstood oscillation between authenticity and inauthenticity. The feeling that nothing in the world matters drains motive and concern: "The 'world' can offer nothing more" casts all one's involvements as inauthentic in the sense of *not one's own*, even as nothing matters *except* in the world. In this same moment (hence the pivot), "anxiety throws Dasein back upon that which it is anxious about—its authentic potentiality-for-Being-in-the-world. . . . Anxiety makes manifest in Dasein its *Being towards* its ownmost potentiality-for-Being, that is, its *Being-free for* the freedom of choosing itself and taking hold of itself" (H 187–88). It is in this sense that *Angst* "individualizes Dasein" (H 187). There is no escape from being in a world already made by others, and there is no escape from one's own existence as pure potentiality. Authenticity and inauthenticity—one's ownness and the not-one's-own—are not states or stations but a perpetual oscillation that uniquely contours every life history.

This existential account of *Angst* is eventually complemented by a consideration of *Angst* from the perspective of the question of being in the essays "What Is Metaphysics?" (1929), "Postscript to 'What Is Metaphysics?'" (1943), and "Introduction to 'What Is Metaphysics?'" (1949).[3] The stress now falls on that which we find ourselves in relation to when our interest in everything that is drops or fades away. To cite once again from the 1929 essay:

Anxiety makes manifest the nothing. . . .

Anxiety robs us of speech. Because beings as a whole slip away, so that precisely the nothing crowds around, all utterance of the "is" falls silent in the face of the nothing. That in the uncanniness of anxiety we often try to shatter the vacant stillness with compulsive talk only proves the presence of the nothing. That anxiety unveils the nothing is immediately demonstrated by human beings themselves when anxiety has dissolved. In the lucid vision sustained by fresh remembrance we must say that that in the face of which and concerning which we were anxious was "properly"—nothing. Indeed, the nothing itself—as such—was there.

With the fundamental attunement of anxiety we have arrived at that occurrence in Dasein in which the nothing is manifest and from which it must be interrogated.

How is it with the nothing? . . .

In anxiety beings as a whole become superfluous. In what sense does this happen? Beings are not annihilated by anxiety, so that nothing is left. How could they be, when anxiety finds itself precisely in utter impotence with regard to beings as a whole? Rather, the nothing makes itself known with beings and in beings expressly as a slipping away of the whole. . . .

Da-sein means: being held out into the nothing.

Holding itself out into the nothing, Dasein is in each case already beyond beings as a whole. Such being beyond beings we call *transcendence*. If in the ground of its essence Dasein were not transcending, which now means, if it were not in advance holding itself out into the nothing, then it could never adopt a stance toward beings nor even toward itself.

Without the original manifestness of the nothing, no selfhood and no freedom.[4]

Let's link the two inquiries, the existential and the ontological. From the first angle, *Angst* individuates Dasein insofar as those moments when nothing in the world matters throw Dasein back on its (that is, his or her) condition of existing as potentiality and facing the possibility of acting of one's own accord, acting in one's own name. From the second angle, *Angst* is the condition of ontological inquiry itself, for only as "beings *as a whole* become superfluous" does the question *what is being?* arise, and it arises from, or as, *attunement to the nothing.*

That in turn poses the philosophically intriguing suggestion that *being is nothing.* Vattimo develops this idea in various contexts, sometimes with respect to hermeneutics: "There is a sort of self-contradictory ontology in Heidegger. Ontology means that we want to speak about Being, but Being is nothing but the Logos interpreted as dialogue, *Gespräch*, as the actual discussion among people."[5] And sometimes with respect to nihilism: "The fact is that metaphysics cannot be brought to an end through the 'discovery' of a truer, nonmetaphysical structure of Being, compelling our reverence yet again as an ultimate foundation (reassuring and subjugating, as Nietzsche taught us), but only as the outcome of a process in which, as Heidegger says about nihilism, 'there is nothing to Being itself.'"[6] The pull-and-tug between Heidegger and Nietzsche in the passage on which Vattimo draws—and indeed the pull-and-tug between Vattimo's own thought and Heidegger's—is a rich, still not fully explored arena. Simply to indicate this richness, let me cite a passage from Heidegger's commentary on Nietzsche and nihilism: "Nietzsche acknowledges the being as such. Yet, in such an acknowledgment, does he also recognize the Being of beings, and indeed It itself, *Being*, specifically *as Being*? He does not. . . . Being is already outside the horizon of the *questionability* of the 'as Be-

ing.' There 'is' nothing to Being as such. Being—a *nihil*. . . . The essence of nihilism is the history in which there is nothing to Being itself."[7] The controversy
vacillates between rescuing the question of being from the history of nihilism
or affirming that being is nothing. A further crux of this question is found
near the end of "Introduction to 'What Is Metaphysics?'" (1949), from which
I cited at length above: "How does it come about that beings take precedence
everywhere and lay claim to every 'is,' while that which is not a being—namely,
the Nothing thus understood as Being itself—remains forgotten? How does it
come about that with Being It is really nothing and that the Nothing does not
properly prevail?"[8]

Out of the rich discussion of *Angst*, being, and nothing, Heidegger does
not connect *Angst* to artistic creation, even though from his own perspective
Angst must be the groundless ground of creativity. The attunement to the
nothing should be seen to underlie the Nietzschean grid of the becoming-
creative of affective states discussed in the previous chapter (Dionysian, classical, *ressentiment*, Romantic pessimism). *Angst* is the mood from which other
affective states emerge and differentiate themselves. Drawing on the existential interpretation of *Angst* as the pivot on which authentic activity emerges
from abject inaction, aesthetic theory confronts the question of creativity.
In David Wellbery's comprehensive history of the semantics of *Stimmung*
in German aesthetic thought since the eighteenth century, the culminating
discussion of Heidegger touches on the aversion to Nietzschean *Rausch*. Heidegger understands *Rausch* as "an embodying attunement [*leibendes Gestimmtsein*]," but a tension in his thought emerges as he tries to scrub *Rausch* of
"Nietzsche's physiological terminology." According to Wellbery, this "leads
Heidegger to amend his understanding of *Stimmung* as it was developed in
Being and Time. While the physiological conception of the body is irrelevant
for his understanding of the artistic condition, the phenomenological conception of the lived body is not. Hence *Stimmung*, and the rapture of aesthetic
Stimmung in particular, is always also the life of the lived body."[9] While this
may be what Heidegger implies, or abstractly asserts, it never does overcome
the eschewing of the body.

Moreover, it is the relation of *Angst* (as attunement to the nothing) that is
the overlooked element of artistic creativity to be brought into relation with
Rausch. What lifts the artist from immobility in the face of *nothing matters*
to that activity which produces an artwork? *Lifts* is a questionable term. It is
true that across a long history poetic inspiration has been figured as a rising
or raising, an uplifting, a soaring or flight. In the English tradition, Milton
spiritualizes the in-spiration of the classical muses. He intends to outstrip the
ancient poets as he invokes the Holy Spirit to lift his song in *Paradise Lost* and

names the sacred sites where the "Heav'nly Muse" inspired Moses and the
Hebrew prophets—"*Oreb . . . Sinai . . . Sion* Hill . . . *Siloa's* Brook":

> I thence
> Invoke thy aid to my advent'rous Song,
> That with no middle flight intends to soar
> Above th' *Aonian* Mount, while it pursues
> Things unattempted yet in Prose or Rhyme.
> And chiefly Thou O Spirit, that dost prefer
> Before all Temples th' upright heart and pure,
> Instruct me, for Thou know'st; Thou from the first
> Wast present, and with mighty wings outspread
> Dove-like sat'st brooding on the vast Abyss
> And mad'st it pregnant: What in me is dark
> Illumine, what is low raise and support;
> That to the highth of this great Argument
> I may assert Eternal Providence,
> And justify the ways of God to men. (I.12–25)[10]

At least since Baudelaire, modern writers have often attested to the affective transformation from the immobility of *Angst* to creativity in images that
contrast starkly with Milton's soaring. Kafka's diary in the month of January
1915 vividly records inaction and impasse. January 4: "Great desire to begin
another story; didn't yield to it. It is all pointless." January 6: "For the time
being abandoned 'Village Schoolmaster' and 'The Assistant Attorney.' But almost incapable too of getting on with *The Trial.*" January 18: "Headache. Slept
badly. Incapable of sustained, concentrated work. Also have been in the open
air too little. In spite of that began a new story; I was afraid I should spoil the
old ones." January 20: "The end of writing. When will it catch me again?"
January 29: "Again tried to write, virtually useless." The next day, having written nothing since that "end of writing," Kafka jots down a remarkable image
of the inner movement required to create:

> 30 January. The old incapacity. Hardly ten days interrupted in my writing and
> already cast aside. Once again prodigious efforts stand before me. You have to
> dive down, as it were, and sink more rapidly than that which sinks in advance
> of you.[11]

Unlike the Miltonic soaring above earthly reality, Kafka must sink faster than
the world is sinking away from him. Then he can write. Kafka's *Angst* is debilitating loss of interest, care, and energy. His inspiration, the *Rausch* that transports him into creativity, is, like Milton's, a kind of acceleration inducing an
affective difference in the state-one-is-in, but while Milton soars, Kafka dives

and sinks. Dives and sinks—the very ambiguity in these words between activity and passivity, doing and suffering, suggests the double quality of *Rausch*. Kafka is jarred from the immobility of *Angst* if he can fall more rapidly than the world that eludes him.

Nietzsche's first answer to the question of the sources of artistic creativity were dreaming and intoxication rather than the Holy Ghost. In *The Birth of Tragedy* he sought to contrast "the Apollinian art of sculpture, and the nonimagistic, Dionysian art of music." He saw the Apollonian and Dionysian as "two tendencies": "Let us first conceive of them as the separate art worlds of *dreams* and *intoxication*. These physiological phenomena present a contrast analogous to the Apollinian and the Dionysian." As regards dreaming, he refers to Lucretius's view "that the glorious divine figures first appeared to the souls of men" in dreams and approvingly cites lines from Wagner's *Die Meistersinger von Nürnberg*: "All poems and versification / are but true dreams' interpretation."[12]

Nietzsche maintains the dream/intoxication contrast, with modifications, long after his repudiation of Wagner:

> *Apollinian—Dionysian*—There are two conditions in which art appears in man like a force of nature and disposes of him whether he will or no: as the compulsion to have visions and as a compulsion to an orgiastic state. Both conditions are rehearsed in ordinary life, too, but weaker: in dream and in intoxication.
>
> But the same antithesis obtains between dream and intoxication: both release artistic powers in us, but different ones: the dream those of vision, association, poetry; intoxication those of gesture, passion, song, dance. (*Will to Power* 798)[13]

There are two important shifts. While Nietzsche attributed *Rausch* only to Dionysian frenzy in *The Birth of Tragedy*, he treats the Apollonian and the Dionysian as two manifestations of *Rausch* in *The Will to Power* and a related passage in *Twilight of the Idols*.[14] Heidegger takes particular note of the shift because now *Rausch* becomes "the basic aesthetic state. . . . The Dionysian and the Apollonian are two kinds of rapture, rapture itself being the basic state."[15] Moreover, eros is no longer associated exclusively with the Dionysian. "In the Dionysian intoxication," writes Nietzsche, "there is sexuality and voluptuousness: they are not lacking in the Apollinian."[16]

Sexuality, dream, rapture—these are the elements of creativity that Heidegger prefers to banish from his own aesthetic thought. He openly disputes the pertinence of "physiological" dimensions such as sexuality and intoxication to explain anything about art. As for dreaming, he bypasses the phenomenon altogether. Ordinary dreaming and "the compulsion to have visions," which for Nietzsche are among the "conditions in which art appears in man

like a force of nature," do not square with Heidegger's conception that the artwork discloses the truth of a being and that the origin of the artwork is art.
Or can they be squared? Once again, as with the encounter of Heidegger and
Deleuze, we are faced with the apparent conceptual incommensurability of
sensation and being, vitalism and hermeneutics. The dream might have been
seen as straddling these oppositions had Heidegger availed himself of *The Interpretation of Dreams*. But he could not countenance psychoanalysis, whether
because of his knee-jerk anti-"scientism" or his deep-seated anti-Semitism,
and so missed the linkages that the dream might afford in deepening ties between his and Nietzsche's aesthetic thinking. Nietzsche poses a fundamental
problem for modern thought because in defining the will to power as art, with
dream and intoxication as benchmarks, he locates will (*voluntas*) in emphatically involuntary processes. Kant labored mightily to reconcile will and reason in our capacity to find freedom in the conscious desire to obey a universal maxim. Nietzsche's challenge to this great innovation of Enlightenment
thought anticipates Freud, for whom the strength of the unconscious lies in
the perpetual striving of wish and impulse, desire and drive. Freudian *conatus*
might have shed light on the *Rausch* that arouses creativity out of *Angst*.

Is there an art of dreaming?

Dreams are utterly inconsequential, unless interpreted; otherwise, they do
little more than let you sleep; upon waking, a dream either vanishes or lives
on in interpretation. Such is the upshot, if not the precise thesis, of Freud's
Interpretation of Dreams. Nietzsche's model of the dream as Apollonian creativity seems to eschew in advance the whole Freudian project of interpreting
dreams. Vitalism over against hermeneutics. Moreover, Freud approaches the
dream as a compromise formation in which the unconscious impulses astir
in the dreamer meet the already etched-out boundaries of the ego, subjecting
the dream itself—its very appearance—to the constraining "considerations
of representability." For Nietzsche, the dream's creative force lies in the Apollonian "principle of individuation": the involuntary will to appearance or "illusion" (*Schein*—German's aesthetic word par excellence) forces itself upon
the human being and shapes him "whether he will or no." Nietzsche's Apollo
embodies the divine luminosity of that individuation. At first blush the gap
between the Freudian ego and Nietzschean individuation seems unbridgeable. So within this nest of difficult terms—dream and artwork, compromise
formation and principle of individuation, drive and representability, will to
power and interpretation—lies the problematic of the relation between the
interpretation and the creativity of dreams.

The protocols of dream interpretation that Freud exacts of himself are a
stringent set of imperatives in keeping with his scientific as well as cultural

and aesthetic *Bildung*. First, his theory must discover the essence or singular function of dreams: thus, the dream is the representation of a fulfilled wish. Second, it must identify the principle of dream construction: thus, a dream is composed of a manifest content behind which lie its latent contents. And third, his procedure must be able, in principle, to explain *every* element in a dream and achieve an interpretive synthesis; even when he notes the impossibility of exhaustive interpretation, he attributes the limitation to the complexity of the latent contents, not to any shortcoming or gap in his interpretive procedures. The entire pattern of argumentation in *The Interpretation of Dreams* follows from Freud's embrace of these axioms and protocols. It is only when he has succeeded in carrying them out in detail and parrying every objection he can imagine that he turns to two problems that otherwise might have put the axioms themselves in question and threatened his entire thesis from the outset, namely, "secondary revision" and the distortion that inevitably occurs whenever a dream is recounted.

Secondary revision refers to "interpolations and additions" to the dream's content; it is something like the opposite of the "limitations and omissions" that Freud initially identifies with dream censorship. Such interpolations "are always introduced at points at which they can serve as links between two portions of dream-content or to bridge a gap between two parts of the dream." Often "the dream loses its appearance of absurdity and disconnectedness and approximates to the model of an intelligible experience" as a result of secondary revision. Freud draws two conclusions. First, such revisions are the work of "phantasy." Fantasies, otherwise analogous to daydreams, are defined at this point in Freud's thinking as the "forerunners of hysterical symptoms"; they are, he writes to Wilhelm Fliess in 1897, "psychical façades constructed in order to bar the way to . . . memories [of the primal scene]." Freud further concludes that secondary revision, by filling in a dream's gaps and rendering it intelligible, in effect interpolates an interpretation of the dream into the dream itself. There "are dreams which might be said to have been already interpreted once, before being submitted to waking interpretation." Secondary revision, in sum, is a fantasy that enters into the dreamwork with the force of an interpretation.[17]

It is of course largely but not merely a misinterpretation, since the interpretive fantasy usually has a significance in its own right. Moreover, although he calls the fantasy's interpretive work "secondary revision" and puts it on a par with waking thoughts, Freud emphatically rejects the idea that the other "dream-constructing factors"—such as displacement and condensation, representability, and the censorship imposed by resistance—first "put together a provisional dream-content out of the material provided, and that this content

is subsequently re-cast so as to conform so far as possible to a second agency."
No. "We must assume rather," writes Freud, with his knack for revealing the
rich ambiguity of his most decisive points, "that *from the very first* the demands of this *second* factor constitute one of the conditions which the dream
must satisfy and that this condition operates *simultaneously* . . . in a conducive
and selective sense upon the mass of material present in the dream thoughts"
(my italics). The secondary *revision* is an *originating* force constructing the
form of the dream itself; (mis)interpretation is part of the creative process of
dreaming.[18]

Several pages later Freud introduces the second problem that might have
disturbed his inaugural axioms and thesis, namely, that every recounting of
a dream distorts the actual dream. After all, a visual-auditory hallucination
during sleep is put into words after the fact. Emboldened by his finely crafted
reflection on secondary revision, Freud dispenses with this problem quickly.
Such distortion of the "text of the dream" does not inhibit interpretation but
enables it, since it is "no more than a part of the revision to which the dream-
thoughts are regularly subjected as a result of the dream-censorship. . . . The
modifications . . . are associatively linked to the material which they replace,
and serve to show us the way to that material, which may in its turn be a
substitute for something else." He concludes with an illustration of his technique. Often when the recounting of a dream is "too hard to follow," he asks
the patient to repeat it. The patient "rarely uses the same words. But the parts
of the dream he describes in different terms are by that fact revealed to me
as the weak spot in the dream's disguise."[19] Who can gainsay Freud's pride in
his interpretive virtuosity, especially at this crucial moment of clinching his
overall argument?

I have sketched the movement of Freud's argument, starting from the
axiom that interpretation must hew to its object's essential nature and be capable in principle of synthesizing all its elements. The conceptual sequence
is important: (1) every dream is the condensation and displacement of latent
contents (dream thoughts) into a manifest content and represents a fulfilled
wish; (2) one aspect of the dreamwork is "secondary revision," a kind of false
interpretation woven into the dream itself and deriving from a fantasy; and
(3) the distortions in recounting a dream are continuous with such revision
and therefore a signpost, not a barrier, to interpretation, which ultimately is
capable of the synthesis that shows how the dream represents a fulfilled wish.

A fourth move—that is, a third complication in the original thesis—is introduced by Jacques Lacan, adding yet another twist to the relation of dreaming and interpretation. I know his argument only from a short paragraph of
the Rome Discourse, though I assume it is elaborated in one of the seminars.

He asserts that analysts know from their therapeutic experience "that from the moment an analysis becomes engaged in the path of transference—and this is what indicates to us that it has become so engaged—each of the patient's dreams is to be interpreted as a provocation, a latent avowal or diversion, by its relation to the analytic discourse, and that as the analysis progresses, his dreams become ever more reduced to the function of elements in the dialogue taking place in the analysis."[20]

Accordingly, then, the analytic space itself affects the telling and even the production of dreams. Now turn the whole sequence of arguments around and look at them in reverse order, starting from the transference, since the analytic space was in fact Freud's own concrete starting point. The original thesis regarding the dream's manifest and latent content and its representation of a fulfilled wish is shown in a new light in the reversed sequence: (1) the workings of the transference turn the subject's dreams into a series of rhetorical gestures addressed to the analyst; (2) the distortions in the recounting of the dream open the dream to interpretation; and (3) unconscious fantasies weave interpretation into the very construction of the dream.

The dream never stands on its own in the manner of, say, a poem. Indeed, nowhere does it stand alone as an object, as something to be interpreted, since there is no dream without interpretation. The hallucinatory event of dreaming becomes a rebus, becomes the enfolded relation of manifest to latent contents, and comes into its appearance as the representation of a fulfilled wish only through interpretation. Interpretation is at work as secondary revision in creating the dream, and dreaming itself dreams *toward* interpretation, that is, toward the retelling and the transference. In light of Lacan's reflection, there is not even a way to give these three moments of interpretation—transference, recounting, and secondary revision—a strict logical or temporal order. The dream is at once the effect and trigger of interpretation. The dream is inextricably linked to the transference within the analytic space, at once the site of therapy and source of theory. Moreover, because the transference is the intertwining of the desire of the analysand and the desire of the analyst, the wish whose fulfillment the dream represents lies between or astride analyst and analysand. The Lacanian dictum that desire is the desire of the Other might be said to acquire its fullest and no doubt most enigmatic significance in dream interpretation and transference: the wish distortedly represented as fulfilled in the dream is the desire of the Other. But who is this Other? The Other cannot, by definition, have an identity. It is often better to speak instead of otherness or radical alterity. Insofar as the dream comes to the dreamer as an enigmatic message, the Other is simply the concatenation of the subject's own unacknowledged desires. Insofar as the subject's resistance to acknowledging those desires is intensified by the analyst's presence and purpose, the analyst is the Other. Insofar as a range of other people's desires, demands, affirmations, and disapprovals have inevitably elicited or compelled the subject's response in the course of his or her life, they are the Other. And insofar as the analyst comes to stand in for one or more of them, the analyst is the Other in that guise as well. Desire is the desire of the Other across all these fluctuating inflections of otherness as they play their part in weaving the dream.

Suddenly Freudian theory—and I do not think my secondary revisions stray from Freud's orbit—rejoins Nietzsche. Dreaming is an artistic-aesthetic process. The hallucinatory visual, auditory, and bodily sensations of sleep, themselves a "force of nature," are a striving for individuation in the double sense Nietzsche gives it: the production of an image or illusion and the involuntary shaping of an individual. What else does the analytic space of transference and dream interpretation hope to foster but the unconscious drive toward unforeseen individuation?

The notion that dreams have an aesthetic dimension, indeed that there is a dreaming-toward-art, finds a different and richly suggestive elaboration in the writings of Gaston Bachelard. He contests "classical psychoanalysis" in its identification of the "unconscious meaning" of certain symbols in dreams—as when "the *dream of flight* . . . symbolizes, we are told, sensual desires"—an interpretation that utterly fails to "account for the *aesthetic* character of the dream flight."[21] Left unaddressed are "the *graceful* images of flight." The aesthetic dimension is already in the dream as gracefulness: "Every Bergsonian knows that a gracefully curved trajectory must be traced with a sympathetic inner movement. . . . Dynamic imagination suggests, to one who contemplates a graceful line, the wildest substitution: it is you, dreamer, who are the evolving grace. Feel in yourself the *force of gracefulness*. Realize that you are a reserve of gracefulness, a potentiality of flight."[22] Such gracefulness lies in one's own potentiality as regards, in Bachelard's list, one's goodness or strength or skill or nature. That such an aesthetic dimension is at the same time a hermeneutic one is already in the Wagner lyrics cited by Nietzsche: art interprets "true dreams."

I also associate Bachelard's reflection with another psychoanalytic domain, that of D. W. Winnicott: the realm of children's play, toys and dolls, transitional objects, games and make-believe, the vast "intermediate zone" between fantasy and reality and between the self's inside and outside.[23] This domain altogether escapes Heidegger's notice, just as dreams do, even though it should count as not only a source of artistic creativity but also the seat of Dasein's being-in-the-world. The ready-to-hand (tools) and the immersive,

ontic involvement with the ready-to-hand (practices) are not quite as primordial to Dasein's being-in-the-world as Heidegger envisions. Underlying them
is child's play. In overlooking toys in favor of tools, Heidegger overlooks *how*
Dasein first encounters its thrownness into the world. The difference of the
ontic and the ontological awakened by the hammer's disrepair hides Dasein's
first hammering in the child's pounding a stick into the ground with the palm
of the hand or a peg in a hole with a brightly colored mallet. It can of course
be claimed that the child mimics the adult, the toy imitates the tool. But every
individual—that is, every individuating Dasein—passes from toys to tools. I
recently watched a toddler, so young he was still unsteady on his feet except
when in motion, reach up to the handle on a glass door and pull it down and
push it up and pull it down again over and over. It was not clear whether he
was at all attuned to the door as a passageway or even had the intention of
opening it or desired to be on the other side or indeed was at all aware that the
handle was involved in opening the door. All that was clear was the pleasure,
fascination, and curiosity that this play stimulated—auto-affected—for some
few minutes. Eventually, the continuous action of depressing the handle,
pushing the door open, crossing the threshold, and heading on one's way will
become part of this child's involvement with everyday tools, practices, and
habits. There will be no seam clearly demarcating the passage from play to
use. Playing precedes and prepares practices; it founds ontic involvements,
which imperceptibly become, from the standpoint of adult experience, what
the Wittgensteinian and pragmatist traditions call background and Heideg-
gerians variously encompass as care or circumspection and assignments or
referential structures.[24]

Dreaming, according to Bachelard, and play, according to Winnicott,
reach toward art, the one giving rise to the hallucinatory-kinesthetic experience of gracefulness and the other by arousing creative impulses that connect
the self to reality through activities distinct from reality itself. And yet such
enhancements of life, such psychic enrichments, do not generate art as such.
Baudelaire's poetry neither arose from a *mens sana* nor brought one about. A
surer hypothesis: the therapeutic power of artistic creativity is interrupted or
overridden when the aim of creativity becomes an artwork, as distinct from
an aesthetically pleasing object, for the creation of an artwork—that is, the
embrace of art as vocation—must confront the inexorable demands of form
and the imperative of newness.

Merleau-Ponty states the problem in terms that resonate with Deleuze
as well as Heidegger when he says, apropos of Cézanne and Balzac, that
the artist "speaks as the first man spoke and paints as if no one had painted
before. What he expresses cannot, therefore, be the translation of a clearly

defined thought, since such clear thoughts are those that have already been said within ourselves or by others. 'Conception' cannot precede 'execution.' Before expression there is nothing but a vague fever, and only the work itself, complete and understood, will prove that there was *something* rather than *nothing* to be found there."[25]

Creativity is not a simple continuum running from dream and fantasy to transitional objects, play, and the intermediate space between fantasy and reality and then all the way to art. Better to think of it as a kind of discontinuum, a corrugated surface each of whose peaks or creases is joined to and yet separated from the next. Winnicott marks the gap from the psychoanalytic perspective: "In order to look into the theory that analysts use in their work to see where creativeness has a place it is necessary . . . to separate the idea of the creation from works of art. . . . . The creativity that concerns me here is a universal. It belongs to being alive."[26] Restated from the aesthetic perspective: art would not exist except for those universal sources and forms of creativity, but once the creative aim becomes an artwork, the creative subject puts his or her well-being at risk for the sake of the work. In this way we can once again affirm the Heideggerian claim that "the essence of the work is the origin of the essence of creation." Moreover, somewhere in the "Romantic" transition from neoclassical to modern art, the Kantian association of form predominantly with harmony and arrangement gives way to an aesthetic of dissonance, discord, rift.

Rift-Design

This brings us to the third term to be related to *Angst* and *Rausch*. *Riss* is introduced by Heidegger to describe the earth/world relation as it emerges in the artwork. A being as disclosed by the artwork is the site of the strife and inseparability of earth and world (stone and divinity of the temple, soil and toil of van Gogh's peasant's shoes). The tear that traverses the artwork gives shape to—is the shape of—the rift of earth and world. The event of such disclosure is what Heidegger calls "truth." Recall: "Truth establishes itself as a strife within a being that is to be brought forth only in such a way that the conflict opens up in this being, that is, the being itself is brought into the rift-design."[27]

Rift-design is the term, then, for artistic *form* and for *truth* at once. The artwork is a rifted shape and a shaped rift.

Such an understanding of form is not unique to Heidegger, and it is worth articulating in other terms. I find inspiration in the purport of Adorno's account of form in *Aesthetic Theory*. Adorno's own inspiration comes, I believe, from three sources: expressionism's procedures of montage, assemblage, and the juxtaposition of jarringly heterogeneous materials and modes of representation; dissonance in modern music, even as he struggled to the point of incoherence in seeking a coherent hierarchy by which to rank Schoenberg, Stravinsky, and jazz; and the conviction derived from Marx and Lukàcs that artists' responses to the conflicting social forces of their time are inscribed or embodied in their art itself, often in ways at odds with the individual artist's own political or ideological outlook. As a result, Adorno accords primacy to form in aesthetic theory while rejecting any formalistic conception of form and demands that intrinsic criticism account for the artwork's extrinsic contexts, imperatives, and motives, as these inflect the form itself. Adorno's legacy, then, is a nonformalistic account of form coupled with attention to the becoming internal of the artwork's external determinants.[28]

It is also a fruitful way of construing Nietzsche's maxim that the artist "accords no value to anything that cannot become form" (*Will to Power* 817).[29] The heterogeneous components that become form in the artwork include the artistic materials, the subject matter, the history and connotations of the work's genre and its stylistic and formal features, the structure of feeling prevailing within the artist's lifeworld, and the artist's motives. The artistic imperative is to compose all the components into a unity. The composition of the artwork is thus conceived not as an act of arranging more or less homogenous elements into a pattern but rather as fusing—indeed, forcing the fusion of—utterly heterogeneous elements into a unified assemblage. "Unity" is of course a contested term. Where deconstruction bequeaths to criticism interpretive procedures that first postulate the work's ostensible unity and then disclose its fissures, Adorno, conversely, bequeaths an attentiveness to the heterogeneous imperatives and materials that the work sets about fusing until, in the very achieving of unity, it cracks, fissures, tears. The fissure does not undo the fusion; the fusion produces the fissure. The artwork is at once form and process. This is how I construe *Riss* as the conceptual key to artistic form.

Nietzsche's neglect of form and Heidegger's aversion to rapture begin to be overcome once form as *Riss* (rifted shape) is joined to *Rausch* in keeping with Heidegger's own gloss on Nietzschean *Rausch* as "form-engendering force." Heidegger further interprets Nietzsche as saying that "the essence of creation . . . is the rapturous bringing-forth of the beautiful in the work."[30] What, though, of Heidegger's other requirement, namely, that the rift-design designate not only form but also truth? Here is the area where it is, initially at least, easiest to see how Heidegger saw his essay "The Origin of the Work of Art" as the step beyond Nietzsche, for the last several chapters of the first Nietzsche seminar circle around the discordance of truth and art. But what is the difference between Heidegger's notion that thanks to the artwork "truth establishes itself as a strife within a being that is to be brought forth only in such a way that the conflict opens up in this being" and Nietzsche's notion of the essential strife between truth and art?

The nineteenth chapter of *Nietzsche*, volume 1, *The Will to Power as Art* is titled "The Raging Discordance between Truth and Art," paraphrasing a comment Nietzsche makes in his 1888 notebook with reference to *The Birth of Tragedy* (1872). The unpublished comment will become Heidegger's touchstone:

> We should remember once more Nietzsche's words on the connection between art and truth. He jotted them down in the year 1888 on the occasion of a meditation on his first book: "Very early in my life I took the question of the relation of *art* to *truth* seriously: and even now I stand in holy dread in the face of this discordance."
> The relation between art and truth is a discordance that arouses dread.[31]

Heidegger's translator, David Farrell Krell, offers an illuminating comment on the entire passage by parsing that final phrase, "a discordance that arouses dread": "*Ein Entsetzen erregender Zwiespalt.* In the title of this section, *Der erregende Zwiespalt zwischen Wahrheit und Kunst*, the phrase *erregende Zwiespalt* is actually a condensation of the statement made here. That is to say, discordance between art and truth 'rages' insofar as it *arouses dread.*"[32] So the discordance of art and truth lies, rather ambiguously at first sight, in the precinct of *Rausch* and *Angst*.

However self-dramatizing Nietzsche's notebook statement may be, it is a thought in the making, a dashed-off reminder to himself, and it is pithy enough to leave wide open what is meant by *truth*. Each possible meaning inflects the discord between art and truth in a distinctive way. Heidegger chooses two determinations of truth, both of which Nietzsche regularly excoriates: Platonism and positivism. In Platonism, truth resides in a supersensuous realm apart from earthly realities and hence for Nietzsche is life-denying. His battle cry of reversing or overturning Platonism affirms the sensuous over the supersensuous and enlists art as the sheerest affirmation of the sensuous. In that sense art is in discordance with truth. However, as Heidegger demonstrates through several carefully crafted arguments, a mere affirmation of the sensuous over the supersensuous is difficult to distinguish from positivism. How does the overturning of Platonism not become a simple positivism?

Here Nietzsche's perspectivalism comes into play. What positivism takes to be sensuous reality is but the reduction of multiple perspectives to one and the petrification of that perspective, such that it is no longer a perspective but taken to be reality itself (as mere appearance). Heidegger provides a compact account that resonates with many Nietzsche-inspired—and many Nietzsche-phobic—theoretical initiatives of the past half century:

> Semblance itself is proper to the essence of the real. We can readily see that in the perspectival character of the actual. The following statement provides an opening onto the matter of semblance within the perspectivally constructed actual: "With the organic world begin *indeterminateness* and *semblance*" (XIII, 288; cf. also 229). In the unity of an organic being there is a multiplicity of drives and capacities (each of which possesses its perspective) which struggle against one another. In such a multiplicity the univocity of the particular perspective in which the actual in any given case stands is lost. The equivocal character of what shows itself in several perspectives is granted, along with the indeterminate, which now appears one way, then another, which first proffers this appearance, then that one. But such appearance becomes semblance in the sense of mere appearance only when what becomes manifest in one perspective petrifies and is taken to be the sole definitive appearance, to the disregard of the other perspectives that crowd round in turn.[33]

Semblance arising from the multiplicity of perspectives is more real than the Platonic real of ideal forms, and self-affirming semblance is in perpetual strife with those petrified semblances that deny or mask their semblanceness and so become what is conventionally called reality. Life oscillates between semblance denial and semblance affirmation. Yet no clear line separates them in the processes of the world, since the affirmative will to semblance strives to affix the semblance as reality and mastery of reality.

The notes, fragments, and aphorisms of the late notebooks and *The Will to Power* are Nietzsche's *furious versions* as he wrestles with himself in trying to think the ineluctable, unmasterable strife of being and becoming and to think their strife without giving in to the temptation to announce mere aporia. In an evolutionary frame of mind, he asserts that "it is improbable that our 'knowledge' should extend further than is strictly necessary for the preservation of life" (*Will to Power* 494), a statement that seems to support the oft-cited precept on truth and error: "Truth is the kind of error without which a certain species of life could not live. The value for *life* is ultimately decisive" (*Will to Power* 493).[34] In a deconstructive state-of-mind, he ironizes on how "one can have *faith* in life. 'Life *ought* to inspire confidence': the task thus imposed is tremendous. To solve it, man must be a liar by nature, he must above all be an *artist*. And he *is* one: metaphysics, religion, morality, science—all of them only products of his will to art, to lie, to flight from 'truth,' to *negation* of 'truth'" (*Will to Power* 853).[35] Nietzsche's double bind is palpable here. First bind: he desires to affirm, absolutely and solely, life and this-worldly existence and yet sees all life-preserving knowledges and truths as error. But—second bind—his disdain for all discourses metaphysical, religious, moral, and scientific that in pretending to truth are in flight from truth leads him to call these discourses not merely life-preserving errors but lies, and so he calls upon himself implicitly to affirm truth against lie. The coexistence of these two sets of contraries constitutes Nietzsche's double bind.

It is striking that his attempt to master the most developed contradictions of his own thinking brings him back to *The Birth of Tragedy*. Heidegger is not wrong in showing that the two determinations of truth in relation to which art is for Nietzsche in raging discordance are Platonism and positivism. Art's sensuousness rages against Platonic supersensuous ideal-real, and art's affirmative semblance rages against positivism's congealed mere appearance. But Heidegger's restriction of the enigmatic dictum of "the raging discordance of truth and art" to these considerations misses something. Art's discordance with Platonism and with positivism would more likely stimulate Nietzsche's joy than his horror. A third sense of truth can be seen in the background to Greek tragic drama, where Dasein faces the bleakness of existence and mortality. The landmark for this aspect of the ancient Greek structure of feeling is book 11 of *The Odyssey*, as Odysseus travels to what the shade of Tiresias calls "this joyless kingdom of the dead" and encounters the realm of beings forgotten and forgetful.[36] *The Will to Power* 853 is an extended note on the conception of art in *The Birth of Tragedy*, as Nietzsche returns to the insights of his first work (perhaps as he was planning the preface to the 1886 edition):

> The conception of the work that one encounters in the background of this book is singularly gloomy and unpleasant: no type of pessimism known hitherto seems to have attained this degree of malevolence. The antithesis of a real and an apparent world is lacking here: there is only *one* world, and this is false, cruel, contradictory, seductive, without meaning—A world thus constituted is the real world. *We have need of lies* in order to conquer this reality, this "truth," that is, in order to live—That lies are necessary to live is itself part of the terrifying and questionable character of existence.[37]

And a few paragraphs later a seeming contradiction adds the decisive nuance: "A highest state of affirmation of existence is conceived from which the highest degree of pain cannot be excluded: the *tragic-Dionysian* state." He can then tighten the Gordian knot of his own thinking and assert that *The Birth of Tragedy* "is even anti-pessimistic: that is, in the sense that it teaches something that is stronger than pessimism, 'more divine' than truth: *art*."[38]

Such a reflection aligns with the idea that the ancient Greeks discovered that human existence could justify itself only aesthetically. More to the point here, though, is that these last statements return to the stricter meaning of "art" and the "artist." The tragic work is discordant with the naked truth of the human condition's lack of intrinsic values and goals; it does not deny or protect itself from this truth, but finds or produces the beautiful in its very discordance with it. Deploying his vocabulary of strength and power, Nietzsche asserts that "the feeling of *power* applies the judgment 'beautiful' even to things and conditions that the instinct of impotence could only find *hateful* and 'ugly.' The nose for what we could still barely deal with if it confronted us in the flesh—as danger, problem, temptation—this determines even our aesthetic Yes. ('That is beautiful' is an *affirmation*)" (*Will to Power* 852).[39]

Neither Nietzsche nor Heidegger associates the beautiful with well-formedness or the harmonious arrangement of elements or parts. And Heidegger's own reflection on art draws the conclusion that it is not that the artwork is beautiful, but that it brings forth the beautiful. *Beauty* and *the beautiful* can seem a ridiculously ineffable idea largely out of place in contemporary criticism. It has come to be associated with the retrograde belief in standards for evaluating art. Or else *the beautiful* has been reduced to the idea of formal closure and pleasantness and then devalued in favor of the "sublime." Concepts of form meanwhile are unsettled throughout modern criticism, whether along the polarity between formalist and nonformalist approaches to form or in the differing understandings of formalism itself which postulate either that the purely formal aspects of art are what make it art or, alternatively, that the task of criticism lies in its formalization of its own techniques of analysis.[40] Just as the concept of beauty has nonetheless remained crucial to modern aesthetic theory from Nietzsche to Heidegger, Adorno, and Merleau-Ponty, and has been invariably linked to some conception of form, so too and more importantly modern artists and writers have by no means washed their hands of the problem of beauty and form. To address the fate of beauty, it is perhaps better to set aside the question, *What is beauty?* since that question is indeed ineffable and a bit ridiculous. As Adorno puts it, "beauty cannot be defined, but neither can the concept of beauty be dispensed with altogether."[41] Let's ask instead: How is beauty or the beautiful referred to, alluded to, designated in poetic texts themselves? And how in turn do those references, allusions, and designations relate to the works' own principles of construction? So too, then, with the question, *What is form?*

In that spirit, I find that Percy Bysshe Shelley and Jorie Graham furnish poetic explorations of beauty, form, and the sublime that pose a particularly rich instance of poetry in the act of thinking, that is, thinking via percepts and affects in their coequal and incommensurate relation to philosophy's concepts.

"Hymn to Intellectual Beauty"

Shelley's thought has always been swiftly labeled. He is a Platonist, an atheist, and a revolutionary. That these three commitments—or self-designations—do not fit easily together seldom keeps readers from ignoring the caveat proffered by W. K. Wimsatt regarding "the conflict between French atheism and Platonic idealism which even in *Prometheus Unbound* Shelley was not able to resolve."[42] Platonism seems to announce itself in the very title of "Hymn to Intellectual Beauty," and the exclamation in "Mont Blanc" that "the wilderness has a mysterious tongue" whose teachings, if fully heard, might reconcile man with nature gives the idea of "nature" a force similar to that associated with Rousseau of exposing all societal artifice, convention, and wrong:[43]

> Thou hast a voice, great Mountain, to repeal
> Large codes of fraud and woe; not understood
> By all, but which the wise, and great, and good
> Interpret, or make felt, or deeply feel.

Such a thematic compass turns out to be extremely misleading. The term *Intellectual Beauty* is unquestionably redolent of Platonism and easily raises the expectation of a poem in which the earthly beauty encountered in experience will be the mere material imitation or shadow of the idea or ideal of beauty whose light can only be approached by the mind overcoming the material world itself, and the poem's very first image seems to confirm just this shadow realm whose source will be addressed as Spirit of Beauty and O awful Loveliness:

> The awful shadow of some unseen Power
> Floats though unseen amongst us

Platonism furnishes Shelley's idiom. But an idiom is not necessarily a conviction or controlling doctrine. The Platonic conception comes into his poetry as part of its metaphorical structure. While it may be tempting to take the title "Hymn to Intellectual Beauty" to be the key to the poem's meaning, such a temptation presupposes that the meaning of Intellectual Beauty is already known, whereas what Intellectual Beauty is will only be divulged in the fabric of the poem. It's not the title that names the poem, but the poem as a whole that unfolds the name Intellectual Beauty. Here the fact that in literature the artwork and criticism share the same medium of expression—language—can be a trap, for Platonism turns out not to be the poem's ultimate meaning but rather its means of making meaning. Platonism is more signifier than signified.

The matter/spirit and body/soul dichotomies in Plato's thought have proved a rich resource for poetic language because they so readily lend themselves to the making of metaphor and analogy: the body is to the soul as x is to y. That structure frequently undergoes a meaning-altering twist when *body* appears twice in the analogy, first as body and then as soul. For example, *body:soul::clothes:body* gives rise to motifs such as the empty sleeve as a figure of the body from which the soul, figured as body, has escaped; the bodiless clothing signifies the soulless body. Wallace Stevens draws on the expressive resources of this chiasmic ambiguity in "The Idea of Order at Key West"—

> She sang beyond the genius of the sea.
> The water never formed to mind or voice,
> Like a body wholly body, fluttering
> Its empty sleeve

—as does Yeats in "Sailing to Byzantium," where "a tattered coat" first figures an aging man himself and then his body ("mortal dress"), in which his soul, now figured as a body, might reawaken to "clap its hands" and create new song:

> An aged man is but a paltry thing,
> A tattered coat upon a stick, unless
> Soul clap its hands and sing, and louder sing
> For every tatter in its mortal dress

In short, while such metaphors of body and soul undoubtedly trace their genealogy to Plato, the thought to which the resulting percepts and affects give rise is not necessarily Platonic at all. So it is with Shelley. Only the workings of trope will yield how he *thinks* the beautiful.

The opening stanza is a preamble evoking the "unseen Power." Before the poem turns to apostrophe in the second stanza and addresses this power as Spirit of Beauty, the visitations of the unseen shadow of the unseen Power are likened, via multiple similes, to ephemeral moments such as the invisible breeze stirring a field of flowers:

> The awful shadow of some unseen Power
> Floats though unseen amongst us,—visiting
> This various world with as inconstant wing
> As summer winds that creep from flower to flower.—

> Like moonbeams that behind some piny mountain shower,
>> It visits with inconstant glance
>> Each human heart and countenance;
> Like hues and harmonies of evening,—
>> Like clouds in starlight widely spread,—
>> Like memory of music fled,—
>> Like aught that for its grace may be
> Dear, and dearer still for its mystery. (1–12)

The similes are more than similes. They tip over into a list of actual instances of the appearance of the beautiful. Every such appearance is fleeting—so emphatically fleeting that vanishing is felt to be a part of appearing. In the stanza's controlling trope, the unseen Power is itself figured as fitfully casting its eye on human beings:

> It visits with inconstant glance
> Each human heart and countenance

That beauty appears only intermittently in the heart and face underlies the pathos expressed in the unanswered question addressed to the Spirit of Beauty—

> Why dost thou pass away and leave our state,
> This dim vast vale of tears, vacant and desolate? (16–17)

—unanswered because unanswerable, for the question is as fruitless as all others that wonder why "Doubt, chance, and mutability" (31) rule over human life:

> Ask why the sunlight not forever
> Weaves rainbows o'er yon mountain river,
> Why aught should fail and fade that once is shewn,
>> Why fear and dream and death and birth
>> Cast on the daylight of this earth
>> Such gloom,—why man has such a scope
> For love and hate, despondency and hope?
>
> No voice from some sublimer world hath ever
>> To sage or poet these responses given—
>> Therefore the name of God and ghosts and Heaven,
> Remain the records of their vain endeavour,
> Frail spells— (18–29)

Within the scope of this recognition of inescapable mutability and mortality, Shelley praises the Spirit of Beauty in hyperbole that conveys by negative implication exactly what humankind cannot attain:

> Man were immortal and omnipotent,
> Didst thou, unknown and awful as thou art,
> Keep with thy glorious train firm state within his heart. (39–41)

How, then, to understand the relation of the beautiful, in its appearing and vanishing, and this figure of the Spirit of Beauty? Beauty is transcendent, ideal, and eternal in Plato, and the beautiful is its earthly transitory shadow. But does this hold for Shelley?

The poem contains three discrepant figurations of the relation of the Spirit of Beauty to the transitory shining of the beautiful:

> It visits with inconstant glance
> Each human heart and countenance (6–7)

> Spirit of Beauty, that dost consecrate
> With thine own hues all thou dost shine upon
> Of human thought or form—where art thou gone? (13–15)

> Thou—that to human thought art nourishment,
> Like darkness to a dying flame! (44–45)

The meaning common to all three tropes is that the beautiful is a fleeting lighting or shining of human thought, form, or feeling. The divergence, even contradictoriness unfolds from there, as though each trope were an approximation or new attempt to interpret the source of these transitory flashes. According to the first image, whenever and wherever the Spirit of Beauty casts its eye upon the human world the beautiful occurs. In the second, the beautiful is the occurrence of the Spirit of Beauty's light shining upon and coloring the human. And, finally, in an image whose boldness earns the Shelleyan exclamation point, the Spirit of Beauty is the darkness, the emptiness, the void, against which human thought's "dying flame" flashes into appearance.

This third trope interprets the Spirit of Beauty's transcendence—the transcendence by which it enables the beautiful to appear—not in the Platonic manner of an eternally existing Idea but in a way that suggestively anticipates Heidegger's conceptualization of *Angst* as the attunement to the nothing: "Holding itself out into the nothing, Dasein is in each case already beyond beings as a whole. Such being beyond beings we call *transcendence*."[44] Transcendence pertains not to the Ideal or Real, as in Plato, but to the nothing. In the fable of the cave the material world of human concerns and experiences is represented as the shadows that the real—that is, the ideal—realm of forms casts on the cave's walls. Here, though, the transitory, vanishing, remembered glimmers that constitute the beautiful in earthly experience become apparent on account of the surrounding darkness. That helps make better sense of the poem's enigmatic inaugural image in which the visitations of the Spirit of Beauty are the unseen shadow of an unseen Power.

The first of the three tropes in question is the one that seems to openly contradict the third—except that it can be construed in two quite different ways. On the one hand, "It visits with inconstant glance" says that wherever the Spirit of Beauty looks upon the world the beautiful appears. In that case, the beautiful is gathered into a transcendent unity insofar as what the Spirit of Beauty sees is, taken as a whole, Beauty itself. On the other hand, "It visits with inconstant glance" can be taken as saying that when the Spirit of Beauty looks upon the world and human beings, all that it sees are the intermittent occurrences of the beautiful because it is unable to see all else that makes up the "dim vast vale of tears, vacant and desolate." The beautiful does not form a unity, since it only flashes up intermittently in the midst of all that the Spirit of Beauty is blind to. In that case, the third trope does not really contradict the first but confirms it: the beautiful occurs thanks to the void that lets the transitory flashes and the dying flames shine. The result is a decidedly inside-out Platonism. The transitory and inconstant nature of Dasein—its immersion in "Doubt, chance, and mutability"—is what makes the appearance of the beautiful possible. Human finitude itself is the source of the beautiful. The "Hymn to Intellectual Beauty" thus names Intellectual Beauty: the manifold, passing shinings of the material and human world that flash into appearance thanks to darkness and vacancy are all the beauty there is and all that beauty is.

Jorie Graham, or, The Thing Called Form

Beauty's ineluctable tie to human time, mutability, finitude, enters into the thinking of form in Jorie Graham's poetics. Her is a poetics after Heidegger, for she writes knowledgeably and astutely in the wake of his essays on art and language and responds to the questions regarding art and language differently from Heidegger himself.

Her reflection on beauty, emerging in her 1987 collection *The End of Beauty* and amplified through the next several volumes of poetry, turns on the keyword *shape*—and along with it the word *thing*. Through the continual joining of these two terms, Graham elaborates a conception of the artwork that does not consider form to be the container of content or the pleasing arrangement of matter. In "Self-Portrait of the Gesture Between Them [Adam and Eve]," form is shape, but not shape imposed on a thing:

19
where the form is complete where the thing must be torn off
20
momentarily angelic, the instant writhing into a shape[45]

Form is linked with temporality—"the instant writhing into a shape"—not, I
think, to suggest that time is transformed into space but rather to indicate that
the thing shows itself in its shape, as a shape, fleetingly. "Writhing into a shape"
refers not to the thing's being wrenched out of time but to the thing's becoming-
form *in* time ("momentarily angelic"). "The form is complete" within a complex temporality of urgency ("must be torn off"), precariousness ("the instant"),
and ordeal or strife ("writhing"). Another passage helps clarify this temporality.
Here the poet is in an attitude of attentiveness, as is often the case with Graham.
In this instance, she listens. The poem is called "Annunciation," and its opening
stanza turns on the following phrase:

> listening into the slippery leaping
> of one thing into another
> for *shape* which is a faltering where it suddenly ceases
> to falter (77)

Again *shape* is precarious, here in the bodily, kinesthetic temporality of "a
faltering where it suddenly ceases / to falter." The *thing* is a sound, not noise;
it is something in its sound, a thing not yet heard and not yet named in the
unremitting sensory flow. Is it unnamed because unheard? Or is it unheard
because unnamed? With that question we enter into the problematic of Graham's poetics.

Shape arises from an attentiveness toward things and a discipline in language. The stanza begins with the poet listening for something in the midst
of the things she actually hears, including a chain saw, a bird's trill, an an-
nouncer on a loudspeaker, trucks on the highway (I say "the poet" because
Graham's reference to herself often oscillates between "she" and "I"):

> She's not sure she can hear it outside of the daylight,
> the small sound of matter wanting to be changed,
> she's not sure she can hear it outside of the daylight,
> the small sound of matter wanting to be changed into minutes,
> outside of the lie, the small click where silence slaps
> against that gear (chain saw?), that trill (?),
> outside of *outside* where the voice downtown announces
> over the p.a. the race's arrivals one by one,
> the numbers called out by lungs onto the small

harbor winds, onto the trucks-eight-miles-away-hitting-the-upgrade-on-50. . . .
She's not she sure can, listening into the slippery leaping
     of one thing into another
     for *shape* which is a faltering where it suddenly ceases
          to falter

It is tempting perhaps to discern a sympathetic fallacy in the line "the small
sound of matter *wanting* to be changed into minutes," the projection of the
poet's desire onto nature. But let's resist the temptation. The poem is called
"Annunciation," after all, so all the ambiguity of being addressed, desiring to
be addressed, fearing being addressed is already in play. Let's instead take up
the metaphor of *wanting*. Matter wants to become minutes in the sense that
in the poet's attentiveness matter comes toward her to become tempo and
rhythm in her poetic articulation, but she is not sure she can hear it:

> She's not sure she can, listening into the slippery leaping
>   of one thing into another
>   for *shape* which is a faltering where it suddenly ceases
>   to falter (for a *reason*, is that important?)
>   close by that trill again and the splash where three birds I
>   had altogether missed hit the leaves is that
>   important

The aside—"(for a *reason*, is that important?)"—acknowledges that the poet's
attentiveness is not mere attentiveness: she wants to hear *something* and she
wants to write, she wants to hear because she wants to write. The ambiguity of
annunciation lies in the zone where the desire to hear and the desire to write
meet. That is why she emphatically affirms the importance of the sound of the
three birds splashing into the leaves. She says that she had missed them, not
seeing them before their splash or, perhaps, not hearing the splash until after
it sounded. There is no escape from time and faltering; the very possibility of
writing lies in time and faltering. The belated hearing

>   is that
>   important, not a fullness yet, not a sentence yet, but a thinning,
>   a suggestion of distance in the flat, as where the
>   minute before and the minute before, like so many souls
>   the *under* keeps feeding forth feeding forth, cease.

The syncopated annunciation, the splash heard belatedly in silence, produces
not a fullness, not a whole sentence, but a suggestion. The stanza ends on
the verge of a paradox: "The sound of matter wanting to be changed *into*

minutes" occurs in that moment of syncopation which arrests the steady flow of minutes. That is perhaps how we are to understand shape as "a faltering where it suddenly ceases / to falter."

A third fragment, from "Self-Portrait as Hurry and Delay [Penelope at Her Loom]," linking thing and shape provides another image, this one visual, of the moment where one thing leaping into another ceases: "A shapeliness, / . . . an edge / to the light, / something that is not something else" (50). The line is a very condensed version of a motif in Graham where the light falling on something or illuminating it is figured as the appearance of an edge that cuts the undifferentiated blend and blur of light. The three shape/thing passages I have isolated—"the thing . . . torn off," "a faltering where it suddenly ceases / to falter," and "an edge to the light"—convey a conception and experience of form that does not refer to a shaped thing or the giving of shape to a thing. On the one hand, form is more precarious than that, for it is an instant, a hesitation, an edge. And on the other, the thing takes shape in that moment, suddenly appearing as "something that is not something else."

That the artwork's completion is but the timely breaking-off of the creative process is also attested to by Anselm Kiefer in his extraordinary Collège de France lectures. On *Riss* as form and as process, he says:

> It is in the studio that the reality of an artistic production in its physical and commercial sense is thought out. When I decide to interrupt the process of permanent transformation, which in my case never ends, I rely on the principle that there comes a moment when things have to stop and the ongoing work has to become a product. An artwork? The result, to be sure, is a product, but a product encompassing two different realities: the reality of the finished painting, as I have determined it, and the reality of its method of production. At this point one is able to discern its successive stages in its different pictorial layers: its history can be pieced together.
>
> The object, whose "figuration" is revealed immediately, is only a decoy, a lure. But as one draws close to the image one notices fractures—the upheavals that mark the painting's history. One discerns the hope and the despair that presided over its creation, the wavering, the erasures and other forms of destruction.[46]

The being held out into the nothing by which Heidegger defines *Angst* is internal to creativity, enabling and threatening the artwork until the oscillation of enabling and threatening, that faltering, ceases to falter: "The creation of a painting involves a ceaseless shuttling back and forth between nothing and something, a constant going from one state to the other. Now this process is not guided by any rule; it is as uncontrollable as ventricular fibrillation and for this reason it too can prove fatal. The vibration only ends when the painting leaves the studio, when it begins to circulate in the world and can no longer be worked."[47]

Poets tend to probe the question of form by foregrounding some particular aspect of poetic construction. The sonnet writer—or Wallace Stevens, in a different way—foregrounds the lineaments of the poem as a whole, the whole in relation to its parts. Donne's use of conceit or Coleridge's use of symbol foregrounds the metaphoric webbing of the poem. William Carlos Williams foregrounds the image. Jorie Graham, like Charles Olson in a different way, foregrounds the line, the phrase, the sentence. Hers is a poetics of syntax, and she turns that stress on syntax into the discipline by which she explores all her most compelling themes.

The intensity of the moments where attentiveness and discipline meet—where attentiveness to the leaping of one thing into another meets the discipline of syntax—never adduces a sense of plenitude. Indeed, for Graham, the sensorium—whatever we might try to call it: the world of the senses, nature, reality—is not a plenitude. She celebrates the loss of the Edenic plenitude. She is a poet who affirms fallibility and imbalance and finitude *and* suffers that affirmation. The passage I started with—"where the form is complete where the thing must be torn off / momentarily angelic, the instant writhing into a shape"—is from a poem titled "Self-Portrait as the Gesture Between Them" and subtitled "[Adam and Eve]." The setting is Eden, the protagonist is Eve, and one might conclude that the thing that must be torn off is the apple. But in a reversal characteristic of Graham's engagement with biblical and ancient texts, she turns the metaphorics around: the biblical fruit nowhere appears in the story except as a simile or metaphor for the "gesture between them." Thus:

> 1.
> The gesture like a fruit torn from a limb, torn swiftly.
>
> 8.
> So it was to have freedom she did it but like a secret thought.
> [. . .]
> Like a fruit that grows but only in the invisible.
> [. . .]
>
> 9.
> But a secret grows, a secret wants to be given away.
> For a long time it swells and stains its bearer with beauty.
> It is what we see swelling forth making the shape we know a thing by.
> The thing inside, the critique of the given.

The poem is thus a couple's story played out with reference to two never-quite-congruent couples, Adam and Eve and the couple of the self-portrait to which the poet herself belongs. The reversal I referred to bears on the meaning of *things* in Graham, but also and first of all to the word *thing*. What then is a thing? What is the word *thing*? The word has an ineluctable and delightful absurdity about it. *Thing* can be used to generalize: "the reason for things" (13); to suggest: "the thing toward which you reason" (9); to speculate: "the realm of uncreated things" (45); to specify: "the thing / called future"; to unspecify: "Not quite the thing that's needed" (7). All the examples are of course from Graham's poems. As a word, *thing* tends toward tautology. For example (not from Graham's poetry): Everything is a thing. Nothing is not a thing, that is, no thing is not a thing. Such statements are easily negated and in the process turned into portentous philosophical problems. Thus "Everything is a thing" can be rebutted with "Not everything is a thing." And it is questionable whether the statement "No thing is not a thing" squares with "Yes, but Nothing is not a thing." Games of logic and semantics are of limited interest in themselves and in any case are largely irrelevant to understanding poetry, except as poetry turns nonsense, paradox, illogic, or contradiction into a sharply edged percept and affect. Take the phrase *and nothing is but what is not*. The logicosemantic stress it adduces is turned to trope when put into the mouth of Macbeth at the moment he, having just heard the witches' prophecy that he himself will be king, first imagines gaining the crown by killing the king he has so valiantly served and defended:

> Present fears
> Are less than horrible imaginings:
> My thought, whose murder yet is but fantastical,
> Shakes so my single state of man, that function
> Is smothered in surmise, and nothing is
> But what is not.
> (*Macbeth*, act 1, scene 3, lines 138–43)

"And nothing is / But what is not" has the power to disclose Macbeth's state-of-mind (*Befindlichkeit*) in the midst of the tremor going through him at the picture of himself as a murderer. For he feels that now he is nothing and has nothing until the deed be done. (His Hamletlike hesitation will be short-lived.)

There is something essential in the tendency of the word *thing* to spiral alternately toward nonsense and tautology, synonym of nothing and everything, all-meaningful and meaningless. *Thing* is the word in English that continually marks the possibility latent in any naming that it will miss what it names. Unlike Eden, where "whatsoever Adam called every living creature, that *was* the name thereof" (Genesis 2:19), our world knows no such harmony between language and being. Just as Graham never laments the expulsion from Eden, she never laments the loss of this harmony. When she alludes to the Adamic power of language in "Self-Portrait as the Gesture Between Them"—"as they walked through the fields naming things"—it is part and parcel of the plenitudinous boredom that Eve is overthrowing with her desire, freedom, and error, "loving that error . . . , that break from perfection." Moreover, Graham's very use of the word *thing* in this poem—"the shape we know a thing by," "the thing inside," "the thing . . . torn off"—undoes the naming of Eve's action, that is, the fruit or the apple by which the Bible and tradition designate this *thing*. The word *thing* operates syntactically, displacing and breaking and opening the semantic fullness of *forbidden fruit. Thing* unnames the thing.

By the same token, the desire and discipline of poetry, with its attentiveness to things, aspires to name "something that is not something else." In this way Graham evokes the artwork's truth-event in its power to bring an entity to appearance as what it is, and her designation of artistic form as "a shapeliness, / an edge / to the light, / something that is not something else" also takes us back to Heidegger's thesis that "in fine art the art itself is not beautiful, but is called so because it produces the beautiful."[48] The notion that art does not produce the beautiful by applying a rule or conforming to a standard ultimately points to the beautiful's eventfulness, its unforeseen and unprecedented appearance. In Graham's language, the illumination or shining of this appearing is the "edge / to the light." Such is "the thing called / form."[49]

Anecdote of the Jug

Graham's probing of shape, form, attention, and creation through the semantic and syntactical dexterities of the word *thing*—and so a probing of language in relation to shape, form, attention, and creation—inevitably evokes Heidegger's exploration of things, thinghood, thingliness, and so on, from his reflection on the "mere thing" in "The Origin of the Work of Art" through his commentaries on Kant up to the 1950 essay "The Thing" and its oft-cited response to the question *what is a jug?* As with van Gogh's shoes, Heidegger again chooses equipment, a product of craft and an object of use, now in order to rethink what *craft* and *use* mean, that is, to think *craft* and *use* now from a different angle: "The jug is a thing as a vessel—it can hold something. . . . The jug is not a vessel because it was made; rather the jug had to be made because it is this holding vessel." He shifts attention from the outward look and shape of the jug to the making of the void into which and out of which the jug's contents pour: "The empty space, this nothing of the jug, is what the jug is as the holding vessel."[50] The craftsman's activity has to be understood in relation to this void:

> From start to finish the potter takes hold of the impalpable void and brings it forth as the container in the shape of a containing vessel. The jug's void determines all the handling in the process of making the vessel. The vessel's thingness does not lie at all in the material of which it consists, but in the void that holds.[51]

Applying the Rorty test, so far so good. Heidegger then asks, "How does the jug's void hold?" His answer brings out that the void holds or keeps what is poured in but that the unity of this "taking and keeping" is determined by the pouring out: "To pour from the jug is to give." To summarize the sequence: the essence of the jug is to hold; therefore, the true vessel is the void around which the jug is shaped; the essence of holding is the pouring out, and the essence of pouring out is giving; therefore, "the nature of the holding void is gathered in the giving."[52]

The immediate philosophical stakes of Heidegger's account are succinctly captured by Bill Brown as the jug sharpens the distinction between thing and object, that is, between a thing's "thingliness" and its appearance as an object, between being and instrumentality: "You could say that the jug has a use value that has nothing to do with (its) use (by humans): it is not man who grabs the jug but the jug that gathers man." Here, then, is a decisive moment in "Heidegger's strategy for thinking beyond the Subject, beyond Kant, for whom 'that which is becomes the object of representing that runs its course in the self-consciousness of the human ego.' It concludes his strategy, in search of the Thing, for overcoming the merely ontic and the merely phenomenological: for overcoming the subject and thus any subject-object divide."[53]

Gathered is a charged term, as Heidegger lowers his conceptual bucket deep into the etymological well of *das Ding* and draws up its derivation from Old German *dinc*, meaning "a gathering, and specifically a gathering to deliberate on a matter under discussion, a contested matter."[54] Within a few paragraphs, though, he dispenses with the obviously related *res publica* by which the Romans designated things of common concern and discussion, as well as the Latin *ens*, from Greek philosophy's *on*, to mean "that which is present in the sense of the standing forth here. . . . The jug is a thing neither in the sense of the Roman *res*, nor in the sense of the medieval *ens*, let alone in the modern sense of the object."[55] The "old usage" of *dinc* is deemed relevant for the idea of gathering only so long as it is not a gathering for purposes of deliberation, let alone a gathering of "equals in ruling and being ruled"—to use the terms by which Arendt recovers *res publica* through the lens of ancient Greek democracy. Rather, what the jug gathers is the fourfold of earth and sky, mortals and divinities.

Heidegger rousts all his poetic propensities to describe the gathering effected by the jug's void as water or wine pours into and out of it. The more interesting case is wine, as though what is poured from a simple *pichet* awakens on the modern philosopher's tongue a Dionysian taste of *terroir*:

> The spring stays on in the water of the gift. In the spring the rock dwells, and in the rock dwells the dark slumber of the earth, which receives the rain and dew of the sky. In the water of the spring dwells the marriage of sky and earth. It stays in the wine given by the fruit of the vine, the fruit in which the earth's nourishment and the sky's sun are betrothed to one another. In the gift of water, in the gift of wine, sky and earth dwell. But the gift of the outpouring is what makes the jug a jug. In the jugness of the jug, sky and earth dwell.
>
> The gift of the pouring out is drink for mortals. It quenches their thirst. It refreshes their leisure. It enlivens their conviviality. But the jug's gift is at times also given for consecration. If the pouring is for consecration, then it does not still a thirst. It stills and elevates the celebration of the feast. The gift of the pouring now is neither given in an inn nor is the poured gift a drink for mortals. The outpouring is the libation poured out for the immortal gods.[56]

It is just here, despite the passage's charms and emotional vivacity, that we must take our last step down the path into Heidegger's forest of symbols. For if the thing is neither ancient nor Christian nor modern—where then to place this gift of conviviality and consecration? With the jug, as with the peasant woman's shoes, this most modern of philosophers remains caught in a kind of rejection of the world—not a religious rejection of the world, but a nonreligious rejection of the *modern* world. Yet his thought is not nostalgic, since it seeks or, more accurately, awaits something new, an annunciation of a new epoch of being on the "traces of the fugitive gods." More is at stake than Heidegger's propensity to seek in preindustrial lifeworlds images of a not-yet-emerged beyond-modernity.

There is something worse than nostalgia in modern thought, and that is lyricism. Heidegger lyricizes the jug. Lyricism is not lyric, and great lyrics are not lyrical. Think only of Stevens's Heidegger-foreshadowing poems "Anecdote of the Jar" and "The Snow Man." It is possible to speculate on a biographical source of Heidegger's lyricizing thanks to a letter dated November 7, 1969, in his correspondence with Ernst Jünger. Jünger had written a text, titled "Shuttlecocks," to present to Heidegger on his eightieth birthday, describing it as "a series of notes" that "stem mostly from a stock of critical and self-critical remarks about language and style." A thread, he adds, is his "pleasant surprise" in "feel[ing] comfortable with the Alemannic region" and hence with Heidegger's childhood Swabian dialect. In Heidegger's ensuing comments on the text, his reflections on dialect and his upbringing include an anecdote about his father's two occupations as a cellarman and a sexton. It is a question not of a jug, but of a tub:

> p. 25 "D' Butte" for us is a feminine noun. I still see my father with a double use for (i.e., while carrying) the "tub":
> as a cellarman, "drawing off" the wine from the large barrels into small kegs (so it was done in the cellars of the Messkirch castle, where the *Zimmer Chronicle* was written);
> as sexton, filling the "fonts" with fresh water for sprinkling the morning of Easter Saturday.[57]

The gift of pouring from the jug enacts either conviviality or libation. As a master cooper and the sexton of Messkirch's Saint Martin's Catholic church, Friedrich Heidegger and his tub also knew two pours, wine from barrel to keg and water from well to font. As a master cooper, he crafted the barrels, kegs, and perhaps even the tubs; as sexton, he set up the implements of the priest's ministrations. He thus remains at one remove from gestures of conviviality and from gestures of the sacred. The tub is not a jug. The father is a craftsman and a caretaker, secure in his vocation and modest in his earnings, a modesty that made his son's only path to the education he craved a subsidized preparation for the priesthood. He lived long enough to know and lament his son's break with theology and not long enough to foresee his philosophical future. The father died in 1924; "The Thing" was written in 1950 and the letter to Jünger in 1969. Obviously there is no empirically sure way to link these moments, and a "wild psychoanalysis" is ill-advised. Nonetheless, the striking resonance between the remembrance of the tub and the invention of the jug—and their difference— suggests the kind of transmutation that Kenneth Burke calls the "motive" of symbolic action when it occurs in a poet's work. Does the anecdote of the jug honor the father in an illusory idealization? Or does it entomb the reality of his occupations in a splendid sarcophagus built to display the son's genius? Or does it atone for the son's failure to become the priest whose existence might have spiritually justified the father's earthly labors? Or does it transpose the shame of origins into pride of origin? Or is it the culmination of mourning by which the lost father is preserved within the son's most valued imagery? While these question remain in suspension, it is clear that the jug's fourfold transmutes the tub's workaday equipmentality into lyricism.

My own step away from Heidegger's path does not turn on the figure of the fourfold itself, but on his portrayal of its purported unity: "In the gift of the outpouring earth and sky, divinities and mortals dwell *together all at once*. These four, at one because of what they themselves are, belong together. Preceding everything that is present, they are enfolded into a single fourfold."[58] *At one because of what they themselves are*: the unity is important to Heidegger because it grounds his conclusion that the jug's being shows that the true nature of *things*, of the thingness of things, stands athwart "the countless objects everywhere of equal value" (which is how he characterizes the culture of modern society) and brings mortals into the proximity of divinities, in contrast to "the measureless mass of men as living beings" (which is how he characterizes the whole of modern social life).[59]

How might the fourfold be wrested from Heidegger's lyricized jug? I propose that earth, sky, mortals, and divinities be construed as four inseparable terms always in need of designation and symbolization. To extend the hypothesis, the four terms are designated in distinctive ways through all of Dasein's cultural and historical transformations, and such designations form its stances toward being. Viewed in this way, the four terms in themselves have near-zero semantic content. Compared to archetypes, they are semantically empty. But they are not abstract, like the four corners of Greimas's semiotic square, nor purely logical, as in Graham Harman's appropriation of Heidegger. Rather, they have a bare minimum of meaning in the sense that it is earth–sky–mortals–divinities that are inevitably designated (symbolized), but how they are designated has no preestablished or intrinsic content or transcendental origin or goal. Construed in this way, the fourfold works rather like the four elements of air, water, earth, and fire in Bachelard's criticism or can even be seen as a kind of recuperation of Ernst Cassirer's concept of symbolic forms without the subject-centered, progress-affirming assumptions that Heidegger so aggressively contested in his debates with Cassirer.[60] Modernity itself is what strips the fourfold down to the scantest meaning by casting off the transcendent and authoritative meanings that imbue mythic and religious fourfolds. That's what allows the fourfold to appear *as* a fourfold.

My reading of the fourfold runs counter to Heidegger's own texts. The most extensive and rigorous commentary on the fourfold, Andrew J. Mitchell's, amply demonstrates that Heidegger ultimately attempts to give each of the four terms a specific significance (without acknowledging and affirming the plurality of meanings produced by actual artworks and events). For example, Heidegger develops a particular understanding of mortals as a kind of yet-to-be-realized supersession of humans, in the philosophical tradition's sense of the rational animal. The *mortals* answers to Nietzsche's *Übermensch*, which Heidegger considers a "completion" of metaphysical determinations of human being that nevertheless fails to efface the metaphysical categories of animality and reason themselves. In Mitchell's interpretation, mortals' "being-*in*-death" points beyond Dasein's being-*toward*-death. In this way he demarcates what he takes to be a decisive break between the "early" Heidegger of *Being and Time* and the "later" Heidegger on being, the meaning of being, the history of being.[61] It follows that there is some kind of passage from human to mortal, an interpretation that leans hard on often enigmatic declarations such as the one in the Bremen lecture "The Danger" (1949): "The human is not yet the mortal."[62]

Rather than a passage or anticipated epochal break, I see the human and the mortal as an oscillation akin to that of inauthenticity and authenticity in *Being and Time*. Moreover, it strikes me that insofar as becoming mortals is a task or imperative, it is decidedly within not beyond modernity, since it calls for becoming capable of discarding Christianity's promise of everlasting life and its image of the immortal soul. Dasein's being-toward-death and mortals' being-in-death are, respectively, the existential and the ontological articulations of human mortality. Two perspectives, not an inferior and a superior stance. There is nonetheless an ambiguity in Heidegger, for he continually evokes at once the ancient Greeks and Christian peasants and craftsmen. For the Greeks, *anthropos* is mortal, in contrast to the immortal gods, and has no afterlife except earthly remembrance, while for Christians their earthly labors are a pilgrimage on the path to eternal life. Heidegger's efforts to turn that ambiguity into a synthesis, from the Greek temple and van Gogh's shoes to the tub-turned-jug, try in effect to paganize the everyday practices of Christian farmers and cellarmen. Such an appropriation of pagan ritual and belief ironically mimics the proselytizing strategies of the very Catholicism that Heidegger had turned away from.

"The Thing" is a fragment addressing the question of the meaning of being in lieu of *Being and Time*'s abandoned third part. The original tool analysis (of the hammer) establishes from the standpoint of Dasein's being-in-the-world the ontic jolt by which the interruption of habitual practice opens the ontological question. Subsequently, "The Origin of the Work of Art" credits the artwork with disclosing tool-being in its essence or truth (the peasant's shoes). "The Thing" reverses the standpoint of the first tool analysis. Now Dasein's being-in-the-world is viewed from the standpoint of the question of being. That is why it seems that it is not Dasein but the jug, in fact the jug's void, that gathers the fourfold together or, indeed, that the fourfold gather themselves in the jug or its void. What is the "subject" of the verb *gather*? Dasein, the jug, its void, the fourfold? On the one hand, the fourfold does not preexist Dasein as a transcendent meaning. On the other, the fourfold does not issue pristinely and sovereignly from Dasein. The fourfold comes *to*

Dasein as though from *beyond* Dasein, though it can be nothing other than Dasein's designations and symbolizations.

Modern thought is rich in conceptions that try to capture this recursivity, from the Gadamerian hermeneutical circle to the Derridean trace, from the Freudian navel of the dream to various Lacanian formulations of subjectivity as emerging from and inhabited by otherness, from Merleau-Ponty's chiasmic touch to sensation's asubjective consciousness in Deleuze, and perhaps most vividly of all Nietzsche's figure that "can turn its eyes at will and behold itself."

Two aspects of the anecdote of the jug help de-lyricize the fourfold.

First, tucked away in the fourfold is its own navel, for there is one term utterly unlike the others, and that is *mortals*. Let's say, in keeping with a theme throughout Heidegger's foregrounding of the question of being, that Dasein must encounter the fourfold in pure receptivity, a listening, a heeding of being. In that case, it receives from the fourfold the designation of itself (mortals) enfolded with that of earth–sky–divinities. None among the fourfold is addressed by the fourfold except mortals. Moreover, and conversely, because only mortals engage in acts of designation, Dasein encounters in the fourfold its designation of itself even as it cannot recognize that act of designation as its own. That is how Dasein's authentic/inauthentic oscillation—first analyzed existentially as thrownness and being-with-others—manifests itself from the standpoint of the question of being. And that is why, in my view, the fourfold cannot be a unity "at one because of what they themselves are, belong[ing] together." Mortals are not at one with the others, since Dasein is at once one of the four and the only one of the four that is addressed *by* the fourfold and the sole though un(self)-recognizable author *of* the fourfold.

Second, casting the gatherer of the fourfold as a void signals the fourfold's ungroundedness. Of the three epochal interpretations of being that Heidegger postulates, the ancient and the Christian designate the fourfold in relatively discernible ways. His commentaries on the Greek temple and the peasant's shoes flesh them out to a suggestive degree. In "The Thing," Heidegger engages modernity only by reducing it to the simple negation or forfeiture of being: in his language, the forgetting of being. In light of other strands of his thought, however, modernity marks the impossibility of the fourfold's unity not simply because Cartesian or scientific rationality determines beings as "objects of calculation and control," but because for us moderns being is a *question* and appears as a question thanks to the *Angst* by which we are held out into the nothing. Such, in Heidegger's own terms, is the condition of modern poetry and thought. Stripped of its lyricization, the jug allegory evokes not modernity's negation but modernity itself: ours is the epoch in which the designations and symbolizations of the fourfold arise from *nothing*, the void around which poems and artworks take shape. Modern artists and poets confront this predicament and possibility as *Angst*.

The impasse in Heidegger's response to modern art shows most tellingly in his hesitancy in the face of Hegel's claim that modernity demarcates the end of art. Hegel means that Western culture, in the wake of Christianity and the advent of modern reason, has moved "beyond the stage at which art is the supreme mode of our knowledge of the Absolute. The peculiar nature of artistic production and of works of art no longer fills our highest need. . . . Art, considered in its highest vocation, is and remains for us a thing of the past."[63] The whole of Heidegger's work dissolves the very idea of the Absolute. Being does not give itself over definitively to mind and knowledge. Modern art's vocation must therefore lie elsewhere. Yet in the epilogue to "The Origin of the Work of Art" Heidegger equivocates and defers when referring to this famous passage from Hegel's introduction to his *Aesthetics*. He readily acknowledges that the century and more since Hegel's lectures have of course seen "the rise of many new artworks and new movements. Hegel never meant to deny this possibility. But the question remains: is art still an essential way in which that truth happens which is decisive for our historical existence, or is art no longer of this character? If, however, it is such no longer, then there remains the question why this is so. The truth of Hegel's judgment has not yet been decided."[64]

What is there implicit in the end-of-art formula that Heidegger is reluctant to accept? Hegel sensed, virtually before the fact, that modern art would not anchor, reveal, or incarnate "that truth . . . which is decisive for our historical existence." He thought he himself had hold of art's replacement, namely, reason in its dialectical process of becoming the conjoining of Spirit and Reality in Absolute Knowledge. Insofar as thought dissolves the Absolute, as it does in Heidegger and Nietzsche, the Hegelian end of art in effect signals the advent of *modern* art, that is, art in its freedom from the imperative and role of holding society together or embodying an absolute truth. Invention, revolt, singularity, plurality, and relentless questioning become its provenance.

Modern poetry does indeed engage the fourfold, ever since the Romantics made poetry's language, percepts, and affects turn so thoroughly around keen observation of the physical world and aesthetic responsiveness to weather, landscapes, seascapes, shorelines, clouds, flowers, mountains, meadows and fields, woods and forests, sunrises and sunsets. Let's hold in abeyance for the moment the designation "Nature" for earth and sky, and let's not assume that the fourfold inevitably places divinities in the sky. The female figure in Stevens's "Sunday Morning" spends her sabbath not in worship but enjoying

"Complacencies of the peignoir, and late / Coffee and oranges in a sunny chair," even as "she feels the dark / Encroachment of that old catastrophe" in reveries that carry "her dreaming feet / Over the seas, to silent Palestine, / Dominion of the blood and sepulchre." By means of resymbolization, Stevens counters the ancients' placement of their gods in the sky overlooking earthbound mortals:

> Why should she give her bounty to the dead?
> What is divinity if it can come
> Only in silent shadows and in dreams?
> Shall she not find in comforts of the sun,
> In pungent fruit and bright, green wing, or else
> In any balm or beauty of the earth,
> Things to be cherished like the thought of heaven?
> Divinity must live within herself:
> Passions of rain, or moods in falling snow;
> Grievings in loneliness, or unsubdued
> Elations when the forest blooms; gusty
> Emotions on wet roads on autumn nights;
> All pleasures and all pains, remembering
> The bough of summer and the winter branch.
> These are the measures destined for her soul.

"Divinity must live within herself": her passions, moods, grievings, elations, and gusty emotions. These attain to divinity only so long as "all pleasures and all pains" are remembered and affirmed, as in Nietzsche's *tragic-Dionysian* and *amor fati*.

Graham's poetry also plies the fourfold of earth and sky, mortals and divinities. And like Stevens, she does not lyricize them into a unity. Divinities dissolve, or are transmuted, into the godless sacred. The human gestures by which things and experiences are allotted sacred space do not disappear even as gods and God have disappeared. In all of Graham's poems from which I have cited passages, she unfolds encounters between mortals and divinities, the human and the sacred. The various self-portraits of the couple intertwine with ancient couples, mythic and religious: Mary Magdalene and Christ, Orpheus and Eurydice, the Virgin Mary and Jesus, Apollo and Daphne, St. Theresa and Christ, Adam and Eve. The source of those encounters is always art, from the biblical and Homeric texts to Ovid to Renaissance sculpture and painting. The sacred survives not as a countermovement to modernity but rather thanks to art's secularizing essence, that is, its postmetaphysical vocation of delivering ancient and biblical stories, symbols, and images over to the poetic imagination.

For Heidegger, it will be recalled, world-founding works of past epochs, such as the Bamberg cathedral and Paestum temple, have suffered "world-withdrawal and world-decay. . . . The works are no longer the same as they once were. . . . As bygone works they stand over against us in the realm of tradition and conservation."[65] That too marks the end of art in Hegel's sense. By the same token, though, Heidegger misses that what enables those ancient and medieval works to persevere *as* tradition is the aestheticizing and secularizing power of art itself, and so he misses in turn how modern art's liberation from the task of world-founding lets it, as in Graham's poetry, plumb the expressive possibilities of tradition for new, unprogrammed ends.

The Fate of Beauty

—Will you allow as a certainty that we are at a turning?
—If it is a certainty it is not a turning.
MAURICE BLANCHOT, "On a Change of Epoch"

Mont Blanc

Let's now return to earth and sky in their determination as Nature. Once again the problematic gets framed philosophically by Kant, since nature figures centrally in both the beautiful and the sublime in the *Critique of Judgment*. At the same time, the beautiful and the sublime find a poetic framing in the juxtaposition of Shelley's "Hymn to Intellectual Beauty" and "Mont Blanc."

The beautiful is luminous and fleeting in "Hymn to Intellectual Beauty," a transitory flash occasioned by darkness and void. "Mont Blanc" seems on the face of it to affirm something else. Addressing the mountain in the concluding lines, Shelley asks:

> And what were thou, and earth, and stars, and sea,
> If to the human mind's imaginings
> Silence and solitude were vacancy? (142–44)

The Alps are already a point of reference for Kant, especially because of the German translation of Horace-Bénedict de Saussure's multivolume *Voyages dans les Alpes*. Saussure (1740–1799), a Swiss geologist, ascended Mont Blanc in 1787 around the time Kant began to conceive the *Critique of Judgment*. Kant draws on an anecdote in Saussure's work to illustrate his own notion that the experience and judgment of the sublime in nature requires "a far greater culture" than the experience and judgment of the beautiful: "The good and otherwise sensible Savoyard peasant (as Herr de Saussure relates) had no hesitation in calling all devotees of the icy mountains fools"; what "we, prepared by culture, call sublime will appear merely repellent to the unrefined person. He will see in the proofs of the dominion of nature . . . only the distress, danger, and need that would surround the person who was banished thereto." There is much suggested by the word "banished" here (or the likewise suggestive "exposed," in Bernard's translation). The peasant who inhabits the Alpine valleys and slopes secures there his dwelling, workplace, and livelihood; the glaciers and peaks loom as the inhospitable horizon of his world, a fearsome site of exile and exposure. For the scientist, adventurer, tourist, or poet, by contrast, the same glaciers and peaks arouse a unique sense of grandeur, though Kant does allow that the peasant may be right about foolishness if, unlike Saussure himself, the visitor were to undertake "the dangers to which he there exposed himself, as most travelers usually do, merely as a hobby, or in order one day to be able to describe them with pathos" (§29).[1]

The Alps and the sublime had become an intensely charged element of European culture during the three decades between 1787, when Saussure made what was considered only the second ascent of Mont Blanc, and the summer of 1816, when the Shelleys arrived at Chamonix filled with expectations. They had just toured Lac Léman (Lake Geneva) with Byron, visiting the sites of Rousseau's *Julie, ou, la nouvelle Héloïse* and tracing the fictional footsteps of Julie and Saint-Preux. By a stroke of luck they even managed, like Rousseau's lovers themselves, to sail in a storm on the lake. Simon Schama gives a lively albeit archly ironizing account of the "sublimity tourism on the roads to the Alps" and yet considers Shelley's poem "one of his darkest and most disturbing."[2] Saussure, scientist and mountain climber, was also the great-grandfather of the linguist Ferdinand de Saussure, founder of structuralism. I do not intended to unravel this tangle of geology, philosophy, tourism, language, and poetry so much as to enter into it in the hope of understanding Shelley's poem and Kant's "Analytic of the Sublime" (§§23–29 of the Third Critique).

The philosopher and the poet touch in their respective modes of thinking on the sublime's relation to the beautiful, its antagonism to superstition, its uncanny relation to human dwelling, and its wrenching of the inner/outer boundary. Even though the philosopher's concepts and the poet's percepts and affects will never neatly align, Kant and Shelley share those four themes: inner/outer, beautiful/sublime, sublimity/superstition, poetry/dwelling.

Kant approaches the sublime, the beautiful, and nature through a sequence of interlocking propositions. The capacity for the aesthetic judgment of the beautiful in art is the precondition for apprehending beauty in nature, but this precedence of art over nature in the formation of aesthetic judgment is counterbalanced by the preeminence of natural beauty insofar as it stirs a moral feeling off to the side, so to speak, of aesthetic judgment. While the cultivated capacity for aesthetic judgment of the beautiful is the precondition for the capacity to experience the sublime in nature, the moral dimension is internal to the aesthetic judgment of the sublime, not merely alongside it. Roughly speaking, there is a sequence in which one facet of aesthetic judgment is the precondition for another facet that in some sense outdoes it: *the beautiful in art → the beautiful in nature → the sublime in nature.* The sequence is not a simple succession, however, as all three facets of aesthetic judgment in effect coexist. Kant's procedure for distinguishing among them is designed to account for the underlying harmony among the mind's three distinct faculties: imagination, understanding, and reason.

As with so many other moments in Kant's aesthetics, the account of nature in relation to art, the beautiful, and the sublime often rattles the very concepts and categories he deploys. Let's work through each moment in the sequence.

The beautiful occurs in art and in nature. It is a phenomenon of *technē* and of *physis*. What is the relation? On the one hand, "art can only be called beautiful if we are aware that it is art and yet it looks to us like nature," while nature, on the other hand, is "beautiful, if at the same time it look[s] like art." That is, the beautiful appears in nature thanks to the observers' aesthetic disposition and receptivity as already shaped by art, while the beautiful appears in art only insofar as it looks like nature. Looking like nature, though, is not a question of resemblance or imitation for Kant; rather, "the purposiveness in its form must . . . seem to be as free from all constraint by arbitrary rules as if it were a mere product of nature" (§45).[3] *As if.* On the one hand, we do not "learn from nature what we have to find beautiful," for then "the judgment of taste would be subject to empirical principles" (§58).[4] And on the other, the artwork is organic and autotelic and hence analogous to nature in the effect of its appearance on the observer. It is this aspect of the artwork that is radically rethought by Heidegger and Deleuze as, in the latter's phrase, "the self-positing of the created."[5] It follows from Kant's account, in keeping with the interpretation I have advanced thus far, that human beings experience the beautiful in nature only because they create art and through it develop their aesthetic sensibility and cultivate their judgment as the urge to persuade. Without art, there is no experience of the beautiful in nature.

Traversing the interlocking movement of nature and art in the reverse direction, there is, Kant asserts, a certain "preeminence of the beauty of nature over the beauty of art." The art-dependent responsiveness to "the beautiful *forms* of nature" is accompanied by an interest that does not have a corollary, according to Kant, in the response to art itself. He calls this interest an "intellectual interest," in order to distinguish it from the instrumental interest in the usefulness of natural entities and from those entities' mere sensory "charms," and he sees in it the unqualified affirmation regarding the beautiful in nature *that it be*:

> Someone who alone (and without any intention of wanting to communicate his observations to others) considers the beautiful shape of a wildflower, a bird, an insect, etc., in order to marvel at it, to love it, and to be unwilling for it to be entirely absent from nature, even though some harm might come to him from it rather than there being any prospect of advantage to him from it, takes an immediate and certainly intellectual interest in the beauty of nature. I.e., not only the form of its production but also its existence pleases him, even though no sensory charm has a part in this and he does not combine any sort of end with it. (§42)[6]

Leaving aside possible objections to Kant's assumption that the artwork in producing the beautiful does not awaken an analogous sense of marvel, love, and pleasure in the work's very existence, let's simply follow out his thinking here in order to see the distinction he wants to make regarding the role of the faculties.

The beautiful in nature, as in art, occasions the accord of the faculties of imagination and understanding; that is, it combines the free sensibility to pleasure with the claim to universal agreement. Since no law determines this universality, as the rule derives from the example in the judgment *this is beautiful*, reason (the mind's third faculty) plays no part in the judgment itself. Reason's own judgments yield "pleasure or displeasure" in a "moral feeling" rather than as "taste." However, reason does take an intellectual interest in the beautiful in *nature* because there the disinterestedness and universality of judgment are tied to an "objective reality" in the sense that nature (unlike art) is a law-governed domain of necessity. Reason perks up at the experience "that nature should at least show some trace or give a sign that it contains in itself some sort of ground for assuming a lawful correspondence of its products with our satisfaction that is independent of all interest."[7] Nature otherwise has nothing to do with morality, for it is amoral in itself and is ubiquitously the object of our self-preservative interests and needs. The beautiful in nature lets reason *feel* that disinterestedness and universality belong in the world. Kant puts this somewhat differently, and quite eloquently, in an early work when he says that "beautiful things indicate that the human being fits into the world."[8] The beautiful, it will be recalled, is also a "symbol of morality" (§59) insofar as one's aesthetic judgment esteems the worth of others in claiming their universal agreement. In sum, reason finds an analogy to itself in the beautiful in general and takes an intellectual interest in the beautiful in nature in accordance with its own requirements of freedom, universality, and objectivity. In this way, reason is able to harmonize with the other two faculties, imagination and understanding, even though it has no role in their distinctive interplay in the aesthetic judgment of the beautiful.

The aesthetic judgment of the sublime, by contrast, brings reason into its own interplay with imagination. It hinges on the encounter with nature's magnitudes and its power. The imagination's ordering of sensibility is over-run by extreme magnitude: "What is excessive for the imagination . . . is as it were an abyss, in which it fears to lose itself" (§27).[9] Most especially with ab-solute magnitude: "The infinite, which for sensibility is an abyss" (§29).[10] The very fact that the mind does not simply unravel in the face of this abyss results from its capacity to form a cogent concept of infinity; such conceptualization is the work of the faculty of reason and does not depend upon the imagi-nation's ability to gather sensations ("the real of perception") into sensory-perceptual coherence. Here the inner drama of the faculties, as conceived by Kant, is one in which reason demands of imagination that it endeavor to make the supersensible sensible and then enjoys imagination's failure to do so as an ultimate affirmation of its own unique grasp of the supersensible. In Kant's words: "Yet for reason's idea of the supersensible to produce such an effort of the imagination is not excessive but lawful, hence it is precisely as attractive as it was repulsive for mere sensibility" (§27).[11] The judgment ad-ducing this "conflict" "remains only aesthetic because . . . it represents merely the subjective play and powers of the mind (imagination and reason) as har-monious even in their contrast" (§27).[12] "Harmonious even in their contrast": Deleuze aptly calls this moment, rather, "a discordant accord."[13] The affect peculiar to the sublime is explained by this drama of the faculties: "The mind feels itself *moved* in the representation of the sublime in nature . . . This move-ment (especially in its inception) may be compared to a vibration, i.e., to a rapidly alternating repulsion from and attraction to one and the same object" (§27).[14] Such is the *mathematically sublime*.

The *dynamically sublime* follows a similar but distinct pattern, now with respect to encounters with nature's overwhelming strength and force. The affect in question is a distinctive permutation of fear, the permutation that supposedly goes over the head of the Savoyard peasant. "We can . . . consider an object as *fearful* without being afraid *of* it, if, namely, we judge it in such a way that we merely *think* of the case in which we might wish to resist it and think that in that case all resistance would be futile." The sight of volcanoes, lightning, "hurricanes with the devastation they leave behind, the boundless ocean set into a rage, a lofty waterfall on a mighty river, etc., . . . only becomes all the more attractive the more fearful it is, as long as we find ourselves in safety, and we gladly call these objects sublime because they elevate the strength of our soul above its usual level and allow us to discover within ourselves a capacity for resistance of quite another kind, which gives us courage to measure ourselves against the apparent all-powerfulness of nature" (§28).[15]

What precisely is this other strength? Kant's great innovation is to turn the tables on the superhuman force of natural occurrence as well as the sensible abyss of infinity, for "the irresistibility of [nature's] power . . . at the same time . . . reveals a capacity for judging ourselves as independent of it and a superiority over nature on which is grounded a self-preservation of quite another kind than that which can be threatened and even endangered by nature outside us, whereby the humanity in our person remains undemeaned even though the human being must submit to that dominion." Pushed one step further, this experience of the gap between nature's overweening power and the mind's independence marks out how "nature is judged as sublime . . . insofar as . . . it calls forth our power [*Kraft*] (which is not part of nature) to regard those things about which we are concerned (goods, health and life) as trivial, and hence to regard its power [*Macht*] (to which we are, to be sure, subjected in regard to these things) as not the sort of dominion over ourselves and our authority to which we would have to bow if it came down to our highest principles and their affirmation or abandonment." Self-preservation splits in this conception between life-preserving and value-preserving forces. The sublime affords the experience of this split in a value-heroic fashion: "Thus nature is here called sublime merely because it raises the imagination to the point of presenting those cases in which the mind can make palpable to itself the sublimity of its own vocation even over nature" (§28).[16]

From another angle, Kant's account of the sublime is a philosophical watershed in the process that Max Weber will call the *disenchantment of nature*. For millennia, and throughout the Christian era, lightning and thunder as well as droughts and plagues were experienced as expressions of divine rage. A tradition that pictured the atmosphere and weather as the realm of Satan and his minions, whose evildoings were manifest in fog and foul air as well as hail, sleet, and thunderstorms, lasted well into seventeenth-century Protestantism and reached as far as Milton's *Paradise Lost*.[17] In the change articulated by Kant, the fearful in nature ceases to be experienced as a fear of God. That epochal change is part and parcel of a transformation—a maturation, in Kant's eyes—in the response to God's power and justness. "The right frame of mind to marvel at the greatness of God" cannot be obtained simply by consciousness that one's "contemptible disposition" has "offended . . . a power whose will is irresistible and at the same time just." Rather, only when a person "is conscious of his upright, God-pleasing disposition do those effects of power serve to awaken in him the idea of the sublimity of this being [that is, God], insofar as he recognizes in himself a sublimity of disposition suitable to God's will, and is thereby raised above the fear of such effects of nature, which he does not regard as outbursts of God's wrath." In light of human fallibility and in the face of one's shortcomings and failings, humility too can be "a sublime state-of-mind, that of voluntarily subjecting oneself to the pain of self-reproach in order gradually to eliminate the causes of it." Whereas "fear and anxiety before the being of superior power" are founded on superstition, such humility and the upright disposition are "the way alone" by which "religion internally distinguish[es] itself from superstition" (§28).[18]

The account of nature and God—earth, sky, divinities—in the "Analytic of the Sublime" brings out the radicalness of Kant's thinking. He in effect lays down two conditions that must be fulfilled before there can be an aesthetic experience and judgment of the sublime. The divine and the demonic must be dispelled from the physical world, and fear of divine retribution must dissolve and be supplanted by a disposition of the will attuned solely to being suitable to God's will. Fear of God's righteous wrath is not sublime, and nature's destructive force is not divine. It is Kant's innovation to link these two negations. He conjoins the *disenchantment of nature* with, in the title of the major work after the Third Critique, *religion within the limits of reason alone.* The disappearance of the wrathful God from morality disenchants nature by overcoming the affective foundation of superstition. For later thinkers, a moral disposition suitable to the will of a just God need not ultimately affirm the existence of God at all; Habermas, for example, recasts Kantian morality as the formal pragmatics of communicative action in which the tacit pledge to mutual understanding orients the interlocutors toward what is right and just.[19] Kant's own formulations, by the same token, suggest that morality does not simply and permanently abolish superstition and myth but rather, like enlightenment in general, "is a difficult matter that can only be accomplished slowly" (§40).[20] The upright disposition rises above the fear of nature and of God, and humility subjects oneself to the pain of self-reproach in order to lift one up again. These are processes rather than permanent achievements; while the spontaneity of fear and pain avoidance are overcome by moral action and transformed into respect and self-respect, there is no basis for assuming that such spontaneity can be overcome once and for all.[21]

The sublime stirs turbulence in the conceptual-experiential distinction of inside and outside: "The sublime in nature is only improperly so called, and should properly be ascribed only to the manner of thinking, or rather to its foundation in human nature" (§30).[22] Sublimity belongs to the subject even as he or she attributes it to nature. "Improperly so-called" signifies not a simple mistake, but ineluctable error. The misnomer is a kind of lived metaphor, an experience-structuring trope, which attributes the peculiar quality of elevation in the affect of sublimity to the "object" that occasions it. Recall that *this is beautiful* is also an as-if-objective judgment for Kant in which one "will speak of the beautiful as if beauty were a property of the object and the judgment logical . . . , although [the judgment] is only aesthetic and contains merely a relation of the representation of the object to the subject" (§6).[23] In aesthetic judgment, whether of the beautiful or the sublime, the subject cannot help but attribute to the object the quality of the feelings aroused within by, in Kant's terms, the interplay of the subject's own faculties. By the same token, this interplay of faculties is not purely "subjective" in the ordinary sense because it could not happen without the "object"; likewise, the projected *as if* still distinguishes the beautiful's luminous appearance (*Schein*) from sheer illusion (*Schein*). The Heideggerian lexicon aims at capturing the entwinement of inner and outer by shedding, or suspending, the terms *subject/object* altogether. The Kantian *as if* becomes the being-outside-oneself of attunement and ec-stasis.

In Shelley's "Mont Blanc" the overwhelming of the senses—the exceeding of the imagination's power to give sensory coherence to sensation in Kant's terms—takes the form of an intensification of the senses that culminates in breaching the boundary between what is grasped as the visible outer world and what is sensed as rampant imaginings from within. The vertiginous confusion itself is attributed to the scene ("Dizzy Ravine!") rather than the self:

> Dizzy Ravine! and when I gaze on thee
> I seem as in a trance sublime and strange
> To muse on my own separate phantasy (34–36)

Perception and imagining mingle in an "unremitting interchange" (39), "one legion of wild thoughts" (41) which rises to its climax with the sensation that the mind's imaginings are shadows projected in the "cave of the witch Poesy" (44) through which "some faint image" of the outer scene itself is sought, until abruptly "the breast / From which they fled recalls them, thou art there!" (47–48). "Thou art there!": the outer scene breaks through the poetic spell that it itself set in motion; the sensory overabundance of the Ravine of Arve provokes and then halts the poet's "own separate phantasy."

Such spiraling movements between scene and mind are woven into the figurative pattern of the poem's opening two stanzas, where Shelley pushes his propensity for simile and analogy to the verge of meaningless tautology as the mind is likened to a valley and the valley to a mind: "The everlasting universe of things / Flows through the mind" (1–2) like a river through a valley and produces a torrent of tones "Now dark—now glittering—now reflecting gloom— / Now lending splendour" (3–4) in and to the mind, which itself is like a "feeble brook" feeding and overtaken by "a vast river":

> The everlasting universe of things
> Flows through the mind, and rolls its rapid waves,
> Now dark—now glittering—now reflecting gloom—
> Now lending splendour, where from secret springs
> The source of human thought its tribute brings
> Of waters,—with a sound but half its own,
> Such as a feeble brook will oft assume
> In the wild woods, among the mountains lone,
> Where waterfalls around it leap for ever,
> Where woods and winds contend, and a vast river
> Over its rocks ceaselessly bursts and raves.
>
> Thus thou, Ravine of Arve . . . (1–12)

Through this "many-coloured, many-voiced vale" flows the Arve, like "The everlasting universe of things / Flows through mind," and yet the bursting raving river is itself a *likeness*:

> awful scene,
> Where Power in likeness of the Arve comes down
> From the ice gulphs that gird his secret throne,

at the same time that *sky* provides the image of *earth*: "Bursting through these dark mountains like the flame / Of lightning through the tempest" (15–18). Unlike the Coleridgean model of symbol in which the poetic description of outer nature is at the same time the metaphorical evocation of the poet's inner nature, harmonizing Nature and Self, Shelley's entangled analogies trace the breakdown of inner and outer.

As in Kant's "dynamically sublime," nature is encountered in all its might. Its fearsomeness is immediately, unmediatedly present and yet does not pose a threat. Might inspires awe rather than fear so long as one does not have to flee bodily harm. In the right season and weather, the sublime is an experience that can be sought out in relative security, but the fact that the Shelleys' 1816 travels in the Alps followed an established touring route in no way undercuts the significance of the experience, nor the originality of Shelley's attempt to capture it poetically. It does mean, though, that he arrived with expectations regarding what he would see and an awareness of the literary precedents inspired by that landscape. One of those antecedents he answers intertextually, indeed rebuts, namely, Coleridge's "Hymn before Sun-rise, the

Vale of Chamouni." Many are the images and paradoxes in Coleridge ("most awful Form"; "thy silent sea of pines"; "I worshipped the Invisible alone"; "Motionless torrents! silent cataracts!"; "eagles, play-mates of the storm"; "lightnings"; "thy sky-pointing peaks"; "Thy kingly Spirit enthroned among the hills"; etc.), that Shelley will echo, all the better to reject Coleridge's evocation of God as source of sublimity and creator of the scene. Coleridge:

> Who made you glorious as the Gates of Heaven
> Beneath the keen full moon? Who bade the sun
> Clothe you with rainbows? Who, with living flowers
> Of loveliest blue, spread garlands at your feet?—
> God! let the torrents, like a shout of nations,
> Answer! and let the ice-plains echo, God!
> God! sing ye meadow-streams with gladsome voice!
> Ye pine-groves, with your soft and soul-like sounds!
> And they too have a voice, yon piles of snow,
> And in their perilous fall shall thunder, God!

Where Coleridge has recourse to God as the unmoved mover, Shelley calls the unseen force moving through the earth and human perception "Power." And he attributes the power to name Power solely to the "human mind's imaginings":

> And what were thou, and earth, and stars, and sea,
> If to the human mind's imaginings
> Silence and solitude were vacancy? (142–44)

Shelley's agon with the preceding, still active generation of poets also drives the intertextual moment that concludes "Hymn to Intellectual Beauty," where he affirms his worship of the Spirit of Beauty for its formative role in his youth and prays for its continuing sustenance—

> Thus let thy power, which like the truth
> Of nature on my passive youth
> Descended, to my onward life supply
> Its calm—to one who worships thee,
> And every form containing thee,
> Whom, Spirit fair, thy spells did bind
> To fear himself, and love all human kind (78–84)

—just as Wordsworth affirms his worship of nature in "Tintern Abbey": "Knowing that Nature never did betray / The heart that loved her." Against Wordsworth's Nature, Shelley affirms the beautiful, and against Coleridge's God, the imagination.

The concluding question of "Mont Blanc"—"And what were thou . . . ?"—clinches a motif that runs throughout the poem. The visible adduces a palpable sense of the invisible: "Far, far above, piercing the infinite sky, / Mont Blanc appears,—still, snowy, and serene—" (60–61), while within its visible stillness the ice-encased mountain invisibly gives birth to the roaring Arve. Its glacial landscape is "A desert peopled by storms alone, / Save when the eagle brings some hunter's bone" (67). A series of striking images conveys the perception of imperceptibility:

> In the calm darkness of moonless nights,
> In the lone glare of day, the snows descend
> Upon the Mountain; none beholds them there,
> Nor when the flakes burn in the sinking sun,
> Or the star-beams dart through them:—Winds contend
> Silently there, and heap snow with breath
> Rapid and strong, but silently! Its home
> The voiceless lightning in these solitudes
> Keeps innocently . . . (130–38)

It is now possible to see how the elements of the sublime converge in a new configuration in the three primary events of the Shelleyan sublime: (1) the unmediated contemplation of nature's overawing might volatilizes inner and outer reality; (2) the ecstatic overabundance of the visible makes the invisible palpable; and (3) the mind's imaginative capacity in the face of solitude and silence transforms vacancy into images of the unseen and unheard. It is the pulsation among these three that constitutes the sublime in nature. The imaginative capacity at issue is not the faculty of imagination in the Kantian sense of the mind's power to assemble sensations into sensible coherence through representations of pleasure/displeasure. Or, rather, Shelley's poem's percepts and affects are oblique to Kant's concept. For it is a question now of the artistic or poetic imagination. As Kiefer puts it, the artist (or poet) "directs us to what our senses cannot perceive."[24]

"Mont Blanc" also provides a different angle on Kant's notion that the sublime in nature depends upon the beautiful and that the beautiful in nature depends upon the beautiful in art. That the sublime in nature ultimately originates from art is evinced for Shelley in the experience afforded by his own poetic imagination that silence and solitude in the face of mountain, earth, stars, and sea do not yield vacancy. Without art, mere vacancy. Which is to say that artistic or poetic imagination itself originates from—in the sense of emerges out of—vacancy. Such is the movement of *Rausch* out of *Angst* that

Heidegger fails to articulate. By the same token, imagination is not purely "subjective" or purely the "subject's." It is an ec-stasis—transports of the mind and senses, a dissonant attunement—as "the everlasting universe of things / Flows through the mind." As for the beautiful, it scintillatingly appears—*is* scintillating appearing—according to "Hymn to Intellectual Beauty" thanks to darkness, the Spirit of Beauty being "like darkness to a dying flame." Vacancy and darkness. The nothing and the abyss. These are not simple negations of the cultivated capacity for the experience and judgment of the beautiful and the sublime. They are also its precondition. How is it possible to be both precondition and negation at the same time? Such a notion is implied in Nietzschean *Rausch*; the frenzy of creation and the rapt attentiveness of receptivity cannot be sustained. In Heidegger's terms, the aesthetic attunements and artistic acts that override *Angst* then lapse back into it. Such a rhythmic vacillation is what I have called Dasein's being enfolded-upon-and-in-strife-with-itself. Shelley's two poems disclose the nothing in its double aspect of precondition and negation of the artistic state by evoking the temporality of the beautiful and the sublime. The beautiful is fleeting; the sublime is unendurable.

From yet another angle, what emanates from the configuration in "Mont Blanc" of inner/outer, visible/invisible, vacancy/imagination, is a theme concerning time and formlessness. Mont Blanc rises in majestic stillness and serenity, while

> Its subject mountains their unearthly forms
> Pile around it, ice and rock; broad vales between
> Of frozen floods, unfathomable deeps (62–64)

The sheer formlessness evokes the unimaginable violence of earthquake or volcano hidden in the depths of geological time:

> —how hideously
> Its shapes are heaped around! rude, bare, and high,
> Ghastly, and scarred, and riven.—Is this the scene
> Where the old Earthquake-daemon taught her young
> Ruin? Were these their toys? or did a sea
> Of fire, envelope once this silent snow?
> None can reply—all seems eternal now. (69–75)

The earth's formless forms seem eternal in human perspective; they indeed inform our very sense of eternity while at the same time providing the image of the seismic upheavals and catastrophes that created the landscape we

inhabit. Havoc appears in the guise of permanence, the glacial pace of chaos.
A double paradox is posed by the formlessness in the sublime: the mountains
are *unearthly earth* and their glaciers and ice forms are an *uninhabited city*:

> there, many a precipice,
> Frost and the Sun in scorn of mortal power
> Have piled: dome, pyramid, and pinnacle,
> A city of death, distinct with many a tower
> And wall impregnable of beaming ice.
> Yet not a city, but a flood of ruin
> Is there . . . (102–8)

This passage invites a rethinking of the boundary that Kant draws between
the Savoyard peasant and the cultivated traveler. The peasant's sense of ban-
ishment and exposure as he contemplates "the icy mountains" does not contrast with the Shelleyan sublime so much as give access to it. The emphatic
experience of the divide between the hospitable and habitable and the inhospitable and uninhabitable earth is at the core of Shelley's experience and
symbolization of the sublime. When Kant says that "beautiful things indicate that the human being fits into the world," does he imply, wittingly or
not, that the sublime, in contradistinction to the beautiful, registers our not
belonging-in-the-world?

Mont Blanc gives a glimpse of earth before humankind (the unmeasured
time of "the old Earthquake-daemon") and of earth without humankind ("A
city of death . . . Yet not a city"). Mind encounters earth stripped of mind:

> The works and ways of man, their death and birth,
> And that of him and all that his may be;
> All things that move and breath with toil and sound
> Are born and die; resolve, subside and swell.
> Power dwells apart in its tranquillity
> Remote, serene, and inaccessible:
> And *this*, the naked countenance of earth,
> On which I gaze, even these primaeval mountains
> Teach the adverting mind. The glaciers creep
> Like snakes that watch their prey, from their far fountains,
> Slow rolling on; (92–102)

The predator image likely alludes to the history of the Mer de Glace snaking
down the mountain and causing the village of Le Bois, as well as other settle-
ments, to be abandoned in the early seventeenth century, during the Little Ice
Age. The power of nature to destroy "the works and ways of men" belongs of

course to Kant's dynamically sublime. But the meaning of the inhospitable earth has today acquired new valences. Just two hundred years after the Shelleys visited Chamonix and Percy wrote this poem and Mary conceived the scene where Victor Frankenstein is confronted by his creature on the Mer de Glace itself, the glacier has melted down and shrunk back to but a semblance of its former self. Less an icy predator of villages and villagers than a serpent's shed skin, the Mer de Glace has become Europe's emblem of global warming in the Anthropocene.[25]

The stomach-churning pathos aroused by the receding glacier, whether witnessed firsthand or simply seen in photos and graphs, renders an uncanny inverted twin to the reading of "Mont Blanc." Moving counter to the awe that Shelley evokes with such unmatched intensity and complexity is the dismay and pity that ecological awareness stirs at the sight of the melting glacier. Nor can the glacier any longer stimulate awe in the historically aware spectator in the form of the Kantian feeling of the mind's moral superiority to mere physical force, the superior "strength of our soul" and reason over nature. As the sublime evaporates, a new order of fear and danger unfolds within this pity for nature, since among the victims of the anthropocentric hubris of the industrial, technological, and economic forces that alter climate and extinguish whole species is *anthropos* itself.[26] Dasein—the being that we ourselves are—is the endangering species endangering itself. The very transformations of nature that sustain human life also tear at it; what Marx called humankind's metabolic interchange with nature has unveiled itself as asymmetrical warfare: the more *anthropos* exercises its power over *physis*, that is, its physical rather than its moral power, the more *physis* threatens to overpower *anthropos*. The flaw in the pity-for-nature stance is that nature cannot lose: "Nature cruel in her cheerfulness; cynical in her sunrises," in Nietzsche's words (WP 850).[27]

Anthropos–Physis–Technē

Whatever designations our philosophies dream up, "Nature" (*physis*, "the everlasting universe of things," earth) will outlast "Man" (humanity, humankind, *Homo sapiens*, Dasein). The ancient Greeks understood this because of their experience of sacked cities and gratuitous death, which shaped how city and individual rose up against the inevitable nothing by striving in words and deeds to be remembered. Nietzsche discovered the "raging discordance of art and truth" in Greek tragedy, and Arendt realized that word and deed were the Greeks' value-creating rage against being forgotten. The Greek designation of humans as mortals was transvalued by Christianity, redesignated and

resymbolized in the promise of immortality, first in the vision of the redemption of earthly life in God's kingdom on earth and then in a transcendence of
nature altogether in the immortal soul's ascent to Heaven.

Two vocal sides of the Anthropocene debate find a way to enjoy apoca-
lyptic expectations. A strand of climate-change deniers believes that if human
activity is hastening the end of humankind, it is but the providential instrument of the divinely ordained end times and the separation of the saved and
the damned, while a no less self-assured strand of ecological consciousness indulges in extinction thinking, the gleeful doomsday rhetoric—*We're fucked!*—
that encases extinction thinkers in their own comforting, self-affirming bubble, for while they themselves are subject to merely ordinary mortality, what
is in store for future generations (to which they will not belong) thanks to
past generations (to which they did not belong) is agonizing decline and extinction. The extinction thinkers, being neither responsible for the past nor
doomed to its ultimate consequences, have already outlived the future.

Serious philosophical reflection resists such pseudo-apocalypticisms. Deeply
thought out responses to Heidegger have produced different, conceptually incompatible paths. The contention between them may well shape the existential
and political response to environmental concern and controversy in the coming years.

Object-oriented ontology undertakes the project of rethinking being by
neutralizing and setting aside Dasein. It seeks an ontology that answers the
question of being without reference to the being for whom being is a question.
Its inaugural gesture frequently expresses its own intellectual enthusiasm for
the picture of human insignificance, a gesture that amounts to an exact reversal of Arendt's association of freedom with the infinite improbability of each
individual's birth and of earthly human life itself. Writes Graham Harman:
"The vast majority of relations in the universe do not involve human beings,
those obscure inhabitants of an average-sized planet near a middling sun, one
of 100 billion stars near the fringe of an undistinguished galaxy among at least
100 billion others. If we forget that objects interact among themselves even
when humans are not present, we have arrogated 50 percent of the cosmos
for human settlement, no matter how loudly we boast about overcoming the
subject-object divide. A truly pro-object theory needs to be aware of relations
between objects that have no direct involvement with people."[28] And according to Hannah Arendt: "It is in the very nature of every new beginning that
it breaks into the world as an 'infinite improbability,' and yet it is precisely
this infinitely improbable which actually constitutes the very texture of everything we call real. . . . For from the point of view of the processes in the
universe and in nature, and their statistically overwhelming probabilities, the

coming into being of the earth out of cosmic processes, the formation of organic life out of inorganic processes, the evolution of man, finally, out of the processes of organic life are all 'infinite improbabilities,' they are 'miracles' in everyday language."[29] Perhaps she had Zarathustra's third metamorphosis of the spirit in mind: "The child is innocence and forgetting, a new beginning, a game, a self-propelled wheel, a first movement, a sacred 'Yes.'"[30]

Whether the sensibility that sees humankind's eternal insignificance or the one that senses its infinitely improbable inaugurations is more attuned to the human condition today may well seem undecided. While I share and abide by Arendt's affirmation of unpredictable human inventiveness, it is nevertheless now clear that her *finally*—"the evolution of man, finally, out of the processes of organic life"—is not so final after all. The human capacity to alter the processes of organic life, including human life, and even the global inorganic processes of temperature, winds, storms, rainfall, desertification, river flows, sea levels, and even seismic tremors is ever more manifest. Writing in 1958, Arendt herself suggests in the opening of *The Human Condition* that developments such as Sputnik ("an earth-born object made by man"), "the attempt to create life in the test tube," and the aspiration to alter human cells or extend human life to "more than a hundred years" are all signs of "the wish to escape the human condition." The rudiments of that condition, which she is setting out to explore, are expressed in terms that may well allude to the Heideggerian earth and world, *Erde* and *Welt*, though he is mentioned nowhere in the book: "The earth is the very quintessence of the human condition, and earthly nature, for all we know, may be unique in the universe in providing human beings with a habitat in which they can move and breathe without effort and without artifice. The human artifice of the world separates human existence from all mere animal environment, but life itself is outside this artificial world, and through life man remains related to all other living organisms."[31]

Bill Brown brings Arendt's thinking into dialogue—a necessarily strained dialogue—with object-oriented ontology and with Bruno Latour's ideas regarding technology and ecology. As Brown puts it, a series of developments since the mid-twentieth century has raised doubts about the adequacy and pertinence of the earth/world conception. Consumerism dissolves the everyday object world that for Arendt stabilized human existence through the familiar solidity of one's chair, desk, and household furnishings; objects increasingly become "actants" (Latour) and acquire agency with respect to humans, from earlier automation to the rapidly expanding arenas of robotics, algorithmic calculation, and artificial intelligence (in finance, advertising, social media, war-making, politics); and finally, as ecological crisis is grasped through the notion of the Anthropocene, it is recognized that the link of human/nonhuman to subject/object or agent/object is undergoing radical transformations.

As regards the Anthropocene, Brown paraphrases Latour's appeal to the reimagining of earth as Gaia as follows: "Gaia might be said to name the subject-object . . . of unhuman history, which is a history that, precisely by being unhuman, retains the human within it. This is history in which *anthropos* comes to find itself (and now to recognize itself) relegated to the role of object within a vast assemblage."[32] The paraphrase is a slight but decisive displacement. A history that, precisely by being unhuman, retains the human within it: the human is not liquidated in the unhuman but displaced into a wholly new position regarding, in the previous vocabulary, its objecthood and subjecthood. The ecological-political question does not dissolve *anthropos* but presses for new self-recognition and new forms of agency and action in light of its "role of object within a vast assemblage." Brown asserts this insight even more pointedly in response to object-oriented ontology (Harman) and "speculative realism" (Quentin Meillassoux), which seek to think the being of things without reference to human beings. By contrast, what matters "in Latour's effort to think beyond the human" is "the way in which the human has returned—differently—in his work, and the way in which that return sheds light—the light of history—on various efforts to do without the human-unhuman binary, as on the current attraction to ontology,"[33] that is, object-oriented ontology's aim of effacing the human.

Let's state the stakes, ontological, ecological, and political, even more baldly. *The anthropocenic imagination must be anthropocentric.*

Over against object-oriented ontology I place Peter Sloterdijk's thought. Rather than attempting to liquidate humanism and anthropocentrism from Heidegger's thought, Sloterdijk rethinks Dasein by rethinking "environment" more radically than Heidegger himself does: "Even Heidegger, as much as his significance as a destructor of metaphysics is undeniable, remains partially caught up in a grammar that has for its presupposition a simply untenable ontology and an inadequate logic." Untenable is "a univalent ontology (Being is, non-Being is not)" and inadequate is "a bivalent logic."[34] The extent of artifice is too wide and too inseparable from Dasein to be contained by the ostensibly comprehensive distinction of the human and the natural, *anthropos* and *physis*. Through such a bivalence, Sloterdijk argues, "we cannot appropriately articulate either the basic views about the constitution of natural objects that are valid today or those about the mode of Being of cultural facts. Holding on to traditional conceptual classifications leads to the absolute inability to describe in an ontologically appropriate way 'cultural phenomena' such as tools, signs, artworks, laws, customs, books, machines, and all other artifices, because in constructs of this type the fundamental high-cultural classifications of soul and thing, mind and matter, subject and object, freedom and mechanism, must miss the mark: all cultural objects, according to their constitution, are indeed hybrids with a spiritual 'component' and a material 'component,' and every attempt within the framework of a bivalent logic and a univalent ontology to say what they 'really' are inevitably ends in hopeless reductions and destructive abridgments." For Sloterdijk, "cybernetics as the theory and praxis of intelligent machines and modern biology as the study of unities of system and environment compelled a new account of the 'artificial' as well as the 'natural.'" When, moreover, genetics recuperates the cybernetic conception of information into the understanding of the processes and building blocks of life, the traditional categories explode, and there emerges the necessity of thinking "a third value between the pole of reflection and the pole of the thing, mind and matter, thoughts and states of affairs."[35]

This line of Sloterdijk's thought develops less as an outright challenge to Heidegger than an elaboration of his conception of the spatiality of Dasein's being-in-the-world (in-der-Welt-sein) beyond his own interpretation. Heidegger contests the notion of environment insofar as "talk about 'man's having an environment [Umwelt]' . . . says nothing ontologically as long as this 'having' is left indefinite."[36] When it comes to being-in-the-world or being-in-language as the house of being, Dasein's being-in, Sloterdijk concludes, is a "structure more like that of a ball of care (Sorge) in which existence is spread out in an original being-outside-itself."[37] Dasein's being-outside-itself is at the same time its dwelling-in, and Sloterdijk is thus able to see the anthropos–physis–technē triad as, in his metaphor, the sphere or bubble constituting, to borrow from the traditional grammar, humans' interaction with their "natural" "environment" as well as its perpetual transformation into new "environments." Technē now demarcates at once the tools with which and the dwelling within which Dasein is. Dasein, enfolded-upon-and-in-strife-with-itself, embodies both the anthropocentric attitude that brings about environmental crisis and the anthropocentric attitude that alone can counter it. The pressure to push beyond a "univalent ontology" can also be seen in Vattimo's emphasis, which has guided my own account of Angst, on those moments where Heidegger encounters in Nietzsche the implication that being is nothing, which eludes the univalent ontology of Being is, non-Being is not.

Kant, too, tacitly if inadvertently opens the "bivalent logic" of mind/nature to a triadic structure at the moment in the Critique of Judgment where the judgment of the beautiful in nature is said to derive from the capacity to judge the beautiful in *art*, for there the mental faculty's relation to nature is inseparable from *technē*. The *anthropos–physis–technē* triad is also latent in Heidegger in the unsettled range of meanings of *technē* (craft, art, technology) that continually trouble the earth/world conception itself, as we have seen with respect to "The Origin of the Work of Art" and the Nietzsche seminar.[38]

Latour engages Sloterdijk in elaborating on the import and possibilities of the concept of the Anthropocene, including the need to rethink what is then meant by *anthropos*. It cannot be a capitalized Humanism in which a single-minded humanity acts upon the earth and now has to revamp its actions: "There is no way to *unify* the Anthropos as an actor endowed with some sort of moral or political consistency, to the point of charging it with being a character capable of acting on this new global stage." He draws on Sloterdijk's interrogation of the iconography and representations of the earth as a globe to argue that the globe is always accompanied by a being that holds it, masters it, knows it, or sees it as a whole. Atlas, man, God, and science have variously played this role: "The figure of the Globe authorizes a premature leap to a higher level *by confusing the figures of connection with those of total-ity*." He further draws on Sloterdijk's extension of the concept of "environ-ment" (*Umwelt*) "to all spheres, all enclosures, all the envelopes that agents have had to invent to differentiate their inside and their outside," that is, the "[immunological] envelopes that are indispensable to the perpetuation of life." That mode of thinking, which Latour dubs "the first *anthropocenic* dis-cipline" complements and occasionally inspires his own experiments in con-ceptualizing and representing the "critical zone" within which earthly life is possible.[39]

The array of alternative modes of thought that I have roughly sketched—extinction thinking, Arendtian humanism, object-oriented ontology, Hei-deggerian ontology, Sloterdijk, Latour—suggest how powerfully ecological crisis impinges upon modern and contemporary thought. As the philosophi-cal and political as well as the scientific and technological responses to the escalating global ecological effects in the Anthropocene develop and con-tend with one another, the unique resources of art and poetry, their power to probe the affective-symbolic links of *technē–physis* that constitute Dasein, will inform and enrich those responses, however obliquely. The obliqueness is essential, as can be seen in Shelley's "Mont Blanc," which affords a doubly discordant attunement to earth. It celebrates the disenchantment of nature while at the same time limning the presence of the uninhabitable within our earthly dwelling and, in its resonance beyond its own intention today, point-ing to the rent opened by human dwelling within the human dwelling itself.[40]

Kant's Affects

The analytic of the sublime pushes Kant to distinguish among a plethora of emotions. In the course of just a few pages he refers to "indignation," "anger," "hatred," "enthusiasm," "astonishment," "respect," "affectlessness," "misanthropy," "enraged despair," "sorrow," "visionary rapture," and "vindictiveness." While these terms are all substantives in the grammatical sense, what they refer to and attempt to name are not at all substances or substantive. Simple definitions are likewise inadequate, since what an emotion is cannot be specified in an *énoncé* except through the interpretation of an *énonciation*. The triad mood–understanding–discourse offers no objective standpoint outside the effects of the individual terms' equiprimordial moments on one another. The emotions elucidated in Aristotle's *Art of Rhetoric*, as we have seen, have complex internal structures compounded of imagination, social agons and hierarchies, self-regard, and bonds of kinship and friendship and are inseparable from the unique Attic lifeworld. No less complex are the emotions designated by Kant in §29. But here the attempts at elucidation revolve around the question of the sublime.

At first glance the distinctions are meant to separate genuinely sublime feelings from their easily mistaken neighbors and cousins. Kant introduces surprisingly empirical considerations into what he calls his "transcendental exposition of aesthetic judgments." The transcendental register is, to be sure, the starting point. The different ways of representing an object "in relation to the feeling of pleasure" are carefully sorted by means of a typology that distinguishes four fundamental forms of satisfaction: "The *agreeable* . . . the *beautiful* . . . the *sublime* . . . [and] the (absolutely) *good*."[41] The *good* is the absolutely good in the sense of the morally good, which for Kant rests on "the representation of an *absolutely necessitating law*." He thus distinguishes the universality at stake in moral as distinct from aesthetic judgment as the difference between a *command* and a *claim*. From all that has been discussed thus far, it is clear how the *beautiful*, the *sublime*, and the *good* are said to derive from a transcendental perspective. Not so for the *agreeable*, which, "as an incentive for the desires, is of the same kind throughout, no matter where it comes from and how specifically different the representation (of sense and of sensation, objectively considered) may be."[42] Similarly, Kant earlier distinguishes the *agreeable* from the satisfactions associated with the beautiful or the good on the grounds that the *agreeable* "rests entirely on sensation" (§4).[43] Kant defines sensation "as the real in perception" (§39).[44] It is not so clear, then, whether the *agreeable*—as the feeling of pleasure in general—is completely separate from the transcendentally derived *beautiful*, *sublime*, and *good* or somehow within or beneath them. Since Kant calls "sensation" "the real in perception," if it were to be granted that there is no *beautiful*, *sublime*, or *good* without the real of *sensation*, then the *agreeable* would be folded within those transcendentally determined pleasures, not extraneous to them.

There is thus something unsettled in the distinction of the empirical and the transcendental, which is perhaps why the distinction itself is addressed afresh at the end of §29 in a kind of coda devoted to Edmund Burke. Kant wants to compare his own "now . . . completed" transcendental exposition "with the physiological exposition, as it has been elaborated by a Burke and many acute men among us, in order to see whither a merely empirical exposition of the sublime and the beautiful would lead."[45] Considerable psychological validity is granted to Burke's approach. The sublime entails fear, terror, and pain in the face of a danger that, in not going to the point of violence, releases a distinctive emotion, "a kind of pleasing horror, a certain tranquility that is mixed with terror," while the beautiful induces a kind of swoon in the sense of "the relaxation, loosening and slackening of the fibers of the body, hence . . . a softening, a dissolution, an innervation, a sinking away, a melting away of gratification."[46] Kant acknowledges that these Burkean formulations provide a foundation for further research in "empirical anthropology," and while this acknowledgment is not surprising in light of Kant's lectures and extensive readings in the psychological and anthropological researches of his time, he is obliged to go a step further:

> It cannot be denied that all representations in us, whether they are objectively merely sensible or else entirely intellectual, can nevertheless subjectively be associated with gratification or pain, however unnoticeable either might be (because they all affect the feeling of life, and none of them, insofar as it is a modification of the subject, can be indifferent), or even that, as Epicurus maintained, *gratification* and *pain* are always ultimately corporeal, whether they originate from the imagination or even from representations of the understanding.

This step in effect straddles the empirical and the transcendental standpoints. To say that "all representations in us . . . can . . . subjectively be associated with gratification or pain" is to acknowledge that the pleasure/unpleasure principle that defines the *agreeable*—which "rests entirely on sensation"—is in fact within or underneath the transcendentally defined and differentiated *beautiful*, *sublime*, and *good*. As he proceeds to elaborate on the "feeling of life" and the "ultimately corporeal," Kant's language becomes a strikingly uncanny and anachronistic mix of Spinozan *conatus*, Nietzschean will to power, Bergsonian vitalism, and Heideggerian mood and attunement,

> because life without the feeling of the corporeal organ is merely consciousness of one's existence, but not a feeling of well- or ill-being, i.e., the promotion or inhibition of the powers of life; because the mind for itself is entirely life (the principle of life itself), and hindrances or promotions must be sought outside it, though in the human being himself, hence in combination with his body.[47]

The forces promoting or inhibiting life (Spinoza, Nietzsche) are outside-yet-within (Heidegger) the living-feeling mind-body (Bergson). The body as the outside on the inside accords with the definition of "sensation as the *real* in perception"; the domain of perception and representation ("mind") somehow and ineluctably mixes the real of the bodily sensorium and the real of forces and objects outside the bodily organism.

As regards these two manifestations of the real, Kant introduces a distinction that thereafter acquires an axiomatic aura: the manifestation of the real that is purely outside he calls "outer nature" and the one that is the outside on the inside he calls "inner nature." Inner nature involves not just the receptivity manifest in sensation, but also the active impetus and force that other thinkers variously call striving (*conatus*), desire, instinct, urge (*Drang*), and drive (*Trieb*). While the essential elements of the analytic of the sublime are established in terms of the mind's powers of representation as it encounters outer nature, whether as extreme magnitude or overwhelming power, Kant likewise poses the question of the mind's ability to rise above the forces and impulses of inner nature and, by so rising, achieve sublimity. Starkly stated, "human nature does not agree with [the moral good] of its own accord, but only through the dominion that reason exercises over sensibility."[48] Some formulations strongly suggest that such dominion over inner nature is the precondition of the judgment and experience of the sublime in outer nature insofar as the latter is a question of encountering the fearsome without being afraid: "Viewing mountain ranges towering to the heavens, deep ravines and the raging torrents in them, deeply shadowed wastelands" can arouse "melancholy reflection" and even "*astonishment* bordering on terror," but not actual fear, insofar as such Alpine spectatorship is "only an attempt to involve ourselves in it by means of the imagination, in order to feel the power of that very faculty, to combine the movement of the mind thereby aroused with its calmness, and so to be superior to nature within us, and thus also to that outside us" (§29).[49] Within and thus also outside us.

Kant's first and controlling instance of the sublime in relation to inner

nature ought to unsettle simplistic readings of his great essay on perpetual
peace. In preparing to show that the sublime has nothing to do with fearful-
ness when it comes to our relation to nature or to God, he first exemplifies
this dimension of the sublime with reference to the soldier and martial valor.
Fearlessness, "which is an object of the greatest admiration even to the sav-
age," achieves sublimity "in the most civilized circumstances," where "this ex-
ceptionally high esteem for the warrior remains, only now it is also demanded
that he at the same time display all the virtues of peace, gentleness, compas-
sion and even proper care for his own person, precisely because in this way
the incoercibility of his mind by danger can be recognized." Whatever other
values may distinguish a general and a statesman, "aesthetic judgment de-
cides in favor of" the general. The author of "Perpetual Peace: A Philosophical Sketch" concludes by embracing Prussian military values as firmly as Descartes and Aristotle embrace the martial forms of courage they associate with
virility: "Even war, if it is conducted with order and reverence for the rights
of civilians, has something sublime about it, and at the same time makes the
mentality of the people who conduct it in this way all the more sublime, the
more dangers it has been exposed to and before which it has been able to assert its courage; whereas a long peace causes the spirit of mere commerce to
predominate, along with base selfishness, cowardice and weakness, and usually debases the mentality of the populace" (§28).[50] The stress falls on receptivity, since it is a question of an aesthetic judgment of the conduct of others,
in this case the warrior's; but the true stakes bear on the subject's own capacity
to rise above inner nature in the act of adhering to the moral law.

Let's reset the sequence of Kant's argument regarding the beautiful and the
sublime. Reason (as the faculty capable of producing universal moral maxims) plays no role in the aesthetic judgment of the beautiful whether in art
or nature (the province of the faculties of imagination and understanding).
But reason is interested in the aesthetic judgment of the beautiful in nature
(understood as outer nature). And it joins with imagination in the aesthetic
judgment of the sublime in nature because of its power to elevate the mind
above nature's superior force. A fourth moment in the sequence is the one
that predominates in §29, where the sublime concerns the aesthetic judgment
of those acts carried out in accordance with reason's moral law. In a sense, the
moral law is now accorded primacy over the beautiful, morality over aesthetics, for whereas in the original sequence of arguments the beautiful in art
conditions the beautiful in nature and the beautiful in art and nature conditions the sublime in nature, now the power of the moral law over *inner* nature
is the object of the aesthetic judgment of the sublime. The moral law takes
over at the head of the sequence insofar as the mind is "superior to nature

within us, and *thus also* to that outside us." Does the change of direction indicate the priority of moral over aesthetic judgment? Or does it simply confirm the circular interplay and harmony of all the faculties, now viewed from
the opposite perspective as in a reverse-angle shot?

In either case the discussion of the sublime has been reanchored on reason's relation to inner nature. Reason's successful exercise of dominion over
sensibility, when "judged aesthetically, must not be represented so much as
beautiful but rather as sublime, so that it arouses more the feeling of respect
(which scorns charm) than that of love and intimate affection."[51] Kant is seeking to place the sublime within the bounds of reason alone. But the irrationality of feeling hounds moral reason. For example, what affect does the absolute
good itself arouse? "The idea of the good with affect is called *enthusiasm*. This
state-of-mind seems to be sublime, so much so that it is commonly maintained
that without it nothing great can be accomplished." There is, however, a caveat.
Kant warns that "every affect is blind, either in the choice of its end, or, even if
this is given by reason, in its implementation." Reason cannot be satisfied by
an affect, yet enacted reason arouses affects. Kant senses the problem in the
converse of *enthusiasm*: "(what seems strange) even *affectlessness* (*apatheia*,
phlegma in significactu bono [apathy, being phlegmatic in a positive sense]) in
a mind that emphatically pursues its own inalterable principles is sublime."[52]

To solve this puzzle Kant introduces—of course—yet more distinctions:
emotion, affect, and passion. He offers not clear-cut definitions but various
quantitative and qualitative differences illustrated by examples (hence the
lexicon of emotions I cited at the beginning of this section). The distinction
between emotion and affect seems to be a matter of intensity; Kant speaks
at one point of those "emotions that can reach the strength of an affect."[53] In
turn, affect and passion differ because a passion exceeds, or perhaps over-
takes, feeling through the subjective forces of "the faculty of desire," which
defy the restraints of conformity to moral principle. So, emotion intensified
to some indistinct but qualitatively recognizable level becomes affect, and an
affect that is taken up and sustained by the faculty of desire is transformed
into a passion. Passions "are inclinations that make all determinability by the
faculty of choice by means of principles difficult or impossible." Indignation,
for example, is an affect when it takes the form of *anger* "but as hatred (vindictiveness), it is a passion." In passion, which is "sustained and considered"
in contrast to the "tumultuous and unpremeditated" affects, can be seen the
auto-affection by which a feeling is rekindled, sustained, and intensified.[54]
For Kant, a passion cannot be sublime because it has an aim and inclines to
action. Such a distinction between affect and passion or the permutation of
affect into passion is unknown to Aristotle, for whom anger, indignation, and

hatred are all thymotic emotions inseparable from socially valued forms of
self-esteem; in the ancient Greek structure of feeling, vindictiveness would
undoubtedly have been considered, much like Nietzsche's *ressentiment*, as an
emotion of those whose talents, social standing, or strength is lower than that
of those who have harmed them.

Which affects, then, can be sublime, and which not? Kant sees sublimity in *thymos* but not in *eros*. Having heart, unlike appetite, can attain the
sublime:

> Every affect of the *courageous sort* (that is, which arouses the consciousness of
> our power to overcome any resistance [*animi strenui*] is *aesthetically sublime*,
> e.g., anger, even despair (that is, the *enraged*, not the *despondent* kind). Af-
> fect of the *yielding* kind, however (which makes the effort at resistance itself
> into an object of displeasure [*animum languidum*]), has nothing *noble* in it,
> although it can be counted as belonging to beauty of the sensory kind. Hence
> the *emotions* that can reach the strength of an affect are also quite diverse.
> We have *brave* as well as *tender* emotions. The latter, if they reach the level
> of an affect, are good for nothing at all; the tendency toward them is called
> *oversensitivity*.[55]

But what if tenderness is caught hold of by desire? Would it not then become
a passion, a sexual or a maternal passion? Kant skirts sexuality and sensuality
altogether, an avoidance symptomatically signaled on this same page by the
orientalist tic that afflicts his discourse just as he distinguishes between those
"tumultuous movements of the mind" that qualify as sublime because they
influence "consciousness of [the mind's] strength and resolution in regard to
that which brings with it intellectual purposiveness (the supersensible)" and
those emotional tumults whose "agreeable exhaustion . . . is an enjoyment
of the well-being resulting from the equilibrium of the various vital forces
that is thus produced in us." This nonsublime pleasure, which Kant associates
with the emotional appeal of many edifying sermons, is no different from
what "the voluptuaries of the Orient find so comforting when they have their
bodies as it were kneaded, and all their muscles and joints softly pressed and
flexed."[56] Massage as emblem of the emotive sermon!

This brings Kant back around to the question of enthusiasm and the
blindness of affect. While enthusiasm is distinguished from visionary rapture
as an affect from a passion, both are distinguished from "the pure, elevating,
merely negative presentation of morality" that arouses the true "feeling of
the sublime." Kant stresses again that this feeling must arise in relation to the
mind's disposition toward "maxims for making the intellectual and the ideas
of reason superior to sensibility." A "negative presentation of morality" is one

shorn of inducements, images, perhaps even models. The aesthetic judgment producing the affect of sublimity in relation to the moral aspect of action is a presentation to the mind so abstract that it recalls for Kant the ancient Jewish and medieval Islamic prohibitions on images. He adopts his earlier account of infinity and the sublime, now in terms of the moral law: "The imagination, although it certainly finds nothing beyond the sensible to which it can attach itself, nevertheless feels itself to be unbounded precisely because of this elimination of the limits of sensibility." He continues by adducing the near-paradox of the sublime as presentation of the unpresentable: "That separation is thus a presentation of the infinite, which for that very reason can never be anything but a merely negative presentation, which nevertheless expands the soul"—purely negative in the sense that there need be no sense inducements to morality, none of those "images and childish devices" that Kant's Protestant rigorism undoubtedly associates with Catholicism. He likewise disdains the fact that "even governments have gladly allowed religion to be richly equipped with such supplements and thus sought to relieve the subject of the bother but at the same time also of the capacity to extend the powers of his soul beyond the limits that are arbitrarily set for him and by means of which, as merely passive, he can be more easily dealt with."[57] For Kant, one's need for sensory inducements to act morally amounts to giving one's freedom over to manipulation and control by heteronomous powers.

Drawing out the consequences of the purely negative presentation of morality leads to a pregnant conclusion, rich in possibility and uncertain in outcome: "The *inscrutability of the idea of freedom* entirely precludes any positive presentation; but the moral law is sufficient in itself in us and originally determining, so that it does not even allow us to look for a determining ground outside it." This statement culminates the movement of "The Analytic of the Sublime" from outer to inner nature. Kant first considered the role of reason's interest in the aesthetic judgment of the sublime in nature (where the mind is elevated above outer nature and the affect is vibratory repulsion/attraction) and then moved on to the aesthetic judgment of the sublime with regard to those acts and attitudes that accord with the moral law (where the mind is elevated above inner nature, and the accompanying affects include respect, fearlessness, humility, anger). For Kant, this effectively concludes "the "transcendental exposition" of the sublime.

From a different angle, however, a fracture or fault line shows through. It is said that the idea of freedom is inscrutable and the moral law self-sufficient, its origin and ground lying beyond any cognition, and yet this moral law does not take hold spontaneously. To grasp the moral law—supposedly "sufficient in itself in us"—without the autonomy-robbing supplement of inducements, that is, to embrace it imagelessly, is a rare achievement according to Kant. The commitment to act in accordance with a maxim that applies universally and to adhere to a supersensible universal command, that is, the commitment to an "absolutely necessitating law," is thus not an immediate product of reason. It is a decision. Such a decision to adhere to what Kant calls "pure practical reason" and its squaring of freedom and reason is in itself, it must be emphasized contrary to Kant, irrational. Were the decision to subject oneself to the categorical imperative not irrational, the subject would have to be angelic or enabled by undeserved grace. Angelism and grace, however, are beyond the pale of Kant's own conceptualization. In neither case would rising above the forces of one's inner—that is, one's human—nature be sublime. It would lack value heroism. While Kant is alert to the irrationality of affects—such as, for example, the blindness that he attributes even to enthusiasm for the idea of the moral good—he is blind to the irrationality of the decision for the moral law itself. These two irrationalities trace the fracture or rent in the transcendental exposition.

Form and Formlessness

It was made clear above that Kant's account of the *agreeable* in relation to the *sublime, beautiful,* or *good* straddles the empirical and the transcendental, since the transcendental determination of the *sublime, beautiful,* or *good* nucleates rather than transcends the empirical element of sensation. It is now possible, shifting metaphors to the empirical perspective, to see that the transcendental itself is the effect of a splitting or dispersal of the (merely) *agreeable* into differentiated satisfactions, including those here dubbed the *sublime, beautiful,* or *good.*

Is this to rejoin Deleuze's transcendental empiricism? Perhaps, provided that a clarification and an extrapolation are made. First the clarification. The Deleuzian rat illustrates transcendental empiricism insofar as the most minimal stimulus-response sequence requires that sensation be held for some duration by consciousness, an *asubjective* consciousness, in Deleuze's terms. Such an asubjective consciousness is the transcendental agency that binds the real of sensation and, by binding it, allows it to become part of experience and behavior. It arguably could account for the form of satisfaction/dissatisfaction that Kant attributes to judgment of the *agreeable.* Now the extrapolation. The *sublime, beautiful,* and *good* are at once permutations of the *agreeable* and forms of subjective rather than asubjective consciousness. Because of their empirical nucleus, these forms of satisfaction cannot be derived solely or directly from transcendental structures in Kant's sense, and yet they are not reducible to the *agreeable*.

What, then, conditions and structures the subjectivity that experiences and judges the *sublime, beautiful,* and *good*?

From the standpoint of sensation and asubjective consciousness, the splintering differentiation of the affects associated with the *sublime,* the *beautiful,* and the *good* is an ec-stasis, that is, the ecstasis of the real in perception (sensation) out-of-itself into value-laden perceptions and affects. Those differentiated perceptions and affects are imbued with value and judgment only through discourse. Discourse, much like *technē*, lies scarcely veiled at the very core of the Third Critique. The experience of the beautiful is inseparable from the urge to persuade, and even if my feeling that others must feel the same as I do in the face of a particular appearance does not eventuate in an articulated appeal for their agreement on my part, the rhetoric of persuasion limns my own experience that *this is beautiful*. Moreover, the "faculty" of aesthetic judgment arises thanks to its institutional-discursive instantiation in the incipient public sphere. And since the beautiful in nature (*physis*) is conditioned by the beautiful in art (*technē*), and the sublime by the beautiful, the whole of what Kant calls "aesthetic judgment" lies along the crease in the ontological fold of *physis* and *technē*, indissociable from them despite his efforts to derive it solely from the transcendental agency of a purely mental faculty.

Discourse, *physis, technē*—these terms are at the heart of Heidegger's approach to affect (the equiprimordiality of mood–understanding–speech) and to the artwork (the *technē* by which *physis* is "set forth and used as the self-closing factor" and so set "free to be nothing but itself").[58] I am appropriating Heidegger's notion of ecstasis in order to reformulate Kant's distinction of the *beautiful,* the *sublime,* and the *good* as permutations of the *agreeable*. In Heidegger, time in the sense of its pure flow ecstasizes, goes out of itself, in and as Dasein in the sense that Dasein's understanding orients to the future and "*a potentiality-for-Being*," while its mood is a "*bringing one back to* something."[59] Since mood and understanding are equiprimordial, Dasein's stretching toward the future and toward the past makes it the site of time's ecstasis. Dasein is never synchronized to the clock's tick-tock; rather, it is syncopated with and against itself. Looking at Kant at once from the Deleuzian perspective of sensation and the Heideggerian perspective of being, Dasein can be seen as the site where *physis* ecstasizes out of itself into and as judgment. Sensation as the real in perception belongs to *physis* in the properly comprehensive sense of the term; the ecstasis of the *agreeable* into the *beautiful,* the *sublime,* or the *good* is thus the ecstasis of *physis* into-and-as the very being of Dasein. Kant tacitly recognizes the ecstasis of *physis* in and as the feeling-judging subject but attempts to quell the consequences by calling it *inner nature* and hence something to be brought under the dominion of the faculty of reason and the moral law. Heidegger's own exclusion of the neurobiophysiological aspect of Dasein from his reflections on *physis* flies in the face of the fact that without that aspect it is impossible to postulate the primordiality of mood. In the determination of *physis* as earth in "The Origin of the Work of Art," he largely restricts *physis* to rock, soil, and plant, with scarcely a nod to body, nerve, and brain. And his overreaction to Nietzsche's reductive physiology in turn leaves *Rausch* as the unthought element of artistic creation.

Heidegger's 1929–30 seminar included an extensive reflection on the difference and relation of the human and the animal via a three-part thesis according to which "the stone is worldless, the animal is poor in world, man is world-forming."[60] Giorgio Agamben provides a meticulous commentary on Heidegger's effort to locate and sustain the difference between human and animal. He illuminates how Heidegger casts boredom as the mood in which the human being in effect experiences being poor in world: "The animal environment is constituted in such a way that something like a pure possibility can never become manifest within it. Profound boredom then appears as the metaphysical operator in which the passage from poverty in world to world, from animal environment to human world, is realized: at issue is nothing less than anthropogenesis, the becoming Da-sein of living man. But this passage, this *becoming*-Dasein of living man . . . does not open onto a further, wider, and brighter space, achieved beyond the animal environment, and unrelated to it; on the contrary, it is opened only by means of a suspension and a deactivation of the animal relation with the disinhibitor."[61] (*Disinhibitor* is the term Heidegger coins to recast the pathbreaking zoologist Jakob von Uexküll's *carrier of significance*, that is, those elements in the animal's environment—*Umwelt*, in Uexküll's coinage—to which an animal's species-specific perceptual apparatus responds).[62] That is, Dasein encounters in profound boredom the animal's poverty in world without being- or becoming-animal because, unlike the animal, the human does not thereby become behaviorally instinctual (disinhibited) within an environment. In the midst of profound boredom I experience a world impoverishment that renders the world a (mere) environment while leaving me disempowered to behave instinctually within it and at the same time attuned to this very disempowerment.

Insofar as Heidegger is explicating, still in keeping with the project of *Being and Time*, Dasein as the being which we ourselves are, what has been brought to light is boredom's contribution to Dasein's ever-in-process interpretation of itself; it is one of those moments in which interpreting itself etches an interpretation of its other, in this case its living "animal" others. In that sense, boredom is, as Agamben says, a "metaphysical operator." While this other-than-*anthropos* living being thus becomes evident in its difference or otherness from the human, what it in actuality *is* nonetheless eludes Dasein. Perhaps a bit askance in relation to Agamben's own conclusions, I draw from his commentary the consequence that Dasein's ever-incomplete self-interpretations continually adduce new anthropomorphisms of "man" and so each time simultaneously project a new *morphe* of non-*anthropos*, without ever fully disclosing the nature of that other. If Heidegger supposes that he *defined* the "animal" in his 1929–30 seminar, he misses how the nonhuman eludes definition, since the definition will always be marked by the provisionality of humans' definition of the human, of *mortals* in the fourfold of mortals, divinities, earth, and sky. What this episode of Heidegger's thought demonstrates is how Dasein's being-in-the-world, in this case in a mood and moment where its own world is suddenly impoverished, awakens it to a sense—or questioning—of the nature of the being-alive, of living beings other than itself. However, Heidegger's account still does not account for how Dasein (the being we ourselves are) grasps that its own being is at once *living* and *in-the-world*. Sensation and being. Vitalism and hermeneutics.

Two problems are straining for a solution. On the one hand, how can the Heideggerian triad mood–understanding–speech integrate *physis* from the earth/world conception insofar as mood's bodily nature implies earth, *Erde*, nature? And on the other hand, how can the Kantian conception of reason and morality absorb the inherence of discourse that it steadfastly refuses to acknowledge?

Merleau-Ponty grapples with the first question in lecture notes and the drafts for the unfinished parts of *The Visible and the Invisible*. Like Heidegger, he resituates phenomenology in Dasein's being-*in*-the-world rather than, like Husserl, in consciousness's power to bracket, or to bracket itself off from, such immersion. But while Heidegger leaves unsettled and undeveloped his own notion that Dasein does not "have" a body but is bodily, Merleau-Ponty takes up that notion and proposes "to study the human body as the root of symbolism, as the junction of *physis* and *logos*."[63] The image of nature that he deploys is that of a *feuillet*, that is, a sheet like a folio folded into a four-page booklet or a printer's signature folded into thirty-two pages. Origami would serve as a valid variation of the image, since the issue is to think through the foldings and unfoldings by which the specifically human body arises in/from/as *physis*.

In *Nature: Course Notes from the Collège de France, feuillet* is translated as "leaf"; following from earlier lectures on animality, Merleau-Ponty turns to the human body to consider its inherence in, its meshing or blending—*Ineinander*—with, animality and Nature:

> Evolution marks the transition since the human issues from it.
>
> Our subject: Regarding Nature, the concern was to study it as an ontological leaf [*feuillet*]—and in particular, regarding life, the concern was to study the unfolding of the leaf of Nature—regarding the human, the concern is to take him at his point of emergence in Nature. Just as there is an *Ineinander* of life and physicochemistry, i.e., the realization of life as a fold or a singularity of physicochemistry—or structure, so too is the human to be taken in the *Ineinander* with animality and Nature. . . . Human being is not animality (in the sense of mechanism) + reason.—And this is why we are concerned with the body: before being reason, humanity is another corporeity.
>
> The concern is to grasp humanity first as another manner of being a body—to see humanity emerge just like Being in the manner of a watermark, not as another substance, but as *interbeing*, not as an imposition of a for-itself on a body in-itself.[64]

From these images and concepts Merleau-Ponty manages to sketch angles from which to understand the human body as "the junction of *physis* and *logos*." One can at best approximate by inference the direction of his thought. "Our body is symbolism" in the sense that bodily perception and movement relate to others and things in the world by means of apprehensions, intentionalities, and interactions: "Feeling or pleasure, because the body is mobile, that is, the power to be elsewhere, are the [means of the] unveiling of *something*. An organ of the mobile sense (the eye, the hand) is already a language because it is an interrogation (movement) and a response (perception as *Erfühlung* [fulfillment] of a project), speaking and understanding. It is a tacit language." The body's tacit language intertwines with the conventions of language, which cannot be purely products of mind, since "*convention* itself presupposes a communication with self or other and can appear only as a variant or divergence in relation to a preliminary communication" that itself "is not instituted" or conventional. "The life of language reproduces perceptual structures at another level. We speak in order to fill in the blanks of perception, but words and meanings are not of the absolute positive. What we call mind is again a re-equilibration, a decentralization which is not absolute. . . . There is a Logos of the natural esthetic world, on which the Logos of language relies."[65] At times Merleau-Ponty relates the perceptual-mobile body to language as the visible to the invisible.

Merleau-Ponty's reflection helps elucidate the first problem I raised above, namely, how to integrate *physis* into Heidegger's equiprimordial triad mood–understanding–speech. On the one hand, Merleau-Ponty conceives affective, perceptual, mobile embodiment as *physis* arising or unfolding as Dasein. The human is not animality joined to reason; rather, the human is "another manner of being a body." And, on the other hand, his formulations accord with Heidegger's notion that understanding is equiprimordial with mood. In Merleau-Ponty's version, perception, affect, and movement are themselves interpretations and intentions. Recall Heidegger: "A state-of-mind always has its understanding, even if it merely keeps it suppressed. Understanding always has its mood" (H 142–43). By the same token, inarticulate and unarticulated understanding reaches toward language in becoming interpretation in Heidegger's idiom, and in Merleau-Ponty's idiom it is the tacit language without which speech could not occur.

The second problem has to do with the veiled role of discourse in Kant's conception of reason and morality, as in the aesthetic judgment of the beautiful. There are two paths that can be followed to bring out the discursive nature of reason and morality. One can go *du côté de chez* Habermas or *du côté de chez* Arendt. I have gone Arendt's way, along which the ordeal of universalism in the moral-political realm is shifted from the model of the categorical imperative to that of the aesthetic judgment of the beautiful, from command to claim, from norm-conformative consensus to valuing-positing persuasion. The discursive-rhetorical core of political participation is the act of wooing. The democratic ethos therefore need not deny that its commitment to democracy is, *as* a commitment, in itself irrational, a leap from sheer self-interest or family, clan, or tribal loyalty to an affirmation and embrace of majority decision, minority protections, and individual rights. In fact, acknowledging the irrationality of the decision for democracy grants the passions their legitimate role in political commitment. In place of the inscrutability of freedom in the categorical imperative, there is the ungrounded grounding of the urge to persuade and esteem for others. Nothing guarantees its sustainability except the practice and enjoyment of democratic deliberation and decision. That is why Arendt stresses that power in the political sense of action in concert is but "the fragile and temporary agreement of many wills." The appeal to the agreement of all in the political realm proceeds without a transcendental ground and without an "object of a pure and unconditioned moral satisfaction" and so without any guarantee of the rightness or persuasiveness of one's own claim.

Let's turn back to the sublime. Can it too be wrenched away from the categorical imperative? Kant lodges the categorical imperative in the aesthetic judgment of the sublime as aesthetic responsiveness to moral reason's dominion over inner nature. One path to displacing the categorical imperative lies, via the Nietzschean deconstruction, in Weber's notion of the polytheistic nature of values in modern society. Since the positing of values to live by that overcome or rechannel one's spontaneous impulses defines all manner of life-enhancing practices, the categorical imperative's demand that actions conform to a maxim universally applicable to all is but one such irrational value-positing. If the maxim were stated purely in the first person: *I aspire to live in such a way that a rule fashioned by my conduct could be embraced by all*, that is, as the supreme value that I choose and try to live by, rather than as a disembodied command addressed to all and purporting absolute validity, it would rank as a powerful ethical guide that sought to persuade by example.

Another, complementary kind of dislodging of the categorical imperative from aesthetic judgment is achieved by modern art itself. It interrupts the Kantian itinerary. In "Analytic of the Sublime," the supremacy of the "absolutely necessitating law" over the aesthetic sensibility is established in the step-by-step movement by which the interplay between imagination and understanding is supplanted by moral reason as it passes from its interested observation of the beautiful in nature (where it feels a compatibility with objectivity) to its partnership with imagination in the sublime in nature (where it affirms the superior power of its own seat in the mind alone) and ultimately to an affirmation in aesthetic judgment itself of moral reason's dominion over inner nature. Kant adheres to this trajectory in order to assert the ultimate autonomy of moral reason in relation to art (*technē*). That is also why he initially insists that the sublime occurs in nature and not in art (§26), in *physis* and not in *technē*. That view is shored up with the notion that the beautiful, conditioned as it is by art, is a matter of form, while the sublime opens an aesthetic relation to formlessness. "The judgments of taste" concern "a satisfaction or dissatisfaction in the *form of the object*" and find their "ground in the object and its shape [*Gestalt*]," whereas "only the sublime in nature . . . can be considered as entirely formless or shapeless, but nevertheless as the object of a pure satisfaction" (§30).[66] But the exclusion of the sublime from art does have exceptions: "The presentation of the sublime, so far as it belongs to beautiful art, can be united with beauty in a *verse tragedy*, a *didactic poem*, an *oratorio*; and in these combinations beautiful art is all the more artistic, although whether it is also more beautiful (since so many different kinds of satisfaction are crisscrossed with each other) can be doubted in some cases" (§52).[67]

Let's leave aside the didactic poem and oratorio, as Kant undoubtedly associates them with the sublime because of their moral and religious contents and aims. Aeschylus, Sophocles, Shakespeare, and even Racine, on the other hand, introduce a possibility that Kant's categories of form and formlessness anticipate but do not fully apprehend. Artistic form in these tragic dramatists confronts and exposes the monstrous, a monstrousness that is inseparable from humanity itself. Dasein's monstrosity is indelibly expressed by the chorus in *Antigone* on the nature of *anthropos*: "Many are the wonders, none / is more wonderful than what is man," in David Grene's translation. The word *deinon* refers not just to wonders in the sense of marvels but also to terrors and the terrifying. Translators sometimes unfold *deinon* in two words. For example, Robert Fagles: "Numberless wonders / terrible wonders walk the world but none the match for man." Or Wm. Blake Tyrrell and Larry J. Bennett: "Many things cause terror and wonder, yet nothing / is more terrifying and wonderful than man." What matters is that Dasein is the being who experiences the world's wonders and terrors *and* Dasein is the world's most wondrous and terrible being. Tragic drama pivots on that rent in human existence, its unique and fathomless capacity to be terrified and to terrify. The Sophoclean insight is that, beyond any natural or divine terror, man is man's greatest terror. That is why, in the wake of the disenchantment of nature and the demystification of divine rage, Baudelaire finds inspiration in Racine, and why Nietzsche is fascinated by the Dionysian-Apollonian bond. And why—in the wake of slavery, political terror, genocides, "total war," and Hiroshima and Nagasaki—modern poets and novelists find inspiration in ancient and Shakespearean tragedy.

Kant's formulation that the sublime is "united with beauty" in tragic drama misses what will be disclosed by modern art. If the work of art is to rise to all the demands of modernity—if it is to respond to reality, if it is to be unprecedented, and if it is to unmask truths—it faces the task of conveying the formless through form. Kant's aesthetic horizon was set by eighteenth-century neoclassicism and adhered to the view of form as the harmonious arrangement of homogeneous elements. In the overdetermined moment of Kantian enlightenment, the experience of terror in the face of nature's power became aesthetic at the same time as the response to landscape and well-proportioned art became attuned to one another—hence the link between the picturesque in landscape and well-formedness in art. While it may be tempting to "historicize" this moment in the sense of draining it of validity or casting its self-understanding as mere ideology, it is far better to see it in its genuine complexity as the moment in which the disenchantment of nature, the liberation of art from religious duties, and the intuition that it was possible for an educated public to make claims of universal validity in conversation with one another first jelled.

Kant could imagine that an artwork could be beautiful while representing the sublime, but he could not conceive how formlessness could become internal to form. What is the difference? In Caspar David Friedrich's paint-ings, for example, the sublime enters art as the representation of nature's disorder, magnitude, or power. In Anselm Kiefer's paintings, sculptures, and installations, by contrast, formlessness enters art as the falter, edge, *Riss*, rift of form itself. As Jorie Graham's poetics so emphatically demonstrates, shape is not harmonious arrangement; and as Adorno implies, the achievement of form in the effort to unify the artwork's heterogeneous materials produces the luminous crack that is beauty. The rifted shape or shaped rift suggested by the *Riss* of earth and world in Heidegger brings us closer to modern art and the modern aesthetic experience than Kant's notion that the sublime can be "united with beauty" *or* than any of Heidegger's own commentaries on poems and artworks.

Once art's power to conjoin the sublime with the beautiful is recognized, the very distinction of the sublime and the beautiful begins to fall apart. How, then, to go beyond the distinction, or perhaps even the two terms al-together? Vattimo and Jean-François Lyotard, whose works exert great influ-ence on contemporary aesthetic thought and have certainly shaped my own, have proposed solutions I nevertheless find inadequate. On the one hand, Lyotard's attribution of the sublime to the avant-garde as a kind of negation of beauty and as the power to "represent unrepresentability" touches on the key question of form and formlessness but oversimplifies the artistic field itself, since the avant-gardes do not by any means hold a monopoly on the modern aesthetic imperative of unprecedentedness, and moreover innovation in the arts and literature is never purely a matter of breaking forms but also a ques-tion of creating new ones.[68] Vattimo, on the other, at one point attempts to question the very distinction of art from décor and ornament as part of his deflation of Heidegger's "predilection for a 'strong' notion of the inaugurality of art."[69] Although I subscribe to the endeavor to displace or dissolve Hei-degger's overheated and antipluralistic search for artistic announcements of an epochal turn, I do not see the need or basis for jettisoning a strong notion of the artwork's difference, indeed its active differentiation, from ornament and decoration. The artwork's differentiation from the very locales and sur-roundings within which it appears operates in a manner analogous to the poem's differentiation of itself from language through language. In differen-tiating itself from the world, the artwork or poem does not establish an alter-native world but jolts and alters our attitude *toward* the world and, as poem or artwork, becomes *part of* the world. As to epochal turns, by recognizing that the Hegelian end of art marks instead the inception of modern art, Hei-degger's own epochal expectations for art are dissolved just as decisively as is Hegel's relegation of art to the status of philosophy's outmoded predecessor.

Why not then simply abandon the concept of the "beautiful"? Surely the aesthetic values infused into modern fashion (since Baudelaire's time) and modern design (from Bauhaus to MacBook) can plausibly be seen as the capture of beauty from *technē* in the sense of fine art by *technē* in the sense of engineering. More plausibly, I believe, the beautiful has forked along two quite distinct paths. As well-formedness, the beautiful has migrated to design, from form-follows-function to the elegance and illusory simplicity of a laptop's exterior, screen, keyboard, and graphics. Art still asks something else of itself. It demands that the furthest reaches of form-finding at the same time disclose formlessness. That is palpable in all the poets, writers, and artists I have drawn on to formulate my questions and responses regarding the rhetoric and poetics of affect. It is also at the heart of the aesthetic thinking of Nietzsche, Heidegger, and Deleuze—all of whom, unexpectedly perhaps, draw sustenance from Kant's thinking, against which and thanks to which they grapple with modern art and literature.

The key task of interpretation and analysis becomes the discovery of the formlessness within form—the *Riss*, the shaped rift, the rifted shape. Such is modern criticism's way of claiming *this is beautiful*. The power of the artwork's form to disclose formlessness shares all the predicates of the beautiful we have encountered: scintillating appearance, a configuration of deconcealing and undeconcealing that engages the question of truth, the waking of an urge to persuade out of the feeling that others responding to this particular work must feel the same, and the self-positing of the created. All these predicates obtain in the artwork as distinct from décor, ornament, fashion, or design. Let me evoke once more the Heideggerian triad mood–understanding–discourse. When the discourse is poetic, mood resides in trope and the rhetoric of address, and understanding takes the form of interpretation. The appeal for agreement, that is, for shared understanding and judgment, is without objectivity and yet without caprice. That is why criticism and the domain of letters, broadly conceived, have through a few turbulent centuries prepared and sustained the democratic ethos—whenever, that is, they have allied themselves with universal literacy and the spread of learning. The fragility of aesthetics, literacy, and learning, especially acute again today, still calls upon criticism and theory to fuse innate skepticism and doubt with a passionate, that is, irrational commitment to the ordeal of universalism.

Acknowledgments

The prehistory of this project lay in two opportunities to explore new avenues of research. Zachary Samalin and I curated a seminar series, "Thinking through Affect," under the auspices of the Center for the Humanities at the Graduate Center of the City University of New York with the gracious support of its then-director, Aoibheann Sweeney. Among the dialogues leaving a lasting impression were those prompted by Kyoo Lee on Descartes and Princess Elisabeth of Bohemia, by Nancy Yousef on Hume, and by Federico Luisetti on Deleuze and Spinoza. The second opportunity came when Amanda Anderson invited me to conduct a six-week seminar at the School of Criticism and Theory. The near-magic of the summer at Cornell University came from the engaged and engaging participants in "Philosophy of the Passions, Rhetorics of Affect"; their contributions to the seminar and the unique, wide-ranging discussions at the School's various lectures and discussions pushed my own thinking in new directions.

The decision to undertake a book project came as the result of a brief but intense discussion with Bill Brown, whose editorial acumen and encouragement set things in motion. I benefited immensely from three invitations by Dilip Gaonkar to lecture and make seminar presentations at Northwestern University's Center for Global Culture and Communication and its Summer Institute in Rhetoric and Public Culture.

As the project evolved, challenges and provocations came from various directions. Nasrin Qader pressed me early on to take account of Deleuze's reflections on affect and aesthetics in contrast to Heidegger's. Several conversations with Federico Luisetti on various problems in contemporary philosophy enriched my understanding and helped me to clarify my views; I am especially grateful for his sharing a partial translation of his *Una vita: Pensiero selvaggio e filosofia dell'intensità*, a spirited discussion of Deleuze's relation to Nietzsche and Bergson. Just as Federico's congenial antagonism forced me to sharpen my view of Kant's renewed relevance to aesthetic thinking, Jason Ciaccio's led me to clarify why I dispute characterizations of Heidegger's thought as anti- or posthumanist.

Mark Sussman and Zachary Samalin generously responded with insightful suggestions to nearly every draft of the manuscript. Zach's research on disgust as a socially and politically polyvalent affect in the nineteenth century and Mark's wide-ranging writings on literature and culture have influenced me in various, often subtle ways.

Regular conversations with Benedetto Fontana, Ali Nematollahy, and Sorin Radu Cucu have been a constant source of invaluable feedback. As the manuscript neared completion, I also received helpful responses from Isabel Sobral Campos, Daniel Jacobson, Evan Knight, Jin Chang, and Andrew Dunn. Deeply appreciated is the research assistance I enjoyed from Brian McDonald, Sandra Moyano Ariza, and Emily Price.

I gained a great deal from the responses and suggestions in the readers' reports for the University of Chicago Press. And I am extremely grateful to Alan Thomas, Randy Petilos, and the staff at the press for their care in shepherding *Mood and Trope* to publication.

Notes

Introduction

1. Martin Heidegger, *Being and Time*, trans. John Macquarrie and Edward Robinson (New York: Harper & Row, 1962), 178 (H 138). Hereafter citations of this work will be made parenthetically in the text with the H pagination.

2. See Daniel M. Gross and Ansgar Kemmann, eds., *Heidegger and Rhetoric* (Albany: State University of New York Press, 2005).

3. Martin Heidegger, "The Origin of the Work of Art," in *Poetry, Language, Thought*, trans. Albert Hofstadter (New York: HarperCollins, 2001 [1971]), 85. The statement is made in the 1960 addendum to the 1936 essay.

4. Hubert L. Dreyfus, *Being-in-the-World: A Commentary on Heidegger's "Being and Time," Division I* (Cambridge, MA: MIT Press, 1991), 168–83.

5. Heidegger, "The Origin of the Work of Art," 25–26.

6. The equiprimordial triad's bearing on poetic language and trope anticipates the triad in Paul Ricoeur's classic essay "The Metaphorical Process as Cognition, Imagination, and Feeling," *Critical Inquiry* 5, no. 1 (Autumn 1978): 143–59. As I see the relation of mood to understanding in Heidegger, one concern that Ricoeur expresses is overcome: "We miss, in Heidegger's *Daseinanalyse* itself, the close connections between *Befindlichkeit* and *Versstehen*, between situation and project, between anxiety and interpretation" (158).

7. Gustave Flaubert, "Herodias," in *Three Tales*, trans. Roger Whitehouse (London and New York: Penguin Books, 2005), 87–89.

8. Flaubert has Jokanaan draw his rhetorical inspiration from Isaiah 3:16-24: "Moreover the Lord saith, Because the daughters of Zion are haughty, and walk with stretched forth necks and wanton eyes, walking and mincing *as* they go, and making a tinkling with their feet: Therefore the Lord will smite with a scab the crown of the head of the daughters of Zion, and the Lord will discover their secret parts. In that day the Lord will take away the bravery of *their* tinkling ornaments *about their feet*, and *their* cauls, and *their* round tires like the moon, The chains, and the bracelets, and the mufflers, The bonnets, and the ornaments of the legs, and the headbands, and the tablets, and the earrings, The rings, and nose jewels, The changeable suits of apparel, and the mantles, and the wimples, and the crisping pins, The glasses, and the fine linen, and the hoods, and the vails. And it shall come to pass, *that* instead of sweet smell there shall be stink; and instead of a girdle a rent; and instead of well set hair baldness; and instead of a stomacher a girding of sackcloth; *and* burning instead of beauty."

9. Aristotle, *The Art of Rhetoric*, trans. H. C. Lawson-Tancred (London and New York: Penguin Books, 2004 [1991]), 153.

10. Ibid., 155.

11. Rüdiger Campe, "Presenting the Affect: The Scene of Pathos in Aristotle's Rhetoric and Its Revision in Descartes's *Passions of the Soul*," in *Rethinking Emotion: Interiority and Exteriority in Premodern, Modern, and Contemporary Thought*, ed. Rüdiger Campe and Julia Weber (Berlin and Boston: De Gruyter, 2014), 39.

12. René Descartes, *The Passions of the Soul*, trans. Robert Stoothoff, *The Philosophical Writings of Descartes*, vol. 1, trans. John Cottingham, Robert Stoothoff, and Dugald Murdoch (Cambridge: Cambridge University Press, 1985), 345. My italics.

13. Aristotle, *The Art of Rhetoric*, 154.

14. Daniel M. Gross, *The Secret History of Emotion: From Aristotle's "Rhetoric" to Modern Brain Science* (Chicago: University of Chicago Press, 2006), 1–20. The choice lies between emphasis on the social structure of dominance and inequality (slavery, property, gender) supporting the Greek *polis* and emphasis on the historic creation of the idea of equality in that same *polis*.

15. Raymond Williams, *Marxism and Literature* (Oxford and New York: Oxford University Press, 1977), 128–35.

16. Peter Sloterdijk, *Rage and Time: A Psychopolitical Investigation*, trans. Mario Wenning (New York: Columbia University Press, 2010).

17. Aristotle, *The Art of Rhetoric*, 142–43.

18. Ibid., 156.

19. Sophocles, *Antigone*, in *Sophocles I*, trans. David Grene, 2nd ed. (Chicago: University of Chicago Press, 1991), 174.

20. Aristotle, *Poetics*, trans. Malcolm Heath (London and New York: Penguin Books, 1996), 6–7.

21. Plato, *Laws*, trans. A. E. Taylor, in *The Collected Dialogues of Plato*, ed. Edith Hamilton and Huntington Cairns, Bollingen Series 71 (Princeton, NJ: Princeton University Press, 1961), 1251.

22. Matthew Ratcliffe, "Why Mood Matters," in *The Cambridge Companion to Heidegger's "Being and Time*,*"* ed. Mark A. Wrathall (Cambridge and New York: Cambridge University Press, 2013), 164.

23. Ibid., 170.

24. Gilles Deleuze, "On Nietzsche and the Image of Thought," in *Desert Islands and Other Texts, 1953–1974*, ed. David Lapoujade, trans. Michael Taormina (Los Angeles: Semiotext(e), 2004), 139.

25. Friedrich Nietzsche, *Writings from the Late Notebooks*, ed. Rüdiger Bittner, trans. Kate Sturge (Cambridge: Cambridge University Press, 2003), 96.

26. Ann Cvetkovich, *Depression: A Public Feeling* (Durham, NC: Duke University Press, 2012), 29–82.

27. Brian Massumi, "The Autonomy of Affect," in *Parables for the Virtual: Movement, Affect, Sensation* (Durham, NC: Duke University Press, 2002), 24. For an extensive polemical engagement with Massumi in the larger context of psychological and neurophysiological researches on affect, see Ruth Leys, "The Turn to Affect: A Critique," in *The Ascent of Affect: Genealogy and Critique* (Chicago: University of Chicago Press, 2017). 307–49. The debate set off by the original appearance of Leys's essay can be found in *Critical Inquiry* (Summer 2011 and Summer 2012).

28. Massumi, "The Autonomy of Affect," 28.

29. Ibid., 27.

30. Jacques Derrida, "Freud and the Scene of Writing," in *Writing and Difference*, trans. Alan Bass (Chicago: University of Chicago Press, 1978), 196–231.

31. Massumi, "The Autonomy of Affect," 29.

32. I draw simply from a journalistic report on research on hearing: "Sound Barriers: The Shape of Your Ears Affects What You Hear," *New York Times*, March 13, 2018, D2.

33. Maurice Merleau-Ponty, *Nature: Course Notes from the Collège de France*, ed. Dominique Séglard, trans. Robert Vallier (Evanston, IL: Northwestern University Press, 2003), 208.

34. Lauren Berlant, *Cruel Optimism* (Durham, NC: Duke University Press, 2011), 158. The immediate context of these formulations is a critical reflection on, and homage to, Eve Sedgwick's work on shame.

35. Ibid., 27.

36. Ibid., 15.

37. Ibid., 51–53 and 63–69.

38. Ibid., 15.

39. Ibid., 227.

40. Hans Ulrich Gumbrecht, *After 1945: Latency as Origin of the Present* (Stanford, CA: Stanford University Press, 2013), 31.

41. Martin Heidegger, *The Fundamental Concepts of Metaphysics: World, Finitude, Solitude*, trans. William McNeill and Nicholas Walker (Bloomington: Indiana University Press, 1995), 162–63.

42. Ibid., 163.

43. Ibid., 162.

44. Ibid., 165.

45. I address the import of affect for political theory in "Rhetorics of Affect: Notes on the Political Theory of the Passions," in *The Oxford Handbook of Rhetoric and Political Theory*, ed. Dilip Gaonkar and Keith Topper (New York and Oxford: Oxford University Press, forthcoming).

Chapter One

1. Immanuel Kant, *Critique of Pure Reason*, trans. Norman Kemp Smith (New York: St. Martin's Press, 1965 [1929]), 67.

2. Ibid., 67–68.

3. Ibid., 74–75.

4. Ibid., 77.

5. Ibid., 88.

6. Ibid., 87.

7. Ibid., 88.

8. Maurice Merleau-Ponty, *The Visible and the Invisible, Followed by Working Notes*, ed. Claude Lefort, trans. Alphonso Lingis (Evanston, IL: Northwestern University Press, 1968), 147–48.

9. Ibid., 148.

10. Ibid., 254.

11. Ibid., 133.

12. Daniel Heller-Roazen, *The Inner Touch: Archaeology of a Sensation* (New York: Zone Books, 2007), 36–37. His translations are from Aristotle's *De somno et vigilia* 2.455a12–23.

13. Ibid., 295. The quotation, translated by Heller-Roazen, is from *Metaphysics* 12.7.1072b20–25.

14. Ibid.

15. Ibid., 299. The quotation, translated by Heller-Roazen, is from *Opera Omnia*, vol. 48, 540.

16. Ibid.

17. Ibid., 297.

18. Judith Butler, "Merleau-Ponty and the Touch of Malebranche," in *Senses of the Subject* (New York: Fordham University Press, 2015), 38.

19. Ibid., 47.

20. Ibid., 38.

21. Ibid. 47–48.

22. Ibid., 48. Malebranche's proposition is cited on 42.

23. Cited and translated in Butler, "Merleau-Ponty and the Touch of Malebranche," 50.

24. Ibid., 61.

25. Ibid., 52.

26. Ibid., 62.

27. Heller-Roazen, *The Inner Touch*, 299.

28. Harold Pinter, *Betrayal* (New York: Grove Press, 1978), 37.

29. Ibid., 39–41.

30. Kant, *Critique of Pure Reason*, 88.

31. Slavoj Žižek, *The Ticklish Subject: The Absent Centre of Political Ontology* (London: Verso, 1999), 166–67 and 276–77.

32. Quotations from "The Philosophy of Composition" and "The Raven" are from *Selected Writings of Edgar Allan Poe*, ed. Edward H. Davidson (Boston: Houghton Mifflin, 1956), 452–63 and 36–39, respectively.

33. As the citations from the essay underscore, Poe achieves the appearance of "precision and rigid consequence" through his adroit deployment of hyperbole and absolutes: *the most legitimate, it was clear, must be, inevitably led to, most sonorous, most producible, at once, the very first, infinitely more in keeping with, universal understanding of mankind, obvious reply, only intelligible mode.*

34. On the narrative innovation of "The Black Cat," see my "On Voice," in *Essentials of the Theory of Fiction*, 3rd ed., ed. Michael J. Hoffman and Patrick D. Murphy (Durham, NC: Duke University Press, 2005), 425–29.

35. Sigmund Freud, *Jokes and Their Relation to the Unconscious*, in *The Standard Edition of the Complete Works*, vol. 8, ed. and trans. James Strachey (London: Hogarth Press, 1960), 143.

36. Ibid., 148.

37. Ibid., 148–49.

38. Ibid., 152.

39. Ibid., 155.

40. Stand-up was only just making its first appearance in American vaudeville in the decade or so before Freud was writing. Sometime in the 1880s "Charley Case, who some sources suggest was an African-American who could pass for white, took to the stage for the explicit purpose of telling jokes directly to the audience so as to elicit laughter." Eddie Tafoya, *The Legacy of the Wisecrack: Stand-Up Comedy as the Great American Literary Form* (Boca Raton, FL: Brown-Walker Press, 2009), 111. Stand-up flowered on the radio and in the Borscht Belt thanks to the heirs of the Jewish humor that was a key reference point for Freud. In addition to his vast reading and his collection of jokes from the everyday life of Jewish culture, Freud saw Mark Twain perform at least once in Vienna, in 1898, during the extremely popular humorist's eighteen-month sojourn in the city.

41. Kenneth Burke, *A Rhetoric of Motives* (Berkeley and Los Angeles: University of California Press, 1969 [1950]), 50.

42. Martin Heidegger, "The Origin of the Work of Art," in *Poetry, Language, Thought*, trans. Albert Hofstadter (New York: HarperCollins, 2001 [1971]), 71.

43. Gilles Deleuze and Félix Guattari, *What Is Philosophy?* trans. Hugh Tomlinson and Graham Burchell (New York: Columbia University Press, 1994), 66.

44. Martin Heidegger, *Being and Time*, trans. John Macquarrie and Edward Robinson (New York: Harper & Row, 1962), 102 (H 72). Hereafter citations of this work will be made parenthetically in the text with the H pagination.

45. Translators' note, H 134 n: "'die Stimmung, das Gestimmtsein.' The noun 'Stimmung' originally means the tuning of a musical instrument, but it has taken on several other meanings and is the usual word for one's mood or humour. We shall usually translate it as 'mood,' and we shall generally translate both 'Gestimmtsein' and 'Gestimmtheit' as 'having a mood,' though sometimes, as in the present sentence, we prefer to call attention to the root metaphor of 'Gestimmtsein' by writing 'Being-attuned,' etc."

46. Martin Heidegger, *Nietzsche*, vol. 1, *The Will to Power as Art*, trans. David Farrell Krell (San Francisco: Harper & Row, 1979), 98–99.

47. Avital Ronell, *Crack Wars: Literature, Addiction, Mania* (Urbana: University of Illinois Press, 2004), 33–34.

48. Ibid., 44–45.

Chapter Two

1. Paul de Man, "Spacecritics: J. Hillis Miller and Joseph Frank" (1964), in *Critical Writings, 1953–1978*, ed. Lindsay Waters (Minneapolis: University of Minnesota Press, 1989), 114.

2. See my "Fascist Commitments," in *Responses: On Paul de Man's Wartime Journalism*, ed. Werner Hamacher, Neil Hertz, and Thomas Keenan (Lincoln: University of Nebraska Press, 1989), 21–35.

3. Paul de Man, "Heidegger Reconsidered" (1964), in *Critical Writings*, 105.

4. Ibid.

5. Paul de Man, *Allegories of Reading* (New Haven, CT: Yale University Press, 1979), 151.

6. Paul de Man, "The Concept of Irony," in *Aesthetic Ideology*, ed. Andrzej Warminski (Minneapolis: University of Minnesota Press, 1996), 181.

7. Evelyn Barish, *The Double Life of Paul de Man* (New York: Liveright, 2014). For a review that sees through, and past, the intellectual prejudices that mar this biography, see Louis Menand, "The de Man Case," *The New Yorker*, March 24, 2014.

8. Friedrich Nietzsche, *"On the Genealogy of Morals" and "Ecce Homo,"* ed. Walter Kaufmann, trans. Walter Kaufmann and R. J. Hollingdale (New York: Vintage, 1989 [1967]), 153–54.

9. Jean-Jacques Rousseau, *Discourse on the Sciences and Arts (First Discourse)*, in *The Discourses and Other Early Political Writings*, ed. and trans. Victor Gourevitch (Cambridge: Cambridge University Press, 1997), 23.

10. Jean-Jacques Rousseau, *Essay on the Origin of Languages*, in *The Discourses and Other Early Political Writings*, 253.

11. Jacques Derrida, *Of Grammatology*, trans. Gayatri Chakravorty Spivak, 40th anniversary ed. (Baltimore: Johns Hopkins University Press, 2016), 179–211; and Paul de Man, "The Rhetoric of Blindness: Jacques Derrida's Reading of Rousseau," in *Blindness and Insight: Essays in the*

Rhetoric of Contemporary Criticism, 2nd ed. rev. (Minneapolis: University of Minnesota Press, 1983), 102–41.

12. Rousseau, *Essay on the Origin of Languages*, 254.

13. de Man, *Allegories of Reading*, 152.

14. Paul de Man, "Hypogram and Inscription," in *The Resistance to Theory* (Minneapolis: University of Minnesota Press, 1986), 27–51.

15. Charles Baudelaire, *Oeuvres complètes*, vol. 1, ed. Claude Pichois (Paris: Gallimard, 1975), 11. Hereafter references to this work will be parenthetically in the text, abbreviated *OC I*. Unless otherwise noted, the translations are mine.

16. Paul de Man, "Anthropomorphism and Trope in the Lyric," in *The Rhetoric of Romanticism* (New York: Columbia University Press, 1984), 246.

17. Ibid., 246–47.

18. Ibid., 250. The *locus classicus* for a recognition of the power of syntax over meaning, of the grammatical over the lexical, so essential to the understanding of poetry, is the analysis of *entre* (between) in Jacques Derrida's great essay on Mallarmé, "The Double Session," in *Dissemination*, trans. Barbara Johnson (Chicago: University of Chicago Press, 1981), 173–285.

19. There is nothing far-fetched for a synesthete who "consistently feels the sound of different instruments on different parts of her body—guitars 'brushing' her ankles on up to her shins, violins 'breathing' on her face, cellos and organs 'vibrating' near her navel. . . . 'I love going to the symphony, but afterwards I am exhausted.'" Richard E. Cytowic and David M. Eagleman, *Wednesday Is Indigo Blue: Discovering the Brain of Synesthesia* (Cambridge, MA: MIT Press, 2009), 45.

20. Julia Kristeva, "Baudelaire, or Infinity, Perfume, and Punk," in *Tales of Love*, trans. Leon S. Roudiez (New York: Columbia University Press, 1987, 318–40.

21. For an extensive account of emotion viewed from within the dualities, binaries, and aporias developed in de Man's conception of rhetoric and figurative language, and in deconstruction more generally, see Rei Terada, *Feeling in Theory: Emotion after the "Death of the Subject"* (Cambridge, MA: Harvard University Press, 2001), 48–89 and passim.

22. Susan Stewart, *Poetry and the Fate of the Senses* (Chicago: University of Chicago Press, 2002), 341–42 n. 107.

23. De Quincey, http://www.gutenberg.org/files/2040/2040-h/2040-h.htm.

24. Edgar Allan Poe, *The Complete Tales and Poems* (New York: Modern Library, 1938), 457–58.

25. Charles Baudelaire, *Les fleurs du mal*, trans. Richard Howard (Boston: David R. Godine, 1983), 42–43.

26. Heidegger, "What Is Metaphysics?" trans. David Farrell Krell, in *Pathmarks*, ed. William McNeill (Cambridge: Cambridge University Press, 1998), 89–91.

27. Martin Heidegger, *Being and Time*, trans. John Macquarrie and Edward Robinson (New York: Harper & Row, 1962), 232 (H 187–88). Hereafter citations of this work will be made parenthetically in the text with the H pagination.

28. *Les fleurs du mal*, trans. Howard, 27–28.

29. Maurice Blanchot, "L'échec de Baudelaire," in *La part du feu* (Paris: Éditions Gallimard, 1949), 149.

30. Ibid., 148.

31. Quoted by Marie-Claude Lambotte, *Le discours mélancolique: De la phénoménologie à la métapsychologie* (Paris: Anthropos, 1993), 291. The reference is to Jean Starobinksi, "Les rimes du vide: Une lecture de Baudelaire," *Nouvelle revue de psychanalyse* 11 (Spring 1975): 135.

32. T. W. Adorno, *Aesthetic Theory*, ed. Gretel Adorno and Rolf Tiedman, trans. C. Lenhardt (London: Routledge & Kegan Paul, 1984), 11–12.

33. Jean-Paul Sartre, *Baudelaire*, trans. Martin Turnell (New York: New Directions, 1950), 163–64.

34. Blanchot, "L'échec de Baudelaire," 142.

35. Ibid., 144.

36. Charles Baudelaire, "The Double Room," in *Paris Spleen*, trans. Louise Varèse (New York: New Directions, 1970), 5–7.

37. Blanchot, "L'échec de Baudelaire," 144.

38. Cited in ibid., 145.

39. Erich Auerbach, "The Aesthetic Dignity of the *Fleurs du mal*," trans. Ralph Manheim, in *Scenes from the Drama of European Literature: Six Essays* (New York: Meridian Books, 1959), 207.

40. Ibid., 201–2.

41. Ibid., 205.

42. Ibid., 206–7.

43. Françoise Meltzer, *Seeing Double: Baudelaire's Modernity* (Chicago: University of Chicago Press, 2011), 71. How 1848 formed and deformed Baudelaire's intellectual and poetic sensibility is evident in *My Heart Laid Bare*, the projected autobiography that he thought would rival Rousseau:

> My intoxication in 1848.
>
> What was the nature of that intoxication?
>
> A taste for revenge. The *natural* pleasure of demolition.
>
> [My fury at the coup d'État.]
>
> [How many times I was shot at.]
>
> Literary intoxication; memory of readings.
>
> May 15th.—Always the taste for destruction. Legitimate taste, if everything that is natural is legitimate.
>
> [My fury at the coup d'État]
>
> The horrors of June. The madness of the people and the madness of the bourgeoisie. Natural love of crime.
>
> My fury at the coup d'État. How many times I was shot at! Another Bonaparte! what shame!
>
> —Charles Baudelaire, *My Heart Laid Bare and Other Texts*, trans. Rainer J. Hanshe (NewYork: Contra Mundum Press), 76.

44. Erich Auerbach, *Mimesis: The Representation of Reality in Western Literature*, trans. Willard R. Trask (Princeton, NJ: Princeton University Press, 1953), 459.

45. Meltzer, *Seeing Double*, 223. The insight that drives Meltzer's entire study of Baudelaire is that clarity about the present and the future was in effect impossible in his historical moment. I am less persuaded by her argument that Walter Benjamin, from the vantage point of the Russian Revolution, the further development of capitalism and commodity culture, and the rise of fascism, achieves a valid reading of Baudelaire because he retrospectively grasps the unfolding reality of the nineteenth century that eluded Baudelaire himself. Such an argument presupposes that Benjamin's grasp of the twentieth century, in whose light he interprets the nineteenth, is free from uncertainty about the present and future, the very uncertainty that haunted and

animated the work of Baudelaire, Stendhal, Flaubert, and Zola. I doubt it. A discussion for another occasion.

46. T. S. Eliot, "*from* Henry James (1918)," in *Selected Prose of T. S. Eliot*, centenary ed., ed. Frank Kermode (New York: Harcourt Brace and Farrar, Straus & Giroux, 1975), 151.

47. Li-Young Lee, *The City in Which I Love You* (Brockport, NY: BOA Editions, 1990).

48. *Breaking the Alabaster Jar: Conversations with Li-Young Lee*, ed. Earl G. Ingersoll (Rochester, NY: BOA Editions, 2006), 33–34.

49. Ibid., 38 and 32.

50. Gianni Vattimo, *The Transparent Society*, trans. David Webb (Baltimore, MD: Johns Hopkins University Press, 1992), 10.

51. For three distinct valuations of Lee's poetry in relation to visions of Asian American studies, see Wenying Xu, "An Exile's Will to Canon and Its Tension with Ethnicity: Li-Young Lee," in *Multiethnic Literature and Canon Debates*, ed. Mary Jo Bona and Irma Maini (Albany: State University of New York Press, 2006), 145–65; Steven G. Yao, "The Precision of Persimmons: Li-Young Lee, Ethnic Identity, and the Limits of Lyric Testimony," in *Foreign Accents: Chinese American Verse from Exclusion to Postethnicity* (New York: Oxford University Press, 2010), 147–86; and Dorothy Wang, "Metaphor, Desire, and Assimilation in the Poetry of Li-Young Lee," in *Thinking Its Presence: Form, Race, and Subjectivity in Contemporary Asian American Poetry* (Stanford, CA: Stanford University Press, 2014), 48–92.

52. Xu, "An Exile's Will to Canon," 126.

53. Wang, "Metaphor, Desire, and Assimilation," 49–50.

54. *Breaking the Alabaster Jar*, 31–32.

55. I adapted a few passages from this section for a short article in *Qui parle*'s commemorative issue asking the question, *Qui parle?* "I, Not I," *Qui parle* 26, no. 2 (December 2017): 351–53.

56. G. W. F. Hegel, *Aesthetics: Lectures on Fine Art*, vol. 2, trans. T. M. Knox (Oxford: Clarendon Press, 1975), 1124.

57. Octavio Paz, *The Other Voice: Essays on Modern Poetry*, trans. Helen Lane (New York: Harcourt Brace Jovanovich, 1991), 152.

58. Friedrich Nietzsche, *"The Birth of Tragedy" and "The Case of Wagner,"* trans. Walter Kaufmann (New York: Vintage Books, 1967), 48–52. All citations of Nietzsche in the next few paragraphs are from these pages.

59. Hegel, *Aesthetics*, vol. 2, 1133.

60. Ibid.

61. *Letters of John Keats: A Selection*, ed. Robert Gittings (New York: Oxford University Press, 1970), 157–58. Letter to Richard Woodhouse, October 27, 1818.

62. Paz, *The Other Voice*, 151.

63. *Breaking the Alabaster Jar*, 42.

64. de Man, "Anthropomorphism and Trope," 261.

65. Ibid., 256.

66. Ibid., 261.

67. Ibid., 262. At the outset of the essay, de Man invokes the phrase from Nietzsche's "On Truth and Lie in an Extra-Moral Sense": "What, then, is truth? A mobile army of metaphors, metonyms, and anthropomorphisms—. . . ." In *The Portable Nietzsche*, ed. and trans. Walter Kaufmann (New York: Penguin Books, 1976 [1954]), 46.

68. What *produces* the fallacious reading? Is it the poem "Obsession"? Its space-time-phenomenality? Or the critic's stating the relation in those terms? Or is the difficulty of disambiguating the sentence a sign of the inextricability of those three possibilities?

69. de Man, "Anthropomorphism and Trope," 256.

70. Virginia Jackson and Yopie Prins (eds.), *The Lyric Theory Reader: A Critical Anthology* (Baltimore, MD: Johns Hopkins University Press, 2014), 454.

71. Ibid., 14.

72. Ibid., 272 and 274. Included in the "Post-Structuralist" section with de Man are essays by Jacques Derrida, Harold Bloom, and Barbara Johnson. It is beyond scope of the discussion here to pursue a detailed engagement with Jackson and Prins's tendency to view New Criticism, structuralism, poststructuralism, and Heideggerian and phenomenological criticism—all of which are amply represented in the anthology—as the great modern, now-surpassed deviation in interpreting and thinking about poetry. The essays they anthologize under these rubrics ought to be refutation enough.

73. Jonathan Culler, *Theory of the Lyric* (Cambridge, MA: Harvard University Press, 2015), 82.

74. Cited in ibid., 120.

75. Ibid.

76. Culler himself devotes an important chapter to "Lyric Address," in ibid., 186–243.

77. Immanuel Kant, *Critique of the Power of Judgment*, ed. Paul Guyer, trans. Paul Guyer and Eric Matthews (Cambridge: Cambridge University Press, 2000), 162.

78. Ibid., 101.

79. Ibid., 164.

80. Ibid., 95.

81. Ibid., 96–97.

82. Nietzsche, *The Birth of Tragedy*, 52.

Chapter Three

1. Gilles Deleuze, *Pure Immanence: Essays on a Life*, trans. Anne Boyman (New York: Zone Books, 2005), 30.

2. Ibid., 28.

3. Dickens's account: "The doctor-seeking messenger meets the doctor halfway, coming under convoy of police. Doctor examines the dank carcase, and pronounces, not hopefully, that it is worth while trying to reanimate the same. All the best means are at once in action, and everybody present lends a hand, and a heart and soul. No one has the least regard for the man: with them all, he has been an object of avoidance, suspicion, and aversion; but the spark of life within him is curiously separable from himself now, and they have a deep interest in it, probably because it *is* life, and they are living and must die." Charles Dickens, *Our Mutual Friend*, ed. Michael Costell (Oxford and New York: Oxford University Press, 1998), 443.

4. Deleuze, *Pure Immanence*, 25.

5. Gilles Deleuze and Félix Guattari, *What Is Philosophy?*, trans. Hugh Tomlinson and Graham Burchell (New York: Columbia University Press, 1994), 32.

6. Ibid., 213.

7. Ibid., 211.

8. Ibid., 212–13.

9. Martin Heidegger, *Nietzsche*, vol. 1, *The Will to Power as Art*, trans. David Farrell Krell (New York: Harper & Row, 1971), 115. Heidegger refers here to section 811 of Friedrich Nietzsche, *The Will to Power*, ed. Walter Kaufmann, trans. Walter Kaufman and R. J. Hollingdale (New York: Vintage, 1968), 428–29.

10. Deleuze and Guattari, *What Is Philosophy?*, 177.

11. Ibid., 66.

12. Ibid., 65.

13. Martin Heidegger, "The Origin of the Work of Art," in *Poetry, Language, Thought*, trans. Albert Hofstadter (New York: HarperCollins, 2001 [1971]), 41.

14. Ibid., 33.

15. Heidegger did not visit Greece until 1962.

16. Heidegger, "The Origin of the Work of Art," 41.

17. Ibid., 61.

18. Ibid., 47.

19. Ibid., 45.

20. Ibid., 33.

21. Deleuze and Guatarri, *What Is Philosophy?*, 163–64.

22. Gilles Deleuze, *Francis Bacon: The Logic of Sensation*, trans. Daniel W. Smith (Minneapolis: University of Minnesota Press, 2003), 7.

23. Ibid., 6.

24. Ibid., 79.

25. Ibid.

26. Ibid., 34, 36.

27. Heidegger, "The Origin of the Work of Art," 35 and 36.

28. Ibid., 28.

29. Ibid., 62.

30. Ibid., 44.

31. Ibid., 54.

32. Ibid., 19.

33. Aristotle, *Poetics*, 6–7.

34. Deleuze, *Francis Bacon*, 32.

35. Heidegger, "The Origin of the Work of Art," 56.

36. Ibid., 61.

37. Ibid., 62.

38. Ibid., 63.

39. Philippe Sollers, *Théorie des exceptions* (Paris: Gallimard, 1986), 12.

40. Heidegger, "The Origin of the Work of Art," 63.

41. John Berger, *A Painter of Our Time* [1958] (London: Writers and Readers, 1976), 137.

42. Heidegger, "The Origin of the Work of Art," 69.

43. Ibid., 64.

44. Ibid., 39–40.

45. Ibid., 60.

46. *The Sonnets*, ed. G. Blakemore Evans (Cambridge: Cambridge University Press, 1996), 92.

47. Gilles Deleuze, "Literature and Life," in *Essays Critical and Clinical*, trans. Daniel W. Smith and Michael A. Greco (Minneapolis: University of Minnesota Press, 1997), 5.

48. Heidegger, "The Origin of the Work of Art," 71.

49. Ibid., 49.

50. Ibid., 50.

51. Ibid., 51.

52. Ibid., 52.

53. Ibid., 53.

54. Martin Heidegger, *Being and Time*, trans. John Macquarrie and Edward Robinson (New York: Harper & Row, 1962), 205 (H 162). Hereafter citations of this work will be made parenthetically in the text with the H pagination.

55. Heidegger, "Origin of the Work of Art," 45.

56. Ibid., 70–71.

57. Immanuel Kant, *Critique of Judgment*, trans. J. H. Bernard (New York: Hafner, 1966), 165–66. Occasionally, as here, I cite the older Bernard translation, sometimes on account of its style and sometimes because of phrasings that have long since seeped deep into English-language discussion of Kant.

58. Immanuel Kant, *Critique of the Power of Judgment*, ed. Paul Guyer, trans. Paul Guyer and Eric Matthews (Cambridge: Cambridge University Press, 2000), 203–4.

59. Ibid., 191–92.

60. Ibid., 193.

61. Michel Chaouli, *Thinking with Kant's "Critique of Judgment"* (Cambridge, MA: Harvard University Press, 2017), 186–87.

62. Heidegger, "The Origin of the Work of Art," 71.

63. Roman Jakobson, "Linguistics and Poetics," in *Style in Language*, ed. Thomas A. Sebeok (Cambridge, MA: MIT Press, 1960) 350–77.

64. Heidegger, "The Origin of the Work of Art," 71.

65. Ibid., 70.

66. Ibid.

67. Ibid., 72.

68. Ibid. 71.

69. Ibid., 69.

70. Ibid., 35, 69, 38, 69, 70, 71, 72, 75, 60, and 69, respectively.

71. Gianni Vattimo, "Art and Oscillation," in *The Transparent Society*, trans. David Webb (Baltimore, MD: Johns Hopkins University Press, 1992), 53.

72. Heidegger, "The Origin of the Work of Art," 71.

73. Martin Heidegger, "Letter on 'Humanism,'" trans. Frank A. Capuzzi, in *Pathmarks*, ed. William McNeill (Cambridge: Cambridge University Press, 1998), 239. Addressed as a letter to Jean Beaufret in 1946 and first published in 1947 and 1949, the essay is said by Heidegger to be "based on the course taken by a path that was begun in 1936" (239 n.), that is, at the time of the Nietzsche seminar and "The Origin of the Work of Art."

74. Heidegger, "The Origin of the Work of Art," 70.

75. Ibid., 42.

76. Ibid.

77. Ibid., 61.

78. Ibid., 75, 74.

79. Ibid., 75–76.

80. Ibid., 41.

81. Gilles Deleuze, "An Unrecognized Precursor to Heidegger," in *Essays Critical and Clinical*, 97.

82. Ibid., 98.

83. Ibid., 97.

84. Heidegger, "The Origin of the Work of Art," 74.

85. Ibid., 49.

86. Ibid.

87. Peter Sloterdijk, *You Must Change Your Life: On Anthropotechnics*, trans. Wieland Hoban (Cambridge: Polity, 2013), 162. For Heidegger's commentary, see "Letter on 'Humanism,'" 269–71.

88. Heidegger, "The Origin of the Work of Art," 83.

Chapter Four

1. Immanuel Kant, *Critique of the Power of Judgment*, ed. Paul Guyer, trans. Paul Guyer and Eric Matthews (Cambridge: Cambridge University Press, 2000), 99.

2. Immanuel Kant, *Critique of Judgment*, trans. J. H. Bernard (New York: Hafner, 1966), 50. In the Guyer translation, 101: "There can be no rule in accordance with which someone could be compelled to acknowledge something as beautiful. Whether a garment, a house, a flower is beautiful: no one allows himself to be talked into his judgment about that by means of any grounds or fundamental principles. One wants to submit the object to his own eyes, just as if his satisfaction depended on sensation; and yet, if one then calls the object beautiful, one believes oneself to have a universal voice, and lays claim to the consent of everyone, whereas any private sensation would be decisive only for him alone and his satisfaction."

3. Kant, *Critique of the Power of Judgment*, 102.

4. Ibid., 91.

5. Martin Heidegger, *Nietzsche*, vol. 1, *The Will to Power as Art*, trans. David Farrell Krell (San Francisco: Harper & Row, 1979), 109. It is noteworthy that "The Origin of the Work of Art" is contemporary with the Nietzsche seminar but contains no reference or even allusion to Nietzsche. By the same token, the seminar's far-reaching, lucid commentary on Nietzsche and aesthetics suggests Heidegger's differences but does not spell them out polemically or even argumentatively. As a result of the seminar's indirectness and the essay's silence, several aspects of Heidegger's own view are left undeveloped or ambiguous; his dissatisfactions with Nietzsche are clearer than his alternatives.

6. Kant, *Critique of Judgment*, 69.

7. Ibid., 198–99. The Guyer and Matthews translation reads: "Now I say that the beautiful is the symbol of the morally good, and that only in this respect (that of a relation that is natural to everyone, and that is also expected of everyone else as a duty) does it please with a claim to the assent of everyone else, in which the mind is at the same time aware of a certain ennoblement and elevation above the mere receptivity for a pleasure from sensible impressions, and also esteems the value of others in accordance with a similar maxim of their power of judgment" (227).

8. Hannah Arendt, *Lectures on Kant's Political Philosophy*, ed. Ronald Beiner (Chicago: University of Chicago Press, 1982), 72.

9. Kant, *Critique of the Power of Judgment*, 12. The passage is from the First Introduction (which is not included in the Bernard translation).

10. Ibid., 359 n. 5.

11. Ibid., 12–13.

12. Ibid., 95.

13. Heidegger, *Nietzsche*, vol. 1, 109.

14. Ibid., 110.

15. Ibid., 111.

16. Friedrich Nietzsche, *The Will to Power*, ed. Walter Kaufmann, trans. Walter Kaufman and R. J. Hollingdale (New York: Vintage, 1968), 433. Krell's translation in *Nietzsche* runs as follows: "The firm, the mighty, solid, the life that rests squarely and sovereignly and conceals its strength—that is what '*pleases*,' i.e., that corresponds to what one takes oneself to be" (112).

17. Heidegger, *Nietzsche*, vol. 1, 112.

18. Kant, *Critique of Judgment*, 83. In the Guyer and Matthews translation: "Directly brings with it a feeling of the promotion of life" (128).

19. Ibid., 44.

20. Ibid.

21. Kant, *Critique of the Power of Judgment*, 173–74.

22. Ibid., 174.

23. François Jullien, *On the Universal, the Uniform, the Common and the Dialogue between Cultures*, trans. Michael Richardson and Krzysztof Fijalkowski (Cambridge and Malden, MA: Polity Press, 2014), 95.

24. Ibid., 96 and 94.

25. Ibid., 96 and 97.

26. Ibid., 92.

27. Kant, *Critique of the Power of Judgment*, 174.

28. Kant, *Critique of Judgment*, 136. In the Guyer and Matthews translation: "1. To think for oneself; 2. To think in the position of everyone else; 3. Always to think in accord with oneself. The first is the maxim of the *unprejudiced* way of thinking, the second of the *broad-minded* way, the third that of the *consistent way*" (174).

29. Immanuel Kant, "An Answer to the Question: 'What Is Enlightenment?,'" in *Kant's Political Writings*, ed. Hans Reiss, trans. H. B. Nisbet (Cambridge: Cambridge University Press, 1970), 54.

30. Kant, *Critique of Judgment*, 137n.

31. Kant, *Critique of the Power of Judgment*, 166.

32. Immanuel Kant, "On the Common Saying: 'This May be True in Theory, but It Does Not Apply in Practice,'" in *Kant's Political Writings*, 84–85; Kant's italics. The context of the passage is an argument against what Kant takes to be the implications of Hobbes's conception of sovereignty. I discuss the relation of Hobbes and Kant in *The Cultural Contradictions of Democracy: Political Thought since September 11* (Princeton, NJ: Princeton University Press, 2007), 4–6, 144–46, and 152–57.

33. Kant, "An Answer to the Question: 'What is Enlightenment?,'" 54. The footnoted caveat regarding the three maxims underlying the *sensus communis* quoted above continues: "For not to be passive as regards reason, but to be always self-legislative, is indeed quite easy for the man who wishes only to be in accordance with his essential purpose and does not desire to know what is beyond his understanding. But since we can hardly avoid seeking this, and there are never wanting others who promise with much confidence that they are able to satisfy our curiosity, it must be very hard to maintain in or restore to the mind (especially the mind of the public) that bare negative which properly constitutes enlightenment." *Critique of Judgment*, 137n.

34. Two classic works of scholarship examine the emergence of the social and discursive practices that spawn modern criticism in the Renaissance and the seventeenth century: Baxter Hathaway, *Marvels and Commonplaces: Renaissance Literary Criticism* (New York: Random House, 1968); and Erich Auerbach, "'La cour et la ville,'" trans. Ralph Manheim, in *Scenes from the Drama of European Literature: Six Essays* (New York: Meridian Books, 1959), 133–79. Auerbach also probed medieval developments in language and literature that preformed the public; see his *Literary Language and its Public in Late Latin Antiquity and in the Middle Ages*, trans. Ralph Manheim (Princeton, NJ: Princeton University Press, 1993 [1965]).

35. Hannah Arendt, "The Crisis in Culture: Its Social and Its Political Significance," in *Between Past and Future: Eight Exercises in Political Thought* (New York: Penguin Press, 1977), 221.

36. See Erich Auerbach, *Mimesis: The Representation of Reality in Western Literature*, trans. Willard R. Trask (Princeton, NJ: Princeton University Press, 1953), 454–524; and my "Innovation:

Notes on Nihilism and the Aesthetics of the Novel," in *The Novel*, vol. 2, *Forms and Themes*, ed. Franco Moretti (Princeton, NJ: Princeton University Press, 2006), 808–38.

37. Jacques Rancière, *The Politics of Aesthetics*, trans. Gabriel Rockhill (New York: Continuum, 2004), 21.

38. Ibid., 22–23.

39. Ibid., 23.

40. Jacques Rancière, *Aesthetics and Its Discontents*, trans. Steven Cororan (Cambridge and Malden, MA: Polity, 2009), 99.

41. Ibid., 102–3.

42. Zachary Samalin, "Adorno's Contempt," unpublished manuscript.

43. Max Weber, "Religious Rejections of the World and Their Directions," "Politics as Vocation," and "Science as Vocation," in *From Max Weber: Essays in Sociology*, ed. and trans. H. H. Gerth and C. Wright Mills (New York: Oxford University Press, 1946), 323–59, 77–128, and 129–56.

44. See my " '. . . wrestling with (my God!) my God': Modernism, Nihilism, and Belief," *Qui parle* 21, no. 2 (Spring–Summer 2013): 1–25.

45. Rancière, *The Politics of Aesthetics*, 13.

46. Deleuze and Guattari, *What Is Philosophy?*, 176–77.

47. Jacques Rancière, "The Monument and Its Confidences; or Deleuze and Art's Capacity of 'Resistance,'" in *Dissensus: On Politics and Aesthetics*, ed. and trans. Steven Corcoran (London and New York: Bloomsbury, 2015), 187. See also Jacques Rancière, "Is There a Deleuzian Aesthetics?," trans. Radmila Djordjevic, *Qui parle* 14, no. 2 (Spring–Summer 2004): 1–14.

48. Niklas Luhmann, *Art as Social System*, trans. Eva M. Knodt (Stanford: Stanford University Press, 2000), 142.

49. Rancière, "The Monument and Its Confidences," 181.

50. Arendt, "The Crisis in Culture," 217–18.

51. Hannah Arendt, *Lectures on Kant's Political Philosophy*, ed. Ronald Beiner (Chicago: University of Chicago Press, 1982), 76. The phrase is from part 4 of the introduction to the *Critique of Judgment*.

52. Nathalie Heinich, *Le paradigme de l'art contemporain: Structures d'une révolution artistique* (Paris: Gallimard, 2014), 150–52.

53. Ibid., 89–92.

54. Ibid., 92–93.

55. Holland Cotter, "In the Naked Museum: Talking, Thinking, Encountering," *New York Times*, January 31, 2010; Gillian Sneed, "Tino Sehgal Presents a Work in Progress," *Art in America* "News," http://www.artinamericamagazine.com/news-features/news/tino-sehgal-guggenheim-this -progress/; and Peter Schjeldahl, "Never-Ending Story," Critic's Notebook, *The New Yorker*, February 15, 2010.

56. My thanks to the Marian Goodman Gallery for granting me online access to the video. The transcriptions are my own.

57. Nietzsche, *The Will to Power*, 443–44.

58. Heidegger, *Nietzsche*, vol. 1, 125.

59. Nietzsche, *The Will to Power*, 448.

60. Heidegger, *Nietzsche*, vol. 1, 126.

61. Ibid.

62. Nietzsche, *The Will to Power*, 445–46.

63. Ibid., 446.

64. Nietzsche, *The Birth of Tragedy*, 24–25.

65. Ibid., 26.

66. Friedrich Nietzsche, *"On the Genealogy of Morals" and "Ecce Homo,"* ed. Walter Kaufmann, trans. Walter Kaufmann and R. J. Holingdale (New York: Vintage Books, 1989 [1976]), 274.

67. Ibid., 275.

68. Ibid., 274.

69. Nietzsche, *The Will to Power*, 377.

70. Peter Sloterdijk, *Nietzsche Apostle*, trans. Steven Corcoran (Los Angeles: Semiotext(e), 2013), 33.

71. Nietzsche, *Ecce Homo*, 315; quoted in Sloterdijk, *Nietzsche Apostle*, 37. An allusion to *Faust*, lines 328–29: "A good man, in his dark, bewildered stress, / Well knows the path from which he should not stray."

72. *Ecce Homo*, 303.

73. Friedrich Nietzsche, *Twilight of the Idols*, in *The Portable Nietzsche*, ed. and trans. Walter Kaufmann (New York: Penguin Books, 1976 [1954]), 519–20.

74. Nietzsche, *Twilight of the Idols*, 520.

75. Ibid., 446.

76. Friedrich Nietzsche, *The Gay Science*, trans. Walter Kaufmann (New York: Vintage Books, 1974), 191.

77. Nietzsche, *Nietzsche contra Wagner*, in *The Portable Nietzsche*, 671.

78. Nietzsche, *Ecce Homo*, 243 ("Why I Am so Clever").

79. Heidegger, *Nietzsche*, vol. 1, 128.

80. Nietzsche, *The Will to Power*, 434. The fuller passage reads: "*Pessimism in art?*—The artist gradually comes to love for their own sake the means that reveal the condition of intoxication: extreme subtlety and splendor of color, definiteness of line, nuances of tone: the *distinct* where otherwise, under normal conditions, distinctness is lacking. All distinct things, all nuances, to the extent that they recall these extreme enhancements of strength that intoxication produces, awaken this feeling of intoxication by association: the effect of the work of art is to *excite the state that creates art*—intoxication."

81. Nietzsche, "Attempt at Self-Criticism," in *The Birth of Tragedy*, 23.

82. Milan Kundera, *Testaments Betrayed: An Essay in Nine Parts*, trans. Linda Asher (New York: HarperCollins, 1995), 27, 7.

83. Cf. my "Innovation: Notes on Nihilism and the Aesthetics of the Novel"; and "World and Novel," *Narrative* 24, no. 1 (January 2016): 13–26. Kundera's passing remarks on criticism would aptly apply to the tradition of criticism I outlined above: "We should not denigrate literary criticism. Nothing is worse for a writer than to come up against its absence. I am speaking of literary criticism as mediation, as analysis: literary criticism that involves several readings of the book it means to discuss (like great pieces of music we can listen to time and again, great novels too are made for repeated readings); literary criticism that, deaf to the implacable clock of topicality, will readily discuss works a year, thirty years, three hundred years old; literary criticism that tries to apprehend the originality of a work in order thus to inscribe it in historical memory." *Testaments Betrayed*, 24.

84. Martin Heidegger, "What Is Metaphysics?," trans. David Farrell Krell, in *Pathmarks*, ed. William McNeill (Cambridge: Cambridge University Press, 1998), 88–89.

85. Martin Heidegger, "The Origin of the Work of Art," in *Poetry, Language, Thought*, trans. Albert Hofstadter (New York: HarperCollins, 2001 [1971]), 69; my italics.

Chapter Five

1. Martin Heidegger, *Nietzsche*, vol. 1, *The Will to Power as Art*, trans. David Farrell Krell (San Francisco: Harper & Row, 1979), 115.

2. Martin Heidegger, *Being and Time*, trans. John Macquarrie and Edward Robinson (New York: Harper & Row, 1962), 232 (H 187). Hereafter citations of this work will be made parenthetically in the text with the H pagination.

3. Heidegger, "What Is Metaphysics?"; "Postscript to 'What Is Metaphysics?'," trans. William McNeil; and "Introduction to 'What Is Metaphysics?'," trans. Walter Kaufmann, *Pathmarks*, 82–96, 231–38, and 277–90. Heidegger never wrote the projected third part of *Being in Time* in which presumably the concepts he elaborated in the first part in terms of the basic analysis of Dasein (from which I have just been quoting) and in the second part in terms of Dasein and temporality would be taken up anew in terms of the question and meaning of being. Arguably, the bulk of his seminars and writings after *Being and Time* are avenues and fragments of that problematic. What makes these three essays so interesting is that they represent his only return to the topic of *Angst* and put it in relation to the question of being (and nothing).

4. Heidegger, "What Is Metaphysics?," 88–91.

5. Richard Rorty, Gianni Vattimo, and Santiago Zabala, "Dialogue," in Richard Rorty and Gianni Vattimo, *The Future of Religion*, ed. Santiago Zabala, trans. William McCuaig (New York: Columbia University Press, 2005), 58. Vattimo's comment resonates, unintentionally I am sure, with the remark in the early essay of de Man's that I cited at the beginning of chap. 2: "A text that exists in time cannot be projected in a definitive and well-rounded shape. It has to be integrated into a continuous interpretation, for it is itself a fragment in the incessant interpretation of Being that makes up our history."

6. Gianni Vattimo, "Hermeneutics and Democracy," in *Nihilism and Emancipation: Ethics, Politics, and Law*, ed. Santiago Zambala, trans. William McCuaig (New York: Columbia University Press, 2004), 94–95.

7. Martin Heidegger, *Nietzsche*, vol. 4, *Nihilism*, ed. David Farrell Krell, trans. Frank A. Capuzzi (San Francisco: Harper & Row, 1982), 201.

8. Heidegger, "Introduction to 'What Is Metaphysics?'," 290.

9. David Wellbery, "*Stimmung*," trans. Rebecca Pohl, *New Formations* 93 (Summer 2018): 39.

10. John Milton, *Complete Poems and Major Prose*, ed. Merritt Y. Hughes (Indianapolis: Bobbs-Merrill, 1957), 211–12.

11. Franz Kafka, *Diaries: 1910–1923*, ed. Max Brod, trans. Joseph Kesh and Martin Greenberg with the cooperation of Hannah Arendt (New York: Schocken Books, 1976 [1948–49]), 330. Other cited entries can be found on pp. 324–30.

12. Nietzsche, *The Birth of Tragedy*, 33–34.

13. Friedrich Nietzsche, *The Will to Power*, ed. Walter Kaufmann, trans. Walter Kaufman and R. J. Hollingdale (New York: Vintage, 1968), 419–20.

14. Nietzsche, *The Portable Nietzsche*, 519–20.

15. Heidegger, *Nietzsche*, vol. 1, 97–98.

16. Nietzsche, *The Will to Power*, 420. See Jason Ciaccio, "Between Intoxication and Narcosis: Nietzsche's Pharmacology of Modernity," *Modernism/Modernity* 25, no. 1 (2018): 115–33.

17. Freud, *The Interpretation of Dreams*, 5:489–91. See p. 491 n. for the citation from Freud's letter.

18. Ibid., 499.

19. Ibid., 514–15.

20. Jacques Lacan, "The Function and Field of Speech and Language in Psychoanalysis," in *Écrits*, trans. Bruce Fink in collaboration with Héloïse Fink and Russell Grigg (New York: W. W. Norton, 2002), 222.

21. Gaston Bachelard, *On Poetic Imagination and Reverie: Selections from the Works of Gaston Bachelard*, trans. Colette Gaudin (Indianapolis: Bobbs-Merrill, 1971), 64–65. It must be noted that Freud, unlike those followers whom Bachelard associates with "classical psychoanalysis," grants very few elements in dreams the status of symbols with a fixed meaning. In fact, he rejects that flying or falling is such. Cf. Freud, *The Interpretation of Dreams*, 5:392–95.

22. Ibid., 65–66.

23. D. W. Winnicott, *Playing and Reality* (London and New York: Tavistock/Routledge, 1991 [1971]).

24. Hubert L. Dreyfus, *Being-in-the-World: A Commentary on Heidegger's "Being and Time," Division I* (Cambridge, MA: MIT Press, 1991).

25. Maurice Merleau-Ponty, "Cézanne's Doubt," trans. Hubert Dreyfus and Patricia Allen Dreyfus, in *The Merleau-Ponty Aesthetics Reader: Philosophy and Painting*, ed. Galen A. Johnson and Michael B. Smith (Evanston, IL: Northwestern University Press, 1993), 69.

26. Winnicott, "Creativity and Its Origins," in *Playing and Reality*, 67.

27. Heidegger, "The Origin of the Work of Art," 61.

28. Adorno, *Aesthetic Theory*, 160–66, 203–19, and 252–55.

29. Nietzsche, *The Will to Power*, 433.

30. Heidegger, *Nietzsche*, vol. 1, 115.

31. Heidegger, *Nietzsche*, vol. 1, 142.

32. Ibid., 142 n.

33. Ibid., 213–14.

34. Nietzsche, *The Will to Power*, 272.

35. Ibid., 451.

36. Homer, *The Odyssey*, trans. Robert Fagles (New York: Penguin Books, 1996), 252.

37. Nietzsche, *The Will to Power*, 451.

38. Ibid., 453.

39. Ibid., 450.

40. See Frances Ferguson and John Brenkman, "Introduction," Essays from the English Institute, *ELH* 82 (Summer 2015): 313–18.

41. Adorno, *Aesthetic Theory*, 75–76.

42. W. K. Wimsatt, "The Structure of Romantic Nature Imagery," in *The Verbal Icon* (Lexington: University of Kentucky Press, 1954), 103.

43. *Shelley's Poetry and Prose*, ed. Donald H. Reiman and Neil Fraistat, 2nd ed. (New York: W. W. Norton, 2002), 92–101.

44. Heidegger, "What Is Metaphysics?," 91.

45. Jorie Graham, *The End of Beauty* (New York: Ecco Press, 1987), 6. Hereafter citations from this volume will be made parenthetically in the text.

46. Anselm Kiefer, *L'art survivra à ses ruines/Art Will Survive Its Ruins*, trans. Catherine Métais (French) and Michael Taylor (English) (Paris: Éditions du Regard, 2011), 320–21. Like Graham, Kiefer is an artist complexly *after* Heidegger, working with and against the grain of his thought. See Matthew Biro, *Anselm Kiefer and the Philosophy of Martin Heidegger* (Cambridge: Cambridge University Press, 1998).

47. Kiefer, *L'art survivra à ses ruines/Art Will Survive Its Ruins*, 191.

48. Heidegger, "The Origin of the Work of Art," 36.

49. Jorie Graham, "History," in *Region of Unlikeness* (New York: Ecco Press, 1991), 36.

50. Heidegger, "The Thing," in *Poetry, Language, Thought*, 166–67. In an earlier phenomenological idiom, the fact that the act of pouring is essential to what a jug is distinguishes it as an intentional as distinct from a natural object.

51. Ibid., 167.

52. Ibid., 169.

53. Bill Brown, *Other Things* (Chicago: University of Chicago Press, 2015), 31 and 30. The Heidegger citation is from "The Thing," 174.

54. Heidegger, "The Thing," 172.

55. Ibid., 174–75.

56. Ibid., 170.

57. Martin Heidegger and Ernst Jünger, *Correspondence, 1949–1975*, trans. Timothy Sean Quinn (London and New York: Rowman & Littlefield, 2016), 48, 50. The reference to the *Zimmer Chronicle* is to a sixteenth-century text. The biographical details below can found in the early chapters of two Heidegger biographies: Hugo Ott, *Martin Heidegger: A Political Life*, trans. Allan Blunden (New York: Basic Books, 1993); and Rüdiger Safranski, *Martin Heidegger: Between Good and Evil*, trans. Ewald Osers (Cambridge, MA: Harvard University Press, 1998).

58. Heidegger, "The Thing," 171.

59. Ibid., 180.

60. For the many facets of the Heidegger-Cassirer debates, see Peter E. Gordon, *Continental Divide: Heidegger, Cassirer, Davos* (Cambridge, MA: Harvard University Press, 2010).

61. Andrew J. Mitchell, *The Fourfold: Reading the Late Heidegger* (Evanston, IL: Northwestern University Press, 2015), 211–57.

62. Martin Heidegger, *Bremen and Freiburg Lectures: "Insight Into That Which Is" and "Basic Principles of Thinking,"* trans. Andrew J. Mitchell (Bloomington: Indiana University Press, 2012), 54.

63. Hegel, *Aesthetics: Lectures on Fine Art*, vol. 1, 10–11.

64. Martin Heidegger, "The Origin of the Work of Art," in *Poetry, Language, Thought*, trans. Albert Hofstadter (New York: HarperCollins, [1971] 2001), 78. See also *Nietzsche*, vol. 1, 84–91.

65. Heidegger, "The Origin of the Work of Art," 40.

Chapter Six

1. Immanuel Kant, *Critique of the Power of Judgment*, ed. Paul Guyer, trans. Paul Guyer and Eric Matthews (Cambridge: Cambridge University Press, 2000), 148.

2. Simon Schama, *Landscape and Memory* (New York: Knopf, 1990), 478–90. The citations are from 487 and 489.

3. Kant, *Critique of the Power of Judgment*, 185.

4. Ibid., 224.

5. Deleuze and Guattari, *What Is Philosophy?*, 164.

6. Kant, *Critique of the Power of Judgment*, 178–79.

7. Ibid., 180.

8. Ibid., 380 n. 20.

9. Ibid., 141.

10. Ibid., 148.

11. Ibid., 141–42. The Bernard translation reads: "The transcendent . . . is for the imagination like an abyss in which it fears to lose itself; but for the rational idea of the supersensible it is not

transcendent, but in conformity with law to bring about such an effort of the imagination, and consequently here there is the same amount of attraction as there was of repulsion for the mere sensibility" (97).

12. Ibid., 142.

13. Gilles Deleuze, *Kant's Critical Philosophy*, trans. Hugh Tomlinson and Barbara Habberjam (Minneapolis: University of Minnesota Press, 1984), xi. The "Preface" cited here can also be found as a separate essay: see Gilles Deleuze, "On Four Poetic Formulas That Might Summarize the Kantian Philosophy," in *Essays Critical and Clinical*, trans. Daniel W. Smith and Michael A. Greco (Minneapolis: University of Minnesota Press, 1997), 27–35.

14. Kant, *Critique of the Power of Judgment*, 141.

15. Ibid., 144–45.

16. Ibid., 145.

17. Katherine Cox, "The Power of the Air in Milton's Epic Poetry," *SEL: Studies in English Literature, 1500–1900* 56, no. 1 (Winter 2016): 149–70.

18. Kant, *Critique of the Power of Judgment*, 147.

19. In his later work, Habermas becomes implicitly concerned with an insufficiency of motive in the supposedly intrinsic commitments of the discourse ethic and reaches toward a new dialogue with religion. See my "Nihilism and Belief in Contemporary European Thought," *New German Critique* 119 (40, no. 2) (Summer 2013): 1–29.

20. Kant, *Critique of the Power of Judgment*, 174 n.

21. Nietzsche of course will mock Kantian morality, but from another angle the moral sublimity evoked here is anything but *ressentiment* or simple self-denial and can even be given a Nietzschean tinge and understood as the life-enhancing harnessing of danger and pain to create the higher value of sublimity. (I use the metaphor of the harness as a kind of homage to Kant's father's vocation.)

22. Kant, *Critique of the Power of Judgment*, 160.

23. Ibid., 97.

24. Kiefer, *L'art survivra à ses ruines/Art Will Survive Its Ruins*, 252.

25. See the Bloomberg reporter Helene Fouquet's account comparing the glacier in 2015 to what she saw in 1988 when she visited on a school trip. From the observation post it was then just three steps down to the glacier; new structures have had to be added in the quarter century since, and it now takes 370 steps to reach the rapidly retreating glacier. "Want to See Climate Change? Come with Me to the Mont Blanc Glacier," September 25, 2015. https://www.bloomberg.com /news/features/2015–09–25/climate-change-on-mont-blanc-the-vanishing-mer-de-glace.

26. Rob Nixon, *Slow Violence and the Environmentalism of the Poor* (Cambridge, MA: Harvard University Press, 2011).

27. Nietzsche, *The Will to Power*, 448.

28. Graham Harman, *Immaterialism: Objects and Social Theory* (Cambridge: Polity Press, 2016), 6.

29. Hannah Arendt, "What Is Freedom?," in *Between Past and Future: Eight Exercises in Political Thought* (New York: Penguin Books, 1977), 169–70.

30. Friedrich Nietzsche, *Thus Spoke Zarathustra*, in *The Portable Nietzsche*, 139.

31. Hannah Arendt, *The Human Condition* (Chicago: University of Chicago Press, 1958), 1–2.

32. Brown, *Other Things*, 173. This passage is part of the broader discussion in chap. 5, "The Unhuman Condition (Hannah Arendt/Bruno Latour)," 155–74. These pages are an essential contribution to the question of humanism in the face of the nonhuman, the unhuman, and the posthuman.

33. Ibid., 172.

34. Peter Sloterdijk, "The Domestication of Being," in *Not Saved: Essays after Heidegger*, trans. Ian Alexander Moore and Christopher Turner (Cambridge and Malden, MA: Polity Press, 2017), 136.

35. Ibid., 137. Sloterdijk goes on to acknowledge (138) the range of thinkers who grapple with and contribute to the search for formulations of the *tertium datur*, that is, let's say, the *both-both-human-and natural-and-neither-human-nor-natural*: Adorno, Ernst Bloch, Deleuze, Derrida, Gotthard Günther, Klaus Heinrich, Bruno Latour, Niklas Luhmann, Michel Serres, and Heienz von Foerster.

36. Martin Heidegger, *Being and Time*, trans. John Macquarrie and Edward Robinson (New York: Harper & Row, 1962), 84 (H 57). Hereafter citations of this work will be made parenthetically in the text using the H pagination.

37. Peter Sloterdijk, *Spheres*, vol. 1, *Bubbles: Microspherology*, trans. Wieland Hoban (Los Angeles: Semiotext(e), 2011), 335. See also 333–42 and 625–30 and a version of the former, "'An Essential Tendency toward Nearness Lies in Dasein': Marginalia to Heidegger's Doctrine of Existential Place," in *Not Saved*, 257–62.

38. For an approach to "originary technicity" via Derrida, psychoanalytic theory, and media studies, see Patricia Ticineto Clough, *Autoaffection: Unconscious Thought in the Age of Teletechnology* (Minneapolis: University of Minnesota Press, 2000), 28–45.

39. Bruno Latour, *Facing Gaia: Eight Lectures on the New Climate Regime*, trans. Catherine Porter (Cambridge and Medford: Polity Press, 2017), 121, 130, and 122–23. A striking instance of Latour's imaginative rethinking and visualizing what he there calls the "critical zone" (the narrow band of air, land, and sea that enables life on Earth) is his lecture-performance "Inside," held in Berlin, September 30, 2017, and especially the show's visual art and projected images, created by Alexandra Arènes and Sonia Lévy: http://www.bruno-latour.fr/node/746.

40. Latour's reflex-to-polemicize frequently addles his urge-to-persuade, as when he tromps through a few verses of "Mont Blanc" merely to say that "Shelley would be hard put to sing his song today." Ibid., 108.

41. Kant, *Critique of the Power of Judgment*, 149.

42. Ibid., 150.

43. Ibid., 93.

44. Ibid., 171.

45. Ibid., 158.

46. Ibid. The citations from Burke in the translation vary a bit from those in Kant's text because Guyer draws on an accurate version of Burke's original treatise in English. Cf. ibid., 376 nn. 38 and 39.

47. Ibid., 158–59.

48. Ibid., 154.

49. Ibid., 152.

50. Ibid., 146.

51. Ibid., 153–54.

52. Ibid., 154.

53. Ibid., 155.

54. Ibid., 154 n.

55. Ibid., 154–55.

56. Ibid., 155.

57. Ibid., 156.

58. Martin Heidegger, "The Origin of the Work of Art," in *Poetry, Language, Thought*, trans. Albert Hofstadter (New York: HarperCollins, [1971] 2001), 62. See above, 000.

59. See above, 00–00.

60. Martin Heidegger, *The Fundamental Concepts of Metaphysics: World, Finitude, Solitude*, trans. William McNeill and Nicholas Walker (Bloomington: Indiana University Press, 1995), 169–366.

61. Giorgio Agamben, *The Open: Man and Animal*, trans. Kevin Attell (Stanford, CA: Stanford University Press, 2004), 68.

62. Agamben notes the contrasting philosophical interests aroused by Uexküll, whose "investigations into the animal environment are contemporary with both quantum physics and the artistic avant-gardes. And like them, they express the unreserved abandonment of every anthropocentric perspective in the life sciences and the radical dehumanization of the image of nature (and so it should come as no surprise that they strongly influenced both Heidegger, the philosopher of the twentieth century who more than any other strove to separate man from the living being, and Gilles Deleuze, who sought to think the animal in an absolutely nonanthropomorphic way." Ibid., 39–40.

63. Maurice Merleau-Ponty, *Nature: Course Notes from the Collège de France*, ed. Dominique Séglard, trans. Robert Vallier (Evanston, IL: Northwestern University Press, 2003), 199.

64. Ibid., 208. The editor cites a definition Merleau-Ponty once gave of *Ineinander*: "The inherence of the self in the world and of the world in the self, of the self in the other and the other in the self" (306 n. 15). The image of the *feuilllet* and the concept of *Ineinander* resonate with the intertwining, chiasm, and flesh of the world in *The Visible and the Invisible* discussed in chap. 1.

65. Ibid., 211–12. See also Hubert L. Dreyfus, "Being-with-Others," in *The Cambridge Companion to "Being and Time,"* 145–56.

66. Kant, *Critique of the Power of Judgment*, 160.

67. Ibid., 203.

68. Jean-François Lyotard, "Answering the Question: What Is Postmodernism?" trans. Régis Durand, in *The Postmodern Condition: A Report on Knowledge*, trans. Geoff Bennington and Brian Massumi (Minneapolis: University of Minnesota Press, 1984), 71–82.

69. Gianni Vattimo, "Ornament/Monument," in *The End of Modernity: Nihilism and Hermeneutics in Postmodern Culture*, trans. Jon R. Snyder (Baltimore, MD: Johns Hopkins University Press, 1988), 81.

Index

Page numbers followed by "f" refer to figures.

Printed in Great Britain
by Amazon

35805941R00167